Management Aesthetics

This edited collection presents the complex theory of kitsch from aesthetic and artistic points of view, transposed into managerial and organisational fields. In the spirit of management aesthetics, on the ground of humanistic management, the central aim of the volume is to show that kitsch is a common phenomenon not only in art and culture but also in management, and its conscious perception and mindful use may be beneficial for achieving organisational and managerial goals efficiently. Due to the diverse research problems covered by particular chapters, no unified methodology is applied in the book; every author applied an optimal method for the selected topic. However, due to the complex and metaphysical character of the kitsch phenomenon, the only common fundament of all chapters is using the kitsch experience theory (Szostak and Sułkowski, 2020). The dominant analytical approach is qualitative, with extensive use of case studies, comparative analyses, and ethnographic focus. Despite this, some chapters also include the application of the quantitative approach for the hypotheses' verification. This book makes a giant step ahead of its competitors by implementing the kitsch theory, especially the kitsch experience theory in a broad spectrum of managerial and organisational fields like marketing, advertising, brand management, business communication, entrepreneurship, leadership, decision-making, human resource management, corporate social responsibility, city space management, management of technology and innovation, and organisational culture. It should be a must-read for researchers, academics, practitioners, and advanced students in these fields.

Michał Szostak is Associate Professor (PhD, Dr. habil.) of Management and Vice Rector for Scientific Research and Head of the Institute for Management Research at Collegium Civitas in Warsaw, Poland. He conducts interdisciplinary research in the intersection of management, art, and aesthetics, the results of which are published in international publishing houses and journals. He is a graduate of doctoral studies (management) and master's studies (management and marketing). He conducts teaching activities in finance, management aesthetics, humanistic management, and art marketing.

Humanistic Management

Series Editors: Michael Pirson, Erica Steckler, David Wasieleski, Benito Teehankee, Ricardo Aguado and Ernestina Giudici

Humanistic Management draws together the concepts of social business, sustainability, social entrepreneurship, business ethics, conscious capitalism and cooperative capitalism to present a new humanistically-based research paradigm. This new paradigm challenges the prevailing neo-liberal 'economistic' approach that dominates twentieth-century management theory and practice, and instead emphasises the need to protect human dignity and wellbeing as well as economic drivers.

Humanistic Tourism
Values, Norms and Dignity
Edited by Maria Della Lucia and Ernestina Giudici

Humanistic Management in Latin America
Edited by Consuelo A. García-de-la-Torre, Osmar Arandia and Mario Vázquez-Maguirre

Alternative Theories of the Firm
Edited by Michael Pirson, David M. Wasieleski and Erica L. Steckler

Love and Organization
Lessons of Love for Human Dignity, Leadership and Motivation
Edited by Michael Pirson

Humanistic Management, Organization and Aesthetics
Art of Management and Management of Art
Michał Szostak

Management Aesthetics
Kitsch and Modern Organisations
Edited by Michał Szostak

For more information about this series, please visit: www.routledge.com

Management Aesthetics

Kitsch and Modern Organisations

Edited by Michał Szostak

Routledge
Taylor & Francis Group
NEW YORK AND LONDON

First published 2025
by Routledge
605 Third Avenue, New York, NY 10158

and by Routledge
4 Park Square, Milton Park, Abingdon, Oxon, OX14 4RN

Routledge is an imprint of the Taylor & Francis Group, an informa business

Library of Congress Cataloging-in-Publication Data
Names: Szostak, Michał, author.
Title: Management aesthetics : kitsch and modern organisations / edited by Michał Szostak.
Description: New York, NY : Routledge, 2025. | Series: Humanistic management | Includes bibliographical references and index.
Identifiers: LCCN 2024032201 | ISBN 9781032823300 (hbk) | ISBN 9781032825137 (pbk) | ISBN 9781003504931 (ebk)
Subjects: LCSH: Management. | Organizational effectiveness.
Classification: LCC HD31.2 .S95 2025 | DDC 658—dc23/eng/20240923
LC record available at https://lccn.loc.gov/2024032201

ISBN: 978-1-032-82330-0 (hbk)
ISBN: 978-1-032-82513-7 (pbk)
ISBN: 978-1-003-50493-1 (ebk)

DOI: 10.4324/9781003504931

Typeset in Times New Roman
by Apex CoVantage, LLC

Contents

Contributors

David M. Atkinson, PhD, is a lecturer in business and management, teaching a broad range of subject areas at both undergraduate and postgraduate levels. As an ex-Royal Air Force Communications Engineering Officer, with a specialisation in software engineering management, he has also gained significant experience of serial entrepreneurship in multiple sectors, and he brings the benefit of a wide range of leadership and management perspectives from the world of real work to his teaching. In his latest research, he has turned to the application of negative dialectic thinking to the study of socio-economic systems, including enterprise and entrepreneurship. He completed his PhD in critical management studies at Lancaster University Management School in 2006, winning two international awards for research excellence, including First Prize in the 2007 European Doctoral Association for Management and Business Administration – Outstanding Thesis Awards. He is an openly autistic person and provides specialist study skills support to autistic students in higher education.

Aleksandra Chmielewska, PhD, is Doctor of Social Sciences in the discipline of economics and finance. She defended her dissertation in 2021 at the Warsaw School of Economics at the Economic and Social College. She also holds two master's degrees in economics, a first degree in special education, specialising in art therapy, and postgraduate studies in internet marketing at the Warsaw School of Economics. She is professionally related to the media market. During many years of work at Telewizja Polska SA, she was responsible for broadcasting projects, including, as a coordinator, supervising digital transformation projects and introducing media products, among others: the new TVP.pl portal, applications for smart TV, cross-media websites for the Great Tests in cooperation with TVP1, and special websites for live television theatres and mobile applications. She was also co-responsible for the HALO POLONIA programme, introducing the first fully interactive programme on TVP Polonia. Then, as Digital Media Director at PMPG, she participated in the group's digital transformation. At Gemius SA, she is responsible for television projects, introducing products based on RPD data. She is a media market manager and entrepreneur. She authored the book *Television Market. Loyalty in the era of technological change*, Warsaw 2022.

Justyna Dziedzic, PhD in humanities, specialising in management sciences, is interested in cultural management processes, including organisational culture and identity, sustainability, brand management, media management, and higher education. She completed doctoral studies at the Faculty of Management and Social Communication of the Jagiellonian University, graduate studies in European studies and creative and media education, postgraduate studies in culture management, and an Executive MBA. She also has experience as a journalist in the cultural sphere. She has conducted interviews with numerous artists and literary authors. She transferred her interests in art and culture to research in culture management. She has conducted research in EU institutions such as the European Commission and the European Parliament and carried out research grants in supranational organisations. She is the author of a scientific monograph on organisational culture in the institutions of the European Union and the perception of the audiovisual sector. She was the editor of the special issue of *Sustainability in Organizational Culture and Intercultural Management.*

Aneta Ejsmont, PhD, Dr. habil., is Associate Professor at the WSB Merito University in Poznan, and Faculty of Entrepreneurship and Innovation in Warsaw. She is habilitated doctor in the field of social sciences in the discipline of economics and finance, employed as a university professor at the Casimir Pulaski Radom University, at the Faculty of Economics and Finance in the Department of Finance, Insurance and Accounting. He specialises in research cooperative connections between enterprises, which are the main determinant of the development dynamics of enterprises in the SME sector. She is the author of over 80 publications in this field, both domestic and foreign. She also deals with practice on a daily basis. In the years 2015–2022, she was a member of the Supervisory Board at the Water and Sewerage Company in Suwałki. He teaches accounting, corporate finance, and international trade. As part of the Erasmus programme, she gave lectures in English at several foreign universities. She participated in European and other international and national programmes.

Magdalena El Ghamari, PhD, is Doctor of Social Sciences, in the field of peacekeeping and conflicts in the Middle East and North Africa, specialising in analyses of the relationship between socio-religious and political factors/policymaking. She is an expert in the radicalisation process in a diverse cultural environment – high-risk area. She is Assistant Professor at the Institute of Political Sciences and International Relations at Collegium Civitas and Head of the Cultural Security Department (Warsaw, Poland). She is Member of the UN Peacekeeping Veterans Association (PL) and The Society for

Libyan Studies (UK). Her research interests and specialisations are terrorism, migration processes, radicalisation, and public policies during and after conflicts in the MENA area, with a focus on Libya issues.

Andrzej Kisielewski, PhD in art history, is a graduate of the Institute of Art History of the University of Warsaw, obtained his doctorate at the Institute of Art of the Polish Academy of Sciences in Warsaw, and habilitated at the University of Warsaw at the Faculty of History. He deals with the history and theory of art of the 20th and 21st centuries, cultural theory, and contemporary visual culture studies. He is the author of books and articles on contemporary art, the relationship between modern art and popular culture and "primitive" art, as well as industrial design, advertising, and other manifestations of contemporary commercial visual culture. He has published, among others, books: *Ludzie lubią obrazy... Studia o komercyjnej kulturze wizualnej i sztuce* (2021) [*People Like Images... Studies on Commercial Visual Culture and Art*]; *Prymitywizm w sztuce awangardy pierwszej połowy XX wieku. Mitologie i obrazy pierwotności* (2013) [*Primitivism in Avant-Garde Art of the First Half of the 20th Century. Mythologies and Images of Primitiveness*]; and *Sztuka ireklama. Relacje między sztuką i kulturą* (1998) [*Art and Advertising. Relations between Art and Culture*].

Andrzej Kondej, PhD, Doctor in economic sciences. His special area of scientific interest is modern marketing and trade organisation and management. He is the author of numerous scientific and popular science publications mainly in the field of trade-related topics. He is currently engaged in research of modern solutions applied in the subject of distribution and display with the application of metaverse and IA solutions. He is employed at Collegium Civitas in Warsaw as an assistant professor. Andrzej Kondej serves as deputy chairman of the Department of Management. He teaches at WSB Merito University in Warsaw and the University of Bialystok as well. In addition, he is very active in social media in the form of running the Vibes of Life website, where issues concerning various aspects of life in the VUCA world are covered.

Marlena Kondrat, PhD in social sciences in the discipline of economics and finance, is a lecturer at Collegium Civitas, University of Warsaw, and SWPS University. Her research interests include the impact of the silver tsunami on economic processes. She publishes on the impact of new technologies on selected social groups, taking into account age, gender, and place of residence. She is Board Member at the National Institute for the Senior Economy in Poland, where she is responsible for the area of digital inclusion of elderly people. She visits Third Age Universities and Senior Citizens' Homes to educate seniors around improving digital competence. She is a speaker at national scientific conferences on the challenges of an ageing society. She creates recommendations for the government on solutions for raising the digital competences of seniors (e.g. recommendations included in the Report "Time for Digital Economy" prepared by Digital Poland). She is a co-initiator of projects related to the activation of elderly people in the digital world.

Olga Kosińska, PhD candidate, is an Assistant Professor at the Institute of Culture at the Faculty of Management and Communication of the Jagiellonian University. She is a graduate of cultural studies (specialisation: comparative studies of civilisations) and culture and media management (specialisation: cultural management). Her research interests focus primarily on non-institutional circulations of culture and culture management, as well as digital activities related to the culture sector. She also researches online communities such as fandoms. Currently, she focuses on the phenomenon of anthropomorphic virtual influencers.

Iga Maria Lehman, PhD, is the head of the Department of English Studies and the Department of Intercultural Communication at the University of Social Sciences in Warsaw. She is Editor-in-Chief of the multidisciplinary journal *Discourses on Culture*. In her research, she adopts a critical, language-centred approach to analyse issues related to socio-linguistic marginalisation, diversity of discourse communities, discursive leadership, dialogical communication, and authorial uniqueness in scholarly writing. She has published books, articles, and chapters in books from the fields of applied linguistics, management communication, and organisation studies, including such outlets as *Ibérica*, *International Review of Pragmatics*, *Innovations in Education and Teaching International*, *Journal of Management Education*, *Management Communication Quarterly*, and *Organization*. Her latest book, *Charismatic Leadership in Organizations: A Critique of Texts*, presents, and empirically defends, an analytic framework conceived of rhetorical charismatic tactics which provides guidance for academic authors seeking to present themselves as convincing and engaging writers.

Artur Modliński, PhD, Dr. habil., is Assistant Professor and Head of the Artificial Intelligence and Cybercommunication Research Center, Department of Management Theory, Faculty of Management, University of Lodz. He is a researcher at the CITAD International Research Center in Lisbon, expert at the R. del Bianco Foundation in Florence and at the Urban Sensorial Laboratory at Lusiada University. He conducts research in the area of the application of artificial intelligence in management, human–machine communication, and virtual work. He is a laureate of over 40 scholarships and scientific awards (including a two-time Scholarship of the Minister of Science and Higher Education, a Scholarship of the first degree of the Marshal of the Łódź Voivodeship, a VIP Scholarship of the DAAD Foundation, and a Santander Scholarship); he organised numerous industry conferences (including in Oxford, Lisbon, and Florence). He conceptualised such constructs as the phenomenon of techno-empowerment, technosis, technologically sustainable organisations, technoisation, organisational anastomosis, bifurcation structure, and carnal collapse effect. During field research, he observed the phenomenon of HRR (human robbing robot), conceptualised the re-manualisation of automated processes, and described the conflict of organisational roles between human and machine (human–machine trans role conflict [HMTRC]). Together with the posthumanist Matthew Gladden, he created a metaphor for the organisation as a cyborg.

Wioletta Małota, PhD, is Assistant Professor and Head of "International Business" Specialisation at the Management Faculty at Collegium Civitas in Warsaw. She earned her PhD in organisational behaviour. She is an interculturalist and strategist. Her areas of expertise are organisational culture and behaviours, management in multicultural environments, global leadership, intercultural negotiations, Oxford debates, consumer behaviour, and strategies for country and city branding. She worked as Visiting Professor in France at Paris Business School, IUT2 Grenoble, ILERI Lyon; in Italy at Altis Business School, Milan; Sapienza University, Rome; at Sogang University Seoul, South Korea; and at Beijing International Studies University, Beijing, China. Before her academic career, she worked for a global corporation in a managerial position in the marketing department. She is the author of three books: *How From a Manager Become a Leader? The Guidebook for Managers and Coaches* (2012); *South Korea. Economy, Society, K-Culture* (2019); and *Paris Culture Architecture Innovative City. What Should You Know to Enjoy the City? An Example of Successful Branding* (2023). She likes modern architecture and travelling to experience different cultures. As a blogger, she shares her cultural experience at www.crossculturemanagement.online and as a visual storyteller on the YouTube channel "Culture and Architecture".

Ada Florentyna Pawlak, PhD, is graduated in law and anthropology at University of Lodz and in communication in business at the Faculty of Political Science at the National Defence University in Warsaw. She is a lecturer in psychology and computer science at SWPS University, trendwatching and future studies at AGH University of Science and Technology, business process automation at the University of Lodz, and business AI at Kozminski University in Warsaw. Her courses cover topics such as the anthropology of technology and digital culture, techno-intimacy, and human–machine collaboration. She is a founding member of the Polish Transhumanist Association and organises the annual scientific conference "Transhumanism: Ideas, Strategies, Doubts". Additionally, she is a regular columnist for the "Domain" magazine of the Polish Information Processing Society (PIPS). Recognised by "Forbes Women" as one of the 22 most influential Polish women in science and business in 2022, she was also listed in the Top 100 Women in AI in Poland.

Weronika Pokojska, PhD, holds master's degrees in cultural management and in media management from the Jagiellonian University in Krakow. In 2019, she successfully defended her doctoral thesis at the Faculty of Management and Social Communication at the Jagiellonian University in the field of humanities in discipline of management sciences. The work concerned the use of corporate heritage in the German automobile industry. She participated in courses and trainings organised by varied universities and research institutes; she also completed a two-year scientific internship (2021–2023) at the TECHNOSEUM State Museum for Technology and Work in Mannheim, Germany. Since 2024, she has been an academic employee at the University of Heidelberg, Germany. She is an active member of the Humanistic Management Network (HMN) and the leader of the Polish Chapter of the Network. She was the co-organiser of the 2019 Humanistic Management Conference (HMC) in Kraków, Poland. Furthermore, she hosts and organises panel discussions at HMCs and seminars within the network. She is a co-author of various analyses linking management and contemporary phenomena related to the culture and heritage sector (including social media).

Michał Szostak, PhD, Dr. habil., is Associate Professor of Management and Vice Rector for Scientific Research and Head of the Institute for Management Research at Collegium Civitas in Warsaw, Poland. He conducts interdisciplinary research in the intersection of management, art, and aesthetics, the results of which are published in international publishing houses and journals. He is graduate of doctoral studies (management) and master's studies (management and marketing). He conducts teaching activities in finance, management aesthetics, humanistic management, and art marketing. He is also a guest lecturer at foreign universities and has experience in the administration of teaching and scientific processes and projects. He has been a business practitioner in managerial positions in an international environment. He has experience in the financial and organisational optimisation of processes and organisations, mergers, divisions, separations, and acquisitions of enterprises, and in implementing and maintaining certified management systems. Moreover, he earned a musical arts doctorate, specialising in organ performance and improvisation. He records on CDs and conducts a lively international concert activity, performing several dozen recitals annually. More at: www.michalszostak.org.

Foreword

The collapse of facades

Kitsch is a concept that has developed across fields over a century and a half. It is absolutely familiar to everyone and a mainstay of popular culture. Yet it is commonly misunderstood, and its range and power remain underappreciated. At a time when considerable changes in communicative and representational technologies provide unparalleled scope for the creation and propagation of "fakes" and "simulations" of great sophistication, there is a need for a rejuvenation of kitsch scholarship. From Benjamin's "dream kitsch", where even the unconscious is fake, to the political oppression of Kundera's "totalitarian kitsch", to the big data-driven computer-generated worlds of "hyperkitsch", the phenomenon continues to evolve, and research has failed to keep up.

This book is an important contribution to redressing this issue. There are two most pressing considerations: one is to map the history and genealogy of the concept across time and disciplines, contributing to a detailing of the current terrain; the second is to focus more closely on the fine grain of how kitsch works, the mechanics of its reproduction, through institutions, organisations, and management practice, showing how even science and theory can be kitsch.

Together, these constitute a daunting project. Thankfully, Michal Szostak and his colleagues have undertaken to develop the foundations of such a project under the auspices of the Institute for Management Research at Collegium Civitas in Warsaw. In the first volume to come from this project, *Management aesthetics: Kitsch in modern organisations*, contributors recognise that kitsch has always faced in two directions. One with which we are most familiar is the cheapening of high art, but its original sense was in the cheap and clumsy copying of high *craft*, skilled artisanal productions, for mass circulation to tourists. Such original works had the quality of the closeness of the craftsperson to the materials of experience; the cheap copies picked up only on superficial signs from the object, and abandoned the experiential qualities, including skills, associated with *making*, rather than mere production. Combating kitsch then requires attention in detail to the conditions of its production – Heidegger's *dwelling*, lingering with the object, taking time to reflect, to "listen" to the material and to carefully analyse when this is not happening. The contributions to this book on kitsch in management are focused on managerial and organisational issues (including organisational culture, entrepreneurship, advertising, brand management, and human resource management) and fill what has been a noticeable empirical gap in showing how kitsch creeps into and overtakes management processes.

Kitsch is about sentiment; kitsch makes us feel we are doing the right thing and that our community agrees with us. It makes us feel comforted and satisfied with, or even good about, ourselves. However, management, as we are taught, is rational and objective. Feelings have no place in the efficient deployment of resources. Yet, in practice, management is at least as much an art as a science and is almost never fully rational – indeed, the more rational it gets, the more likely it is to create crises as it develops.

Let me illustrate. Currently in the British and international press are reports from an inquiry into the UK Post Office, where hundreds of innocent postmasters found themselves unjustly accused of theft from their branches due to massive bugs in the PO's computer system, Horizon, over two decades from 1999. The PO told each of them they were the only person with a problem, deliberately lying so that the postmasters would not form any sense of collective justification and begin to organise. This would not have been a kitsch sentiment of justification: it had genuine substance, experiences that could be shared, and hence was dangerous. The PO brought criminal charges against over 500 of them; many were sent to jail, and others lost their savings, jobs, houses, and marriages. One committed suicide and three others died without having their name cleared. All were innocent.

Problems had surfaced from the introduction of the system in 1999, and by 2001, bug reports were coming in daily. They were familiar issues in the industry. Fujitsu, the contractor, had provided a system for the National Health Service, which cost £12 billion and ultimately had to be withdrawn as useless, so rationality would have considered the likelihood of a repetition. Even when Fujitsu and independent consultants raised concerns with the PO, they continued to blame and persecute the Postmasters. When the courts cleared the first group of postmasters, the PO challenged the impartiality of the judge and tried to get him replaced. Why did they double-down? Why did they not come clean? And why, when others not directly involved with the system itself saw the consequences, did they not ask questions: such as, if all these postmasters are corrupt, how did the PO come to hire so many corrupt recruits, all at around the same time? Postmasters traditionally were the heart of their communities, friendly, honest, and respected. Rationality would have demanded an answer to what went wrong in Human Resources as the outcomes were improbable – in actuality, they were impossible.

The inquiry continues, but one aspect is that at the crucial period in this saga, the PO was being split from Royal Mail in the next phase of the privatisation of postal services. Raising of any doubts about its governance and systems would have killed this initiative. A lesser subsequent factor was that non-existent financial deficits were recovered from postmasters who were pressured to pay in order to avoid court proceedings and legal costs. These "recovered" funds were being paid as bonuses to senior managers who had an obvious interest in maintaining this brutal situation. However, the major factor seems to be a "belief in technology", or at least, our *need* to believe in technology. People in the wider company, shareholders, and even the public needed to preserve the collective sense that everyone shared the same view and feeling of security, were all under the same safe umbrella of technology, and that technology could be trusted. They would, therefore, be happy to accept the denial or minimisation by PO managers of any accusations that this was not the case. Almost none of those people had the means or capacity to check the reasons for the system's actions or the rationality behind it. They could only trust the system, trust the word of the PO and Fujitsu, and trust that it was rational and efficient. They were operating from a sentimental belief in technology – if the computer says no, it must be correct. In other words, the unjust treatment of the postmasters was enabled by *sentiments of rationality* typical of a *kitsch response to reality*.

So kitsch has an impact which goes beyond style right to the heart of institutional practice. Furthermore, it also extends to theory – in a paper in 2002, I demonstrated how the work of Abraham Maslow, still taught in every business school globally, and the cultural excellence school inspired by Peters and Waterman (1982) were examples of kitsch management and organisation theory. Luc Peters (2016) prefers the term cliché, but his message is the same. Much work remains to be done to continue exposing the increasing surface sophistication of kitsch in constructing the frames and formulae that constitute management knowledge. This book is an exciting and important contribution to that endeavour.

Stephen Linstead

References

Linstead, S. A. (2002) Organizational Kitsch *Organization* 9,4: 657–684.

Peters, L. (2016) *Cliché and Organization: Thinking with Deleuze and Film* Newcastle-upon-Tyne: Cambridge Scholars Publishing.

Peters, T. and Waterman, R. (1982) *In Search of Excellence* New York: Harper and Row.

Foreword

Managing beyond kitsch

In the "liquid era" of neoliberal capitalism (Bauman, 2000), management has become divorced from responsibility, and executives have become idols and celebrities, deserving of admiration and imitation (Bloom and Rhodes, 2018) without regard for how they actually perform their pivotal role as takers of responsibility for the good of different organisations and as connectors and communicators (Mintzberg, 2015). Yet management science is, from Mary Parker Follett (1919, 1940) to Henry Mintzberg (2023), well aware of the need to acknowledge and pay close attention to the complexity and dynamics of organisations.

Kitsch is an idea coined by late 19th-century artists from Munich and traditionally defined as "useless painting, literary work, film; cf. junk-art" (Kopaliński, 1970: 376). Indeed, it can be "technically skilful art, but superficial, operating with external effects – stereotypes, easy ornamentation, calculated for fast effect, appealing to not too refined tastes" (Głowiński, 1994: 108).

In *The unbearable lightness of being*, Milan Kundera (1990) explains that "kitsch the answers are known a priori and exclude any questions" (p. 172). It does not signify "bad taste" but is unifying and simplifying the complexities of the human condition by "authoritative approval" (ibid.: 174). It enforces the acceptance of received ideas by translating them into a language that is simultaneously highly emotive and strongly normative in claiming "beauty and feeling" (p. 163). However, real beauty is unsettling, amazing, and multifaceted, as is the endless complexity we call truth. But beauty astonishes; it is dazzling. The linearity of kitsch makes it both powerful and effective and feeble and unstable.

That is why kitsch is used as a powerful managerial dispositive, as at the same time an authoritarian tool of simplification and ordering typical of greedy organisations (Coser, 1974), and a kind of libertarian seduction.

> The corporate image is a means to capitalise on the fundamental drive of ontological *lack*, the desire for the other which drives social structure, by manufacturing a synthetic lack which is engineered by consumerism and which

> offers access to the desired world of the other (implicitly, at an ontological level) through access to the desired world of a particular social milieu. ... The corporate image, or corporate culture, is a seductive device designated to operationalise manufactured lack into a desire willingly to be controlled.
>
> (Linstead, 1993: 61–61)

In this sense, it is a form of totalising managerial ideology that can be used in any socio-economic system (Kostera, 1997). Kitsch-organisations are managed in a way that practically precludes individuation, dissent, or real difference. Experience, time, and engagement are all equally streamlined. In this land of total linearity (Burrell, 1997), the only effective work organisation is not creative emergence but conformism and bullshit jobs (Graeber, 2018).

> Surprise takes time, creation is timeless – both do not fit in the kitsch-organizations' map of reality. The kitsch reality is two-dimensional, like an animated movie. Everything that happens: pain, happiness, ambition, dignity, etc., has two correlates and can be presented in a quantitative mode. There is just one rationality reigning in those organizations, and that Rationality is god. The god worshipped in the "surrogates for churches" is omnipotent, but one-dimensional.
>
> (Kostera, 1997: 173)

This is an ideal setting for micromanagement, total organisations, or algorithmic management procedures. Kitsch is "the transit station between being and forgetting" (Kundera, 1989: 189).

Graffiti, mural art, and other forms of urban art, despite their frequent use of simplifications and aim for fast effects, stand out as anti-kitsch. Their unique appeal lies in their ability to transcend traditional notions of aesthetics. Even if, at first glance, the creation appears "kitschy", naïve, or sometimes even ugly, the difference lies in the statement that it is making. It expresses the political, social, and cultural values of the groups and individuals oppressed and excluded by the dominant system. For this reason, it has not even been considered art by recognised art institutions (Rolston, 2012).

Urban art is the voice of those who are otherwise unheard, those who are disadvantaged and repressed. It is an act of rebellion against the dominant views, and as such, it breaks the omnipotence of kitsch. Urban art is authentic, which contradicts kitsch, which, by definition, is fake and superficial. This act of rebellion is necessary to break the pervasiveness and oppression of kitsch, as described by Kundera, by disturbing the pleasant, easy, and numbing feeling of the recipients.

This disturbance is necessary to prevent kitsch's greatest danger in art or management, which is an imposition of a single-view, one-size-fits-all approach. According to Johan Galtung, the founder of peace studies, the singularity of a dominant view in culture gives legitimacy to structures of exploitation and marginalisation of non-dominant groups, which further leads to acts of direct violence in the form of alienation and repression, which brings benefits to some but harm and suffering to others (Galtung, 1990).

The opposition to violence is peace. Following Galtung's definition, a peaceful organisation is a system that can deal with occasional violence, understood as an avoidable insult to basic human needs, in a nonviolent way, and can restore itself after a violent shock (Galtung, 1996). To do this, organisations need to be complex and inclusive, and the role of management is to embrace this complexity to deal with inevitable conflicts that it creates without suffering or harm.

There exist different forms of artistic expression, as well as of management. Between them lies a whole spectrum of presenting the universe's complexity. Managing beyond kitsch means accepting diverse voices, self-expression, sensitivity, and vulnerability of people in organisations, thus creating organisational peace. What is needed to transcend the temptation to be seduced by kitsch (Linstead, 1993) is not so much artistic taste as a managerial openness that Ghislain Deslandes (2020) labels weak management. Based on the poetics of negative capability, it opens the managerial mind to doubt, helps to avoid fast categorisations, and ultimately to pay attention to weak signals. Renouncing aspirations to omnipotence and omniscience may help managers reclaim the genuine responsibility that flourishes with engagement for and with peace.

This is an important calling and a good reason why humanistic management is concerned with human complexity and dignity (Pirson, 2017), as well as with art and aesthetics (Szostak, 2023). Indeed, management is an art "focused on the universal values of truth and beauty, and art, accumulating the most abstractly advanced products of humanity – is the quintessence and emanation of humanity" (Szostak, 2023: 3).

Monika Kostera and Ilona Hunek

References

Bauman, Zygmunt (2000) *Liquid modernity*. Cambridge: Polity.

Bloom, Peter and Carl Rhodes (2018) *CEO society: The corporate takeover of everyday life*. London: Zed Books.

Burrell, Gibson (1997) *Pandemonium: Towards a retro-organization theory*. London: SAGE.

Coser, Lewis A. (1974) *Greedy institutions: Patterns of undivided commitment*. New York: Free Press.

Deslandes, Ghislain (2020) "Weak Theology and Organization Studies." *Organization Studies*, 41(1): 127–139.

Follett, Mary Parker (1919) "Community Is a Process." *Philosophical Review*, XXVIII: 576–588.

Follett, Mary Parker (1940) *Dynamic administration: The collected papers of Mary Parker Follett* (eds. H.C. Metcalf and L. Urwick). New York: Harper & Row.

Galtung, Johan (1990) "Cultural Violence." *Journal of Peace Studies*, 27(3): 291–305.

Galtung, Johan (1996) *Peace by peaceful means: Peace and conflict, development and civilization*. London: Sage Publications.

Głowiński, Michał, Teresa Kostkiewiczowa, Aleksandra Okopień-Sławińska and Janusz Sławiński (1994) *Podręczny słownik terminów literackich* (*The handbook of literary terms*). Warszawa: Open.

Graeber, David (2018) *Bullshit jobs*. New York: Simon & Schuster.

Kopaliński, Władysław (1970) *Słownik wyrazów obcych i zwrotów obcojęzycznych* (*The dictionary of foreign words and terms*). Warszawa: Wiedza Powszechna.

Kostera, Monika (1997) "The Kitsch Organization." *Studies in Culture, Organizations and Societies*, 3: 163–177.

Kundera, Milan (1989) *Nieznośna lekkość bytu* (*The unbearable lightness of being*). Translated from Czech into Polish by Agnieszka Holland. Wrocław: IWA.

Kundera, Milan (1990) *The art of the novel*. Translated by Linda Ascher. London and Boston: Faber and Faber.

Linstead, Steve (1993) "Deconstruction in the Study of Organizations." In: John Hassard and Martin Parker (eds.) *Postmodernism and organizations*. London, Newbury Park and New Delhi: Sage, pp. 49–70.

Mintzberg, Henry (2015) *Rebalancing society: Radical renewal beyond left, right, and center*. Oakland: Berrett-Koehler Publishers.

Mintzberg, Henry (2023) *Understanding organizations: Finally*! Oakland: Berrett-Koehler Publishers.

Pirson, Michael (2017) *Humanistic management*. Cambridge: Cambridge University Press.

Rolston, Bill (2012) "Re-Imaging: Mural Painting and the State in Northern Ireland." *International Journal of Cultural Studies* 15(5): 447–466.

Szostak, Michał (2023) *Humanistic management, organisation and aesthetics: Art of management and management of art*. New York: Routledge.

Introduction

Michał Szostak

Research procedure course

The term "kitsch" is traditionally associated with art and aesthetics, describing objects considered to be of poor taste because of excessive garishness or sentimentality but sometimes appreciated ironically or knowingly (Broch, 1969; Dorfles, 1969; Kulka, 1996; Kjellman-Chapin, 2023). There is a relatively limited sort of publications that take kitsch discussions outside of aesthetics and art; however, kitsch has been used in debates on bullshitting, academia, or deculturation (Botz-Bornstein, 2015, 2019, 2021; Ryynänen and Barragán, 2023). In managerial and organisational studies, kitsch refers mainly to adopting superficial, oversimplified, or overly sentimental approaches and practices that may lack substantive value (Kostera, 1997; Linstead, 2002; Ciupka, 2020); however, these analyses are done rather from subjectivistic point of view than based on objective criteria with the use of formalised analytical tools.

This book is an extensive development of the monograph *Humanistic Management, Organisation and Aesthetics: Art of Management and Management of Art* (Szostak, 2024) that built theoretical scientific fundaments for deep (in opposition to superficial) aestheticisation of managerial and organisational phenomena. Chapter 6 of that book, titled "Kitsch and Ignorance in Management", following the kitsch experience theory described firstly in conference proceedings (Szostak and Sułkowski, 2020) and then developed in a Polish-language monograph (Szostak, 2023), provided an analytical structure for more profound studies of kitsch in managerial and organisational contexts. Seeing the potential of the kitsch experience theory for further development, in October 2023, I invited international scholars from varied fields and disciplines to participate in a scientific project ("Kitsch in Management: Determinants and Functions, Carriers and Propagators") held at the Institute for Management Research at Collegium Civitas (a non-public university) in Warsaw to investigate kitsch in varied managerial and organisational dimensions. After a few months of joint research work, a precise shape of this book started to arise. The kitsch experience theory inspired and allowed us to analyse kitsch in

DOI: 10.4324/9781003504931-1

organisational culture, marketing, advertising, human resources, communication, leadership language, entrepreneurship, and others – in business entities, as well as in more extensive and less formalised organisations like religious or political groups.

The conceptualisation and realisation phases of the research process were composed in the following way. Initially, a general literature review on kitsch was undertaken; kitsch is present mainly in publications from arts, culture, and aesthetics; Just a limited number of researchers have transposed the concept into varied fields and disciplines but they analyse kitsch from the perspectives of their disciplines, not from the aesthetic perspective. In the second step, a detailed analysis of the literature on kitsch in aesthetics and arts was undertaken to define general directions within these analyses. Following this, theories and approaches to kitsch in management and organisation were defined, analysed, and synthesised based on the managerial literature review. Finally, the kitsch experience theory (Szostak and Sułkowski, 2020) was verified and evaluated as a tool for analysing kitsch in varied managerial and organisational contexts and issues. Figure 0.1 depicts the research process stages.

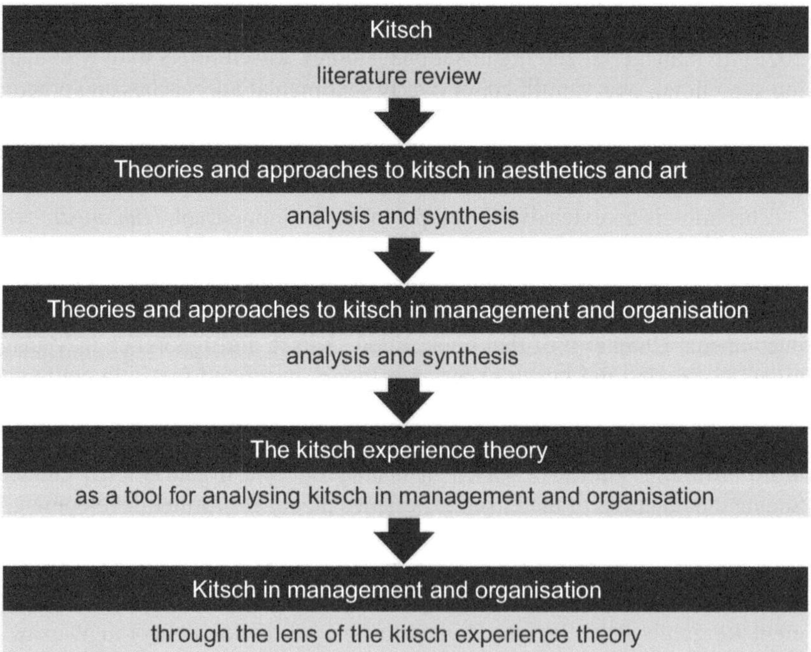

Figure 0.1 The research process

Source: own elaboration

Research gaps, research problems, objectives, and theses

The subsequent *research gaps* were identified during the conceptualisation process of this research project. The research gap at the *epistemological* level can be defined as the following: in the literature on the aesthetics of management and organisation, there is a lack of extensive description of managerial and organisational kitsch with the use of well-defined and repetitive analytical tool. The research gap at the *empirical* level can be defined as the lack of deep exemplifications of managerial and organisational kitsch based on extensive empirical research instead of indication of examples based on individual assumptions and particular aesthetic criteria. The research gap at the *practical* level refers to the lack of structured concepts of managerial and organisational kitsch that organisational actors can apply in everyday situations to understand the contexts of actions broader and function more efficiently in an organisation. This book intends to fill these epistemological, empirical, and practical research gaps around managerial and organisational kitsch.

The fundamental *research problem* of the whole book can be formulated in the following manner: How to provide contemporary organisations' managers and stakeholders with an extensive but at the same time a coherently focused set of examples of managerial and organisational kitsch to give them theoretical background for conscious recognition of managerial and organisational kitsch in their daily practice? Two *objectives* will be fulfilled by solving this problem:

1. the consciousness of *kitsch in management* phenomenon, that is, kitsch as a result of oversimplification, superficiality, or dehumanisation (van de Klundert and van Boeschoten, 2017);
2. *the management of kitsch*, that is, conscious use of organisational kitsch (its presence or lack, its character, scope, form, and intensity) by managers as a means/tool for achieving goals (Szostak, 2024).

After setting the objectives, two *theses* were formulated: T1) the consciousness of kitsch within managerial and organisational contexts allows managers and stakeholders to be more secure, aware, and confident participants of organisational life; T2) conscious use of organisational kitsch (its presence or lack, its character, scope, form, and intensity) by managers as a means/tool may increase efficiency in achieving goals.

Due to the diverse research problems covered by particular chapters, no unified methodology is applied in the book; every author was free to use the most efficient method for the selected topic. However, due to the complex and metaphysical character of the kitsch phenomenon, the only common fundament of all chapters is using the kitsch experience theory (Szostak and Sułkowski, 2020). The dominant analytical approach is qualitative, with extensive use of case studies, comparative analyses, and ethnographic focus. Despite this, some chapters also include the application of the quantitative approach for the hypotheses verification. The conclusions of a particular chapter may be generalised and transposed to other areas of organisational life with appropriate rigour and relevance levels. Every chapter lists the limitations of the applied methodology and suggests future research directions in the elaborated area.

Structure

The book starts with two forewords written by fundamental names for aesthetical approaches to management and organisations, Professor Stephen Linstead and Professor Monika Kostera. Next, 13 chapters analyse kitsch in selected management subdisciplines, mainly through the lens of the kitsch experience theory (Szostak and Sułkowski, 2020). The order of chapters is not crucial for internalising the idea of the book; after the Introduction, chapters can be read in varied order.

Chapter 1, "From kitsch phenomenon, through kitsch experience, to kitschy management and management of kitsch" by Michał Szostak, aims to execute a synthetic review of the literature about aesthetic and artistic approaches to kitsch and provide a reductionistic division of these concepts and views based on repetitive criteria. Next, an analysis of these theories' usefulness in the face of efficient application for managerial and organisational kitsch is provided. The research questions that will be answered through these analyses are the following: RQ1. What are the main factors that distinguish approaches to kitsch in the literature on aesthetics and art? RQ2. What is the applicability of defined groups of approaches to kitsch that can be used to analyse the managerial and organisational kitsch efficiently? The primary research method applied in these analyses is the critical analysis of the literature. As the result of analyses, kitsch theories are first categorised into five main groups based on disciplinary focus: 1) aesthetic and formal, 2) psychological and emotional, 3) sociological and cultural, 4) philosophical and existential, and 5) ethical and ideological, and then they are classified based on the substance of their interest: 1) descriptive focus on kitsch phenomenon versus kitsch artefact; 2) substantive character of descriptive narration: black-and-white versus grey scale; and 3) dynamics of the phenomenon: kitsch as a phenomenon (state) versus kitsch as an experience (process). Summing up all kitsch approaches and theories, three dichotomic classifications are made: 1) descriptive focus on kitsch phenomenon versus kitsch artefact; 2) substantive character of descriptive narration: black-and-white versus grey scale; and 3) dynamics of the phenomenon: kitsch as a phenomenon (state) versus kitsch as an experience (process). In the end, an assessment of the applicability of these kitsch theories for efficient analysis of the kitsch phenomenon in the managerial and organisational areas is provided.

Chapter 2, "Kitsch in organisational culture: challenges and opportunities in the work environment" by Justyna Dziedzic, provides practical guidance for companies seeking to avoid or eliminate kitsch from their managerial practices and organisational culture by presenting fundamental concepts and identifying specific kitsch aspects in management. The chapter recognises elements of behavioural and physical artefacts at the symbolic level, as well as norms and values. It also delves into hidden cultural assumptions deeply embedded in the consciousness of organisational members, which may draw connections to experiences within the realm of kitsch. Based on the comparative analysis of the case study, seven types of kitsch in organisational culture were put forward to describe the kitsch practices present in organisational culture: innovative, exploratory, inspirational, sustainable, social, environmental, and ethical. The study uncovers these seven types of kitsch, highlighting how they are not only pervasive across various aspects of organisational life but also closely tied to the underlying cultural assumptions of its members, thereby offering a nuanced perspective on the multifaceted roles kitsch can play within corporate environments.

Chapter 3, "Kitsch in organisational governance: management through simplified edicts and superficial interpretations in religious fatwas" by Magdalena El Ghamari, investigates the intersection between religious fatwas and the phenomenon of kitsch, with the primary objective of illuminating the potential implications arising from simplified rulings and shallow interpretations within religious discourse. The core of this research study involves an in-depth exploration of the consequences associated with this convergence, accentuating the inherent risks linked to oversimplification and the conceivable distortion of religious principles. This study employs a comprehensive analysis encompassing diverse fatwas from various religious contexts to assess the authenticity and scholarly rigour underpinning simplified rulings critically. Furthermore, the presence of kitsch within religious fatwas, as illuminated in this research, carries significant relevance to the concurrently examined case study, which scrutinises the prevalence of simplified religious fatwas disseminated through social media platforms. The specific case study focused on social media platforms serves as a distinctive exemplar of the overarching phenomenon, spotlighting how kitsch becomes ingrained within religious discourse due to simplification driven by the constraints imposed by such platforms. This chapter also evaluates the role played by mass media and popular culture in shaping these interpretations, ultimately aspiring to foster an enriched comprehension of the intricate interplay between kitsch and religious guidance within contemporary society.

Chapter 4, "Kitsch in HRM: the role of communication in managing generational diversity in an organisation", prepared by Marlena Kondrat, aims to find elements of kitsch experience theory in managing generational diversity in an organisation. It points out that different generations have different aesthetic preferences and values, which can lead to conflicts and communication difficulties. At the same time, kitsch can be a source of innovation and creativity if adequately utilised. The chapter also discusses strategies for managing generational diversity with consideration for kitsch. It emphasises the need to understand and accept the differences between generations, as well as the necessity of creating flexible and open work environments. Examples of best practices and tools to help organisations effectively manage generational diversity are presented. The chapter concludes that managing generational diversity in organisations requires taking kitsch into account as an essential factor. With the right approach, kitsch can become a driving force for innovation and harmonious collaboration among different generations in the workplace.

Chapter 5, "Kitsch in managerial language: rhetorical manifestations of kitsch in scholarly writing" by Iga Maria Lehman, aims to show how scholarly text production can be approached as an act of leadership in which text can be perceived as a "kitsch artefact" and its author as a "kitsch producer". It begins with the argument that the relationship between leaders and followers is similar to that between mainstream disciplinary journal gatekeepers and academic writers. In each case, the former party is the agenda setter. Then, the academia's publishing culture is reflected upon along with its consequences for management and organisation scholars who must conform to the exigencies of mainstream journals in the field. The author argues that privileged rhetorical norms of scholarly writing contribute to the kitsch experience as texts in which these norms are employed are jargon-ridden, pretentious, complex, and consequently meaningless to anyone outside the narrow confines of these disciplines. The chapter ends with examples of such writing translated into readable English to show its artificiality, rendering it less accessible to a broader and more diverse audience.

Chapter 6, "Kitsch in marketing: merchandising and promotional activities in the retail sphere", written by Andrzej Kondej, investigates merchandising solutions that fulfil a kitsch experience's hallmarks. The author attempts to find answers to the following research questions: 1) What merchandising and sales promotion activities can be categorised as kitsch in trade? 2) What are the reasons and justification for using kitsch-like solutions in merchandising? and 3) To what extent does the use of kitsch in the commercial sphere meet consumers' expectations? After a broad review of the literature with analytical and synthetic approaches, the author concludes that the characteristics of kitsch are well suited to achieve the goals set for merchandising. The positive reception of the content and forms of kitsch by a significant proportion of buyers is also a favourable factor. However, ethical concerns arise regarding how buyers are misled in purchasing decisions.

Chapter 7, "Kitsch in advertising: a field of postmodern market communication battle" by Andrzej Kisielewski, is devoted to kitsch in advertising, which is treated as its primary tool to increase the sale of mass-produced goods. The text analyses advertisements that are well known have received awards and are considered a permanent element of advertising history. They are often treated as a testimony to artistry, albeit with the caveat that it is the art of advertising. The central theme of this chapter is the problem of formal solutions developed in modern art being appropriated by advertising and transformed into kitsch. Analyses of the advertisements referred to here are meant to show the point of view of both the creators of the advertisements and the perspective of the recipients and answer the question of whether their perception is connected only with the experience of kitsch or whether it allows for an aesthetic experience. They are also meant to answer the question: is advertising doomed to kitsch? These questions are also associated with a broader nature: does modernity, especially late modernity, mandate a constant kitsch experience? Advertising is the field of these inquiries.

Chapter 8, "Kitsch in brand management: impact of aesthetic truth and false in advertising strategies" by Aleksandra Chmielewska, examines kitsch's role in the evolution of advertising aesthetics and its impact on brand management strategies. It analyses the use of kitsch to communicate and shape brands' identities and discusses consumer reactions to such strategies. Using kitsch in advertising strategies is empirically analysed through successful and unsuccessful case studies through the lens of the kitsch experience theory. Particular attention is paid to how kitsch affects consumer experience, taking into account psychological and cultural aspects. An interdisciplinary approach combining media theory, consumer psychology, and brand management allows us to comprehensively examine the complexity and consequences of using kitsch in advertising. Three main research questions focus on the impact of kitsch on brand perception, its application in the digital era and effective marketing strategies. The research procedure comprises a critical literature review, a detailed analysis of advertising development and public discourse regarding advertising. The research results contribute to a better understanding of the impact and effectiveness of kitsch use in advertising and media, allowing marketers to better adapt their strategies to changing trends and consumer expectations.

In Chapter 9, "Kitsch in entrepreneurship: meal kits, taste and the art of socio-economic enterprise", David M. Atkinson argues that while the overtly kitsch may find its niche, a normalised entrepreneurship practice – fashioned through a contemporary dialectic-informed, capitalistic education – risks promoting a more subtle yet insidious form of kitsch in enterprise. Here, given the consensus that socio-economic entrepreneurship (and therefore its education) is vital to the growth of capitalist economies, any deviation from a potential universal value of truth, understood in the theme of this present work, as intended action on the part of the entrepreneurship practitioner towards the realisation of something of the absent other – truth in a value exchange between producer and consumer – tends to the kitsch in enterprise. Invoking a methodology of applied analytical philosophy, the author views the case of the meal kit through the lens of a faux-art of enterprise. The author argues that this faux entrepreneurial phenomenon favours appearance and external form, an enterprising value transaction that preys on convenience, prettiness, and pleasure, as an exemplar of entrepreneurial enterprise for enterprise's sake.

Chapter 10, "Kitsch in decision-making: financial destabilisation of joint-stock companies by boards of directors" by Aneta Ejsmont, investigates the kitsch characteristics of decisions made by the boards of directors of large joint-stock companies regarding their financial condition examined in the face of a global economic crisis. The research hypothesis is as follows: the strength of cooperative ties promotes the stability of the financial condition of the companies under study. The research method used in the chapter is an econometric model, in which the explanatory variable will not be the financial condition measured by the value of monthly turnover in the period from 1 January 2021 to 31 December 2023, but the same financial condition, but measured by the value of daily turnover recorded in the period between 1 September 2023 and 15 March 2024 in the joint-stock companies included in the WIG20 index on Warsaw Stock Exchange. Considering the explanatory variables, the original idea was to study the impact of the capitalisation of domestic and foreign companies listed on the primary and regulated markets. However, because of current events (military conflict in Ukraine, energetic crisis) that we see in the media daily, the chapter intends to study the impact of the turnover of the companies under study on the overall value of the WIG20 index.

Chapter 11, "Kitsch in new technologies management: design practices and user experiences", written by Artur Modliński and Ada Florentyna Pawlak, explores the principles governing kitsch aesthetics in the context of new technologies, focusing on design practices and user experiences. By examining trends such as wearable technology, biohacking, digital augmentation of androids, and the design of virtual agents, the study aims to understand how designers and users contribute to creating kitsch in the technology field. The application of artificial intelligence, generative art, and deep fake culture is discussed in the context of information saturation and content overload, potentially introducing kitsch elements into user experiences. There are cases of technological kitsch as a marketing strategy, deliberately evoking emotions and consciously combining outdated elements with modernity. Technological kitsch raises questions about the sustainability of design trends and the inherent tension between innovation and sentimentality. Simultaneously, it provides insight into the complex interaction between technological evolution and cultural nostalgia, encouraging critical analysis of our collective aspirations and uncertainties in the ever-changing innovation landscape. Through the analysis of various cases and design practices, the chapter contributes to understanding the role of kitsch aesthetics in today's technological environment and its impact on user perception, experiences, and interactions. It also names and analyses features of new technology management using the kitsch experience theory.

Chapter 12, "Kitsch in city space management: beauty and functionality of public space" by Wioletta Małota, discusses the possible sources of kitsch experience in urban city management, analysing the Targowek case of urban space redevelopment in a Warsaw district, Poland's capital. Two main research questions were addressed: 1) Which factors in creating, planning, implementing, and evaluating a public space redevelopment project might determine that kitsch experience would occur? and 2) What can be a kitsch experience in public space – the artworks themselves, their creation process, or narration? To answer these questions, specific requests about the four phases of urban project management in a public space were formulated, including its conception, preparation, implementation, and evaluation. The occurrence of kitsch experience was analysed through the aesthetic and kitsch experience theories and the model of city development concepts. The theory was an analysis tool to assess the quality of management of the four project phases. The model of the city development concepts was used to compare modern city concepts with those implemented in the concept of the Targowek project. The Targowek case study was a pretext to formulate potential places of kitsch experience components' appearance in the model of urban project management of a public space.

Chapter 13, "Kitsch in social media: self-optimisation gurus on Instagram" by Olga Kosińska and Weronika Pokojska, analyses self-proclaimed self-optimisation gurus whose actions are prominent, especially on social media such as Instagram. Many of their posts not only contain advice but also operate with a range of attributes that construct a model of success that users should strive to achieve – also employing visuals, as Instagram is an image-centred medium, they suggest potential success scenarios to users by showing specific aesthetics. We argue that they are kitsch producers using certain kitsch artefacts that often-spread shallow concepts with many quick and simple rules to flatter their audience. In this chapter, we conduct a netnographic study of selected examples of female Instagram self-optimisation gurus and try to find answers to the following research questions: 1) What makes a self-management or self-optimisation guru on Instagram? 2) What are the attributes of success as described by self-optimisation gurus? and 3) What makes self-optimisation gurus kitsch producers?

References

Botz-Bornstein, T. (2015) 'Kitsch and Bullshit', *Philosophy and Literature*, 39(2), pp. 305–321. https://doi.org/10.1353/phl.2015.0053.

Botz-Bornstein, T. (2019) 'Kitsch: An "Alternative Aesthetic Truth"', in *The New Aesthetics of Deculturation*. Bloomsbury Publishing Plc, pp. 43–60. https://doi.org/10.5040/9781350086371.0008.

Botz-Bornstein, T. (2021) '"Bullshit Art" and Non-Fungible-Tokens', *Polish Journal of Aesthetics*, 63(4), pp. 69–83. https://doi.org/10.19205/63.21.4.

Broch, H. (1969) 'Evil in the System of Artistic Values', in Dorfles, G. (ed.) *Kitsch: The World of Bad Taste*. New York: Universe Books, pp. 68–76.

Ciupka, S. (2020) 'Pathologies and Kitsch in the Workplace – Theoretical Perspective', *ASEJ Scientific Journal of Bielsko-Biala School of Finance and Law*, 24(1), pp. 26–30. https://doi.org/10.5604/01.3001.0014.1347.

Dorfles, G. (1969) *Kitsch: An Anthology of Bad Taste*. New York: Universe Books.

Kjellman-Chapin, M. (2023) *Kitsch: History, Theory, Practice*. Newcastle upon Tyne: Cambridge Scholars Publishing.

Kostera, M. (1997) 'The Kitsch-Organisation', *Studies in Cultures, Organizations, and Societies*, 3(2), pp. 163–177. https://doi.org/10.1080/10245289708523494.

Kulka, T. (1996) *Kitsch and Art*. University Park: Pennsylvania State University Press.
Linstead, S. (2002) 'Organizational Kitsch. The Aesthetic Turn in Management', *Organization*, 9(4), pp. 657–682. https://doi.org/10.4324/9781351147965-4.
Ryynänen, M. and Barragán, P. (eds) (2023) *The Changing Meaning of Kitsch. From Rejection to Acceptance*. Cham: Palgrave Macmillan. https://doi.org/10.1007/978-3-031-16632-7.
Szostak, M. (2023) *Sztuka zarządzania – zarządzanie sztuką*. Łódź-Warszawa: Wydawnictwo Społecznej Akademii Nauk.
Szostak, M. (2024) *Humanistic Management, Organisation and Aesthetics: Art of Management and Management of Art*. New York City: Routledge. https://doi.org/10.4324/9781003458029.
Szostak, M. and Sułkowski, Ł. (2020) 'Kitsch in Management: Characteristic Forms, Carriers and Propagators', in *Education Excellence and Innovation Management: A 2025 Vision to Sustain Economic Development During Global Challenges: Proceedings of the 35th International Business Information Management Association Conference (IBIMA)*. Sevilla: IBIMA, pp. 7584–7598. Available at: https://depot.ceon.pl/handle/123456789/19173.
van de Klundert, M. and van Boeschoten, R. (2017) *Organisations and Humanisation. Perspectives on Organising Humanisation and Humanising Organisations*. London and New York: Routledge.

1 From kitsch phenomenon, through kitsch experience, to kitschy management and management of kitsch

Michał Szostak

Introduction

Aesthetics named the concept of kitsch as the phenomenon of departing from artistic values in favour of simplifying features. As an aesthetic defence against reality, kitsch seemingly normalises painful episodes of history, neutralising, trivialising, commercialising, and exploiting them (Saltzman, 2001). Kitsch consists of sentimentalised and unreflective manipulation of emotions, distortion of perception, limiting rationality and understanding, and avoiding or suppressing unpleasant or disturbing aspects of reality. Unreflective and uncritical kitsch quickly succumbs to propaganda and group thinking. It is mistaken for entertainment, attractiveness, or fame, masks personal flaws, and serves to cajole. Moreover, kitsch as dogma diverts attention from essential issues underlying reality, especially those contradictory and conflicting, preferring compliance, and maintaining the status quo (Kulka, 1996; Solomon, 1997). Kitsch is usually figurative, drawing on conventions rather than abstract styles. One of its most characteristic features is the use of standard and tried-and-tested canons of representation rather than esoteric, idiosyncratic, original, or innovative styles (Kulka, 1996). All this is to achieve unquestionable and easy identification of the object by its recipients. The aesthetic conservatism of kitsch, though stylistically reactionary, implies its accessibility and comprehensibility by recipients. Its expressiveness and one-dimensionality (lack of ambiguity, nuances, uncertainties, or hidden meanings) usually allow only one interpretation, emphasising its fundamentality and dogmatism. As "art" is pre-digested and presented to the viewer, kitsch saves its effort, providing instant pleasure without the trouble of interpretation, an immanent art feature. Kitsch, being mechanical, works by formulas; being a vicarious experience and a feign of sensation, it changes according to fashion, although, in essence, it always remains the same (Greenberg, 1985). Kitsch is the epitome of falsehood because, pretending to be valuable, it demands money from its consumers. However, on the other hand, money – measuring the relative value of objects – reduces an individual's artistic activity to the margin of alienation. As a result, works of art are increasingly

DOI: 10.4324/9781003504931-2

evolving towards a closed world, with fewer and fewer points where the subjective viewer can develop his will, reflection, and feelings in a multi-level process of contemplation. In this way, economic modes of interaction replace socially rooted ones, transforming every aspect of life to fit the logic of market exchange through commodification (Samier, 2008).

The *research questions* this chapter will answer are the following: RQ1. What are the main factors that distinguish approaches to kitsch in the literature on aesthetics and art? RQ2. What is the applicability of defined groups of approaches to kitsch that can be used to analyse the managerial and organisational kitsch efficiently?

The primary *research method* applied in these analyses is the critical analysis of the literature (monographs and articles) written mainly in English and Polish in the 20th and 21st centuries. The central sources of articles were scientific bases such as Google Scholar, SCOPUS, Web of Science, Mendeley, and JSTOR. The chapter will not analyse all concepts and theories around the kitsch phenomenon; there is much fresh and extensive research on that (Kjellman-Chapin, 2023; Ryynänen and Barragán, 2023). Instead, the chapter synthesises existing theories on aesthetic and artistic kitsch from a historical point of view of their development from the end of the 19th century until today, and it synthesises methodologies applied in studying kitsch; next, kitsch is categorised into main groups based on disciplinary focus, and then these groups are classified in a dichotomic manner based on the substance of their interest and validated for their adaptivity to describing the kitsch phenomenon in the managerial and organisational area.

Classifications of kitsch theories

Summing up all approaches and theories about kitsch, the following dichotomic classifications can be made: 1) descriptive focus on kitsch phenomenon versus kitsch artefact; 2) substantive character of descriptive narration: black-and-white versus grey scale; and 3) dynamics of the phenomenon: kitsch as a phenomenon (state) versus kitsch as an experience (process).

Phenomenon (in general) versus artefact (result)

The concept of kitsch is analysed through two primary approaches: as a phenomenon and as an artefact. These approaches help delineate kitsch's broader implications in cultural and artistic contexts, offering insights into its nature, impact, and manifestations.

Kitsch as a phenomenon encompasses the cultural and societal processes that give rise to kitsch, viewing it as a pervasive aspect of modern life rather than just specific objects. This approach examines how kitsch reflects and influences cultural values, tastes, and behaviours. As a phenomenon, kitsch is seen as a product of specific cultural and social conditions. The rise of kitsch is tied to the industrialisation and democratisation of culture. With mass production and the spread of consumer culture, art became more accessible, leading to the proliferation of aesthetically pleasing but shallow cultural products. This democratisation, while positive in some respects, also meant that art was increasingly produced for mass consumption, often sacrificing depth and originality for broad appeal (Greenberg, 1985). Kitsch as a phenomenon also involves understanding the psychological and emotional responses it evokes. It highlights how kitsch plays on collective emotions, creating a sense of communal identity through shared sentimentalism. Kitsch offers comfort and escapism, appealing to a desire for an idealised reality. This emotional manipulation can be seen as a response to the complexities and anxieties of modern life, providing a simplified and comforting alternative (Kundera, 1984). The phenomenon of kitsch is also analysed through its ideological functions. Totalitarian regimes often utilise kitsch to propagate idealised and simplistic images that support their political agendas. In this sense, kitsch becomes a tool for ideological control, shaping public perceptions and maintaining social order through emotionally appealing but intellectually shallow imagery (Kundera, 1984; Kostera, 1997).

Kitsch as an artefact focuses on the specific objects and works of art considered kitsch. This approach examines the characteristics that make an object kitsch and how these objects function within cultural and aesthetic frameworks. Kitsch artefacts are often characterised by their aesthetic and formal properties. Excessive ornamentation, bright colours, and a lack of subtlety typically mark kitsch objects. These characteristics make kitsch easily recognisable and immediately appealing, but also superficial. The aesthetic appeal of kitsch artefacts is based on clichés and familiar motifs, which provide instant gratification without demanding deeper engagement (Moles, 1971). Another defining feature of kitsch artefacts is their reproducibility, which is how the mass production of art leads to kitsch creation. Reproducible art loses its unique "aura", becoming a commodified object designed for mass consumption. Kitsch artefacts, therefore, are often mass-produced, making them accessible to a broad audience but also stripping them of originality and authenticity (Benjamin, 2013). Kitsch artefacts are typically created for specific functions, such as home decoration, entertainment, or souvenir collection. They are designed to be pleasing and comforting, often evoking nostalgia or idealised memories. The primary purpose of kitsch artefacts is to elicit an immediate and uncomplicated emotional response. Unlike high art, which often challenges the viewer and provokes thoughtful reflection, kitsch artefacts aim to be instantly likeable and emotionally gratifying (Kulka, 1996).

Black-and-white versus grey scale

The concept of kitsch can be approached through two distinct lenses: the black-and-white approach and the grey-scale approach. These perspectives offer different ways of understanding and categorising kitsch, each with implications and analysis.

The black-and-white approach to kitsch is characterised by a clear, binary distinction between what is considered kitsch and what is considered genuine art.

This perspective often relies on strict criteria and value judgements to differentiate the two categories. Proponents of this approach argue that kitsch is unequivocally inferior to high art due to its lack of originality, depth, and authenticity. Kitsch is inherently derivative and formulaic, merely imitating the surface effects of genuine art without contributing any substantive innovation or emotional depth. According to this view, kitsch is seen as a cultural pollutant that dilutes the standards of true artistic expression (Greenberg, 1985). The black-and-white approach often incorporates moral and ethical dimensions, viewing kitsch as both aesthetically inferior and ethically problematic. Kitsch represents a counterfeit aesthetic experience that deceives viewers by offering false beauty and sentimentality; by presenting a sanitised and idealised version of reality, kitsch undermines authentic engagement with the complexities and challenges of human existence (Broch, 1933, 1969b). This approach emphasises a clear demarcation between high art and kitsch, often relegating kitsch to a lower cultural status. Kitsch is part of the culture industry's effort to standardise and commodify cultural products, reinforcing social conformity and passive consumption (Horkheimer and Adorno, 2002).

In contrast, *the grey-scale approach* to kitsch recognises a continuum between kitsch and high art, emphasising the fluidity and contextuality of aesthetic value. This perspective challenges the rigid distinctions of the black-and-white approach and acknowledges the complexity of cultural production and reception. The grey-scale approach suggests that kitsch and high art are not mutually exclusive categories but exist on a spectrum. What might be considered kitsch in one context could be appreciated as genuine art in another, depending on factors such as cultural context, individual taste, and historical period. This approach allows for a more nuanced understanding of aesthetic value, recognising that tastes and cultural standards evolve (Kulka, 1996). This perspective also highlights the importance of context in defining kitsch. What is considered kitsch in one culture might be revered in another, and vice versa. In a postmodern world, the lines between kitsch and high art are increasingly blurred; all cultural products are part of a system of signs and meanings that can shift depending on the context, thus challenging the rigid distinctions upheld by the black-and-white approach (Baudrillard, 1994). The grey-scale approach is often more inclusive and democratic, recognising the value of diverse forms of cultural expression. It challenges elitist notions of aesthetic hierarchy and acknowledges that mass-produced and popular culture can have significant artistic and emotional value. This perspective is aligned with contemporary cultural studies, emphasising the legitimacy of studying popular culture alongside traditional high art.

Phenomenon (state) versus experience (process)

Understanding kitsch can be approached through two distinct lenses: kitsch as a phenomenon and kitsch as an experience. These perspectives offer different ways of analysing and interpreting kitsch's nature, impact, and reception.

Kitsch as a phenomenon refers to the widespread cultural, social, and economic processes that give rise to kitsch. This approach examines how kitsch functions within larger societal structures and its implications for culture and art. When viewed as a phenomenon, kitsch is seen as a product of specific historical and cultural contexts. The rise of kitsch is tied to the democratisation of culture brought about by industrialisation and mass production; in a society where art is mass-produced and widely disseminated, kitsch thrives by offering easily accessible, formulaic, and superficially appealing products that cater to the tastes of the masses (Greenberg, 1985). The proliferation of kitsch is closely linked to economic forces and the mechanisms of mass production that change the nature of art by making it more accessible but also more commodified. As a phenomenon, kitsch emerges from this context, where the emphasis on commercial viability produces aesthetically pleasing but shallow and derivative works. These works prioritise marketability over artistic integrity, reflecting broader capitalist dynamics (Benjamin, 2013; Ergül, 2016). Kitsch as a phenomenon also encompasses its role in maintaining social control and reinforcing dominant ideologies. The culture industry produces standardised cultural goods that serve to pacify and manipulate the masses. In this sense, kitsch functions ideologically by providing comforting and familiar images that prevent critical engagement with social and political realities. It reinforces the status quo by offering an escapist alternative to the complexities and challenges of real life (Horkheimer and Adorno, 2002).

Kitsch as an experience focuses on the subjective reception and emotional responses of individuals engaging with kitsch. This approach examines how kitsch affects viewers on a personal and emotional level. Kitsch is often defined by its ability to evoke strong, immediate emotional responses. It is criticised for its sentimentalism, arguing that it manipulates emotions by presenting idealised and overly simplistic images that evoke nostalgia, comfort, and sentimentality. This emotional manipulation is problematic because it offers a superficial sense of beauty and happiness, avoiding the more profound and often more challenging truths of human existence (Kundera, 1984). One of the critical characteristics of kitsch as an experience is its accessibility. Kitsch is designed to be immediately pleasing and easily understood, requiring little intellectual or emotional effort from the viewer. This immediate gratification can be appealing, providing a quick and easy emotional reward. However, it also means that kitsch lacks the depth and complexity that encourage prolonged reflection and engagement (Kulka, 1996). Kitsch as an experience plays a role in shaping personal and cultural identities. Baudrillard's concept of hyperreality suggests that in a postmodern world, people's experiences are increasingly mediated by images and representations. Kitsch contributes to this hyperreality by offering familiar and comforting images that resonate with individual and collective identities. These experiences can be meaningful to people, even based on superficial or idealised representations (Baudrillard, 1994). The newest broad addition to analysing kitsch as an experience is the theory built by Szostak and Sułkowski on the fundament of Maria Gołaszewska's theory of aesthetic experience (Gołaszewska, 1984b), reversed into an opposite-to-art state of kitsch and then developed by application of kitsch phenomenon descriptions (Szostak and Sułkowski, 2020a).

Kitsch theories' application within managerial and organisational studies

Following the definition of management as an art of achieving goals efficiently (Szostak, 2024, p. 53), the following is an assessment of different kitsch theories and their applicability within managerial and organisational contexts. Traditionally studied within art and culture, kitsch can also provide valuable insights when applied to management and organisational studies (Szostak, 2024, pp. 233–260). Understanding kitsch through various theoretical lenses can help managers and organisations navigate various issues.

Kitsch as a phenomenon: cultural and economic dynamics. Understanding kitsch as a phenomenon influenced by mass production and cultural dynamics is highly relevant in managerial and organisational contexts. This approach can be applied to branding and marketing strategies where companies must appeal to mass markets. For instance, recognising the appeal of kitsch in consumer goods can help managers develop products that resonate emotionally with a broad audience. This theory is applicable because it aligns with consumer culture theories, highlighting the importance of emotional engagement and mass appeal in marketing. The cultural and economic forces that drive kitsch are analogous to market forces that shape consumer preferences and behaviour. Brands like Coca-Cola or Disney have successfully leveraged kitsch aesthetics to create a sense of nostalgia and emotional connection with their consumers (Solomon, 1997, 2019; Holt, 2002, 2004).

Kitsch as an experience: emotional and psychological perspectives. Kitsch has an emotional and psychological appeal and is particularly useful in organisational behaviour and human resource management. Understanding how kitsch creates solid emotional responses can aid in designing organisational cultures and employee engagement strategies that foster a sense of belonging and emotional well-being. This theory is applicable because emotional engagement is critical in motivating employees and enhancing job satisfaction. Creating an organisational culture that evokes positive emotions through symbolic elements (e.g. corporate storytelling, office decor, and rituals) can strengthen employee loyalty and productivity (Kahn, 1990; Ashkanasy, Zerbe and Härtel, 2016).

Kitsch and ideological functions: organisational control and branding. The ideological functions of kitsch, mainly its role in reinforcing social norms and ideologies, can be applied to corporate branding and internal communications. Organisations can use kitsch to promote company values and create a unified corporate identity. This theory is applicable because it aligns with strategic management practices that use corporate culture to align employees with organisational goals. By leveraging kitsch aesthetics, companies can create powerful symbols that embody corporate values and inspire collective identity among employees (Hatch, 1993; Schein and Schein, 2004; Schein, 2013).

Kitsch as inauthenticity and ethical concerns. The critique of kitsch as inauthentic and ethically problematic has limited direct applicability in a managerial context, except in areas concerned with corporate ethics and authenticity in branding. While the ethical implications of kitsch are essential, the focus on inauthenticity might not translate well into practical managerial strategies. However, this perspective can serve as a cautionary framework, reminding managers to avoid overly simplistic or manipulative branding practices that could backfire regarding consumer trust and brand reputation (Macdonald, 2001; Solomon, 2019).

Kitsch and aestheticisation of everyday life (aesthetics of superficiality). The concept of kitsch contributing to the aestheticisation of everyday life is applicable in organisational design and workspace management. Creating visually appealing and emotionally comforting environments can enhance employee satisfaction and productivity. This theory is applicable because the physical and aesthetic aspects of the workplace significantly impact employee well-being and productivity. Incorporating kitsch elements like nostalgic decor or playful design can create a more engaging and pleasant work environment (Duffy, 1997; Becker, 2004). On this occasion, it should be mentioned that the aesthetics of superficiality is a consequence of the aesthetics of depth (Welsch, 2005; Szostak, 2024, p. 124).

Kitsch and self-awareness. Self-awareness is the foundation of self-management and self-organisation, where self-awareness and the ability to reflect play key roles (Kostera, 2014, 2019). Self-management is fundamental to managing other individuals, groups, and organisations. Within this issue, kitsch may depict dominant egoism, exaggeration of self, or grandiosity (Szostak and Sułkowski, 2020a).

Applying kitsch theories in managerial and organisational contexts offers valuable insights into branding, consumer behaviour, employee engagement, and organisational culture. Theories focusing on kitsch as a phenomenon and experience are particularly relevant, providing practical frameworks for creating emotionally engaging and culturally resonant corporate strategies. While some aspects of kitsch, such as its inauthenticity and ethical concerns, have limited direct applicability, they are important considerations for maintaining authenticity and integrity in organisational practices. Kitsch theories enrich our understanding of the interplay between culture, aesthetics, and management, offering diverse tools for enhancing organisational effectiveness and cultural resonance.

Managerial and organisational kitsch in the scientific literature

The literature review on kitsch within managerial and organisational contexts shows two main groups of discourse: 1) kitsch as a defined and named phenomenon and conscious analysis of its character, features, roots, and consequences (Kostera, 1997; Linstead, 2002; Ciupka, 2020; Szostak and Sułkowski, 2020a); 2) description of kitschy issues without using the word "kitsch"; in this case, authors omit, consciously or unconsciously, a complicated issue of defining kitsch; however, their narrations and intentions balance around the kitsch phenomenon clearly and/or intuitively (Taylor and Hansen, 2005). The below synthesis draws from both discursive groups of sources and is divided into the following sections: 1) main research problems within the literature on managerial and organisational kitsch, 2) applied methodologies within the literature on managerial and organisational kitsch, 3) key conclusions within the literature on managerial and organisational kitsch, 4) specific examples used to describe managerial and organisational kitsch, and 5) implications of kitsch for managers, employees, managerial process, managerial methods, and managerial techniques and whole organisations.

The main *research problems* around kitsch present in the literature on managerial and organisational kitsch are described as follows:

1. the difficulty in defining and recognising kitsch within organisational contexts, avoiding, at the same time, its simplifying, simulating, and sentimentalising tendencies (Linstead, 2002);
2. impact on authenticity and knowledge; kitsch obscures the processes of construction, making artificial experiences appear natural and glossing over inevitable gaps; it can make ignorance appear as knowledge, blocking new insights and silencing critique (Linstead, 2002);
3. emotional and theoretical numbing; kitsch blunts our capacities to respond to our ontical situation by perpetually taking the emotionally and theoretically easy way out (Linstead, 2002; Hochschild, 2012);
4. empty rhetoric and superficial practices that characterise organisational life (in general or particular areas), disconnecting managerial rhetoric from practice (Bolton and Houlihan, 2007; Hochschild, 2012; Alvesson, 2013);
5. the tension between authenticity and superficiality in modern organisations and workplaces (Fleming, 2009);
6. focusing on narrow managerial or organisational issues like theatrical and often kitsch-like nature of business presentations (Biehl-Missal, 2011);
7. kitsch as a negative side of aesthetic awareness of organisational phenomena (Strati, 1999, 2009);
8. the role of organisational culture and identity in unity and diversity management (Parker, 2000);
9. the influence of postmodern aesthetics and superficiality in organisational settings, especially organisational culture and employee experiences (Hancock and Tyler, 2001);
10. impact of aesthetics, including kitsch, into organisational life (Warren, 2008).

Methodologies applied while researching managerial and organisational kitsch are diverse, mainly mixing varied qualitative approaches:

1. comparative analysis of kitsch in different arenas, such as classical organisation theory and applied simplified quasi-theories (Linstead, 2002);
2. historical and conceptual tracing to understand kitsch's core characteristics and its response to modernism (Linstead, 2002);
3. metaphorical analysis; the kitsch metaphor is used to analyse organisations, emphasising the construction and collectivist dimensions and drawing attention to the significance of façades (Kostera, 1997; Linstead, 2002; Szostak, 2023);
4. ethnographic methods, including extensive fieldwork in organisations (Parker, 2000; Hancock and Tyler, 2001; Alvesson, 2013);
5. sensory ethnography and visual analysis (Warren, 2008);
6. case studies (Parker, 2000; Hochschild, 2012);
7. content analysis (Bolton and Houlihan, 2007; Biehl-Missal, 2011);
8. a multidisciplinary approach, combining insights from varied subdisciplines like marketing, management, and cultural studies (Kornberger, 2010) or even different fields like management and art or aesthetics (Strati, 1999; Minahan, 2020; Szostak, 2022, 2024);
9. critical theory (Hancock and Tyler, 2001);

A synthesis of *key conclusions* on managerial and organisational kitsch touches on the following issues:

1. pervasiveness and adaptability; kitsch is adaptable and constantly changing at a superficial level; it can achieve cheap artistic, social, and political effects by selling ideas and feelings (Linstead, 2002; Hochschild, 2012);
2. human-centeredness and narcissism; kitsch is human-centred, proposing that the world is as we want it to be; it positions humanity at the centre of creation and fosters a narcissistic adoration of the familiar (Linstead, 2002);
3. defence mechanism; kitsch acts as a collective defence mechanism, providing a mask for materiality and the anguishes of being and defending against the abject (Linstead, 2002);
4. simplification and translation; kitsch simplifies and translates complex theories into more digestible forms, often underweighting theory in the process (Linstead, 2002);
5. illusory arrangements created by organisations to present an appealing surface to external groups, which may not reflect the actual functioning of the organisation (Linstead, 2002; Alvesson, 2013);
6. kitsch as a symptom of deep structural issues within modern organisations, such as the pursuit of image over substance and the focus on short-term gains; the prevalence of kitsch contributes to a culture of emptiness, where

employees are disengaged and organisational values are hollow (Alvesson, 2013);

7. commodification of emotional expressions in organisations leading to kitsch-like representations of genuine human interactions; this commodification can create a façade that masks the true emotional state of employees, potentially leading to emotional exhaustion and a lack of authentic engagement in the workplace (Hochschild, 2012);
8. superficiality of communication in business contexts; presentations prioritising style over substance, turning them into performances rather than genuine information exchanges; this leads to a disconnect between presentation content and actual organisational practices (Biehl-Missal, 2011, 2015);
9. while aesthetically pleasing elements can enhance the workplace environment, an overemphasis on kitsch (superficial and overly simplistic design choices) can detract from critical thinking and genuine innovation (Taylor and Hansen, 2005);
10. the commercialisation and branding of organisational culture often introduce kitsch elements, such as overly simplistic and emotionally charged brand narratives; these elements create a superficial corporate culture that emphasises image over substantive values, potentially leading to a lack of authenticity and deeper employee engagement (Kornberger, 2010);
11. pursuing a unified organisational culture may lead to adopting superficial symbols and rituals to create a sense of belonging and unity but often fails to address deeper issues of identity and division within the organisation; it can result in a veneer of cohesion that masks underlying conflicts and discontent (Parker, 2000);
12. overly simplistic and sentimental initiatives can create a façade of care and engagement, while in reality, these practices often lack genuine impact and fail to foster authentic satisfaction and engagement (Bolton and Houlihan, 2007);
13. postmodern influences lead to the incorporation of kitsch elements (themed workspaces, sentimental corporate values) in organisational culture; their lack of depth and their role in creating a disingenuous work environment can undermine genuine employee engagement and organisational authenticity (Hancock and Tyler, 2001);
14. many organisational practices aimed at promoting authenticity are, in fact, kitsch by involving overly sentimental or simplistic approaches that fail to resonate with employees on a deeper level; the result is a superficial culture that can lead to employee cynicism and disengagement (Fleming, 2009);
15. kitsch in organisational aesthetics (such as motivational posters and themed environments) serve more as superficial decorations than meaningful influences on organisational culture and contribute to a disconnection between the visual appeal of the workplace and the actual experiences and sentiments of employees (Warren, 2008).

As *specific examples* for illustrating kitsch in managerial and organisational theory are used:

1. Maslow's hierarchy of needs; this hierarchy simplifies Freudian desire into a more digestible form for management students and is often used to illustrate reasons for all organisational problems related to human issues (Linstead, 2002);
2. oversimplified wellness programmes (like step challenges, meditation sessions, and healthy eating seminars) aiming to promote employee well-being but often failing to address deeper issues such as workplace stress, job insecurity, and work-life balance (Bolton and Houlihan, 2007);
3. Peters and Waterman's "excellence" literature (Peters and Waterman, 2012); the success of this book is seen as a testament to its kitsch qualities, translating the whole academic theory about leadership into a simple set of rules applicable to every managerial problem (Linstead, 2002);
4. themed workspaces and office decor (open-plan offices with bean bags, slides, and quirky decor) intended to create a fun and engaging work environment but overshadowing the need for functional and supportive workspaces with ergonomic workstations, adequate meeting spaces, and quiet areas for focused work (Hancock and Tyler, 2001);
5. motivational slogans and corporate mantras (such as "Work hard, play hard" or "We are a family") intended to foster a sense of unity and motivation among employees but lack substantive meaning and are perceived as empty rhetoric (Fleming, 2009);
6. sentimental corporate rituals (such as team-building retreats, award ceremonies, and holiday parties) that aim to foster camaraderie and loyalty but are overly sentimental and fail to address employees' real challenges (Warren, 2008).

Researchers show the following *implications* of kitsch presence in management and organisations:

1. cultural and social critique; kitsch in organisations can be used to critique the superficiality and lack of depth in modern organisational practices, highlighting the need for more substantial and critical approaches (Linstead, 2002);
2. educational impact; the idealised images of working life presented in media, management books, and public appearances can influence education and create a disconnect between theory and practice (Linstead, 2002; Alvesson, 2013);
3. superficial engagement, for example, in HRM practices that aim to create an illusion of care and engagement without addressing the deeper needs of employees; such practices can include oversimplified wellness programmes, clichéd motivational initiatives, and sentimental corporate values that do not translate into meaningful action (Bolton and Houlihan, 2007);

4. disingenuous organisational culture, for example, themed workspaces, sentimental rituals, and superficial corporate narratives, can create a disingenuous sense of unity and cohesion; these elements often mask underlying issues and fail to address the natural dynamics within the organisation (Hancock and Tyler, 2001);
5. undermining *authenticity, developing* cynicism and disengagement; overly sentimental or simplistic approaches to fostering authenticity can be seen as disingenuous, leading to cynicism and disengagement among employees (Fleming, 2009);
6. aestheticisation *without substance, fostering a* disconnect between appearance and reality; visually appealing but functionally insignificant elements, such as motivational posters and themed office environments, can create a disconnect between the visual appeal of the workplace and the actual experiences and sentiments of employees (Warren, 2008).

As a final remark of the literature review, it can be said that approaches to managerial and organisational kitsch are twofold:

1. kitsch as a result of oversimplification, superficiality, or dehumanisation (van de Klundert and van Boeschoten, 2017); in this case, we can analyse *kitsch in management*;
2. kitsch as a means for achieving goals – conscious use of organisational kitsch by managers to lead an organisation in a particular way (Szostak, 2024); in this case, we can analyse *the management of kitsch*.

The concept of kitsch in managerial and organisational contexts highlights the tension between appearance and substance in contemporary corporate life. The works reviewed here illustrate that while kitsch can create an appealing veneer, it often fails to address underlying issues and can lead to disengagement and disillusionment. These studies collectively advocate for a more authentic and substantive approach to management that values genuine engagement and meaningful practices over superficial and sentimental gestures.

Metaphor: an organisation as a work of art

Researchers have created many metaphors for the organisation, which is the essential field for processes and phenomena related to management (Sułkowski, 2011). Some metaphors also refer to the world of art, for example, an organisation as an orchestra or jazz band (manager as conductor), an organisation as theatre (manager as an actor) or an organisation as history (Biehl-Missal, 2011). The shadow of the "organisation as a work of art" metaphor was outlined by the team J. Reckhenrich, M. Kupp, and J. Anderson (Reckhenrich, Kupp and Anderson, 2009) while its full development with

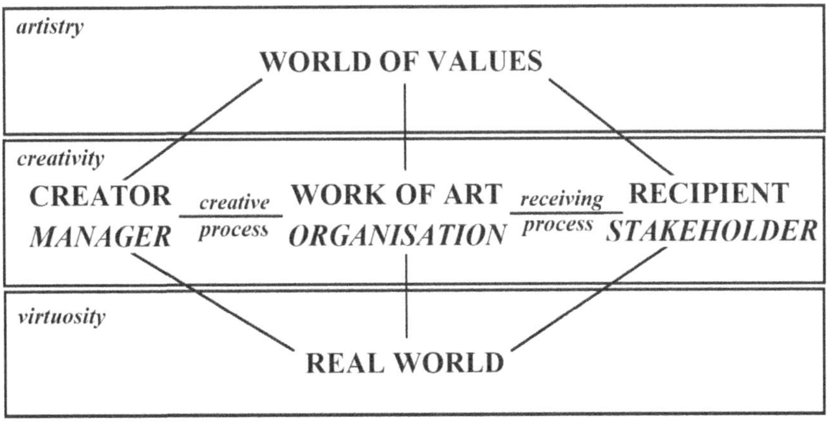

Figure 1.1 Application of M. Gołaszewska's theory of the aesthetic situation in a managerial context

Source: (Szostak, 2024, p. 126)

extensive use of the achievements of aesthetics – in the form of an organisation as a product of the "creator" (manager), which is created (modelled and managed) for the needs of "recipients" (stakeholders) according to specific "universal values" within the "real world" – was presented only in 2020 (Szostak and Sułkowski, 2020b).

The assumptions of the theory of "aesthetic situation", which translates the theory of "axiological situation" into the field of aesthetics, may be summed up in the following form: the creator in the creative process creates a work of art; the recipient contemplates the work of art in the process of reception; all these elements (creator, work, recipient) have connections and interactions with the world of universal values and take place in the real world, determining the type of art, but also creative methods and techniques. Although the most important from the point of view of aesthetics are universal values, and the most noticeable manifestation of creativity is the work itself, in the person of the creator (in consciousness, subconsciousness), there are fundamental processes that make up the phenomenon of creativity (Figure 1.1).

The kitsch experience theory

Based on the theory of the aesthetic situation, the problem of the "kitsch experience" can be presented, showing its opposition to the "aesthetic experience". A kitsch product is called a "kitsch artefact", and a kitsch maker is called a "kitsch producer", distinguishing it from aesthetic experience. A synthesis of the discussed phenomena is presented in Table 1.1.

Table 1.1 Differences between aesthetic experience and kitsch experience

Component	*Aesthetic experience*	*Kitsch experience*
Creator/Producer	focus on universal values	targeting a mass audience
	creative inventiveness	duplication, copying
	open to criticism and discussion	open to criticism and discussion
Work/Artefact	an advantage over the recipient	dominated by the desires and needs of the recipient (most often patriotic, religious, sexual, or political)
	extending the recipient's existence	confirms the recipient's habits
	cohesion	pretentiousness
	filling the future based on the past	fulfilling the present
Recipient	submission to a work of art	willingness to interact with the artefact
	exclusiveness	egalitarianism, mass scale
	willingness to contemplate the work from all sides/ dimensions	selection of elements to be considered from the desires of the recipient
	participation of thought, consciousness, and will	avoidance of thought, awareness, and will (lack of thought, credulity, irrationality)
	deep emotions, feelings	shallow and fleeting experience, sentimentalism
	inner contemplation	external experience
	the need for solitude	the need for community
World of values	dominant: true	dominant: prettiness and pleasure
Real world	source of creative inspiration	source of impulses to satisfy

Source: (Szostak and Sułkowski, 2020a) based on (Broch, 1933; Banach, 1968; Gołaszewska, 1984a, 1984b, 1986; Adorno, 2002)

A dependable *art creator* who prioritises universal values is receptive to criticism and dialogue about his work because these interactions allow him to understand what the audience (including critics, who are a distinct type of audience) perceives in his work and what resonates with them. Conversely, the *producer of kitsch* – mimicking either his or others' ideas and patterns – caters to the mass audience and shuns criticism, viewing it as an assault on his independence. A critical examination of kitsch swiftly exposes a lack of values, thereby explaining the aversion to criticism and discourse. One of the motives behind the creation of kitsch is to fabricate an appearance and impression that makes something seem more valuable than it is. Thus, kitsch is a deceptive and disguised imitation masquerading as art (Calinescu, 1987). A genuine *work of art* is coherent, possesses an advantage over the audience, and, by bridging the future with the past, enriches the audience's present (filled with their past experiences, the audience approaches the artwork and shapes their future through the act of reception).

The *kitsch artefact* is often shaped by the recipient's patriotic, religious, sexual, or political desires and needs; it affirms the recipient's habits and fills the present only with the superficial glitter of its pretentiousness. The *recipient of true art* is submissive to the work, granting it exclusivity and enabling it to be considered from every angle and aspect. To fully appreciate art, the recipient must engage reason, awareness, and will to contemplate the values, deep emotions, and feelings embedded within the work. Kitsch artefacts, however, lack essential aesthetic values such as unity, balance, or harmony, which comprise the internal logic of structure and style, complexity, multidimensionality, richness, the fusion of heterogeneous forms, and detailed elaboration. Furthermore, kitsch lacks the artistic value of contributing creatively and innovatively to art history by opening up new possibilities and suggesting solutions to current artistic challenges (Kulka, 1996). While seemingly original, a kitsch artefact does not enhance the recipient's associations with objects or themes; instead, it is parasitic, as it fails to create intrinsic beauty. A kitsch artefact, despite being imitative, has no true provenance – it is detached from the original's essence and ignores the original's contexts.

The *kitsch consumer* engages with kitsch artefacts driven by a sense of mass-scale egalitarianism; they choose things based on their desires, avoiding more profound thought, consciousness, and will, and focus on external, fleeting, and sentimental experiences, preferably shared with others in similar situations. The consumer finds kitsch easy to understand. Kitsch does not challenge sociopolitical realities or specific interests, does not require significant intellectual effort, and avoids unpleasant conflicts. It promises a happy ending while reinforcing prejudice. The allure of kitsch for the consumer lies not in its maker, origin, contribution to the development of art, or even its social status. Kitsch is consumed as an end in itself because it immediately satisfies desires without conflicting with the consumer's feelings and beliefs. It targets universal rather than individual emotions, relying on the "most common" denominator possible (Samier, 2008); it is emotionally stirring but empty, serving primarily as a distraction. Unlike art, kitsch does not accept the nature of things in light of their critical or revealing attributes; it only covers, protects, relieves, and comforts (Gregotti, 1969). Kitsch does not directly question the fundamental metaphysical and moral assumptions of human existence, the meaning of human effort, the adopted moral code, or the meaning of life – it simply disregards these phenomena (Broch, 1969a; Kulka, 1996). Regarding *the world of values*, the aesthetic experience is dominated by truth and beauty, whereas the kitsch experience is dominated by pleasure and prettiness. The *real world* serves as a source of creative inspiration for aesthetic experiences and a source of impulses to be satisfied in a kitsch experience.

Conclusion

Answering RQ1 (What are the main factors that distinguish approaches to kitsch in the literature on aesthetics and art?), it can be said that there are key points that can be found within the aesthetic and artistic discourse on kitsch: 1) historical and etymological origins of kitsch; 2) criticisms of traditional theories on kitsch; 3) modern theories and reinterpretations of traditional theories on kitsch; 4) empirical aesthetics and processing dynamics; 5) functional and social models of kitsch; and 6) contemporary re-theorisation of kitsch. On the other hand, analysing kitsch theories based on disciplinary focus, five main disciplinary perspectives can be identified: 1) aesthetic and formal, 2) psychological and emotional, 3) sociological and cultural, 4) philosophical and existential, and 5) ethical and ideological. For all approaches and theories about kitsch, the following dichotomic classifications can be made: 1) descriptive focus on kitsch phenomenon versus kitsch artefact; 2) substantive character of descriptive narration: black-and-white versus grey scale; and 3) dynamics of the phenomenon: kitsch as a phenomenon (state) versus kitsch as an experience (process).

Answering RQ2 (What is the applicability of defined groups of approaches to kitsch that can be used to analyse the managerial and organisational kitsch efficiently?), the following issues can be conceptualised: 1) kitsch as a phenomenon determining cultural and economic dynamics within organisations and environment shaping managerial practices; 2) kitsch as an experience (process) shaping emotional and psychological perspectives of managers and organisation's stakeholders; 3) kitsch and its ideological functions determining organisational control power distribution, including branding of individuals and products; 4) kitsch as inauthenticity and ethical concerns flowing from this perspective; 5) kitsch and aestheticisation of everyday life (aesthetics of superficiality versus aesthetics of depth); and 6) kitsch within self-awareness allowing to define and control negative aspects of personality like egoism, exaggeration of self, or grandiosity.

The field of kitsch aesthetics presents several *challenges*, primarily due to its complex relationship with cultural and artistic values (not easy to define and analyse) and the evolving nature of contemporary organisations: 1) defining kitsch as consistently and universally acceptable, understanding its role and impact in modern mass culture, and reconciling its perceived negative connotations with its widespread prevalence and acceptance (Klimova and Klimov, 2019; Ortlieb and Carbon, 2019); 2) developing empirical methods to study kitsch could enhance understanding of its psychological and sociological impacts, and bridge the gap between theoretical discussions and empirical evidence, providing a more rounded understanding of kitsch's role in art perception and aesthetic experience (Ortlieb and Carbon, 2019); reevaluating kitsch within various cultural contexts could provide insights into how different societies perceive and integrate kitsch into their cultural and artistic practices; this could challenge the predominantly Western perspective and explore kitsch's role in non-Western cultures (Hoberman, 2005); and 3) integrating kitsch into aesthetic education could help demystify and destigmatise it, allowing for a more inclusive understanding of different aesthetic values; this could also help students appreciate a broader spectrum of artistic expressions (Morreall and Loy, 1989); exploring kitsch in the context of posthuman aesthetics could open new avenues for understanding how kitsch interacts with contemporary issues such as gender, identity, and technology; this kind of re-theorisation could transform the perception of kitsch from mere cultural trash to a valuable tool in cultural critique and artistic expression (Casey, 2019).

References

Adorno, T. W. (2002) *Essays on Music*. Berkeley, Los Angeles and London: University of California Press.

Alvesson, M. (2013) *The Triumph of Emptiness: Consumption, Higher Education, and Work Organization*. Oxford: Oxford University Press.

Ashkanasy, N. M., Zerbe, W. J. and Härtel, C. E. J. (eds) (2016) *Research on Emotion in Organizations*. Leeds: Emerald Group Publishing Limited. https://doi.org/10.1108/S1746-979120160000012018.

Banach, A. (1968) *O kiczu*. Kraków: Wydawnictwo Literackie.

Baudrillard, J. (1994) *Simulacra and Simulation*. Ann Arbor, MI: University of Michigan Press. https://doi.org/10.3998/mpub.9904.

Becker, F. (2004) *Offices at Work: Uncommon Workspace Strategies That Add Value and Improve Performance*. Jossey-Bass.

Benjamin, W. (2013) *The Work of Art in the Age of Mechanical Reproduction*. Hoboken, NJ: Penguin Books. https://doi.org/10.4324/9780203124291-54.

Biehl-Missal, B. (2011) *Wirtschaftsästhetik. Wie Unternehmen die Kunst als Inspiration und Werkzeug nutzen*. Wiesbaden: Gabler Verlag.

Biehl-Missal, B. (2015) 'Finding Form: Gestalt as a Development of Aesthetic Approaches to Organisation and Management', *Dialogue and Universalism*, 25(4), pp. 163–172. https://doi.org/10.5840/du201525492.

Bolton, S. C. and Houlihan, M. (eds) (2007) *Searching for the Human in Human Resource Management: Theory, Practice and Workplace Contexts*. New York: Red Globe Press.

Broch, H. (1933) *Das Böse in dem Wertsystem der Kunst*. Berlin: S. Fischer. https://doi.org/10.1515/9783111502489-168.

Broch, H. (1969a) 'Evil in the System of Artistic Values', in Dorfles, G. (ed) *Kitsch: The World of Bad Taste*. New York: Universe Books, pp. 68–76.

Broch, H. (1969b) 'Notes on the Problem of Kitsch', in Dorfles, G. (ed) *Kitsch: An Anthology of Bad Taste*. New York: Universe Books, pp. 49–67.

Calinescu, M. (1987) *Five Faces of Modernity: Modernism, Avant-Garde, Decadence, Kitsch, Postmodernism*. Durham: Duke University Press.

Casey, K. (2019) 'On Kitsch in Nature & Technology: Redefining Kitsch for Posthuman Feminist Aesthetics', *International Visual Culture Review*, 1, pp. 9–15. doi: 10.37467/gka-visualrev.v1.1747.

Ciupka, S. (2020) 'Pathologies and Kitsch in the Workplace – Theoretical Perspective', *ASEJ Scientific Journal of Bielsko-Biala School of Finance and Law*, 24(1), pp. 26–30. https://doi.org/10.5604/01.3001.0014.1347.

Duffy, F. (1997) *The New Office*. London: Conran Octopus.

Ergül, A. (2016) *Walter Benjamin and Kitsch Politics in the Phantasmagorical Age*. Ottawa and Ontario, Canada: Carleton University.

Fleming, P. (2009) *Authenticity and the Cultural Politics of Work*. Oxford: Oxford University Press. https://doi.org/10.1093/acprof:oso/9780199547159.001.0001.
Gołaszewska, M. (1984a) *Estetyka rzeczywistości*. Warszawa: Instytut Wydawniczy PAX.
Gołaszewska, M. (1984b) *Zarys estetyki*. Warszawa: PWN.
Gołaszewska, M. (1986) *O naturze wartości estetycznych*. Kraków: Uniwersytet Jagielloński.
Greenberg, C. (1985) 'Avant-Garde and Kitsch', in Frascina, F. (ed) *Pollock and After: The Critical Debate*. New York City: Harper and Row.
Gregotti, V. (1969) 'Kitsch and Architecture', in Dorfles, G. (ed) *Kitsch: The World of Bad Taste*. New York: Universe Books.
Hancock, P. and Tyler, M. (2001) *Work, Postmodernism and Organization: A Critical Introduction*. London: SAGE Publications Ltd. https://doi.org/10.4135/9781446218365.
Hatch, M. J. (1993) 'The Dynamics of Organizational Culture', *Academy of Management Review*, 18(4), pp. 657–693.
Hoberman, R. (2005) 'Aesthetic Taste, Kitsch, and the Years', in *Woolf Studies Annual*. New York City: Pace University Press, pp. 77–98. Available at: https://www.jstor.org/stable/24906571.
Hochschild, A. R. (2012) *The Managed Heart: Commercialization of Human Feeling, The Managed Heart*. Berkeley, Los Angeles and London: University of California Press.
Holt, D. B. (2002) 'Why Do Brands Cause Trouble? A Dialectical Theory of Consumer Culture and Branding', *Journal of Consumer Research*, 29(1), pp. 70–90. https://doi.org/10.1086/339922.
Holt, D. B. (2004) *How Brands Become Icons: The Principles of Cultural Branding*. Boston: Harvard Business School.
Horkheimer, M. and Adorno, T. (2002) *Dialectic of Enlightenment: Pfilosophical Fragments, Вестник Росздравнадзора*. Edited by G. Schmid Noerr. Stanford: Stanford University Press.
Kahn, W. A. (1990) 'Psychological Conditions of Personal Engagement and Disengagement at Work', *Academy of Management Journal*, 33(4), pp. 692–724. https://doi.org/10.2307/256287.
Kjellman-Chapin, M. (2023) *Kitsch: History, Theory, Practice*. Newcastle upon Tyne: Cambridge Scholars Publishing.
Klimova, G. P. and Klimov, V. P. (2019) 'Kitsch's Casus in Modern Culture', *Interactive Science*, 9(43), pp. 27–29. https://doi.org/10.21661/r-508103.
Kornberger, M. (2010) *Brand Society: How Brands Transform Management and Lifestyle*. Cambridge: Cambridge University Press. https://doi.org/10.1017/CBO9780511802881.
Kostera, M. (1997) 'The Kitsch-Organisation', *Studies in Cultures, Organizations, and Societies*, 3(2), pp. 163–177. https://doi.org/10.1080/10245289708523494.
Kostera, M. (2014) *Occupy Management! Inspirations and Ideas for Self-Organization and Self-Management*. London: Routledge. https://doi.org/10.4324/9780203795033.
Kostera, M. (2019) *Organize Ourselves! Inspirations and Ideas for Self-Organization and Self-Management*. Mayfly Books. Available at: https://ruj.uj.edu.pl/xmlui/bitstream/handle/item/72058/kostera_organize_ourselves_2019.pdf?sequence=1&isAllowed=y.
Kulka, T. (1996) *Kitsch and Art*. University Park: Pennsylvania State University Press. Available at: https://books.google.rw/books?id=lEu4oFo_SWQC&printsec=frontcover#v=onepage&q&f=false.
Kundera, M. (1984) *The Unbearable Lightness of Being*. New York City: Harper & Row.
Linstead, S. (2002) 'Organizational Kitsch. The Aesthetic Turn in Management', *Organization*, 9(4), pp. 657–682. https://doi.org/10.4324/9781351147965-4.
Macdonald, D. (2001) *Masscult and Midcult. Against the American Grain*. New York City: Da Capo Press.

Minahan, S. (2020) *Aesthetic Turn in Management*. New York: Routledge. https://doi.org/10.4324/9781351147965.
Moles, A. (1971) *Kitsch: The World of Bad Taste*. New York City: Universe Books.
Morreall, J. and Loy, J. (1989) 'Kitsch and Aesthetic Education', *The Journal of Aesthetic Education*, 23(4), pp. 63–73.
Ortlieb, S. A. and Carbon, C. C. (2019) 'Kitsch and Perception: Towards a New "Aesthetic from Below"', *Art and Perception*, 7(1), pp. 1–26. https://doi.org/10.1163/22134913-00001091.
Parker, M. (2000) *Organizational Culture and Identity: Unity and Division at Work*. London: SAGE Publications Ltd. https://doi.org/10.4135/9781446217214.
Peters, T. and Waterman, R. (2012) *In Search of Excellence*. New York: HarperCollins.
Reckhenrich, J., Kupp, M. and Anderson, J. (2009) 'Understanding Creativity: The Manager as Artist', *Business Strategy Review*, 20(2), pp. 68–73.
Ryynänen, M. and Barragán, P. (eds) (2023) *The Changing Meaning of Kitsch. From Rejection to Acceptance*. Cham: Palgrave Macmillan. https://doi.org/10.1007/978-3-031-16632-7.
Saltzman, L. (2001) 'Avante-Garde and Kitsch Revisited: On the Ethics of Representation', in Kleeblatt, N. (ed) *Mirroring Evil*. New Brunswick: Rutgers University Press.
Samier, E. (2008) 'On the Kitschification of Educational Administration: An Aesthetic Critique of Theory and Practice in the Field', *International Studies in Educational Achievement*, 36(3), pp. 3–18. https://doi.org/10.1016/b978-0-08-037268-6.50001-7.
Schein, E. H. (2013) 'The Role of Art and the Artist', *Organizational Aesthetics*, 2(1), pp. 1–4. https://doi.org/10.1162/152417301750385495.
Schein, E. H. and Schein, P. (2004) *Organizational Culture and Leadership*. John Wiley & Sons, Ltd. Available at: http://books.google.com/books?id=xhmezDokfnYC&pgis=1%5Cnhttp://www.loc.gov/catdir/bios/wiley047/2004002764.html.
Solomon, M. R. (2019) *Consumer Behavior: Buying, Having, and Being*. London: Pearson Education.
Solomon, R. (1997) 'Kitsch', in Goldblatt, D. and Brown, L. (eds) *Aesthetics: A Reader in Philosophy of the Arts*. Upper Saddle River: Prentice Hall.
Strati, A. (1999) *Organization and Aesthetics*. London: SAGE Publications Ltd. Available at: https://sk.sagepub.com/books/organization-and-aesthetics.
Strati, A. (2009) 'Do You Do Beautiful Things? Aesthetics and Art in Qualitative Methods of Organization Studies', in *The Sage Handbook of Organizational Research Methods*. SAGE Publications, pp. 230–245. https://doi.org/10.13140/RG.2.1.1309.3849.
Sułkowski, Ł. (2011) 'Metafory, archetypy i paradoksy organizacji', *Organizacja i Kierowanie*, 145(2), pp. 55–70.
Szostak, M. (2022) 'Co estetyka może wnieść do teorii zarządzania?', *Przegląd Organizacji*, 5(988), pp. 3–10. https://doi.org/10.33141/po.2022.05.01.
Szostak, M. (2023) *Sztuka zarządzania – zarządzanie sztuką*. Łódź-Warszawa: Wydawnictwo Społecznej Akademii Nauk.
Szostak, M. (2024) *Humanistic Management, Organisation and Aesthetics: Art of Management and Management of Art*. New York City: Routledge. https://doi.org/10.4324/9781003458029.
Szostak, M. and Sułkowski, Ł. (2020a) 'Kitsch in Management: Characteristic Forms, Carriers and Propagators', in *Education Excellence and Innovation Management: A 2025 Vision to Sustain Economic Development During Global Challenges: Proceedings of the 35th International Business Information Management Association Conference (IBIMA)*. Sevilla: IBIMA, pp. 7584–7598. Available at: https://depot.ceon.pl/handle/123456789/19173.
Szostak, M. and Sułkowski, Ł. (2020b) 'Manager as an Artist: Creative Endeavour in Crossing the Borders of Art and Organizational Discourse', *Creativity Studies*, 13(2), pp. 351–368. https://doi.org/10.3846/cs.2020.11373.

Taylor, S. S. and Hansen, H. (2005) 'Finding Form: Looking at the Field of Organizational Aesthetics', *Journal of Management Studies*, 42(6), pp. 1211–1231.

van de Klundert, M. and van Boeschoten, R. (2017) *Organisations and Humanisation. Perspectives on Organising Humanisation and Humanising Organisations*. London and New York: Routledge.

Warren, S. (2008) 'Empirical Challenges in Organizational Aesthetics Research: Towards a Sensual Methodology', *Organization Studies*, 29(4), pp. 559–580. https://doi.org/10.1177/0170840607083104.

Welsch, W. (2005) 'Procesy estetyzacji. Zjawiska, rozróżnienia, perspektywy', in *Estetyka poza estetyką: o nową postać estetyki*. Kraków: Universitas, pp. 31–73.

2 Kitsch in organisational culture

Challenges and opportunities in the work environment

Justyna Dziedzic

Introduction

Key to the chapter is the crucial demonstration of the main challenges associated with kitsch elements in organisational culture and identifying opportunities it creates for companies in the management domain. Analysing the impact of behavioural and physical artefacts at the symbolic level on the perception of kitsch in organisations allows an understanding of how these elements influence interpretation by employees and external stakeholders. Furthermore, identifying the interaction of norms, values, and hidden cultural assumptions with the emergence of kitsch enables defining strategies for managing kitsch in organisational culture.

The focus of the study revolved around three research questions: 1) What are the main challenges associated with kitsch elements in organisational culture, and what opportunities does it present for companies in terms of management? 2) How do behavioural and physical artefacts at the symbolic level influence the perception of kitsch in organisations by employees and external stakeholders? and 3) In what ways do norms, values, and hidden cultural assumptions in an organisation interact with the emergence of kitsch, and what strategies exist for eliminating kitsch from deeply rooted beliefs held by members of the organisation?

The methodology used in the chapter focuses on two main elements: the literature review and the case studies. The literature review forms the foundation of the analysis, allowing the identification of relevant theories, key concepts, and previous research on kitsch in the context of organisational culture. The literature was selected based on its relevance to kitsch, organisational culture, and aesthetics. This review made the study theoretically grounded, setting the framework for further empirical analysis. The case studies, the second key element of the methodology, serve as a tool to explore and illustrate how kitsch manifests itself in practical organisational contexts. The cases were selected based on their ability to demonstrate kitsch's diverse presence and impact on organisational culture. Each case was analysed based on available information, such as descriptions of organisational practices, examples of cultural artefacts and other relevant elements to understand the role of kitsch in shaping organisational culture.

DOI: 10.4324/9781003504931-3

The study delves into the complex interplay of kitsch within organisational culture, examining its challenges and opportunities for management, the influence of behavioural and physical artefacts on perceptions of kitsch among internal and external stakeholders, and the interaction between organisational norms, values, and the emergence of kitsch, alongside strategies for its mitigation within entrenched organisational beliefs.

Literature review: theories of organisational culture with kitsch perspective

Organisational culture has been the subject of numerous studies in the field of management (Cameron & Quinn, 2011; Deal & Kennedy, 2008; Handy, 1995; Hatch, 1997; Hofstede, 1984; Hofstede et al., 2010; Schein, 2009, 2010; Trompenaars & Hampden-Turner, 1997) and constitutes a complex set of values, norms, beliefs, language, and symbols that are shared among the members of a particular organisation. It articulates the organisation's distinct ethos, moulding its members' cognitive and behavioural patterns and capturing the entity's unique identity. This cultural framework reflects the organisation's historical lineage and traditions while outlining its future ambitions and objectives encapsulated within the organisational vision. Furthermore, it is a pivotal factor in facilitating the complexities of intra-organisational interactions and shaping the nature of relationships with the external environment and the vast array of stakeholders.

Organisational culture is shared values, beliefs, norms, and behaviours (Akpa et al., 2021; Cicea et al., 2022; Schein, 1996; Teehankee, 1994). It is how things are done in the organisation, encompassing both formal and informal aspects of the organisational environment. Organisational culture influences how employees interact with each other, how they perceive their work, and how they behave in the workplace (Akpa et al., 2021). Organisational culture is seen as the "software" of an organisation, shaping how employees think, feel, and react in different situations within the workplace. The collective programming of the mind distinguishes members and influences their behaviour (Sun & Milosevic, 2006).

Furthermore, organisational culture plays a crucial role in guiding behaviour, influencing decision-making processes, promoting employee motivation and morale, improving productivity and efficiency, fostering innovation and creativity, and shaping employee attitudes in the workplace (Sun & Milosevic, 2006). An organisational culture is the collective mindset and behaviour patterns that define how individuals interact with one another, external stakeholders, and the organisation's overall mission and goals. It is a fundamental aspect of organisational identity that influences performance, employee satisfaction, and overall success (Bigliardi et al., 2012). This perspective on organisational culture underscores its role not merely as a collection of shared values, norms, and beliefs among the members of an organisation but also as a process through which individuals are intricately woven into a community. This "collective programming of the mind" differentiates members within the community, shaping how they perceive their environment, make decisions, and act. In this view, organisational culture is pivotal in fostering a sense of belonging and identity, influencing efficiency, motivation, and employee satisfaction.

Consequently, culture emerges as an invisible force that directs actions and interactions within the organisation, crafting a unique identity and operational ethos (Ogbonna, 1992). This interpretation underscores the integrative function of culture, binding individuals to a communal identity and shared consciousness.

Foundations and evolution of organisational culture theories

The construct of organisational culture encompasses myriad interpretations and dimensions, reflecting the complexity of the fabric that constitutes organisational life. Academicians and practitioners alike have delved into the essence of this construct, yielding diverse but complementary perspectives that underscore its multifaceted nature.

In synthesis, the interpretations above and dimensions reveal that organisational culture is not a monolithic entity but a dynamic and complex system. It is a force that shapes the behaviours and attitudes of individuals within the organisation and the processes and outcomes that define organisational success and adaptability. Through this lens, the significance of organisational culture is truly illuminated, as it is woven into the fabric of daily operations and strategic initiatives. The scholarship on this topic, thus, provides a foundational understanding that is critical for both the scholarly exploration of organisational phenomena and the practical management of organisational life. This body of work encourages a nuanced appreciation of the various forces at play within organisational settings, as well as the myriad ways in which culture manifests and influences the collective behaviour of its members. It invites leaders and managers not only to contemplate the static elements of culture but also to engage with its dynamic aspects, shaping and reshaping the cultural contours of their organisations in pursuit of excellence and coherence in a constantly evolving business landscape.

From an academic perspective, organisational culture is perceived as a "soft" aspect of management that exerts "hard" effects on efficiency, productivity, and overall performance. Edgar H. Schein (1996, 2009, 2010) is a seminal figure in exploring organisational culture, with his groundbreaking works on the subject first appearing in the 1980s (Schein, 1987, 1983). Edgar H. Schein's (1983) investigation into founders' significant role in shaping their cultures reveals the deep-rooted influence of founders' actions, beliefs, and assumptions on establishing an organisation's initial cultural ethos. Schein contends that organisational culture extends beyond mere visible artefacts or stated philosophies, embodying a deeper set of assumptions that direct behaviour and decision-making within the company. He elucidates the complexity of organisational culture, focusing on the challenges of external adaptation and internal integration, and discusses the evolution of cultures from their inception under a founder's guidance to the transition to new leadership, emphasising the importance of preserving the cultural core that underpins the organisation's success. Schein's work is pivotal for understanding organisational culture's genesis and leadership's critical role in its ongoing development and maintenance.

Beyond Edgar Schein's seminal contributions, the field of organisational culture has been enriched by the scholarly endeavours of a distinguished cohort of researchers, each bringing profound insights and expanding the breadth of knowledge within this discipline. Esteemed scholars such as Geert Hofstede (1984), Charles Handy, along with Robert E. Quinn and Kim S. Cameron (2011), Fons Trompenaars with Charles Hampden-Turner (1997), Mary Jo Hatch (1993), and the duo of Terrence E. Deal and Allan A. Kennedy (1982), have all contributed significantly. Their theories and models have deepened our comprehension of organisational culture and broadened the horizons of this intricate field of study.

Geert Hofstede, eminently recognised in academic and professional domains for his pioneering contributions to cross-cultural research, has profoundly shaped the understanding of cultural dynamics within organisational settings. As a Dutch social psychologist, Hofstede's (Hofstede et al., 2010) extensive investigation into national and organisational cultures culminated in formulating a dimensional model of culture. Initially identifying four dimensions – individualism versus collectivism, uncertainty avoidance, power distance, and masculinity versus femininity – his model was expanded to encompass six dimensions, offering a more nuanced lens to examine and comprehend intercultural variations. Hofstede's scholarly endeavours underscore the imperative of acknowledging and valuing cultural diversity, particularly in managing international enterprises, emphasising the critical role that cultural insight plays in navigating the complexities of global organisational environments.

Hofstede's seminal work 1984 posited organisational culture as the collective programming of the mind that distinguishes the members of one human group from another (Hofstede, 1984). This definition heralds culture as a set of collective mental imprints that guide and distinguish the behaviour of individuals within organisational boundaries. Similarly, Edgar H. Schein (Schein, 1996) eloquently delineates organisational culture as an intricate mindset characterised by the collective norms, values, and underlying assumptions that guide individuals' perceptions, cognitive processes, and actions within the organisational milieu. Schein posits that to grasp the essence and breadth of organisational culture truly, one must go beyond mere quantitative assessments and observe tangible behaviours manifested within the organisational setting. This approach underscores the critical importance of a nuanced, qualitative understanding of the dynamic interplay between individual actions and the overarching cultural framework, enriching the discourse on organisational studies with a deeper, more holistic comprehension of culture's pivotal role in shaping organisational identities and practices.

When considering the dimensions of organisational culture, scholarly works have identified a broad spectrum of facets such as Performance Orientation, Uncertainty Avoidance, Team Orientation, Gender Egalitarianism, Assertiveness, Future Orientation, and Humane Orientation, among others (Gutterman, 2017). These dimensions, derived from societal culture studies, significantly influence the attributes of organisational identity. The intricate tapestry of organisational culture is also woven from patterns of development, shared values, beliefs, meanings, and customs held in common among organisation members (Akpa et al., 2021).

Furthermore, the adaptive and consistent nature of organisational culture, along with the fundamental beliefs, assumptions, values, attitudes, and behaviours of organisational members, is hypothesised to play a critical role in defining organisational processes (Shamsudin, 2021). This holistic view suggests that culture is not merely a backdrop but a dynamic and influential actor in uniting abilities, resolving problems, and either hindering or facilitating the achievement of organisational goals. Similarly, Charles Handy (Handy, 1993, 1995) has significantly contributed to the discourse on organisational culture by delineating four distinct cultural archetypes: Zeus, Apollo, Athena, and Dionysus (Handy, 1995). The Zeus archetype encapsulates a power-centric approach characterised by decision-making concentrated at the organisational pinnacle, fostering centralisation and pronounced leadership. Contrarily, the Apollo archetype embodies a procedural ethos, emphasising harmony, and systemic order underpinned by structured decision-making protocols and formal organisational frameworks.

Furthermore, the Athena archetype highlights a competency-based culture, valorising expertise, and knowledge, thereby granting significant decision-making leverage to specialists and experts within the organisation. Lastly, the Dionysus archetype celebrates the primacy of individual autonomy and creative expression, prevalent in entities within the creative and innovation-driven sectors, advocating for a milieu of independence and adaptability. This typological framework not only delineates the underlying values and operational tenets of diverse organisational cultures but also suggests the strategic alignment of these cultural dimensions with organisational goals and environmental exigencies, enhancing organisational agility and effectiveness. Each archetype delineates a unique organisational modus operandi, elucidating the influence of power structures, decision-making processes, and employee motivations on organisational functionality. Handy's theoretical framework facilitates a deeper understanding of how prevailing cultural norms within an organisation can affect its operational efficacy, adaptability, and overall workplace milieu. Through their seminal works, both Hofstede and Handy have indelibly enriched the academic and practical understanding of cultural phenomena in organisational contexts, highlighting the intricate interplay between cultural values, organisational structures, and management practices (Handy, 1995; Hofstede, 1984).

Dimensions and dynamics of organisational culture

Understanding organisational culture is crucial to effectively managing and leading change in any institution, as has been widely studied and described by many business theorists and practitioners. Among them, Robert E. Quinn and Kim S. Cameron (2011), Fons Trompenaars with Charles Hampden-Turner (1997), Mary Jo Hatch (1997), and Terrence E. Deal with Allan A. Kennedy (1982) make essential contributions to the theory of organisational culture, presenting a variety of models and perspectives to help understand its complexity and impact on organisational performance.

Robert E. Quinn and Kim S. Cameron (2011) created the Competitive Values Model, classifying organisational cultures into four types: clan, adhocracy, market, and hierarchy. The model provides a tool for diagnosing and understanding organisational culture and serves as a guide for managing cultural change. Each culture type represents a distinct approach to management, leadership, and the value and belief system necessary for organisational success.

Fons Trompenaars, in collaboration with Charles Hampden-Turner, developed the Seven Dimensions of Culture model, as detailed in their seminal work "Riding the Waves of Culture" (Trompenaars & Hampden-Turner, 1997). Their publication is renowned for illustrating how a profound understanding of these differences can enhance effective management and communication in diverse international environments. Trompenaars and Hampden-Turner emphasise the importance of tailoring business strategies to cultural diversity, which ensures an organisation's global effectiveness.

Mary Jo Hatch emphasises the interplay between culture, identity, symbols, and leadership, a theme she elaborates on in detail in her book "Organisation Theory: Modern, Symbolic, and Postmodern Perspectives" (Hatch, 1997), illustrating the dynamics of organisational culture and its impact on organisational change processes. Moreover, she highlights the crucial role of narratives, rituals, and ceremonies in developing and maintaining organisational culture. Hatch elucidates how leaders can intentionally craft these elements to bolster the pursuit of organisational objectives (Hatch, 1993).

In their seminal work "Corporate Cultures: The Rites and Rituals of Corporate Life," Terrence E. Deal and Allan A. Kennedy (1982) illuminate the essential role rituals, ceremonies, narratives, and symbolic elements play in forging organisational culture. Their insightful theory delineates the profound influence these "soft" facets of an organisation's framework exert on its success. They contend that robust organisational cultures serve as a bedrock, fostering heightened productivity and facilitating a more agile response to the vicissitudes of market dynamics.

The insights from eminent scholars' collective bodies reveal organisational culture's intricate complexity and multifaceted nature, highlighting its pivotal role in shaping an organisation's strategic direction, structural configuration, procedural flows, communicative dynamics, and overall performance metrics. Organisational culture is inherently dynamic, perpetually morphing in response to an amalgam of internal dynamics and external environmental pressures. Table 2.1 synthesises the contributions of foremost thinkers in organisational culture, encapsulating their seminal discoveries alongside the critical avenues of their scholarly exploration. This aggregation of academic endeavours offers a rich tapestry of research that sheds light on the nuanced dimensions of organisational culture, delineating its influence on internal behavioural norms and the broader spectrum of intercultural and communicational exchanges.

Table 2.1 The landscape of organisational culture: a comparative analysis of research directions

Researcher and methodological approach	*Key findings*	*Cultural dimensions*
Edgar H. Schein: Qualitative case studies	Developed a model of organisational culture that includes three levels: artefacts, espoused values, and basic underlying assumptions. Highlighted the role of leadership in shaping culture	Leadership and change management: Focuses on the impact of leadership styles and strategies on organisational culture and its adaptation to change.
Geert Hofstede: Survey-based research	Identified four (later expanded to six) dimensions of culture that help understand cross-cultural differences: Individualism versus Collectivism, Uncertainty Avoidance, Power Distance, and Masculinity versus Femininity.	Explores how the search dimensions influence organisational behaviour and interpersonal relations within different cultural contexts.
Charles Handy: Theoretical analysis	Introduced the concept of four types of organisational cultures: power culture, role culture, task culture, and person culture.	Analyses the predominance of power dynamics, organisational roles, task orientation, and individual personality within organisational cultures.

(*Continued*)

Table 2.1 (Continued)

Researcher and methodological approach	*Key findings*	*Cultural dimensions*
Robert E. Quinn and Kim S. Cameron: Mixed methods	Developed the Competing Values Framework, which describes four types of organisational cultures: clan, adhocracy, market, and hierarchy.	Describes organisational cultures based on familial (clan), innovative (adhocracy), competitive (market), and structured (hierarchy) characteristics.
Fons Trompenaars: Cross-cultural comparison	Developed a model of seven dimensions of culture that analyses cultural differences and their impact on business behaviour.	Relationship with Nature, Time, and People: Investigates cultural variations in the perception and management of environmental factors, temporal aspects, and human relations.
Mary Jo Hatch: Ethnography, case analysis	Proposed a model of organisational culture that links culture with identity, symbols, and leadership.	Examines the role of symbols, narratives, and corporate identity in shaping organisational culture.
Terrence E. Deal and Allan A. Kennedy: Observational studies	Highlighted the importance of rituals, ceremonies, stories, and other symbolic elements in shaping organisational culture.	Focuses on the significance of rituals, myths, and symbolic elements in creating and reinforcing an organisation's culture.

Source: own elaboration

Every scholar studying organisational culture has made a unique contribution to management and organisational psychology, devising intricate models and conceptual frameworks that offer a profound understanding of culture's effect on organisations and its malleability under leadership. Within their scholarly contributions, recurring themes emerge, highlighting the critical influence of leadership in moulding organisational culture, the integral role of symbols and rituals in embodying cultural essence, and culture's consequential impact on organisational efficacy and communicative processes. These academic endeavours emphasise organisational culture's intricate complexity and rich multidimensionality, presenting strategic insights for leaders and managers on effectively navigating and sculpting organisational culture to bolster performance, foster adaptability to transformative dynamics, and secure organisational triumph. This scholarly dialogue enriches the textbook narrative, providing a nuanced lens through which the interplay between organisational culture and leadership can be examined, understood, and applied towards achieving sustainable organisational excellence.

Organisational culture is inherently dynamic and susceptible to various fluctuations, such as integrating new personnel, strategic shifts, technological advancements, or alterations in the market landscape. In an era of globalisation and escalating cultural heterogeneity, organisational culture's comprehension and adept management have become increasingly intricate yet pivotal for organisational triumph. The emergence of global, digital, and technologically driven cultural paradigms amplifies organisational endeavours to adapt to these challenges and harmonise divergences within their cultural milieu. This alignment is essential for fostering innovation, adaptability, and fortifying competitive prowess globally. Organisational culture assumes the role of a strategic asset, exerting pervasive influence across all facets of organisational operations. It presents a dual facet, posing challenges and opportunities for leaders and managers. Their stewardship in cultivating a conducive work environment can yield productivity, innovation, and alignment with organisational values and objectives. Thus, organisational culture is a fundamental determinant of organisational success, demanding astute leadership and managerial acumen to harness its potential effectively.

Theoretical foundations of kitsch experience in organisational culture

Within aesthetic theory and cultural philosophy frameworks, kitsch is frequently regarded as the antithesis of "high" culture and art. This stance emanates from its proclivity for simplification, its penchant for surface-level appeal, and its tendency to cater to mass taste, all pursued at the cost of sacrificing depth and originality (Attfield, 2006). In the organisational context, this inclination towards simplification can distort the company's values and objectives, contributing to the emergence of a corporate culture perceived as either untrustworthy or incongruent with the actual practices and aspirations of the organisation. Kitsch in organisational culture, characterised by simplification, grandiosity, and a sense of artificiality, refers to the phenomenon of depriving the managerial experience of beauty and surprise, involving behaviours, manifestations, activities, and attitudes within an organisation that deviate from universal values of truth, favouring appearances and external forms (Szostak & Sulkowski, 2020). In such a culture, individuals are not expected to experience genuine emotions or personal growth; instead, they are encouraged to conform, adapt, and exclude their participation in the organisation from their private lives. "Kitsch-Organisation is what it is meant to represent: immortal, eternal, but this is the immortality of kitsch: infinite because of the failure to come alive or to die, infinite because it is an on-being" (Kostera, 1997, p. 173). The organisation is portrayed as immortal and eternal, representing a sense of infinite existence without genuinely being alive or having any real essence (Kostera, 1997).

Kitsch is viewed as an elusive phenomenon, continually evolving and eliciting mixed responses, oscillating between acceptance and rejection (Attfield, 2006; Tiffany, 2013). While contemporary discourse is predominantly linked with material or visual culture, the origins of kitsch trace back to poetry, a domain that has significantly contributed to shaping its historical contours. Comprehending kitsch demands an analytical lens focused on the interplay of lexicon, connotations, and narratives, collectively revealing its intricate origins and development (Tiffany, 2013). Critical considerations of kitsch reveal its diverse interpretations and implications across various semantic contexts. It has been utilised for propagating ideologies, subjected to rigorous critique by art historians, and employed to challenge elitism in art. Furthermore, kitsch has been reappropriated in contemporary discourse to question hierarchical notions of taste and cultural expression (Attfield, 2006).

Kitsch, a form of art or aesthetics characterised by exaggeration and a lack of authenticity, has permeated many aspects of contemporary life, including organisational culture (Kostera, 1997). The aesthetics of kitsch have gained significance as a domain of cultural analysis, undergoing continuous redefinitions and blurring the boundaries between high and low culture, contributing to its increased appeal as a source of inspiration (Stępień, 2014).

Any attempts to comprehend kitsch through so-called deflationary approaches (Emmer, 2014) lead to the conclusion that kitsch should either be dismissed as a concept or that we should unreservedly indulge in the pleasure derived from kitschy objects. Kitsch is treated as an insignificant element or, if acknowledged, as something to which one can freely surrender, being one of the many available forms of culture. Thus, the deflationary approach (Emmer, 2014) to kitsch may suggest that its presence in the workplace should not be the subject of excessive criticism or analysis but instead accepted as an element of cultural diversity. From this perspective, kitsch, viewed as an aspect of culture with little artistic or aesthetic value, could be considered a form of expression or humour that does not adversely affect the work environment (Emmer, 2014). However, a balance between acceptance and critical evaluation of kitsch in organisational practice may be crucial for maintaining professionalism and brand authenticity, indicating the need for a more nuanced approach to its role and impact on organisational culture.

Within the cultural diagnosis of Theodor Adorno and Max Horkheimer (Adorno, 1973; Adorno & Horkheimer, 2002), recognising the impact of the culture industry and its associated kitsch aesthetics on organisational structures and practices becomes paramount. Analysing the dynamics of mass society, Adorno and Horkheimer unveil the mechanisms through which the culture industry standardises entertainment, transforming art into a product amenable to commercialisation (Adorno, 1973; Adorno & Horkheimer, 2002). Such a process not only homogenises the aesthetic preferences of the mass audience but also fosters the spread of conformism by promoting the unreflective consumption of cultural products, thereby deepening the crisis of values in society (Adorno, 1973; Adorno & Horkheimer, 2002). Transposing this perspective to the realm of organisational culture allows for an illustration of how these mechanisms are reflected in corporate practices. The standardisation, proliferation of schematic solutions, and promotion of conformist attitudes within organisations can be viewed as expressions of the dominance of kitsch aesthetics. This manifests through external corporate attributes, such as design or marketing strategies, and simplified communication and intra-organisational interactions, often contributing to an organisational culture needing more depth and authenticity. Such phenomena are particularly prevalent in the standardised aesthetics of corporate culture.

In the context of Theodor Adorno's theoretical framework (Adorno, 1973, 1992; Adorno & Horkheimer, 2002), organisations are confronted with the imperative challenge of cultivating a culture predicated on authenticity, individuality, and aesthetic commitment. This paradigm necessitates an organisation's dual approach: an introspective examination of its cultural practices and a deliberate orchestration of the organisational milieu to accommodate and nurture individual and heterogeneous aesthetic perspectives.

Adorno (1992) posits that contemporary art responds to the loss of tradition, shedding its former certainty in its approach to subject matter, materials, and employed techniques, necessitating profound introspection. As traditional foundations of art are questioned or abandoned, what was once deemed indisputable through tradition now reveals itself as emptiness and the illusory nature of outdated conventions, rendering what was previously considered immutable and evident as hollow and inauthentic. Thus, in the light of Adorno's theory (Adorno, 1992), organisations face the challenge of creating a culture that opposes dominant aesthetic and cultural schemas, promoting authenticity and individuality as the foundations for a rich and diverse organisational space. This approach necessitates their conscious shaping of an environment that facilitates the exploration and expression of varied aesthetics, contributing to developing an organisational culture that reflects deeper critical reflection and aesthetic engagement. Responding to the challenges of the culture industry and the dominance of kitsch aesthetics in organisations requires critical reflection and an active search for new forms of expression that can break through schematics and conformism, fostering a rich and diverse organisational culture.

Kitsch in organisational theory serves as a multifaceted response to modernity. It is characterised by establishing an illusory unity between the individual and the world, which conceals the experience of existence. Instead of merely being a matter of style, kitsch is considered one of the fundamental philosophical problems of modernity that organisation theory should take seriously (Linstead, 2002; Szostak & Sulkowski, 2020). Overall, it reflects a superficial and inauthentic approach to organising, focusing on appearances rather than genuine experiences, values, and truths.

Discussion: kitsch in organisational culture, views, and implications

A multifaceted exploration assesses how kitsch, often dismissed for its superficiality, significantly impacts organisational culture's formation and perception. From decorative excesses to the rhetoric of mission statements, kitsch can reflect and shape a corporation's cultural underpinnings. In an organisational context, Kitsch is not just a questionable taste but reveals fundamental conflicts between individual creativity and corporate uniformity, potentially influencing innovation and ethical practices. This discourse explores the layers beneath the glaring surface of kitsch, examining its impact on organisational dynamics, employee engagement, and broader cultural implications in the corporate sphere.

Kitsch in the culture of the organisational sphere: from superficiality to dysfunction

Kitsch transcends ordinary classifications of objects, referring to a specific, often negatively judged relationship with objects that cannot be unequivocally defined through the context of their production or their place in material culture (Tiffany, 2013).

This concept is dynamically influenced by intricate and evolving aesthetic preferences that transcend mere economic considerations, deriving its attributes from the fluidity and transformation within societal perceptions and tastes (Tiffany, 2013). The aesthetic preferences of organisation members, often an amalgamation of personal inclinations and cultural influences, are subject to continuous changes, responding to external trends and internal group dynamics. This evolution of preferences can lead to conflicts between individual and corporate aesthetic choices, which affects the formation of organisational identity and how it is perceived externally.

Kitsch is manifested as a tendency to adopt and propagate aesthetics or practices that are widely considered banal or tacky, which can lead to the creation of a superficial, rather than deeply rooted, organisational identity, understood as a social construct and collective understanding of an organisation's characteristics as a meta-theory of a social actor, referring to a symbolically constructed organisation based on mutual contracts and networks (Haslam et al., 2017). Kitsch's organisational identity can manifest as overly simplified symbols, slogans, or initiatives that do not reflect the actual value or mission of the organisation but rather reflect fleeting trends. As a result, kitsch in organisational culture may be perceived as a need for deeper understanding and commitment to the authentic values of the organisation, leading to a culture based on superficial imagery and aesthetics, which does not support sustainable development.

Kitsch within an organisation can manifest in various forms, ranging from overly simplified motivational messages through tacky office decorations to practices internally inconsistent with the company's mission. Examples of kitsch in organisations and their manifestations in culture include creating mascots and company songs through executive decision rather than emerging naturally from the culture; the "one best way" claim; simplification; grandiosity; organisational cynicism; functional stupidity; bullshit jobs; and seeming management (Szostak & Sulkowski, 2020). Kitsch can be perceived not only as an aesthetic faux pas but also as an indicator of deeper structural and value-based issues within the organisation. Its infiltration into the workspace suggests a lack of aesthetic sensitivity and may reflect a superficial approach to management, corporate culture, and relationships with employees and clients. Embracing kitsch in corporate spaces may signal an attempt to substitute substance and authenticity with easy, empty gestures to quickly achieve a positive impression at the expense of deeper values.

Kitsch's organisational culture can lower employee morale and commitment and negatively affect employee perception, engagement, and effectiveness, disrupting innovation. Organisational culture plays a significant role in driving innovation success, with specific cultural values promoting innovative behaviours and developmental culture, emphasising external orientation and flexibility, which is deemed most conducive to fostering innovation within organisations (Büschgens et al., 2013; Chen et al., 2018; Szczepańska-Woszczyna, 2014). Several factors within kitsch in organisational culture can negatively influence innovation, including a hierarchical culture characterised by stability and a preference for rules and procedures over experimentation and change (Büschgens et al., 2013). In such cultures, an emphasis on detailed procedures and regulations can decrease organisational creativity and hinder the implementation of new developments. A culture that values stability and security over innovation can inhibit innovative behaviours within an organisation, and organisational members may feel constrained and limited in their ability to explore new ideas and take risks if the culture prioritises stability and resists change (Büschgens et al., 2013). An inflexible organisational culture that values stability, strict procedures, and control rather than cultivating cultural values and fostering a creative environment for creative behaviour can negatively affect organisational innovation (Chen et al., 2018; Li et al., 2018).

Andreea Ivan points out that literary critics transform short-lived bestsellers into enduring classics through subtle manipulation of their reception (Ivan, 2016). The author uses Pierre Bourdieu's theory to demonstrate that this process constitutes a form of kitsch aesthetic recuperation, where critics influence the cultural value of works and assign them a place in the literary canon. Ultimately, the transformation of these novels exemplifies kitsch, wherein critics' actions can impact the perception of artworks and their status as classics. Analysing the mechanisms of critical reception in literature can help understand analogous processes in organisational culture, which are responsible for the critical reception and interpretation of organisational actions and decisions (Ivan, 2016). These mechanisms may be similar to those observed in the critical reception of literature, including manipulation of perception, control of information, and influence on interpreting actions and events within the organisation.

Tadeusz Ciupka discusses the phenomenon of kitsch in the workplace, exploring various pathologies such as corruption (violation of ethical standards for personal gain), employee anomie (lack of moral norms and mutual trust), cynicism (loss of confidence in management and oneself), discrimination (unequal treatment based on various factors), workaholism (excessive focus on work leading to negative consequences), and dysfunctional inter-domain transfer (uncritical imitation of principles from other domains) (Ciupka, 2020). The intertwining of kitsch and organisational culture introduces a complex dynamic within workplaces. Kitsch, often associated with superficiality and artificiality, can infiltrate organisational cultures, leading to a proliferation of detrimental pathologies. Corruption, as a form of kitsch, distorts the ethical fabric of organisations, eroding trust and integrity. Similarly, employee anomie fuelled by kitsch fosters a culture of indifference towards ethical norms, perpetuating a cycle of dishonest behaviour. Furthermore, the emergence of cynicism in response to kitsch-infused environments reflects a systemic breakdown of trust in leadership and organisational values. Addressing these pathologies requires a nuanced understanding of how kitsch operates within organisational cultures, necessitating comprehensive strategies to promote ethical conduct and foster a culture of authenticity and integrity.

The classification of kitsch may vary across social and cultural contexts; it serves as a conduit for personal expression, identity formation, and political commentary (Attfield, 2006). Dlatego negatywny odcień kiczu może znaleźć swoje odzwierciedlenie również w sferze organizacji realizujących polityki publiczne jako narzędzie propagandy, wykorzystując łatwo rozpoznawalne i zrozumiałe formy sztuki, by wpływać na kształtowanie opinii społecznej (Lugg, 1999). The accessibility of kitsch in everyday life, serving as a symbol that bridges history and culture with an emotional message, enables quick engagement with audiences and evokes specific reactions from them. While kitsch may sometimes unsettle, it often provides comfort and solace for the observer (Lugg, 1999). Creators of kitsch consciously exploit this, engaging emotions, and bypassing intellect, which makes kitsch a form of cultural anaesthesia. This ability to create and utilise cultural myths and easily manipulate complex history assigns kitsch a significant role in constructing political narratives, underscoring its influence on public policy directions (Lugg, 1999).

Leaders, by choosing proposals containing elements of kitsch, employ them to simplify complex social issues, offering the electorate easily digestible messages (Lugg, 1999). Consequently, kitsch is deployed as a potent instrument of propaganda and the manipulation of societal perceptions, affording authorities the means to regulate and influence public opinion, thereby bolstering their political credibility. This strategic approach to leadership involves the shrewd utilisation of simplistic cultural motifs to shape public image, and the utilisation of kitsch by leaders does not necessarily denote a deficiency in leadership prowess. Still, it underscores the pivotal role of kitsch as a formidable instrument in sculpting the political landscape (Lugg, 1999). CEOs and owners who dishonestly focus solely on maximising revenue and profits while pretending to engage in the organisation's mission contribute to organisational kitsch by prioritising external attractiveness over genuine value (Szostak & Sulkowski, 2020). In the context of public-sector organisations, which frequently grapple with multifaceted social and political challenges, leadership must prioritise genuine and substantive engagement with these issues, eschewing simplistic narratives and vacuous promises.

M. Szostak and Ł. Sułkowski point to the components of kitsch experience; concerning this concept, the components of kitsch in organisational culture can be pointed out: creators of kitsch in organisational culture, recipients of Kitsch in organisational culture, and reference to the world of universal values (Szostak & Sułkowski, 2020). Creators of organisational kitsch often focus on mass recipients rather than universal values. They tend to duplicate or copy established patterns, practices, or ideas rather than fostering originality and creative reliability. These creators are typically closed to criticism and discussion. They might seek to make things appear more valuable or important than they are, essentially opting for deceptive aesthetic manipulation rather than truthfulness or functionality. Recipients or consumers of organisational kitsch are generally willing to engage with and even interfere with kitschy artefacts without critical evaluation. They embrace egalitarianism and mass-scale production, often choosing to consider items from a surface level that aligns with their desires, which aligns with the avoidance of deep thought, consciousness, and will. This results in shallow and fleeting experiences, sentimentalism, and a preference for external experiences over internal contemplation. In the realm of universal values, kitsch in organisational culture often eschews truth for beauty (or rather, prettiness) and pleasure.

Table 2.2 analyses the concept of kitsch in organisational culture, focusing on its impact on creators/producers, works/artefacts, receivers/recipients, and

Table 2.2 Characteristics of kitsch within organisational settings

Element	*Kitsch in organisational culture*
Creator/Producer	Focus on the mass recipient, duplication, copying, and closing for criticism and discussion in the work environment.
Work/Artefact	Dominated by the receiver's desires, habit confirmation, pretentiousness, and presence-oriented in organisational decisions.
Receiver/Recipient	Interference with the artefact, mass-scale egalitarianism, selective consideration based on desires, avoidance of cognitive effort, and shallow experiences in organisational collaboration.
World of Values	The dominance of pleasure and satisfaction of impulses in the work environment.

Source: own elaboration after (Szostak & Sulkowski, 2020).

prevailing values. It highlights vital aspects such as the dominance of the receiver's desires, mass appeal, and avoidance of cognitive effort, which influence decision-making processes and collaboration within an organisation.

This summary underscores the pervasive influence of kitsch across various dimensions of organisational culture. Organisations may inadvertently foster environments where superficiality trumps depth and critical engagement by prioritising surface-level appeal and immediate gratification. The focus on replicating popular trends and satisfying ephemeral desires shapes the creation and reception of organisational artefacts and reinforces values that emphasise prettiness and pleasure over substantive, meaningful engagement. Consequently, this phenomenon could challenge cultivating innovative, critical, and authentic cultures within organisations, suggesting a need for a more nuanced understanding and strategic management of kitsch's role in shaping organisational dynamics and identities.

When kitsch aesthetics become a tool for external and internal communication, public-sector employees can feel discouraged from expressing new ideas or challenging existing practices, ultimately inhibiting innovation and adaptability in the organisation. To counteract these adverse effects, public organisations should promote a culture based on transparency, transparency, and critical thinking, and it is then crucial to develop spaces for open discussion and critical analysis and to involve employees and citizens in decision-making processes, which can help break the patterns of thinking imposed by kitsch and build a more sustainable and deep organisational culture.

Reinterpreting kitsch: benefits for organisational culture

It cannot be overlooked that kitsch, despite its negative connotations, may also serve certain positive functions within organisational culture. It can indeed function as a tool for building camaraderie among employees or serve as a form of escape from the daily work routine, offering light-hearted and non-committal elements of humour or decoration that can provide momentary relief and enhance the workplace atmosphere. D. Tiffany (2013) argues that the aesthetic ideology of kitsch, challenging to reassess, combines the naive joy characteristic of childlike contentment with a tendency to create social divisions and express disdain. Attributing negative connotations to kitsch occurs unequivocally, without self-critical reflection, especially by individuals seeking deeper cultural aesthetic values (Tiffany, 2013).

Although kitsch is subject to criticism and mixed feelings – ranging from fascination to contempt – its nature is more complex and not entirely harmless, contrary to common beliefs (Tiffany, 2013). In organisational culture, the tendency to unilaterally assess kitsch may reflect deeper tensions between the pursuit of unique identity and conformity, influencing how values and aesthetics are negotiated and manifested in the workplace. Kitsch, although seemingly harmless as an aesthetic addition, can carry the potential to evoke discomfort and challenge accepted norms, acting as a subtle dissident (Tiffany, 2013). This phenomenon in organisational culture can lead to considerations of how aesthetic elements influence perceptions of professionalism and corporate identity. Kitsch may lead to superficial rejection and subtle forms of rebellion. In an organisational context, such dynamics can catalyse discussions about the diversity of aesthetic preferences and their impact on creating an inclusive work culture, emphasising how aesthetic choices can reflect and influence broader organisational values.

Labelling something as kitsch often stems from alienation and distrust, which blocks the possibility of a positive connection between a person and objects frequently considered of little value (Tiffany, 2013). Social mechanisms based on exclusion and disapproval in the context of organisational culture may manifest as distance and scepticism towards cultural elements perceived as inconsistent with entrenched norms and values, thereby inhibiting the potential for building positive relationships between employees and new, potentially groundbreaking ideas or practices. Consequently, achieving a balanced approach to kitsch in organisational culture becomes crucial, allowing for utilising its potentially positive aspects while avoiding the pitfalls associated with its negative consequences. This requires leaders and cultural managers to have a deep understanding of the values and identity of their organisation and the ability to use aesthetics in a way that supports the authentic expression of these values rather than their distortion.

Redefining organisational aesthetics: the role of cultural kitsch

Organisational culture is becoming a key differentiating element for companies in the market; there is an inevitable phenomenon of kitsch within it. This case study focuses on analysing and identifying the various forms of kitsch manifested in the organisational culture of modern companies. Through the prism of seven categories – from innovative kitsch to ethical kitsch – we explore how overemphasising specific values without real support from the organisational structure, false declarations of sustainability, or creating the illusion of an online community can affect employees' and external stakeholders' perception of the company. Examples from companies such as WeWork, Uber, Tesla, Facebook, Twitter, Apple, Nestlé, Monsanto, Shell, Johnson & Johnson, and Enron serve as evidence, shedding light on the complex nature of kitsch in organisational culture and its potential effects. This study uncovers hidden cultural assumptions and offers insights into how kitsch can be understood and managed in a corporate context, highlighting its challenges.

The comparative study in Table 2.3 reveals the complexity and pervasiveness of kitsch in the organisational culture of contemporary companies, identifying seven key categories in which this phenomenon manifests itself. Each category highlights the diverse ways in which kitsch can influence the perception and operation of companies, and these are Innovative Kitsch, Exploratory Kitsch, Inspirational Kitsch, Sustainable Kitsch, Social Kitsch, Environmental Kitsch, and Ethical Kitsch. The cases of companies such as WeWork, Uber, Tesla, and Facebook highlight how an excessive fascination with specific ideas, without real actionable support, can lead to organisational dysfunction, highlighting the importance of authenticity and an honest approach to the values promoted by organisations. The study not only reflects on the challenges associated with the presence of kitsch in organisational culture but also points to the need for a deeper

Table 2.3 Kitsch trends in organisational culture: compilation of data from case studies

Type of kitsch in organisational culture	*Description*	*Case studies of kitsch in organisational culture*
1. Innovative kitsch in organisational culture	Excessive emphasis on innovation and enthusiasm without real support from the organisational structure.	WeWork creates an atmosphere of innovation but faces financial problems and controversial management decisions (Zeitlin, 2019). Apple's decision-making is influenced more by aesthetics than genuine innovations (Abboud & Wagstaff, 2015)
2. Exploratory kitsch in organisational culture	False emphasis on market exploration, overlooking essential managerial and ethical issues.	Uber's global expansion ignores safety, ethical labour practices, and competition issues (Wilson, 2023). Enron utilising artificial accounting methods to manipulate financial results (Segal, 2023).
3. Inspirational kitsch in organisational culture	Excessive focus on inspiration and vision despite internal issues related to personnel management.	Tesla promotes revolutionary projects but faces production, personnel management, and communication problems (Furr & Dyer, 2020). Theranos creates a vision for revolutionary medical research but is involved in fraud and lacks technological effectiveness (Bilton, 2016).
4. Sustainable kitsch in organisational culture	Creating the appearance of a sustainable business despite criticism of resource exploitation practices and ethical choices.	Nestlé has been criticised for using water resources and unethical practices in production and marketing (Lurie, 2019). Volkswagen has been criticised for concealing actual emissions during tests (Leggett, 2018).

(*Continued*)

Table 2.3 (Continued)

Type of kitsch in organisational culture	*Description*	*Case studies of kitsch in organisational culture*
5. Social kitsch in organisational culture	Creating the illusion of an online community while facing data management and disinformation issues.	Facebook has privacy controversies, content manipulation, and influence on online community life (Newcomb, 2018). Twitter had problems managing hate speech and harmful content (Counts & Nakano, 2023).
6. Environmental kitsch in organisational culture	Abusing ecological concepts to mask controversies related to environmental and health safety.	Monsanto was criticised for its environmental impact and controversies regarding the safety of pesticides and GMOs (Dewey, 2018). Shell was accused of pollution and failure to adhere to ecological standards (Gaughran, n.d.).
7. Ethical kitsch in organisational culture	Creating the appearance of ethics despite crisis management issues and ethical ties to products	Johnson & Johnson, scandal related to inadequate crisis management, issues with breast implants, and baby powder (Pierson, 2023). Enron's financial manipulation led to the company's downfall and contributed to the loss of public trust in the security of the stock exchange (Constable, 2021).

Source: own elaboration

understanding and management of this phenomenon to avoid potential adverse effects and capitalise on identifiable benefits. Thus, while kitsch in organisational culture can be perceived as harmful or destructive, a proper understanding and conscious management can lead to a more conscious and sustainable corporate culture.

Conclusion

Kitsch in organisational culture can arise for a variety of reasons, being, for example, the result of attempts to build a positive corporate image using inappropriate means of expression, a manifestation of the dehumanisation of the organisation as well as being a consequence of insufficient reflection on the values and goals of the organisation, leading to the adoption of inauthentic solutions. Nevertheless, although kitsch is often viewed negatively in organisational culture, it can also reflect some positive aspects of organisational culture; for example, it can serve as a tool for building camaraderie among employees or as a form of escape from the daily routine of work, offering elements of humour or decoration to improve the atmosphere in the workplace. Recognising its adverse effects and potential positive aspects is crucial for effective organisational culture management. It poses a significant challenge and requires implementing conscious and thoughtful management strategies based on authenticity, transparency, and employee engagement, constituting an organisational culture based on well-being and truth.

This chapter provides answers to three key research questions by considering the challenges associated with the presence of kitsch elements in organisational culture, the impact of behavioural and physical artefacts at the symbolic level on the perception of kitsch in organisations by employees and external stakeholders, and the interaction between norms, values, and implicit cultural assumptions in organisations and the emergence of kitsch, presenting strategies for eliminating kitsch from the deeply held beliefs of organisational members. 1) The main challenges associated with elements of kitsch in organisational culture include the risk of creating a superficial identity for the organisation, which can be perceived as inconsistent with the company's fundamental mission and vision and lead to the dehumanisation of the organisation being the result of insufficient reflection on values, leading to the adoption of insincere solutions. On the other hand, kitsch can also offer some management opportunities, for example, by creating a sense of community among employees or as a form of escape from the daily routine of work by offering elements of humour or decoration that can improve the atmosphere in the workplace. 2) Behaviours and physical artefacts at the symbolic level can significantly influence the perception of kitsch in organisations by employees and external stakeholders. Using simplistic motivational messages, tacky office decorations, or practices consistent with the company's mission can lead to an organisational culture perceived as inconsistent or harmful. Such artefacts and behaviours can signal a lack of aesthetic sensitivity and a superficial approach to management, corporate culture, and employee and customer relations. 3) Norms, values, and hidden cultural assumptions in an organisation interact with the emergence of kitsch due to an illusory image, often at the expense of authentic experiences, values, and truths. Strategies for eliminating kitsch from deeply rooted beliefs of organisational members include promoting authenticity, transparency, and employee engagement, which allows for building an organisational culture based on well-being and truth.

The study on kitsch's role in organisational culture has several limitations that must be considered when interpreting the results. The limitation of this study is the focus mainly on the literature and case studies, which may not fully capture the complexity and dynamics of the phenomenon of kitsch in diverse contexts of organisational cultures. The analysis was based on available publications and examples, which may limit the universality of the conclusions. Although an effort was made to select examples that illustrate different aspects of kitsch in organisational culture, the selection of case studies may be limited. It may only exhaust some possible kitsch manifestations in a corporate culture environment. Despite these limitations, the study provides valuable insights into the complex relationship between kitsch and organisational culture.

Given the existing limitations, future research should focus on expanding the scope and depth of the analysis of the phenomenon of kitsch in organisational culture. It could be essential to deepen the understanding of the impact of kitsch on individual and group behaviour of employees, as well as their commitment, job satisfaction, and organisational effectiveness. Research could examine how the perception of kitsch affects employee motivation and their identification with the organisational culture, as well as how kitsch can be managed to bring positive effects within the organisation. Additionally, future studies should focus on developing kitsch management strategies and tools in the corporate culture environment. It would be valuable to identify decision-making practices that organisations can use to minimise the negative aspects of kitsch and use its potential positive sides to build a solid and authentic organisational culture.

References

Abboud, L., & Wagstaff, J. (2015, October 5). Legal Troubles, Market Realities Threaten Uber's Global Push. *Reuters*. Retrieved from https://www.reuters.com/

Adorno, T. W. (1973). *Negative Dialectics* (E. B. Ashton, Trans.). Continuum.

Adorno, T. W. (1992). On Tradition. *Telos: Critical Theory of the Contemporary, 94*, 75–82.

Adorno, T. W., & Horkheimer, M. (2002). *Dialectic of Enlightenment: Philosophical Fragments* (E. Jephcott, Trans.). Stanford University Press.

Akpa, V. O., Asikhia, O. U., & Nneji, N. E. (2021). Organisational Culture and Organisational Performance: A Review of Literature. *International Journal of Advances in Engineering and Management (IJAEM)*, *3*(1), 361–372. https://doi.org/10.35629/5252-0301361372

Attfield, J. (2006). Redefining Kitsch: The Politics of Design. *Home Cultures*, *3*(3), 201–212.

Bigliardi, B., Dormio, A. I., Galati, F., & Schiuma, G. (2012). The Impact of Organizational Culture on the Job Satisfaction of Knowledge Workers. *VINE*, *42*(1), 36–51.

Bilton, N. (2016, September 6). Exclusive: How Elizabeth Holmes's House of Cards Came Tumbling Down. *Vanity Fair*. Retrieved from https://www.vanityfair.com/news/2016/09/elizabeth-holmes-theranos-exclusive

Büschgens, T., Bausch, A., & Balkin, D. B. (2013). Organisational Culture and Innovation: A Meta-Analytic Review. *Journal of Product Innovation Management*, *30*(4), 763–781. https://doi.org/10.1111/jpim.12021

Cameron, K. S., & Quinn, R. E. (2011). *Diagnosing and Changing Organisational Culture: Based on the Competing Values Framework* (3rd ed.). Jossey-Bass.

Chen, Z., Huang, S., Liu, C., Min, M., & Zhou, L. (2018). Fit Between Organisational Culture and Innovation Strategy: Implications for Innovation Performance. *Sustainability (Switzerland)*, *10*(10). https://doi.org/10.3390/su10103378

Cicea, C., Ţurlea, C., Marinescu, C., & Pintilie, N. (2022). Organisational Culture: A Concept Captive between Determinants and Its Own Power of Influence. In *Sustainability (Switzerland)* (Vol. 14, Issue 4). MDPI. https://doi.org/10.3390/su14042021

Ciupka, S. (2020). Pathologies and Kitsch in the Workplace – Theoretical Perspective. *ASEJ Scientific Journal of Bielsko-Biala School of Finance and Law*, *24*(1), 26–30. https://doi.org/10.5604/01.3001.0014.1347

Constable, S. (2021, December 2). How the Enron Scandal Changed American Business Forever. *Time*. Retrieved from https://time.com/6125253/enron-scandal-changed-american-business-forever/

Counts, A., & Nakano, E. (2023, July 19). Harmful Content Has Surged on Twitter, Keeping Advertisers Away. *Time*. Retrieved from https://time.com/6295711/twitters-hate-content-advertisers/

Deal, T. E., & Kennedy, A. A. (1982). *Corporate Cultures: The Rites and Rituals of Corporate Life*. Addison-Wesley.

Deal, T. E., & Kennedy, A. A. (2008). *The New Corporate Cultures: Revitalising the Workplace after Downsizing, Mergers, and Reengineering*. Perseus Books.

Dewey, C. (2018, June 4). Why 'Monsanto' Is No More. *The Washington Post*. Retrieved from https://www.washingtonpost.com/news/wonk/wp/2018/06/04/why-monsanto-is-no-more/

Emmer, C. E. (2014). Traditional Kitsch and the Janus-Head of Comfort. In J. Stępień (Ed.), *Redefining Kitsch and Camp in Literature and Culture* (pp. 23–40). Cambridge Scholars Publishing.

Furr, N., & Dyer, J. (2020, February 12). Lessons from Tesla's Approach to Innovation. *Harvard Business Review*. Retrieved from https://hbr.org/2020/02/lessons-from-teslas-approach-to-innovation

Gaughran, A. (n.d.). Shell's Niger Delta Pollution: The Good, the Bad and the Ongoing Quest for Justice. *Amnesty International*. Retrieved from https://www.amnestyusa.org/updates/shells-niger-delta-pollution-the-good-the-bad-and-the-ongoing-quest-for-justice/

Gutterman, A. S. (2017). *Sustainable Entrepreneurship Project Organizational Culture: A Global Survey of Theory and Research*. www.seproject.org

Handy, C. (1993). *Understanding Organisations*. Penguin Books.

Handy, C. (1995). *Gods of Management: The Changing Work of Organizations*. Oxford University Press.

Haslam, S. A., Cornelissen, J. P., & Werner, M. D. (2017). Metatheories and Metaphors of Organisational Identity: Interacting Social Actor Perspectives Within a Social Interactionist Model. *International Journal of Management Reviews*, *19*(3), 318–336.

Hatch M. J. (1993). The Dynamics of Organizational Culture. *Academy of Management Review*, *18*(4), 657–693.

Hatch, M. J. (1997). *Organisation Theory: Modern, Symbolic, and Postmodern Perspectives*. Oxford University Press.

Hofstede, G. (1984). *Cultural Consequences: International Differences in Work Values*. Sage.

Hofstede, G., Hofstede, G., & Minkov, M. (2010). *Cultures and Organisations: Software of the Mind*. McGraw-Hill.

Ivan, A. (2016). Kitsch as Aesthetic Recuperation. *Bulletin of the Transilvania University of Braşov Series VII: Social Sciences Law*, *9*(58), 143–150.

Kostera, M. (1997). The Kitsch-Organisation. *Studies in Cultures, Organisations, and Societies*, *3*(2), 163–177. https://doi.org/10.1080/10245289708523494

Leggett, T. (2018, May 5). How VW Tried to Cover Up the Emissions Scandal. *BBC News*. Retrieved from https://www.bbc.com/news/business-44005844

Li, W., Bhutto, T. A., Nasiri, A. R., Shaikh, H. A., & Samo, F. A. (2018). Organisational Innovation: The Role of Leadership and Organisational Culture. *International Journal of Public Leadership*, *14*(1), 33–47. https://doi.org/10.1108/ijpl-06-2017-0026

Linstead, S. (2002). Organisational Kitsch. *Organisation*, *9*(4), 657–682. https://doi.org/10.1177/135050840294008

Lugg, C. A. (1999). *Kitsch: From Education to Public Policy*. Routledge.

Lurie, T. (2019, October 29). The Fight to Stop Nestlé from Taking America's Water to Sell in Plastic Bottles. *The Guardian*. Retrieved from https://www.theguardian.com/environment/2019/oct/29/the-fight-over-water-how-nestle-dries-up-us-creeks-to-sell-water-in-plastic-bottles

Newcomb, A. (2018, March 24). A Timeline of Facebook's Privacy Issues – and Its Responses. *NBC News*. Retrieved from https://www.nbcnews.com/tech/social-media/timeline-facebook-s-privacy-issues-its-responses-n859651

Ogbonna, E. (1992). Managing Organisational Culture: Fantasy or Reality? *Journal of Human Resource Management*, *3*(2), 42–54.

Pierson, B. (2023, October 3). Court Tosses $223.8 Million Verdict Against J&J in Talc Cancer Case. *Reuters*. Retrieved from https://www.reuters.com/markets/us/court-tosses-2238-million-verdict-against-jj-talc-cancer-case-2023-10-03/

Schein, E. H. (1983). The Role of the Founder in the Creation of Organizational Culture. *Organisational Dynamics*, *12*(1), 13–28.

Schein, E. H. (1987). *The Clinical Perspective in Fieldwork*. Sage.

Schein, E. H. (1996). Culture: The Missing Concept in Organization Studies. *Administrative Science Quarterly*, *41*(2), 229–240.

Schein, E. H. (2009). *The Corporate Culture Survival Guide*. Jossey-Bass.

Schein, E. H. (2010). *Organisational Culture and Leadership*. Jossey-Bass.

Segal, T. (2023, December 22). Enron Scandal: The Fall of a Wall Street Darling. *Investopedia*. Reviewed by J. Mansa, Fact-checked by M. Reeves. Retrieved from https://www.investopedia.com/updates/enron-scandal-summary/

Shamsudin, S. (2021). Organisational Culture and Performance: An Examination of Relative Effects of Culture Factors in IT Industry in India Organisational Culture and Performance: An Examination of Relative Effects of Culture Factors in IT Industry in India. *XIlkogretim Online – Elementary Education Online*, *20*(5), 3460–3465. https://doi.org/10.17051/ilkonline.2021.05.380

Stępień, J. (2014). *Redefining Kitsch and Camp in Literature and Culture*. Cambridge Scholars Publishing.

Sun, S., & Milosevic, D. (2006). Organisational Culture and Its Themes. *International Journal of Business and Management*, *3*(12), 137–143.

Szczepańska-Woszczyna, K. (2014). The Importance of Organizational Culture for Innovation in the Company. *Innovations, Entrepreneurship and Economic Growth*, *2*(3), 27–39.

Szostak, M., & Sulkowski, Ł. (2020). 'Kitsch in Management: Characteristic Forms, Carriers and Propagators,' in *Education Excellence and Innovation Management: A 2025 Vision to Sustain Economic Development During Global Challenges: Proceedings of the 35th International Business Information Management Association Conference (IBIMA)*, Sevilla: IBIMA, pp. 7584–7598. Available at: https://depot.ceon.pl/handle/123456789/19173.

Teehankee, B. (1994). Organisational Culture: A Critical Review of Literature. *Dialogue: An Interdisciplinary Journal for Cultural Studies*, *27*(1), 68–92.

Tiffany, D. (2013). *My Silver Planet: A Secret History of Poetry and Kitsch*. Hopkins University Press.

Trompenaars, F., & Hampden-Turner, C. (1997). *Riding the Waves of Culture: Understanding Cultural Diversity in Global Business*. Nicholas Brealey.

Wilson, M. (2023, June 5). Apple Is No Longer a Design-Led Company. *Fast Company*. Retrieved from https://www.fastcompany.com/

Zeitlin, M. (2019, December 20). Why WeWork Went Wrong. *The Guardian*. Retrieved from https://www.theguardian.com/business/2019/dec/20/why-wework-went-wrong

3 Kitsch in organisational governance

Management through simplified edicts and superficial interpretations in religious fatwas

Magdalena El Ghamari

Introduction

The phenomenon of kitsch is a cultural aesthetic marked by shallow sentimentality and lacking depth. It involves mass-produced sentimental or clichéd imagery that appeals to popular taste but lacks genuine emotional or aesthetic value. Kitsch spans various forms such as art, literature, music, fashion, and religious expression, often associated with consumer culture and mass media. It prioritises immediate gratification over critical engagement and can serve as cultural shorthand for familiar themes and symbols. However, perceptions of kitsch vary widely, with some embracing or subverting it intentionally (Hawkins, 1998). In religious contexts, kitsch can be contentious, criticised for prioritising external displays of piety over genuine spiritual engagement, yet some argue it aids emotional connection or accessibility to religious teachings. The diversity of interpretations within Islamic jurisprudence refers to the wide range of understandings and opinions among Islamic scholars regarding religious texts, principles, and legal rulings.

Conducted research on analysing the phenomenon of kitsch in religious fatwas is crucial for several reasons. Firstly, it addresses a significant gap in the scholarly literature by exploring the intersection of religious guidance and the phenomenon of kitsch. While there is ample research on kitsch in various cultural and artistic contexts, its manifestation within religious discourse needs more study. By focusing specifically on religious fatwas, which carry considerable authority and influence within religious communities, this research sheds light on a vital aspect of contemporary religious practice. Secondly, the study's emphasis on critically examining simplified rulings and superficial interpretations within religious fatwas is timely and relevant. In an age marked by information overload and the proliferation of digital media platforms, there is a growing concern about the oversimplification of complex religious concepts and the potential distortion of religious principles. By scrutinising the impact of kitsch on religious fatwas, this research contributes to ongoing discussions surrounding the authenticity and integrity of religious guidance in the modern era. Research also has practical implications for

DOI: 10.4324/9781003504931-4

religious leaders, scholars, and practitioners. By identifying the presence of kitsch within religious fatwas and assessing its implications, this study provides valuable insights for promoting more nuanced and informed approaches to religious interpretation and communication.

The intersection between religious fatwas and the phenomenon of kitsch presents a compelling area of inquiry, encapsulating the complexities of contemporary religious discourse and its interaction with popular aesthetics. This research chapter critically examines the convergence between religious decrees and kitsch, aiming to shed light on the implications stemming from simplified rulings and superficial interpretations within religious discourse. With its hallmark traits of low artistic merit, sentimentality, and superficial aesthetics, kitsch has not merely entered but ingrained itself within the realm of religious fatwas (Buang, 2002; Hosen, 2008). It has wielded considerable influence over how religious guidance is communicated and understood by the broader populace.

The presence of kitsch within religious fatwas marks a notable departure from the traditional norms and standards that have historically governed religious discourse. In traditional modes of religious discourse, such as those found in classical theological texts and scholarly discussions, there was a profound emphasis on scholarly rigour and depth of understanding. Religious scholars and theologians dedicated extensive time and effort to analyse religious texts meticulously, engage in rigorous debates, and uphold the intellectual integrity of their interpretations. For example, in classical Islamic jurisprudence, scholars meticulously analysed primary religious texts such as the Quran and Hadiths to derive legal rulings (fatwas) on various aspects of life. For example, renowned jurists like Imam Abu Hanifa, Imam Malik, and Imam Shafi'i developed comprehensive legal methodologies grounded in rigorous textual interpretation, linguistic analysis, and jurisprudential reasoning. Their works, such as Hanafi fiqh, Maliki fiqh, and Shafi'i fiqh, are characterised by extensive discussions, debates, and references to foundational sources, demonstrating a commitment to scholarly rigour and depth of understanding. In Medieval Christian theology, during the Middle Ages, Christian theologians such as Thomas Aquinas, Augustine of Hippo, and Origen of Alexandria produced seminal works that exemplify the emphasis on scholarly rigour in traditional Christian discourse. For instance, Aquinas's "Summa Theologica" is a comprehensive treatise that systematically addresses theological topics ranging from the existence of God to moral philosophy. Aquinas employs rigorous logical argumentation, dialectical reasoning, and extensive engagement with philosophical and theological sources to elucidate complex theological concepts, demonstrating a deep commitment to intellectual rigour and depth of understanding. However, with the infiltration of kitsch into religious fatwas, there has been a noticeable shift away from this tradition of scholarly rigour. With its emphasis on sentimentality, superficiality, and mass appeal, kitsch prioritises emotional impact over intellectual depth. As a result, religious fatwas may sacrifice the careful analysis and nuanced interpretation characteristic of traditional religious discourse in favour of simplistic, emotionally resonant messaging. This departure from traditional modes of religious discourse has significant implications for interpreting and disseminating religious guidance. Instead of engaging with religious texts and principles rigorously and intellectually stimulatingly, individuals may be presented with watered-down, easily digestible versions of religious teachings that cater to mass sensibilities. This can lead to a deeper understanding of religious concepts and principles and a dilution of the richness and complexity inherent in religious traditions. Moreover, the presence of kitsch within religious fatwas may undermine the authority and credibility of religious institutions and leaders. Traditional religious authorities are often esteemed for their expertise, scholarly credentials, and adherence to rigorous interpretive methodologies. However, when religious fatwas are infused with kitsch, they may be perceived as pandering to popular tastes or engaging in superficial appeals for relevance, thereby eroding trust and confidence in religious leadership.

This infiltration of kitsch into religious fatwas has far-reaching consequences that form the focal point of my research. At its core, I seek to unpack the myriad ramifications associated with this convergence. Integrating kitsch elements into religious decrees raises the risk of oversimplification – a reduction of complex theological concepts into easily digestible but often shallow forms. This oversimplification runs the peril of diluting the richness and depth of religious principles and opens the door to potential distortions of these principles. The influence of kitsch on religious fatwas extends beyond mere aesthetic considerations. It can also shape individuals' emotional and psychological responses to these rulings. The sentimentality inherent in kitsch can evoke strong emotional reactions, potentially clouding individuals' critical faculties and leading them to accept simplified interpretations uncritically. Furthermore, the superficial aesthetics associated with kitsch may overshadow the substantive content of religious fatwas, diverting attention away from the core principles they seek to elucidate (Hirschkind, 2006). This diversion of focus can contribute to a surface-level understanding of religious guidance, lacking the depth and nuance necessary for proper comprehension and application in diverse contexts. In essence, the infiltration of kitsch into religious fatwas represents a departure from the rigorous intellectual traditions that have historically underpinned religious scholarship. It underscores the need to critically examine how religious guidance is presented and consumed in contemporary society. By illuminating these dynamics, we aim to underscore the importance of preserving scholarly rigour and depth in religious discourse while also interrogating the implications of simplified interpretations for individuals and communities navigating complex religious landscapes.

The "kitsch experience" theory – as elucidated by prominent aesthetics and cultural studies scholars, offering a compelling framework for understanding the multifaceted nature of kitsch and its impact on individuals' aesthetic sensibilities (Szostak & Sułkowski, 2020, Szostak, 2021) – will be the main analytical tool for analysing kitsch components in religious fatwas.

Methodology

This study adopts a comprehensive analytical approach, drawing upon a diverse selection of fatwas from various religious contexts to assess critically the authenticity and scholarly rigour underpinning these simplified rulings. I have applied two methods: 1) literature review and 2) comparative analysis based on a qualitative approach (using some basic quantitative metrics). As revealed in this research, the presence of kitsch within religious fatwas holds significant relevance to the concurrently examined case study, which scrutinises the prevalence of simplified religious fatwas (Nawi & Hamzah, 2014) disseminated through social media platforms. Within the broader framework of this paper, kitsch serves as a lens through which to examine the broader issue of oversimplification and superficial interpretation of religious tenets and aesthetics. The specific case study focused on social media platforms serves as a distinct exemplar of this overarching phenomenon, illustrating how kitsch becomes entrenched within religious discourse due to the constraints imposed by such platforms. The research delves into the role played by mass media and popular culture in shaping these interpretations, seeking to enrich our understanding of the intricate interplay between kitsch and religious guidance within contemporary society. The main research questions were formulated as follows:

1. How has the phenomenon of kitsch influenced the formulation and dissemination of religious fatwas in contemporary society?
2. What are the potential consequences of oversimplified religious rulings and superficial interpretations for religious communities and their faith?
3. To what extent do mass media and popular culture contribute to the proliferation of kitsch in religious fatwas?

Through addressing these questions, the research contributes to a nuanced understanding of the dynamics at play within the intersection of religious discourse, aesthetics, and popular culture, ultimately seeking to inform discourse surrounding the interpretation and dissemination of religious guidance in contemporary society.

Literature review

Functions of fatwas

Islamic jurisprudence, known as fiqh, is derived from the Quran (Ali, 2011; Nasr, Dagli, Dakake, Lumbard & Rustom, 2015), the Hadith (Saloot, Idris, Mahmud, Ja'afar, Thorleuchter & Gani, 2016; Brown, 2009, 2017) (sayings and actions of the Prophet Muhammad), scholarly consensus (ijma), and reasoning (ijtihad) (Brown, 2014). However, interpreting these sources can lead to different conclusions due to varying methodologies, perspectives, and cultural contexts among scholars.

This diversity is evident in multiple schools of thought (madhhab) within Sunni Islam, such as the Hanafi, Maliki, and Shafi'i (Imam Al shafi'i, 2019), and Hanbali schools, each with its approach to interpreting Islamic law. There are diverse scholarly traditions within Shia Islam, including the *Ithna Ashari*, Ismaili, and Zaidi schools, each with its legal framework and interpretations. The diversity of interpretations within Islamic jurisprudence can lead to differences in legal rulings (fatwas) on various issues, ranging from personal matters like prayer and fasting to broader societal issues like governance and finance (Hassan & Khairuldin, 2020). These differences reflect the richness and dynamism of Islamic legal tradition and challenge consistency and coherence in legal rulings, especially in contemporary contexts where new challenges and circumstances arise. Navigating this diversity requires a nuanced understanding of Islamic jurisprudence principles and respect for differing opinions and scholarly methodologies. It also underscores the importance of consulting knowledgeable scholars and seeking a balanced approach to interpreting and applying Islamic law using the principles of justice, compassion, and wisdom. The issue with interpretation and understanding fatwas lies in their potential to be oversimplified or misinterpreted, leading to misunderstandings or misapplications of religious rulings. Fatwas are complex legal opinions issued by Islamic scholars based on their interpretation of religious texts and principles. However, due to the diversity of interpretations within Islamic jurisprudence and the complexities of contemporary issues, fatwas can sometimes be presented that need to consider the nuances of the situation or the broader context in which the ruling applies. There may be variations in fatwas issued by different scholars or schools of thought, leading to consistent guidance on certain matters. This can result in confusion among individuals seeking religious guidance, especially when faced with conflicting opinions from different sources. The accessibility of fatwas on digital platforms and social media, like Facebook, Twitter, TikTok, and Instagram, can further complicate matters, as oversimplified or sensationalised interpretations may spread rapidly without proper context or scholarly oversight. This can exacerbate misunderstandings and contribute to the dissemination of inaccurate information. Overall, the issue with understanding fatwas underscores the importance of seeking guidance from qualified religious authorities, critically evaluating sources of religious information, and fostering an environment of informed dialogue and inquiry within religious communities.

Religion and kitsch

Authors like Jean Baudrillard delve into the phenomenon of kitsch simplifying complex ideas (Baudrillard, 1998). Baudrillard argues that in contemporary culture, there is a proliferation of simulations or copies that need more depth and authenticity of the original (O'Reilly, 1992). This concept applies to Kitsch (Lane, 2008), who often presents shallow imitations of profound ideas. For instance, in religious fatwas, complex theological concepts may be reduced to clichéd phrases or oversimplified narratives, diminishing their richness and depth. Similarly, Susan Sontag, in "Notes on 'Camp'," discusses how kitsch operates through simplification, transforming complex cultural phenomena into easily digestible forms (Sontag, 2018). In religious fatwas, this could manifest as reducing intricate religious doctrines into simplistic slogans or sentimental imagery, lacking the intellectual rigour and nuance required for a comprehensive understanding. These examples illustrate how kitsch tends to oversimplify complex ideas within religious discourse, resulting in a loss of depth and nuance. The insights provided by Theodor Adorno and Milan Kundera shed light on the reliance of kitsch on sentimentality and emotional manipulation within religious discourse (Adorno, 1997; Kundera, 2020). In "Aesthetic Theory," Adorno critically examines kitsch's role in contemporary culture, highlighting its propensity to exploit sentimental emotions for mass appeal (Kimbrell, 2002). Within religious fatwas, this reliance on sentimentality can be observed in using emotionally charged narratives or imagery to elicit immediate and uncritical responses from the audience (Huhn & Zuidervaart, 1997; Adorno, 1997; Stan, 2018). For example, a fatwa may employ poignant anecdotes or dramatic storytelling to sway followers' emotions and garner support for a particular religious interpretation or practice. Similarly, Milan Kundera's exploration in "The Unbearable Lightness of Being" delves into the manipulation of emotions inherent in kitsch. Kundera illustrates how kitsch creates an illusion of depth and meaning through superficial sentimentality, masking the absence of genuine substance (Kundera, 2020; Sewlall, 2013). In religious fatwas, this manipulation of emotions can manifest in presenting simplistic solutions to complex spiritual or moral dilemmas, appealing to followers' emotions rather than engaging in thoughtful theological discourse. It demonstrates how kitsch within religious fatwas relies on sentimentality and emotional manipulation to evoke immediate, uncritical responses from its audience. By understanding these mechanisms, scholars can critically analyse the impact of kitsch on religious discourse and work towards fostering more authentic and intellectually rigorous interpretations within religious communities.

Fredric Jameson's analysis in "Postmodernism, or, The Cultural Logic of Late Capitalism" (Jameson, 2016) and Walter Benjamin's (Benjamin, 2018) exploration in "The Work of Art in the Age of Mechanical Reproduction" provide valuable insights into the role of superficial aesthetics in kitsch within religious discourse. Jameson examines how postmodern culture, influenced by late capitalism, prioritises surface appearances over substance, resulting in a proliferation of kitsch aesthetics. Within this framework, kitsch is characterised by its visually striking but intellectually shallow content, designed to appeal to mass audiences. In the context of religious fatwas, this emphasis on superficial aesthetics can be observed in the use of flashy graphics, catchy slogans, and simplistic imagery to convey religious messages. For example, a fatwa disseminated through social media platforms may employ vibrant colours and eye-catching design elements to attract attention but need more substantive theological content.

Similarly, Walter Benjamin's exploration of the impact of mechanical reproduction on art sheds light on how kitsch utilises visual appeal to cater to mass tastes (Peim, 2007). Benjamin argues that the reproducibility of art diminishes its aura and authenticity, leading to the proliferation of superficial and commercially driven aesthetics. In the realm of religious fatwas, this commodification of visual imagery can manifest in promoting religious merchandise or using aesthetically pleasing but intellectually vacuous symbols to represent complex theological concepts. For instance, a fatwa endorsing a particular religious product may emphasise its attractive packaging or design, prioritising consumer appeal over theological depth. These examples illustrate how Jameson and Benjamin's analysis of superficial aesthetics provides insights into the mechanisms through which kitsch operates within religious discourse. By highlighting the appeal of visually striking but intellectually shallow content to mass audiences, these scholars contribute to a deeper understanding of the role of aesthetics in shaping religious fatwas and their reception.

Naomi Klein's "No Logo" (Klein, 2010, 2014) and David Morgan's (Morgan, 1997, 2005) "The Sacred Gaze: Religious Visual Culture in Theory and Practice" offer valuable insights into how kitsch contributes to the commodification of spirituality within religious discourse. Klein's exploration focuses on the pervasive influence of branding and consumerism on various aspects of contemporary culture, including religion (Klein, 2010). She discusses how corporations exploit religious symbols and experiences as part of their marketing strategies, turning spirituality into a commodity for profit. In the context of religious fatwas, this commodification can be observed in promoting and selling religious artefacts, such as prayer beads, religious clothing, or even virtual blessings offered for purchase online. These commodified religious products often prioritise marketability over authenticity, catering to consumerist impulses within religious communities.

David Morgan's work delves into the intersection of religion and visual culture, examining how religious imagery and artefacts are consumed and commodified within religious communities (Morgan, 2005). He discusses how religious objects and experiences are marketed and sold to believers, transforming sacred practices into commercial transactions. In religious fatwas, this commodification may manifest in promoting religious pilgrimage packages, where individuals can purchase pre-packaged experiences of spiritual fulfilment for a fee. Additionally, the commercialisation of religious rituals, such as the sale of blessings or religious services, further underscores the commodification of spirituality within religious discourse. Examples of such commodification include the sale of religious-themed merchandise, such as t-shirts, keychains, or home decor featuring religious symbols, which are marketed as expressions of faith but are often mass-produced for profit (Taylor, 2007). Additionally, promoting exclusive religious experiences, such as VIP access to sacred sites or private audiences with religious leaders, for a premium price further illustrates the commercialisation of spirituality within religious fatwas. These examples highlight how Klein and Morgan's analyses provide insights into how kitsch contributes to the commodification of spirituality within religious discourse, emphasising the role of consumerism in shaping contemporary religious practices and experiences.

Martha Nussbaum (Nussbaum, 2003) and Alain de Botton (De Botton, 2012) have critiqued the oversimplification of ethical and moral guidance in kitsch-infused religious messaging, highlighting its failure to address the complexities of moral dilemmas and human experience. Scholars like Edward Said in "Orientalism" (Said, 1977) and Jacques Derrida in "Of Grammatology" (Derrida, 2016) offer critical perspectives on the erosion of scholarly rigour and intellectual depth within kitsch-infused discourses, shedding light on the necessity of critical engagement and rigorous analysis in understanding complex cultural phenomena. Said's examination of Orientalism reveals how Western representations of the East often rely on simplistic stereotypes and distortions (Said, 2023; Macfie, 2014; El Ghamari, 2017), lacking scholarly integrity and depth. In the context of religious fatwas, this can manifest as oversimplified and essentialised depictions of non-Western cultures or religious traditions, perpetuating misconceptions and reinforcing power dynamics. Qualitative data collection focused on the content analysis of sampled fatwas, examining the language, imagery, and themes employed to convey religious messages. Researchers documented oversimplification, sentimentality, and superficiality in presenting religious rulings. Similarly, Derrida's deconstructionist approach to language and meaning challenges the notion of absolute truth and authority in discourse (Cunningham, 2015). Derrida critiques the tendency of kitsch-infused discourses to prioritise emotional appeal over critical engagement, emphasising the importance of rigorous analysis and scholarly integrity in understanding complex cultural phenomena. In the context of religious fatwas (Agrama, 2010), this may involve deconstructing the language and rhetoric used to convey religious messages and uncovering underlying power dynamics and ideological biases. For example, Said's critique of Orientalism exposes how kitsch-infused representations of Islam often rely on simplistic dichotomies between the "East" and "West," failing to acknowledge the diversity and complexity within Muslim societies (Asad, 2003). Similarly, Derrida's deconstruction of religious rhetoric may reveal how kitsch-infused fatwas employ binary thinking and emotional manipulation to reinforce religious orthodoxy and control. These examples demonstrate how Said and Derrida's analyses contribute to a deeper understanding of the erosion of scholarly rigour and intellectual depth within kitsch-infused discourses, underscoring the importance of critical engagement and rigorous analysis in deciphering complex cultural phenomena. By applying their insights to the study of religious fatwas, scholars can uncover the underlying mechanisms through which kitsch operates within religious discourse and work towards fostering more authentic and intellectually rigorous interpretations within religious communities (Juergensmeyer, 2017; Kepel, 2002).

By drawing on the insights of these authors, the literature review provides a nuanced understanding of the various behaviours and issues associated with kitsch in religious fatwas, shedding light on the challenges posed by oversimplification, emotional manipulation, and the loss of scholarly integrity within contemporary religious discourse.

Empirical support: kitsch of religious fatwas in social media

In recent years, the advent of social media platforms has revolutionised the dissemination of information, including religious guidance, to a global audience. This case study focuses on the phenomenon of simplified religious fatwas proliferating on social media, highlighting their impact on religious discourse and community engagement.

Social media platforms, such as Facebook, Twitter, Instagram, and TikTok, have become increasingly popular avenues for religious authorities to reach their followers directly. With millions of users worldwide, these platforms offer unprecedented access to diverse audiences, making them invaluable religious communication and outreach tools. Facebook was chosen for its widespread popularity and diverse user base, making it an ideal platform for reaching a broad audience with religious content. Religious authorities often use Facebook to share fatwas, engage with followers through live streams or Q&A sessions, and create religious communities through groups and pages dedicated to spiritual discussions. Twitter's real-time nature and character limit make it suitable for concise and immediate communication of religious rulings. Religious scholars and organisations frequently use Twitter to share quick updates, inspirational quotes, and links to longer-form content, including fatwas and scholarly articles. The platform's hashtag feature also facilitates categorising and discovering religious discussions on various topics. Instagram's visual nature makes it an ideal platform for sharing aesthetically pleasing religious content, including inspirational quotes, artwork, and short videos. Religious influencers and organisations often use Instagram to share daily reflections, promote religious events, and showcase religious rituals or practices through visually engaging posts and stories. TikTok's format, characterised by short, engaging videos, lends itself well to disseminating simplified religious messages and fatwas. Religious scholars and influencers leverage TikTok's creativity and entertainment value to share bite-sized religious teachings, answer common questions, and engage with younger audiences through trends and challenges related to faith and spirituality.

Comparative analysis employs a mixed-methods approach, combining qualitative analysis of religious fatwas shared on social media with quantitative data on audience engagement metrics (Table 3.1). Researchers analyse a sample of religious fatwas across various platforms, examining their content, presentation, and reception.

Table 3.1 Methodological approaches in analysing simplified religious fatwas on social media platforms

Case study methodology	*Research objectives*	*Specificity*
Sampling strategy	The research utilised purposive sampling to select a diverse range of social media platforms for analysis, including but not limited to Facebook, Twitter, Instagram, and TikTok. Platforms were chosen based on their popularity, user demographics, and relevance to religious communication.	Within each platform, a combination of religious authorities, organisations, and influencers known for disseminating religious fatwas was identified for inclusion in the study. This ensured a comprehensive examination of different voices and perspectives within religious discourse.
Data collection	The research team employed quantitative and qualitative data collection methods to gather information on the prevalence and nature of simplified religious fatwas on social media platforms.	Quantitative data collection involved the systematic collection of fatwas shared by selected accounts over a specified period, capturing metrics such as likes, shares, comments, and engagement rates. This quantitative analysis provided insights into the reach and popularity of simplified fatwas.
Content analysis	The collected fatwas were subjected to thorough content analysis guided by the research questions and objectives. Researchers identified patterns, themes, and trends in the presentation and reception of simplified religious fatwas on social media platforms.	Qualitative coding techniques were employed to categorise fatwas based on their level of simplification, emotional appeal, and adherence to scholarly rigour. This allowed for a nuanced understanding of the strategies used to convey religious guidance and their impact on audience perceptions.
Comparative analysis	By comparing simplified religious fatwas across different social media platforms, I am examining variations in content, presentation style, and audience engagement.	By comparing fatwas from diverse religious contexts and platforms, researchers sought to identify commonalities and differences in the manifestation of kitsch aesthetics and oversimplified interpretations within religious discourse.

Source: Own research form media platforms Facebook, Twitter, Instagram, and TikTok

The study uncovers a notable proliferation of simplified religious fatwas across social media platforms. These fatwas condense intricate theological concepts into easily digestible messages, often relying on catchy slogans, emotive imagery, and oversimplified interpretations to captivate audiences. Consequently, simplified religious fat garnered substantial engagement on social media, evidenced by metrics such as likes, shares, and comments. However, despite their popularity, these fatwas face criticism for their potential to distort religious teachings and promote shallow understanding among followers. Critics argue that prioritising emotional appeal over scholarly rigour may lead to misconceptions and misinterpretations. Moreover, the study underscores the influential role of social media algorithms in shaping the visibility and dissemination of religious fatwas. These algorithms prioritise content that generates high engagement, incentivising religious authorities to prioritise simplified messages to reach broader audiences.

The prevalence of simplified religious fatwas on social media platforms carries significant implications for religious discourse and community dynamics. While these fatwas may enhance accessibility and outreach, they also raise concerns about the erosion of scholarly rigour, the distortion of religious teachings, and the reinforcement of superficial understanding among followers.

Facebook is utilised for sharing simplified religious messages and fatwas with daily inspirational posts, live-streamed sermons or lectures, Facebook groups for religious discussion, scheduled Q&A Sessions with religious scholars, and Facebook events for religious workshops or retreats with the following examples:

- A religious organisation shares daily inspirational posts on its Facebook page featuring quotes from religious texts or teachings. These posts offer brief messages of encouragement, reflection, or guidance to uplift and inspire followers throughout the day. By incorporating visually appealing graphics or images, the organisation enhances the impact and engagement of these posts.
- A religious leader broadcasts live sermons or lectures on their Facebook page, allowing followers to participate virtually in religious gatherings. During these live streams, the leader delivers teachings, answers questions from viewers, and offers spiritual guidance in real-time. Followers can interact through comments, likes, and shares, fostering community and connection.
- A religious community creates a Facebook group to discuss specific religious topics or teachings. Group members can share insights, ask questions, and engage in dialogue with fellow believers and religious scholars. The group provides a supportive space for deeper exploration of religious concepts and fosters mutual learning and growth.
- A religious organisation hosts scheduled question-and-answer sessions with renowned religious scholars on its Facebook page. Followers can submit their questions in advance or during the session, and the scholars provide insightful

responses, offering clarity on complex religious issues or theological debates. These sessions facilitate direct engagement and promote understanding among followers.
- A religious centre creates Facebook events to promote upcoming workshops, seminars, or retreats focused on spiritual development. The events provide details about the programme, speakers, and registration information, allowing followers to express interest, RSVP, and share the event with their networks. Facebook events serve as valuable tools for community building and outreach.

These examples demonstrate how Facebook serves as a dynamic platform for sharing simplified religious messages and fatwas, fostering engagement, community building, and spiritual growth among followers. By leveraging features such as daily posts, live streaming, groups, Q&A sessions, and events, religious leaders and organisations can effectively communicate key teachings and principles while nurturing meaningful connections with their audience.

Twitter is sharing simplified religious messages and fatwas with threaded explanatory tweets, daily inspirational tweets, live-tweeting of religious events, and Twitter polls on religious topics with the following examples:

- A religious scholar creates a Twitter thread to offer a simplified explanation of a religious concept or ruling. The thread breaks down complex topics into concise tweets, each building upon the previous one to provide a comprehensive overview. For instance, they might explain the significance of certain religious rituals or clarify misconceptions about specific religious practices.
- A religious organisation shares daily inspirational tweets featuring quotes from religious texts or teachings. These tweets offer brief messages of encouragement, reflection, or guidance to uplift and inspire followers throughout the day. By incorporating relevant hashtags and mentions, the organisation increases the visibility of its tweets and encourages engagement from the Twitter community.
- During religious events or gatherings, such as sermons, conferences, or workshops, religious leaders or organisations live-tweet vital points, insights, or quotes shared during the event. This allows followers who cannot attend in person to participate virtually and stay informed about the proceedings in real-time. Live-tweeting enhances engagement and fosters a sense of community among followers.
- A religious figure conducts Twitter polls to gauge followers' opinions or preferences on religious topics or practices. For instance, they might ask followers to vote on their favourite spiritual practices during the holy month of Ramadan or to share their views on contemporary ethical issues from a religious perspective. Twitter polls encourage interaction and provide valuable insights into followers' beliefs and attitudes.

These examples demonstrate how Twitter serves as a platform for sharing simplified religious messages and fatwas in a format that is concise, accessible, and conducive to engagement. By leveraging threaded tweets, daily inspiration, live-tweeting, and polls, religious leaders and organisations can effectively communicate critical teachings and principles while fostering meaningful dialogue with their followers.

Instagram is sharing simplified religious messages and fatwas with visual quote posts, story highlights for religious education, behind-the-scenes content, interactive question-and-answer sessions, and weekly reflection posts:

- A religious influencer creates visually appealing quote posts featuring short excerpts from religious texts or teachings. These posts combine inspiring messages with aesthetically pleasing graphics or imagery, making them engaging and shareable. For instance, they might share a quote about gratitude accompanied by a serene nature scene or a call to prayer overlaid on a minimalist background.
- A religious organisation creates *Instagram Story Highlights* dedicated to religious education. Each Highlight covers a specific topic, such as prayer, fasting, or charity, and includes short videos or graphics providing simplified explanations and practical guidance. Followers can easily access these Highlights for quick reference and continuous learning.
- A religious leader shares behind-the-scenes glimpses of their daily life and activities on Instagram Stories. These candid moments humanise the religious figure and offer followers a more personal connection. For instance, they might share Stories of preparing for a religious event, spending time with family, or engaging in acts of charity, accompanied by captions reflecting on the spiritual significance of these moments.
- A religious scholar hosts interactive question-and-answer sessions on Instagram Live. Followers can submit their questions in real-time, and the scholar responds to them live on camera, offering simplified explanations and insights into various religious topics. These sessions encourage direct engagement and foster a sense of community among followers.
- A religious organisation shares weekly reflection posts on their Instagram feed, providing followers with thought-provoking prompts or questions about spirituality and personal growth. Followers are encouraged to engage with the posts by sharing their reflections in the comments or through direct messages. This interactive approach promotes self-reflection and deeper engagement with religious teachings.

These examples demonstrate how Instagram serves as a versatile platform for sharing simplified religious messages and fatwas through visually engaging content, interactive features, and behind-the-scenes glimpses into the lives of religious figures and organisations. By leveraging Instagram's diverse features and formats, religious leaders and organisations can effectively communicate critical teachings and principles while fostering meaningful connections with their followers.

TikTok is sharing simplified religious messages and fatwas with brief explanatory videos, inspirational quotes and reminders, interactive Q&A sessions, challenges, or Trend Participation, with the following examples:

- A religious scholar creates short TikTok videos explaining common religious concepts or addressing frequently asked questions. For instance, they might provide a simplified explanation of the significance of fasting during Ramadan or offer guidance on performing daily prayers. These videos are concise, engaging, and tailored to TikTok's format, making them accessible to a younger audience.
- A religious influencer shares motivational quotes or reminders related to faith and spirituality through TikTok videos. These short clips may feature uplifting messages from religious texts or personal reflections on gratitude, patience, or perseverance. TikTok videos' simplicity and visual appeal make them practical for quickly inspiring viewers.
- A religious figure hosts live Q&A sessions on TikTok, inviting followers to submit questions about Islamic teachings or religious practices. During these sessions, the host provides concise answers to inquiries ranging from theological debates to practical guidance on religious rituals. Viewers can engage directly by commenting or submitting questions in real-time, fostering interactive dialogue within the TikTok community.
- Religious individuals or groups participate in TikTok challenges or trends by incorporating religious themes or messages into their content. For instance, they might create a video showcasing the acts of kindness inspired by religious teachings or share personal stories of faith and spiritual growth. By aligning with popular TikTok trends, religious content creators can reach a wider audience and spark meaningful conversations about faith.

These examples demonstrate how TikTok is a platform for sharing simplified religious messages and fatwas in a format that resonates with younger audiences. Through creative and engaging content, religious influencers and scholars can effectively convey essential religious teachings and principles, fostering a sense of community and connection among viewers.

In analysing the case study regarding disseminating simplified religious messages and fatwas on social media platforms, it becomes evident that various theoretical frameworks can help elucidate the underlying dynamics at play. The phenomenon aligns closely with theories on the impact of mass media and popular culture on religious discourse, as articulated by authors such as Jean Baudrillard and Walter Benjamin. Baudrillard's concept of the hyperreal, where simulations and representations come to replace reality itself, finds resonance in the oversimplified and commodified representations of religious teachings often encountered on social media. Likewise, Benjamin's notion of the aura being stripped away in the age of mechanical reproduction sheds light on how religious content on these platforms can become detached from its original context and significance, reduced to easily digestible soundbites or images. The utilisation of emotional manipulation and sentimentality in religious messaging, as discussed by scholars like Theodor Adorno and Milan Kundera, is evident in the strategies employed by religious authorities on social media. Adorno's critique of the culture industry and its propensity for manufacturing standardised, emotionally charged content finds relevance in the proliferation of simplified religious messages designed to evoke immediate, uncritical responses from audiences. Kundera's exploration of the "unbearable lightness of being" also resonates, as the superficiality of these messages may contribute to a shallow understanding and engagement with religious principles. Additionally, the role of social media algorithms in shaping the visibility and dissemination of religious content echoes theories on the algorithmic logic of late capitalism put forth by scholars like Fredric Jameson. Jameson argues that these algorithms prioritise content that generates high levels of engagement, perpetuating a cycle of oversimplified content creation aimed at maximising likes, shares, and comments. This can distort religious teachings and reinforce superficial understanding among followers, as content creators prioritise virality over substantive engagement. The case study findings underscore the complex interplay between social media, religious discourse, and cultural production. By drawing on theoretical frameworks from scholars such as Baudrillard, Benjamin, Adorno, Kundera, and Jameson, we can gain deeper insights into the mechanisms through which simplified religious messages proliferate on social media platforms and their broader implications for religious communities and practices.

In an era where social media platforms have become ubiquitous channels for communication and discourse, the intersection of religion and online spaces presents opportunities and challenges. The following examples (Table 3.2) delve into the complexities of how religious fatwas, traditionally vehicles of scholarly guidance and moral instruction, navigate the digital landscape of platforms like Facebook, Twitter, TikTok, and Instagram. I embark on a journey to explore the multifaceted dynamics at play when religious guidance intersects with social media's fast-paced, visually driven world. My research exploration will reveal instances where the integrity and depth of religious discourse may be compromised, influenced by factors ranging from commercialisation to the oversimplification of complex theological concepts. Through the lens of various examples, I will witness the promotion of exclusive religious experiences for profit, where spiritual journeys are marketed as luxury commodities attainable at a premium. Additionally, I will uncover instances where the moral compass provided by fatwas may falter, offering simplistic solutions to intricate ethical dilemmas without fully grappling with the depth of human experience. Furthermore, I will examine

Table 3.2 Analysis of kitsch behaviours in religious fatwas across social media platforms

Kitsch behaviours	*Fatwas identify-specific instances*	*Facebook examples*	*Twitter examples*	*TikTok examples*	*Instagram examples*
Oversimplification of complex ideas	Reduction of intricate theological concepts into clichéd phrases or oversimplified narratives.	A fatwa distils a complex theological concept into a catchy meme with a simplistic slogan, such as "Love thy neighbour," without delving into the deeper theological implications.	A fatwa reduces nuanced religious teaching into a brief, 280-character tweet, lacking the depth required to fully understand the context and significance of the guidance provided.	A fatwa uses short, visually engaging videos to convey religious rulings, but these videos may gloss over the intricacies of the underlying theological principles, focusing instead on surface-level interpretation.	A fatwa is shared as a visually appealing graphic with a brief caption, but this format may sacrifice the depth of understanding by simplifying complex ideas into easily digestible soundbites or quotes.
Use of sentimental imagery or slogans	Employing emotionally charged narratives or imagery to elicit immediate and uncritical responses from the audience.	A fatwa accompanies a heartwarming story or image, invoking emotions of compassion or empathy to garner support for a particular religious interpretation or practice.	A fatwa uses emotionally charged slogans or hashtags to convey religious messages, aiming to evoke immediate reactions from followers without encouraging critical reflection.	A fatwa features emotionally compelling videos with sentimental music or imagery, tapping into the platform's short-form content to convey religious teachings in a way that resonates with users' emotions.	Fatwas are shared alongside aesthetically pleasing visuals, such as serene landscapes or uplifting quotes, designed to evoke feelings of spirituality or reverence in the audience.

(*Continued*)

Table 3.2 (Continued)

Kitsch behaviours	*Fatwas identify-specific instances*	*Facebook examples*	*Twitter examples*	*TikTok examples*	*Instagram examples*
Manipulation of emotions	Presenting simplistic solutions to complex spiritual or moral dilemmas, appealing to followers' emotions rather than engaging in thoughtful theological discourse.	A fatwa presents a straightforward solution to a complex moral issue, accompanied by emotionally charged language or imagery designed to evoke fear or guilt in followers who may question the ruling. Twitter.	Fatwas utilise emotionally manipulative language to sway followers' opinions, framing the religious guidance in a way that appeals to their emotions rather than encouraging critical thinking or theological debate. TikTok.	A fatwa uses dramatic storytelling or visual effects to elicit strong emotional reactions from viewers, steering them towards a predetermined interpretation of religious teachings without considering alternative perspectives.	Fatwas employ sentimental imagery or anecdotes to reinforce a particular religious viewpoint, playing on followers' emotions to discourage dissent and promote conformity to the established doctrine.
Emphasis on superficial aesthetics	Use of flashy graphics, catchy slogans, and simplistic imagery to convey religious messages, prioritising visual appeal over theological depth.	Fatwas utilise eye-catching graphics and bold fonts to convey religious messages, prioritising the visual appeal of the post over the depth of theological content.	A fatwas presented with a flashy image or GIF, accompanied by a short, attention-grabbing slogan, focusing more on the aesthetic impact of the tweet rather than the theological significance of the message.	Fatwas rely on visually stimulating effects and trendy music to capture viewers' attention, sacrificing theological depth for the sake of creating engaging and entertaining content.	Fatwas feature aesthetically pleasing photos or videos with minimal text, emphasising the visual appeal of the post while neglecting to provide substantive theological analysis or context.

(*Continued*)

Table 3.2 (Continued)

Kitsch behaviours	*Fatwas identify-specific instances*	*Facebook examples*	*Twitter examples*	*TikTok examples*	*Instagram examples*
Commodification of spiritual experiences	Promoting and selling religious artefacts or experiences, such as prayer beads, religious clothing, or virtual blessings, turning spirituality into a commodity for profit.	A fatwa promotes the sale of exclusive religious experiences, such as virtual blessings or personalised prayers, offered for a fee, transforming spirituality into a commercial transaction.	A fatwa endorses the purchase of religious merchandise, such as prayer beads or religious clothing, implying that these items hold spiritual significance and can enhance one's connection to faith.	A fatwa features influencers promoting religious pilgrimage packages or guided spiritual experiences, emphasising the luxurious amenities and exclusive access available for purchase.	A fatwa advertises the sale of branded religious products, such as candles, incense, or meditation apps, framing these items as essential tools for spiritual growth and well-being while prioritising profit over genuine religious practice.
Lack of scholarly integrity and depth	Oversimplified and essentialised depictions of non-Western cultures or religious traditions, perpetuating misconceptions and reinforcing power dynamics.	A fatwa oversimplifies complex theological concepts or historical events, presenting them in a manner that lacks scholarly rigour and depth, thereby perpetuating misconceptions about non-Western cultures or religious traditions.	A fatwa propagates essentialised stereotypes or generalisations about certain religious practices or communities, failing to engage in nuanced discussion or provide adequate context, undermining scholarly integrity and depth.	A fatwa glosses over the intricacies of religious doctrines or ethical principles, opting instead for superficial explanations or sensationalised narratives that appeal to viewers' emotions but lack the depth necessary for scholarly discourse.	A fatwas perpetuates power dynamics by presenting a one-sided interpretation of religious texts or teachings without acknowledging diverse perspectives or engaging with critical scholarship, thereby contributing to the erosion of scholarly integrity within religious discourse.

(*Continued*)

Table 3.2 (Continued)

Kitsch behaviours	*Fatwas identify-specific instances*	*Facebook examples*	*Twitter examples*	*TikTok examples*	*Instagram examples*
Promotion of exclusive religious experiences for profit	Offering VIP access to sacred sites or private audiences with religious leaders for a premium price, highlighting the commercialisation of spirituality within religious fatwas.	Fatwas advertise exclusive guided tours to sacred sites led by renowned religious figures, with premium packages offering private audiences or personalised blessings for an additional fee, turning spiritual experiences into luxury commodities. Twitter	Fatwas could endorse paid memberships or subscriptions that grant followers access to exclusive online seminars or virtual meetings with religious leaders, creating a tiered system where access to spiritual guidance is determined by financial status.	Fatwas feature influencers promoting high-end retreats or workshops promising transformative spiritual experiences, with VIP packages offering perks such as front-row seating or exclusive meet-and-greets with religious celebrities, catering to affluent followers seeking privileged access. Instagram	Fatwas showcase luxury travel packages to religious pilgrimage sites, emphasising deluxe accommodations and VIP treatment while downplaying the spiritual significance of the journey in favour of promoting an extravagant lifestyle associated with exclusive access to religious experiences for profit.

(Continued)

Table 3.2 (Continued)

Kitsch behaviours	*Fatwas identify-specific instances*	*Facebook examples*	*Twitter examples*	*TikTok examples*	*Instagram examples*
Failure to address complexity in moral guidance	Critiqued for overlooking the complexities of moral dilemmas and human experience, resulting in shallow ethical and moral guidance.	Fatwas offer simplistic solutions to complex moral dilemmas, such as issuing blanket statements or prohibitions without considering the nuanced circumstances or ethical considerations involved, leading to shallow and inadequate moral guidance.	Fatwas provide brief, one-size-fits-all answers to intricate ethical questions, lacking the depth necessary to thoroughly examine the moral complexities and implications of various scenarios, resulting in superficial moral guidance.	Fatwas present overly simplified moral teachings or commandments in short, entertaining videos, failing to address the intricate nuances of real-life ethical dilemmas and human experiences, which can lead to shallow and inadequate moral guidance.	Fatwas offer concise but superficial moral advice in visually appealing posts, focusing on catchy slogans or inspirational quotes rather than engaging with the complexities of ethical decision-making, resulting in moral guidance that lacks depth and nuance.

Source: Own research form media platforms Facebook, Twitter, Instagram, and TikTok

the allure of superficial aesthetics, which often precedes theological substance, as religious messages are packaged in visually striking yet intellectually shallow formats. My exploration will also unveil the subtle manipulation of emotions, as fatwas leverage emotionally charged narratives to elicit immediate responses, sometimes at the expense of critical reflection.

Lastly, I will confront the commodification of spiritual experiences, witnessing how religious artefacts, services, and experiences are commercialised within the digital realm, blurring the lines between sacred guidance and consumerist ventures. As I embark on this exploration, I invite readers to critically engage with the examples presented, reflecting on the implications of these phenomena within the broader landscape of contemporary religious discourse. Through thoughtful analysis and dialogue, I endeavour to shed light on the complexities and nuances inherent in the intersection of religion and social media, paving the way for a deeper understanding of the challenges and opportunities ahead.

The examples illustrate various ways religious fatwas can deviate from scholarly integrity and depth, often succumbing to commercialisation, oversimplification, and moral superficiality on social media platforms such as Facebook, Twitter, TikTok, and Instagram. Firstly, promoting exclusive religious experiences for profit is highlighted, where fatwas may endorse luxury packages offering VIP access to sacred sites or private audiences with religious leaders, turning spiritual experiences into commodities available for purchase. The failure to address complexity in moral guidance is evident, with fatwas offering simplistic solutions to intricate moral dilemmas without adequately considering the nuances of human experience or ethical considerations. These examples illustrate the emphasis on superficial aesthetics, where fatwas prioritises visual appeal over theological depth by using flashy graphics, catchy slogans, and simplistic imagery to convey religious messages, often neglecting substantive theological content. Moreover, those showcase the manipulation of emotions, where fatwas employ emotionally charged narratives or imagery to elicit immediate and uncritical responses from the audience, bypassing critical reflection and thoughtful engagement. Lastly, the commodification of spiritual experiences is depicted, with fatwas promoting and selling religious artefacts, experiences, or services for profit, thereby turning spirituality into a commercial transaction driven by consumerist impulses. These examples underscore the challenges posed by the intersection of religious discourse and social media, highlighting the need for critical engagement and scholarly integrity in navigating complex religious issues within online platforms.

Discussion

The theoretical framework of the "kitsch experience" theory encompasses several components, including kitsch creators, kitsch recipients, and the world of universal values.

Kitsch creators produce and disseminate simplified, emotionally manipulative, and superficial content, often aiming to evoke immediate emotional responses or appeal to mass audiences. In the context of religious fatwas on social media platforms, kitsch creators may include religious authorities, organisations, influencers, or individuals seeking to promote specific religious interpretations or practices. These creators may employ catchy slogans, sentimental imagery, and oversimplified narratives to convey religious messages, often prioritising visual appeal and emotional impact over theological depth and scholarly rigour.

On the other hand, kitsch recipients are the audience or followers who consume and engage with kitsch content. They may be drawn to kitsch due to its accessibility, emotional resonance, or entertainment value. In the context of religious fatwas, kitsch recipients may include devout followers seeking guidance, individuals exploring spirituality, or casual observers encountering religious content on social media. These recipients may be more susceptible to kitsch due to its ability to simplify complex ideas, evoke emotional responses, and offer quick solutions to moral or spiritual dilemmas.

Each social media platform, including Facebook, Instagram, Twitter, and TikTok, offers unique strengths for sharing simplified religious messages and fatwas. Facebook's diverse features, such as daily posts, live streaming, groups, events, and Q&A sessions, facilitate comprehensive engagement and community building. Instagram's visual nature allows for visually appealing content like quote posts, story highlights, and behind-the-scenes glimpses, enhancing engagement through visual storytelling (Table 3.3). Twitter's real-time communication and character limit enable concise messaging, ideal for threaded tweets, daily inspiration, live-tweeting of events, and polls. TikTok's short video format caters to bite-sized teachings, inspirational messages, and interactive challenges or trends, particularly appealing to younger audiences. Each platform's distinct characteristics provide religious communicators with opportunities to tailor their content effectively and engage with their audience meaningfully, fostering connections and facilitating spiritual growth within their communities.

Across online platforms such as Facebook, Instagram, Twitter, and TikTok, the dissemination of simplified religious messages and fatwas can be contextualised within the framework of the "kitsch experience" theory, as articulated by scholars like Jean Baudrillard, Susan Sontag, Theodor Adorno, and Milan Kundera. The oversimplification observed in these messages, evident in the reduction of complex religious concepts to easily consumable forms, resonates with Baudrillard's exploration of simulacra and the superficiality inherent in kitsch. Additionally, Sontag's observations on the sentimentality and emotional manipulation employed in kitsch align with the strategies used to evoke immediate, uncritical responses from audiences on social media platforms. Adorno's critique of aesthetic theory highlights the potential consequences of

Table 3.3 Effectiveness of social media platforms in facilitating religious communication

Social media	*Strengths*	*Example*
Facebook	Facebook offers a wide range of features, including daily posts, live streaming, groups, events, and Q&A sessions, making it versatile for sharing simplified religious messages and facilitating community engagement.	Daily inspirational posts, live-streamed sermons, Facebook groups for religious discussion, scheduled Q&A sessions with scholars, and events for religious workshops.
Instagram	Instagram's visual nature is well suited for sharing visually appealing content, such as quote posts, story highlights, behind-the-scenes glimpses, and interactive question stickers.	Visual quote posts, story highlights for religious education, behind-the-scenes content, interactive Q&A sessions, and weekly reflection posts.
Twitter	Twitter's real-time nature and character limit allow for concise and immediate communication of religious teachings, making it effective for threaded explanatory tweets, daily inspiration, live-tweeting of events, and Twitter polls.	Threaded explanatory tweets, daily inspirational tweets, live-tweeting of religious events, and Twitter polls on religious topics.
TikTok	TikTok's short video format lends itself well to sharing bite-sized religious teachings, inspirational messages, and participatory challenges or trends, making it engaging for younger audiences.	Brief explanatory videos, inspirational quote videos, interactive challenges, and live Q&A sessions.

Source: Own research form media platforms Facebook, Twitter, Instagram, and TikTok

oversimplification and emotional manipulation in religious messaging. At the same time, Kundera's examination of kitsch's "unbearable lightness" emphasises its superficiality and lack of depth. By referencing these theorists, religious communicators can critically assess the implications of their messaging strategies within the broader context of contemporary digital discourse and the kitsch phenomenon.

The world of universal values represents the broader context within which kitsch operates, encompassing fundamental ethical principles and spiritual beliefs shared across cultures and societies. Kitsch often appeals to superficial and stereotypical clichés about sexuality, politics, patriotism, and religion instead of universal values such as love, compassion, and morality. It does so in a superficial and manipulative manner, exploiting these values for emotional impact rather than genuine engagement with their complexities.

Positive consequences of kitsch in religious fatwas may include increased accessibility and outreach, as simplified messages and emotionally engaging content can attract a wider audience, including those who may not typically engage with religious discourse. Kitsch may also offer comfort, inspiration, or guidance to individuals seeking spiritual fulfilment or reassurance in uncertain times. Additionally, kitsch can foster a sense of community and connection among followers who resonate with its messages, providing a supportive space for shared beliefs and experiences.

However, there are also negative consequences associated with kitsch in religious fatwas. Oversimplification of complex theological concepts may lead to shallow understanding and misinterpretation of religious teachings, perpetuating misconceptions and reinforcing dogmatic beliefs. Emotional manipulation tactics used in kitsch content may exploit vulnerable individuals or promote uncritical acceptance of religious authority, potentially leading to psychological harm or manipulation. Furthermore, the commodification of spirituality within kitsch can undermine the authenticity and integrity of religious practices, reducing sacred rituals to commercial transactions and prioritising profit over genuine spiritual growth.

Conclusions

Analysing kitsch in religious fatwas reveals a spectrum of phenomena that not only simplify but also distort the depth and nuance of religious principles and practices. One instance may involve fatwas dictating strict and superficial guidelines regarding Islamic dress, often without consideration for individual circumstances or cultural contexts. Such rulings, while aiming to promote modesty and adherence to religious tradition, may inadvertently reduce the rich tapestry of Islamic attire to a mere checklist of prescribed garments, neglecting the broader spiritual and cultural significance attached to modes of dress. In another scenario, fatwas may use sentimental appeals or emotional manipulation to reinforce religious obligations rather than foster genuine understanding or personal conviction. This approach risks reducing religious duties to acts of compliance devoid of sincere faith or spiritual engagement. Consequently, individuals may adhere to religious practices not out of genuine belief or conviction but rather out of fear, guilt, or societal pressure, undermining the essence of religious devotion and sincerity. Some fatwas may oversimplify complex social interactions and ethical dilemmas, providing overly prescriptive guidance that fails to address the multifaceted nature of human relationships and moral decision-making. By offering black-and-white solutions to nuanced issues, these rulings overlook the moral agency and critical thinking essential for navigating the complexities of contemporary life by Islamic principles. In summary, while kitsch in religious fatwas may offer certain benefits such as accessibility and emotional resonance, it also poses significant risks, including shallow understanding, emotional manipulation, and commodification of spirituality. By critically examining the role of kitsch creators, kitsch recipients, and universal values in shaping religious discourse, researchers and practitioners can better understand the implications of kitsch and work towards fostering more authentic and intellectually rigorous interpretations within religious communities.

Furthermore, instances of fatwas endorsing the commercialisation of religious practices or rituals raise concerns about the commodification of spirituality. When religious experiences are marketed as consumer goods or services, the focus shifts from inner spiritual growth and devotion to external displays of wealth or status. This phenomenon not only distorts the essence of religious practice but also reinforces materialistic values incompatible with the spiritual teachings of Islam. Lastly, fatwas that discourage critical inquiry or independent thinking within religious communities perpetuate an environment of intellectual stagnation and conformity. By equating questioning or dissent with disobedience or heresy, these rulings inhibit the intellectual curiosity and diversity of thought necessary for a vibrant and dynamic religious discourse. Instead of fostering an atmosphere of open dialogue and scholarly inquiry, such fatwas foster an environment of intellectual rigidity and dogmatism, hindering the evolution and adaptation of religious teachings to contemporary contexts.

In conclusion, examples of kitsch in religious fatwas underscore the importance of critically evaluating the content and presentation of religious rulings to ensure that they uphold the principles of intellectual rigour, ethical integrity, and genuine spiritual guidance. By acknowledging the complexities of religious interpretation and practice, religious authorities can strive to offer rulings that promote holistic understanding, ethical reflection, and sincere devotion among believers. It is crucial to clarify that "kitsch fatwas" is not a standard category within Islamic jurisprudence or scholarship. Instead, "kitsch" refers to art, objects, or cultural products characterised by their superficiality, sentimentality, or lack of artistic merit. However, in the context of the research topic, a "kitsch fatwas" could be understood as a fatwas that exhibits characteristics of a kitsch in its formulation or presentation. Examples studied illustrate this concept:

- The superficial interpretation of a complex issue – fatwas that oversimplifies a complex ethical or legal matter, such as prohibiting certain forms of music without considering their cultural context.
- Emotional manipulation in religious rulings is a fatwa that uses fear-based rhetoric to enforce compliance rather than present reasoned arguments.
- The commodification of spiritual practices – a fatwas that promotes the commercialisation of religious rituals, such as endorsing expensive pilgrimage packages.

- Oversimplified rulings on contemporary issues – a fatwa that offers simplistic solutions to complex modern problems, like blanket bans on digital communication, without considering their nuanced implications.

These examples illustrate how certain fatwas might exhibit characteristics of kitsch, such as oversimplification, sentimentality, or superficiality, in their formulation or presentation.

In conclusion, this study has delved deep into the intricate relationship between religious fatwas and the "kitsch experience" theory, shedding light on the multifaceted implications of simplified religious messaging and superficial interpretations within contemporary digital discourse. Through an exhaustive review of the literature, we have identified and expounded upon a diverse array of kitsch behaviours and issues prevalent in the dissemination of religious fatwas, drawing upon the seminal works of renowned theorists such as Jean Baudrillard, Susan Sontag, Theodor Adorno, and Milan Kundera. These behaviours encompass a spectrum of phenomena, including the simplification of complex religious concepts, the insidious use of emotional manipulation, the cultivation of superficial aesthetics, the rampant commodification of spirituality, and the gradual erosion of scholarly rigour, each posing significant challenges to the integrity and authenticity of religious discourse in contemporary society. Moreover, a discussion has underscored the imperative of complementing theoretical insights with empirical research and case studies, allowing for a more nuanced understanding of how kitsch manifests and operates within real-world contexts. By juxtaposing theoretical frameworks with empirical findings, I have elucidated the practical manifestations of kitsch within religious communication, highlighting the need for critical engagement with digital platforms such as Facebook, Instagram, Twitter, and TikTok. While offering unprecedented opportunities for disseminating religious messages and fostering community engagement, these platforms also present unique challenges in oversimplification, sentimentality, and the commodification of spirituality, all of which can potentially undermine the substantive depth and intellectual rigour of religious teachings. In navigating these challenges, religious leaders and organisations must exercise discernment and foresight, leveraging the affordances of digital platforms while remaining vigilant against the pitfalls of kitsch-infused communication. By embracing a multifaceted approach that balances accessibility with intellectual rigour, they can cultivate authentic connections with their audience, fostering meaningful dialogue and spiritual growth in an increasingly interconnected world. Ultimately, the insights gleaned from this study serve as a clarion call for renewed attention to the ethical imperatives and intellectual responsibilities inherent in religious communication, urging practitioners to uphold the dignity and integrity of religious teachings amidst the complexities of the digital age.

While the analysis presented offers valuable insights into the intersection of religious fatwas and the "kitsch experience" theory, several limitations exist. Firstly, the study focuses on the content and presentation of religious fatwas on social media platforms, potentially overlooking other forms of religious communication or interpretations within offline contexts. Additionally, examining kitsch behaviours in religious fatwas may be constrained by the availability and accessibility of data, particularly regarding the motivations and intentions of kitsch creators. Furthermore, the study may need to fully capture kitsch recipients' diverse perspectives and experiences, as individual interpretations and responses to religious messaging can vary significantly based on cultural background, religious affiliation, and personal beliefs. Further research is needed to address these limitations and deepen our understanding of the implications of kitsch in religious fatwas. Future studies could explore the long-term effects of kitsch-infused religious messaging on individual beliefs, attitudes, and behaviours, utilising qualitative methods such as interviews or focus groups to capture nuanced perspectives and experiences.

Additionally, comparative analyses across different religious traditions and cultural contexts could provide valuable insights into the universality or specificity of kitsch phenomena within religious discourse. Moreover, interdisciplinary approaches integrating insights from psychology, sociology, and communication studies could enrich our understanding of the psychological mechanisms underlying the reception and impact of kitsch in religious communication. By addressing these gaps in knowledge, researchers can contribute to more comprehensive and nuanced discussions on the role of kitsch in shaping religious discourse and community dynamics in social sciences.

References

Adorno, T. W. (1997). *Aesthetic theory*. A&C Black.

Agrama, H. A. (2010). Ethics, tradition, authority: Toward an anthropology of the fatwa. *American Ethnologist*, *37*(1), 2–18.

Ali, M. M. (2011). *Holy Quran*. Ahmadiyya Anjuman Ishaat Islam Lahore USA.

Asad, T. (2003). *Formations of the secular: Christianity, Islam, modernity*. Stanford University Press.

Baudrillard, J. (1998). *Jean Baudrillard. Simulacra and simulations*. Jean Baudrillard selected writings. SMITH.

Benjamin, W. (2018). The work of art in the age of mechanical reproduction. In *A museum studies approach to heritage* (pp. 226–243). Routledge.

Brown, J. A. (2009). *Hadith*. Oxford University Press.

Brown, J. A. (2014). *Misquoting Muhammad: The challenge and choices of interpreting the legacy*. Simon and Schuster.

Brown, J. A. (2017). *Hadith: Legacy in the medieval and modern world*. Simon and Schuster.

Buang, A. H. (2002). Analisis Fatwa-Fatwa Semasa Syariah di Malaysia. *Jurnal Syariah*, *10*(1), 39–52.

Cunningham, D. (2015). Logics of generalisation: Derrida, grammatology and transdisciplinarity. *Theory, Culture & Society*, *32*(5–6), 79–107.

De Botton, A. (2012). *Religion for atheists: A non-believer's guide to the uses of religion*. Vintage.

Derrida, J. (2016). *Of grammatology*. Jhu Press.

El Ghamari, M. (2017). Bezpieczeństwo kulturowe a orientalizm: konieczność współczesności? *Security Review*, *1*(2), 8–21.

Hassan, S. A., & Khairuldin, W. M. K. F. W. (2020). Research design based on fatwa making process: An exploratory study. *International Journal of Higher Education*, *9*(6), 241–246.

Hawkins, P. (1998). *Visual piety: A history and theory of popular religious images*. University of California Press.

Hirschkind, C. (2006). *The ethical soundscape: Cassette sermons and Islamic counterpublics*. Columbia University Press.

Hosen, N. (2008). 9. Online fatwa in Indonesia: From fatwa shopping to googling a Kiai. In Fealy, G. & White, S. (Eds.), *Expressing Islam: Religious life and politics in Indonesia* (pp. 159–173). ISEAS Publishing. https://doi.org/10.1355/9789812308528-013.

Huhn, T., & Zuidervaart, L. (Eds.). (1997). *The semblance of subjectivity: Essays in Adorno's aesthetic theory*. MIT Press.

James, K. A. (2014). *How (not) to be secular: Reading Charles Taylor*. Wm. B. Eerdmans Publishing.

Jameson, F. (2016). Postmodernism, or the cultural logic of late capitalism. In *Postmodernism* (pp. 62–92). Routledge.

Juergensmeyer, M. (2017). *Terror in the mind of God: The global rise of religious violence*. University of California Press.

Kepel, G. (2002). *Jihad: The trail of political Islam*. Harvard University Press.

Kimbrell, G. (2002). Existential investigation: The unbearable lightness of being and history. *Chrestomathy: Annual Review of Undergraduate Research at the College of Charleston*, *1*, 66–82.

Klein, N. (2010). *No logo*. Vintage Canada.

Klein, N. (2014). *No logo: Mærkerne, magten, modstanden*. Klim.

Kundera, M. (2020). *The unbearable lightness of being*. Faber & Faber.

Lane, R. J. (2008). *Jean Baudrillard*. Routledge.

Macfie, A. L. (2014). *Orientalism*. Routledge.

Morgan, D. (1997). *Visual piety: A history and theory of popular religious images*. University of California Press.

Morgan, D. (2005). *The sacred gaze: Religious visual culture in theory and practice*. University of California Press.

Nasr, S. H., Dagli, C. K., Dakake, M. M., Lumbard, J. E., & Rustom, M. (2015). The study Quran. *A New Translation and Commentary*, *19*.

Nawi, A. M., & Hamzah, M. I. (2014). Mobile fatwa (M-Fatwa): The integration of Islamic fatwa through mobile technologymohd. *Turkish Online Journal of Distance Education*, *15*(2), 108–116. https://dergipark.org.tr/en/pub/tojde/issue/16892/175951.

Nussbaum, M. C. (2003). *Upheavals of thought: The intelligence of emotions*. Cambridge University Press.

O'Reilly, J. A. (1992). *The vanishing of Jean Baudrillard* (Doctoral dissertation, University of Warwick).

Peim, N. (2007). Walter Benjamin in the age of digital reproduction: Aura in education: A rereading of 'the work of art in the age of mechanical reproduction'. *Journal of Philosophy of Education*, *41*(3), 363–380.

Said, E. W. (1977). Orientalism. *The Georgia Review*, *31*(1), 162–206.

Said, E. W. (2023). Orientalism. In *Social theory re-wired* (pp. 362–374). Routledge.

Saloot, M. A., Idris, N., Mahmud, R., Ja'afar, S., Thorleuchter, D., & Gani, A. (2016). Hadith data mining and classification: A comparative analysis. *Artificial Intelligence Review*, *46*, 113–128.

Sewlall, H. (2013). Contested epistemological and ethical spaces: The place of non-humans in Milan Kundera's the unbearable lightness of being and JM Coetzee's disgrace. *English Academy Review*, *30*(1), 76–91.
Sontag, S. (2018). *Notes on camp*. Penguin UK.
Stan, C. (2018). Identity in the unbearable lightness of being by Milan Kundera. *Cultural Intertexts*, *8*(8), 148–155.
Szostak, M. (2021). Artistry, management, and creativity: Links and common denominators. *Discourses on Culture*, *16*(1), 23–54.
Szostak, M. and Sułkowski, Ł. (2020). Kitsch in Management: Characteristic forms, carriers and propagators. In *Education Excellence and Innovation Management: A 2025 Vision to Sustain Economic Development During Global Challenges: Proceedings of the 35th International Business Information Management Association Conference (IBIMA)* (pp. 7584–7598). IBIMA. Available at: https://depot.ceon.pl/handle/123456789/19173.
Taylor, C. (2007). *A secular age*. Harvard University Press.
وسام محمود الطيطي, & عبد الله علي الصيفي. (2019). Imam Al shafi'i and his efforts in the science of jurisprudential rules. *IUG Journal of Sharia and Law Studies*, *27*(3).

4 Kitsch in HRM

The role of communication in managing generational diversity in an organisation

Marlena Kondrat

Introduction

The modern workplace is a very diverse and demanding place. Numerous challenges are faced by both managers, who are obliged to improve their managerial skills continuously, and employees, who are required, among other things, to adapt to working with people presenting a different attitude to their professional duties. The diversity of needs and behaviours of employees representing different communication styles affects their working approach, which requires the employer to consider these factors, for example, by creating an appropriate space for cooperation and efficient communication. In order to do this, it is worth considering kitsch in age diversity management, particularly in intergenerational communication, which will translate into a more effective creation of the strategies and solutions necessary for generational dialogue in the organisation. This paper aims to assess the impact of kitsch on intergenerational communication in an organisation, pointing out the different communication styles determined by the trends in which employees of different generations grew up.

The research questions included in this chapter are as follows: 1) What strategies are used to manage generational diversity in an organisation to prevent conflicts between representatives of different age groups? 2) How does kitsch affect communication between representatives of different generations, and can it lead to organisational conflicts? and 3) Can kitsch be a source of innovation and creativity in organisations?

The chapter uses non-reactive research methods based on an analysis of literature and foundational data on managing diversity in organisations. The combination of considerations of kitsch and its role in the efficient communication of representatives of different generations can inspire the exploration of research on effective strategies to manage teams in contemporary workplaces effectively.

DOI: 10.4324/9781003504931-5

Literature review

Generational diversity in the workplace – attitude to work of representatives of selected generations

Generational diversity in the workplace means optimising productivity by employing people of different ages. Ensuring appropriate working conditions for all employees promotes using their potential, which consists, among other things, of acquired education, intrinsic motivation and mental abilities (Gajda, Seroka-Stolka, 2014). This is important in recruiting quality staff, which reduces staff turnover and absenteeism costs. Training and development programmes contribute to improving management styles, developing skills and increasing productivity in various management areas. The age diversity of the workforce and its associated potential benefit the company's adaptation to changing market expectations, as it creates opportunities to create innovative solutions, meeting the needs of equally diverse customers. As a result, the competitiveness and economic efficiency of the company increase, which translates into increased customer satisfaction. In addition, introducing age management and implementing good practices in this area ensure compliance with legislation prohibiting age discrimination. Companies that engage in age management and implement good practices are aware of the importance of the company's image and reputation in the market. However, mixed teams also have many other benefits, such as combining the dynamism and creativity of the younger generation with the balanced impact assessment and pragmatic approach of the boomer generation, leveraging the experience and knowledge of mature employees and the millenials' familiarity with new technologies, developing relationship-building skills along with youthful assertiveness, benefiting from mentoring and peer learning, and creating synergistic added value (Przetacka, 2009).

The attitude towards work of people representing given age groups differs significantly from that of others due to the cultural, social and economic context in which they grew up. As Stanislaw Wojnicki notes, 'a generation in the sociological sense is defined by the whole set of cultural, social and economic factors accompanying the growing up of its members and forming their common experience defining consciousness – including collective consciousness' (Wojnicki, 2015).

Although distinguishing generations by date of birth is not fully legitimate according to sociologists, many researchers use the criterion of age when classifying generations. Depending on the calculations of various researchers, different age matches between specific age groups and generations can be found in the literature. Today, four generations active in the labour market are distinguished:

- Baby boomers (1945–1969);
- Generation X (1970–1979);
- Generation Y (1980–1990) (Sztajerowska, 2019);
- Generation Z (people born after 1990, sometimes referred to as Generation C from the English word *change* or *connected*) (Waśko, 2016).

Table 4.1 External and internal benefits of generational diversity for organisations

External benefits	*Internal benefits*
Creating an image of the organisation as modern and tolerant, following the demands of modern times	Peer support for staff to share differing experiences and knowledge. More conscious and professional meeting of the needs of customers of different ages by employees representing all age groups of generations
Creating a positive image as an employer that takes into account the needs of its employees and is open to diversity.	Older generations can act as an authority for younger workers to acquire the knowledge necessary to perform the job duties.

Source: own compilation based on A. Jagoda (2016, pp. 209–218).

The demographic changes seen in the labour market mean that modern organisations are characterised by the age diversity of their workforce, which is a valuable resource for organisations (Waligóra, 2018).

Companies with age-diverse employees should provide them with a comfortable working environment while showing that age is not a factor in evaluating their work. For this reason, organisations should continually develop their awareness of creating friendly workplaces for people representing different generations (Jagoda, 2016). Building companies that consider generational differences brings numerous internal and external benefits, as Table 4.1 indicates.

Characteristics of Generation X

Generation X is communicative and entrepreneurial. Generation X people value the opportunity to gain unique work experience. Sometimes, they work for more than one company at the same time. They change careers several times during their working lives, unlike representatives of older generations (Baby Boomers), who have worked 30–40 years for one company. Temporary or contract work has allowed them to move between employers (Beutell, Wittig-Berman, 2008).

This generation is distinguished by its loyalty to its employer. Most of its representatives have stable and permanent jobs and like interesting challenges. However, adaptation to change is a problem compared to younger generations. 'The characteristic feature of Generation X concerning attitude at work is independence and resourcefulness' (Krawczyńska-Zaucha, 2020). The difficult times they had to start their careers and the associated job insecurity created a sense of constant fear and anxiety in the generation concerned about the possibility of losing their jobs. These individuals do not accept multitasking; they are patient, do not start many tasks simultaneously and follow instructions sequentially. They want their work to be socially relevant and have a deeper meaning, and they expect continuous feedback on their performance at work (Para, 2015).

Due to the family situation of Generation X, the primary motivator for them to work is money, including systematic pay rises. A salary increase is not necessarily linked to a simultaneous promotion, which is a less important value for them. From their employer, they mainly expect respect and a good atmosphere in the workplace. They are the oldest working generation; therefore, family is more important in their value system than work. They are much less likely to be professionally mobile than younger generations (Krawczyńska-Zaucha, 2020).

Characteristics of Generation Y

Generation Y includes people born after 1980. 'Generation Y has been shaped by events and phenomena such as political transformation, globalisation and integration, computerisation, and the development of new technologies'. For this reason, representatives of the generation follow new technologies and support innovation, which is also linked to their tendency to multitask – they are not in the habit of pursuing only one goal at a time. Their quick adaptation to new working conditions is also important (Para, 2015).

Generation Y is highly ambitious, focused on goals and achievements and confident in themselves and their abilities. 'Technology is not a tool to just get more work done or to balance private and professional life – it is an integral part of the members of this group, and working with technology has become second nature to them' (Espinoza, Ukleja, 2018). This generation cannot imagine working without being able to use new technologies (e-mail, social media and mobile phones), allowing them to get work done efficiently. If their current job does not meet their expectations (which may be manifested, for example, by a lack of promotion in the long term), they quickly decide to leave it. Unlike Generation X, they are not strongly tied to a particular workplace. Writing about Generation Y, Ulrich Beck draws attention to the negative consequences of high job mobility, which are associated with deteriorating family relationships. What matters to Generation Y is their job satisfaction, as they are aware of their abilities and competencies. They care about their professional development, which is manifested by continuing their education in postgraduate studies and courses and using the support of career counsellors. For this reason, it may be essential for them to have a mentor assisting them in developing their talents (Beck, 2004).

Generation Y values teamwork and expects quick and frequent feedback on their work (Para, 2015, p. 98). They are also the first generation to place a high value on language learning, which enables them to improve their skills abroad. This, in turn, helps them to find a rewarding job and ensures that they can choose from a range of offers (Kisiolek, 2019).

Characteristics of Generation Z

There is no consensus in the literature on the timeframe of Generation Z. There is also no consensus on its occurrence as a separate generation. According to some sources, Generation Y and Generation Z appear as one Millennial generation. Other terms for Generation Z include Gen Tech, Post Gen, e iGeneration, Gen Wii, Net Gen, Digital Natives and Gen Next (Żarczyńska-Dobiesz, Chomątowska, 2014). Many of this generation do not know or remember a world without a computer, telephone or internet. There is no clear boundary between the virtual and real worlds for their representatives, and the two universes complement each other. Communicating with others at any time, 'being online' 24 hours a day, seven days a week, or having trouble establishing social interactions in the real world sets this generation apart from previous ones. The marked technological leap that occurred while they were growing up has made the intergenerational gap much more visible than for other generations (Żarczyńska-Dobiesz, Chomątowska, 2014). Generation Z is the youngest in the labour market, including people born after 1990. This generation values, above all, the opportunity to develop their interests and passions in the workplace. For them, the greatest value is personal development and a job fitting their personality, not the salary. Because of their needs, representatives of this generation have no problem showing high expectations of their employers despite their lack of work experience (Gajda, 2017). Generation Z are good listeners, creative, accustomed to providing input, and constantly learning-oriented but have poor writing skills (due to growing up in an era of shorthand via social media: emoticons, abbreviations and lack of punctuation marks are advantageous on social media but can raise issues at work). They know the importance of in-person communication and their shortcomings in this area (Racolta-Paina, Irini, 2021).

Efficient management of a generationally diversified workforce

In the literature, the issues of age management and managing generational diversity are emphasised. *Age management* consists of activities that make it possible to use human resources in organisations more effectively and rationally. It refers primarily to the conditions and potential of employees of different ages (Litwinski, Sztanderska, 2010). A good age management strategy considers the fact that demographic changes associated with an ageing society (also known as the silver tsunami trend) are inevitable and affect all companies. Although the literature on age management often focuses on ways to retain older employees (who have valuable work experience), it is worth paying attention to the potential of employees representing different age groups. It is therefore essential to get an idea of the intergenerational relationships within a company to make proper use of their potential (Pawlak, 2016). The benefits of age management stem from the following:

- retaining older employees with experience from many years in the organisation. This experience is unquestionable and unrivalled, often unknown to competitors, and it takes a huge amount of time and cost to attract people with such knowledge and familiarity with the company's operations;

- reduced labour costs, with low absenteeism among older workers resulting from developed preventive health care and the use of flexible working arrangements;
- reduced training expenses – older employees can share their knowledge and experience with younger colleagues;
- increase in the number of customers – the ageing population is causing a change in the consumer market by increasing the number of customers among older people. Mature employees are more familiar with the needs of customers of a similar age, which promotes better communication between them (Adamska-Chudzińska, 2016).

Issues of managing generational diversity are a crucial stage in the training of future and current managers. They require training and knowledge in new approaches to employees. Appropriate management of generational diversity positively impacts potential candidates or business partners and the local community. An implemented diversity policy effectively improves employee communication, positively impacts the workforce's openness and builds an atmosphere conducive to knowledge sharing. A good collaborative climate depends on a willingness to understand the expectations and needs of the employee team (Robak, 2021).

Traditional management methods in organisations (e.g. the Michigan model representing a hardline approach to HR management and viewing employees as a means to achieve company goals, which is used like other organisational resources) are no longer sufficient in the current labour market. Companies are becoming more open to a diverse workforce due to the possibility of better reaching out to generationally different consumers. In such a situation, the whole organisation's functioning system is changing and taking shape, as each generation requires different motivation and gratification from management. The prerequisites for the successful performance of managers are the creation of a friendly atmosphere in the workplace and opportunities for them to develop their leadership skills. This behaviour leads to decreased motivation and willingness to educate employees for the company's benefit further. The manager should also know how to motivate employees of different age groups (Hysa, 2016).

The transfer of knowledge and experience from older to younger employees plays an important role in intergenerational relations. To this end, a culture of trust should be created in the organisation, one manifestation of which is helping experienced employees to solve the problems of those who are less experienced and who make more mistakes and are therefore less apprehensive about talking about them. One way to do this is to offer human resource management courses to employees, where they can learn the principles of communication that do not violate the other person's dignity, resolve disagreements constructively and focus on subordinates' strengths. These courses can help them understand the benefits of listening to subordinates' communicated needs, refraining from rash opinions without first knowing the problem, or building subordinates' commitment by learning about the factors that motivate them to work. Creating a culture of trust in the organisation fosters the building of a value base by management that will motivate ethical action among all employees regardless of age. It will also facilitate shared team goals, which should be consistent and clear to all employees in the company (Wojnicki, 2015).

Another important aspect is to formulate the company's strategy properly and to make sure that it is known to all employees, thus fostering the achievement of the set goals. A vital element of the organisation's culture is the belief that a lack of specific knowledge or experience does not indicate weakness on the part of the employee, who can always make up for deficiencies in this area with the help offered by older, more experienced colleagues. The practice of asking for and providing help from more experienced people is a pillar of an effective knowledge management policy in an organisation. A key challenge is knowledge transfer. However, it cannot occur without mutual trust and a sense that asking for advice or help is normal, not derogatory, and that providing help is the responsibility of everyone in the organisation.

Based on S. Wojnicki's analysis, it is, therefore, possible to list the processes for the effective management of a diversified workforce: 1) creating trust and identification with the company; 2) creating a company strategy based on a common goal; 3) building values that are consistent across the workforce; 4) the practice of asking for and giving help; and 5) building a good practice based on senior knowledge (Wojnicki, 2015).

Strategies for managing age diversity in organisations

Managing age diversity is a key strategy that assumes that a company's growth and business goals will be more effective if it takes advantage of the different needs and experiences within and around the organisation. There is widespread acceptance in Western literature that properly managed workforce diversity can be a source of tangible benefits for modern organisations (Waligóra, 2018).

In managing generational diversity, proactive practices that develop the organisation are necessary. Some of the opportunities for effective multigenerational integration in an organisation are 1) creating awareness of the value generation, 2) promoting openness and respect by implementing an appropriate organisational culture, 3) introducing an organisational culture based on trust, 4) breaking stereotypes in the perception of representatives of different generations, and 5) mentoring and development programmes.

Creating awareness of the value generation that occurs due to effective diversity management: Employees must be aware of the benefits of age diversity and understand how different generations can complement each other. The organisation can organise training or workshops to help increase knowledge and understanding of generational differences (Sidor-Rządkowska, 2018).

Promoting openness and respect by implementing an appropriate organisational culture: The organisation should create a culture where all employees, regardless of age, feel respected and valued. Openness to diverse perspectives and experiences should be promoted, and age stereotypes should be avoided (Walczak, 2011).

Introducing an organisational culture based on trust: Many problems of managing generational diversity in an organisation can relate to a lack of trust between representatives of different generations. According to Patrick Lencioni, when co-workers are afraid to talk honestly with each other and do not clearly express their problems, it leads to unhealthy rivalry and conflict. Building trust between generations at work is key to understanding and respecting differences due to the different circumstances in which representatives of each generation grew up (Lencioni, 2002).

Breaking stereotypes and the perception of representatives of different generations: In the social space, measuring oneself against stereotypes of various kinds has become an everyday occurrence. Regarding generational changes, finding common ground proves to be a major challenge. Each incoming generation brings with it a certain freshness of outlook and many unknowns. Hence stereotyping becomes a tool for defending more experienced employees. According to Chip Espinoza, template thinking is an obstacle that should be faced not only by supervisors and managers but also – and perhaps especially – by the youngest participants in the labour market. Breaking stereotypes can be made easier by finding similarities between generations. It is important to integrate co-workers with shared passions, experiences, similar character traits and soft skills to join project teams, charity work or social events, leading to intergenerational bonds.

Mentoring and development programmes: Mentoring is now recognised as the most effective proactive method for managing generational diversity in an organisation. Older employees can act as mentors to younger team members, sharing their knowledge and experience. The organisation can also introduce development and training programmes to help younger employees develop skills and gain experience. The definition adopted by the European Mentoring Centre states that 'mentoring is the voluntary assistance, independent of the service hierarchy, given by one person to another so that he or she can make significant progress in knowledge, professional work or thinking' (Clutterbuck, 2002). Mentoring is based on a master–student relationship (Oleksyn, 2010). The mentor in the indicated relationship has a specific, greater body of knowledge, while the student is a person who is open to developing his or her skills within the mentor's knowledge (Moczydłowska, 2014).

Mentors command general respect and appreciation, have authority and a large body of knowledge and experience, and can be role models for younger employees. Older employees can also learn much from younger people (e.g. technological development). Such relationships develop the company very well by increasing efficiency and productivity. Mentoring can be divided into three separate categories that are most relevant when working with a generationally diversified workforce, viz.:

- *Classical mentoring* (so-called traditional mentoring) – the introduction of younger people with no work experience into an organisation. It is provided by senior employees and usually by age. The mentor supports the apprentice in breaking down barriers, providing advice and contacts in the industry,
- *Reverse mentoring* – this is the swapping of master and apprentice roles. In this situation, a younger employee becomes a mentor for an older one in order to teach him or her how to use new technologies or how to use the internet, among other things.
- *Intermentoring* (so-called reciprocal mentoring) – this type of mentoring is distinguished by a relationship that is two-way, with different generations learning from each other. In a given mentoring, there is an exchange of knowledge and experience between employees (Baran, 2015).
- *Flexible working arrangements* – adjusting working hours, the possibility to work remotely and flexibility in working time scheduling can help to accommodate the needs of different age groups. The organisation can also introduce work-life balance programmes to help employees of different ages balance work and personal responsibilities (Baran, 2015).
- Kitsch in communication between employees can lead to numerous misunderstandings and, at the same time, generate conflicts, one of the important factors hindering age diversity management, as will be discussed in the next subsection of the chapter.

Discussion

The impact of kitsch on age diversity management and communication between representatives of different generations in the workplace

The contemporary business environment is no stranger to kitsch, defined as an excessive, artificial or inauthentic style, which is gradually permeating various aspects of organisations and social constructs. This subsection will present an analysis of this phenomenon in the context of management, looking at its impact on organisational culture, decision-making processes, interpersonal relationships and, in particular, intergenerational communication, which has a not inconsiderable impact on the management of age diversity in organisations.

In the context of management, kitsch manifests itself in various areas of an organisation's activities, encompassing how it communicates internally, its strategic decision-making process and its external image-building (Szostak & Sułkowski, 2020). One clear example of this phenomenon is the overuse of marketing platitudes and slogans, which have lost their original value and meaning but are still used to evoke certain associations in the audience. Although it can be seen as an attempt to create a positive impression, this action often leads to the perception that the organisation is insincere or lacks authenticity (Jaska, 2016), highlighting that such a practice can negatively affect customer and employee trust, making it difficult to build lasting relationships and achieve long-term success. Therefore, organisations must consciously choose their communication and marketing strategies, avoiding the overuse of kitsch, which can damage their reputation and credibility.

The roots of kitsch in management can be traced to time pressures and competition, which cause managers to be forced to make quick decisions, often based on shallow analyses or thought patterns. As a result, management rules and strategies can become trite, lacking authenticity and effectiveness.

Contemporary organisations often reveal a tendency to adopt the characteristics of kitsch, especially in their corporate culture. This phenomenon is closely linked to the dynamic pace of life and business conduct, which presents managers with increasing challenges. These require quick decisions, searching for simple and universal rules, and a natural response. However, these rules often become a source of kitsch instead of being based on reality. Particularly in the business world, where public figures are sometimes required to speak on topics they do not fully understand, the appearance of nonsense becomes inevitable. Such a situation can be exploited by business people, politicians, PR specialists and consultants, who fear showing their incompetence by not speaking up and are willing to talk nonsense. The concepts they introduce can often be described as 'bullshit management', as they are not necessarily based on real knowledge or experience but are primarily aimed at financial gain and satisfying managers' egos (Szostak, 2021).

The development of the theory of the phenomenon of kitsch in aesthetics can be translated into management theory. The second half of the 20th century transposed the phenomenon of kitsch from the field of art to other areas of social life. Kitsch in management can be considered in two ways: literal and metaphorical. The metaphorical understanding of kitsch is 'just plain management', that is, uncreative and flattering to low motives, devoid of mission – meaningless, linked to the high cynicism of managers in the organisation. This understanding of kitsch in management can also specifically relate to collaboration and communication problems between generations in the workplace.

As Michal Szostak points out, managers have less and less time for adequate analysis; hence, searching for universal and simple rules becomes a natural solution. Managers and subordinates follow templates and established patterns of behaviour, paying little attention to assumptions and beliefs that are important to employees. On the other hand, we have 'management shamans' who, rejecting the theoretical achievements of the discipline, use simple and colloquial linguistic categories, which allows them to attract crowds of followers; they have found their place and fame through simple diagnoses for all organisational problems (Szostak & Sułkowski, 2020).

When discussing intergenerational relations in organisations, it is worth referring to organisational cynicism as a new paradigm of employer-employee relations. A significant percentage of employees are very cynical about their organisations, as well as their colleagues. Organisational cynicism occurs when employees lack trust in their organisation and feel it cannot be trusted (Durrah, Chaudhary, Gharib, 2019). Definitions of organisational cynicism involve emotions such as disillusionment and anger, which can also relate to disillusionment in intergenerational communication when employees feel irritated by not understanding the needs and conditions that have shaped the behaviour of other generations. Unfortunately, a significant percentage of employees are highly cynical about their organisations and their colleagues. When a manager does not set goals or plans for the future, and the organisation operates at its own pace and direction, we speak of sham management. The quixotic manager artificially maintains his position. Suppose one adds to this sham management related to the narcissistic personality of a manager by creating illusions. In that case, this can prove to be a hazardous phenomenon for the organisation, as it lacks focus on the real problems of the employees, overlooking their needs regarding intergenerational communication.

As Michal Szostak points out, stupidity is often associated with low intelligence, but there is no clear link between IQ level and a person's actual thinking and acting in a social context. Intelligent people can do stupid things. Functional stupidity is associated with narrow thinking, in which established frameworks are accepted uncritically. Managers and subordinates follow templates without paying attention to assumptions and beliefs. In the context of kitsch, the main aspects of functional stupidity are a lack of reflexivity, an unwillingness to look for reasons and a lack of substantive justification (Szostak, 2021). The notion of 'functional stupidity' may be reflected in the perpetuation of negative stereotypes about the approach of representatives of different generations to work, attributing specific negative characteristics to given age groups, which creates a false image of them in the eyes of representatives of other generations and leads to mutual prejudice.

In light of the above, an important question arises: Is there a way to avoid kitsch in management, including the management of generational diversity? Are there strategies that allow organisations to avoid falling into the kitsch trap? Or is kitsch an inevitable part of organisational life that is difficult to eliminate?

One area where kitsch in management can negatively impact is interpersonal relationships within an organisation. The excessive use of superficial motivational techniques or artificial forms of recognition can lead to increased cynicism and social disintegration within a team.

In today's world, where people are increasingly overwhelmed by intense, competitive work and interpersonal relationships are disappearing, authentic social contact is becoming valuable. Against the backdrop of the prevalence of kitsch and the omnipresence of stupefying media, genuine culture becomes a distinct and valuable value. In a society where there is an increase in cases of depression every five years, happiness becomes a scarce good, while where emptiness and a lack of understanding of the surrounding reality prevail, wisdom and spirituality become more critical. In the modern economy, 'well-being', in the broadest sense, is becoming the greatest value, and the primary goal of management is to seek its growth – for employees, customers and communities alike. Such a management model does not necessarily lead to an outdated 'welfare state' model, as well-being is not the same as welfare. In properly understood welfare, the fundamental values are knowledge, wisdom, creativity and self-fulfilment at work, not just the accumulation of material goods.

Kitsch manifests in values and preferences, which may differ between generations. For example, younger employees are more likely to prefer modern and original solutions, while older employees may be more conservative and prefer traditional approaches. This can lead to value conflicts and communication difficulties. Among other things, employers should consider the values a company should consider in order to integrate employees, considering that each generation has different values. Because of this, conflicts can arise between co-workers due to a lack of understanding of the needs in this area. These values have been analysed and found to be strongly linked to, among other things, job satisfaction (Parks, Guay, 2009). The value theory proposed by S. H. Schwartz highlights some important aspects: 1) values can be prioritised; 2) values are strongly linked to beliefs; 3) values are used to set standards; 4) values influence goal achievement; 5) values go beyond the specific situation; and 6) values are the foundation of all employees' actions (Schwartz, 1992).

Schwartz highlights the link between values and the achievement of career goals, building job satisfaction or motivation. They are a key factor in workplace satisfaction. By addressing these values, it is possible to create a very loyal and productive team, but it is crucial to reach out to different generations of employees so that everyone understands that the factors that satisfy co-workers can differ significantly (Krawczynska-Zaucha, 2020). The appearance of kitsch in the values and preferences of different generations can lead to frustration and misunderstanding among employees. If kitsch is present in the workplace and one age group accepts it while the other group does not, this can lead to conflict and a lack of willingness to cooperate. Employees may struggle to understand why others have different preferences and why kitsch is accepted or rejected.

The use of emoticons in chat conversations – a popular example is 'xD' – originally a set of letters that connotes a wide-smiling face, in 2017, it was chosen as the Youth Word of the Year. It is intended to emphasise expression, to depict laughter – sometimes more 'hysterical' than out of joy. For employees of the older generation, it can be associated with kitsch, as it has a broad meaning and can replace many other words – it is in circulation virtually constantly, helping young people to express various emotions that are difficult to express, which representatives of the older generation may consider infantile. Observing people from Generation Z, we can see that such an emotional climate – agitation, exaggerated surprise and amusement – is most characteristic of them. Living in a period of constant change – dynamic adolescence, relationships that are in constant transformation – may require slogans that easily help name emotions. This is why 'xD, LOL, OMG' are in constant rotation until they are replaced by other – more common – terms for the same thing. In addition to the indicated examples that are manifestations of kitsch in the eyes of representatives of older generations, other examples can be pointed out:

1. Emoticons and emoji – the younger generation often uses a wide range of emoticons and emoji to express their emotions in text communication. These small images add emotion and expressiveness to text messages.
2. Abbreviations and acronyms – young people often use abbreviations and acronyms to shorten long words or sentences. For example, 'lol' means 'I'm laughing out loud', 'brb' means 'I'll be right back' and 'omg' means 'Oh my God'. These abbreviations describe something sudden, often arousing mixed feelings, astonishing, unexpected.
3. Emotional expressions – young people often use intense emotional expressions such as 'mega', 'super', and 'amazing' to emphasise their feelings. They may also use trending slang expressions that are popular at the time, which is, according to the theory presented earlier, a hallmark of kitsch.
4. Internet memes and slang – the younger generation often uses internet memes and slang in their communication. Memes are images or videos circulated online and often used for humour. Internet slang refers to specific expressions, abbreviations or phrases popular among young people.
5. Multimedia content – young people often use different platforms and tools to communicate through multimedia content. This can be photos, videos, memes, or GIFs that add a visual aspect to communication (Sidor-Rządkowska, 2018).

In turn, the baby boomer generation and people from Generation X often find it difficult to fully understand and accept the new forms of communication that have naturally become part of the everyday life of the younger generations. For many, the digital world and the language of communication within it can seem alien and inaccessible. While efforts to understand and adapt are commendable, specific cultural, technological and linguistic barriers mean that older generations will no longer enter the same virtual communication world as younger generations.

The manifestations of kitsch in the communication of the older generation may differ from those of the younger generation. Here are some examples:

1. Formal language – the older generation may prefer more formal language in communication, using complete sentences and avoiding abbreviations or slang expressions. They may also focus on grammatical correctness and avoid using emotive expressions.

2. Longer forms of communication – representatives of older generations may prefer longer forms of communication, such as letters or long emails, in which they express their thoughts and feelings in more detail. They may avoid short text messages or real-time communication. This approach does not fit contemporary trends and may be kitsch for younger generations.
3. Use of formal forms of politeness – the older generation may place more importance on formal forms of politeness, such as 'Mr/Mrs', 'Please go ahead', and 'Thank you very much'. They may be more inclined to maintain certain rules of etiquette in communication.
4. Lack of use of emoticons and emojis: The older generation may use emoticons and emojis less frequently in communication. They may prefer to express emotions through words or tone of voice rather than using icons or images.
5. Less inclination to use internet memes and slang, often resulting from a lack of understanding of the modern form of communication – the older generation may be less familiar with internet memes and slang that are popular with young people. They may prefer more traditional forms of communication and avoid using expressions with which they are unfamiliar (Litwinski, Sztanderska, 2010).

However, it is worth bearing in mind that these are only general observations and do not apply to everyone belonging to the older or younger generations. Communication style may vary depending on individual preferences and experiences. Rather than striving for total integration, employees representing different age groups must understand and accept that differences in communication styles are a natural part of social and technological evolution. Rather than trying to impose their standards, managers managing age-diverse teams should focus on building bridges of understanding, respecting and appreciating the uniqueness of each generation, and trying to familiarise different age groups with the perspective they present in terms of expressing their thoughts in a way that is typical of their age. It is, therefore, worth building a culture of openness, respect and tolerance that enables dialogue and mutual understanding in everyday work.

Kitsch as a source of innovation and creativity in organisations

Kitsch can be a source of innovation and creativity in an organisation (Szostak & Sułkowski, 2020). Here are some reasons why kitsch can have a positive impact on creativity:

1. Bridge-building opportunities – on the other hand, kitsch can also be a common point that can help build bridges and create bonds between different age groups. If all employees have a sense of humour and are open to different styles, kitsch can serve as a topic of conversation and a way to build relationships.

2. Breaking conventions – kitsch often breaks conventions and norms, which provokes people to think outside the box. This can open the way to new and unusual ideas. If employees are encouraged to experiment and think differently, kitsch can become a source of unconventional solutions and creative ideas.
3. Inspiration and stimulation of the imagination – kitsch can be inspiring and stimulate the imagination. Bright colours, extravagant patterns and unusual combinations represented by representatives of younger generations can stimulate the senses and evoke new thoughts and ideas. This can contribute to discovering new perspectives and generating innovation in the organisation.
4. Creating an atmosphere of openness and spontaneity – kitsch is often associated with a sense of humour, carefreeness and spontaneity. In an environment of openness and acceptance, employees can feel free to express their creativity and experiment with unusual ideas. This can lead to the development of innovative solutions and projects.
5. Building relationships and cooperation – kitsch can also be a tool for building relationships and cooperation within an organisation. If all employees engage in kitsch and have a sense of humour, it can promote unity and cooperation. Creating and sharing kitsch ideas can create a collaborative and inclusive atmosphere (Wojnicki, 2015).

However, it is worth remembering that not all employees react similarly to kitsch. Some may accept and appreciate it, while others may reject it. It is essential to create a space where each employee can express their preferences and ideas.

Conclusion

Based on the considerations in this study, it is possible to answer the research questions posed in the thesis, cited at the beginning of the chapter. The chapter discussed the strategies used in age diversity management, considering those most popular today. These included creating awareness of the value generation that occurs as a result of effective diversity management (Sidor-Rządkowska, 2018), promoting openness and respect by implementing an appropriate organisational culture (Walczak, 2011), introducing an organisational culture based on trust (Lencioni, 2002), breaking stereotypes in the perception of representatives of different generations. One of the critical elements of a strategy to enable effective diversity management in an organisation is both the mentoring and the implementation of various types of development programmes, as highlighted by many researchers (Oleksyn, 2010; Clutterbuck, 2002; Moczydłowska, 2014; Baran, 2015).

This chapter also answers a further research question by addressing the issue related to the impact of kitsch on intergenerational communication and the potential conflicts that kitsch can lead to. One area where kitsch in management can have a particularly negative impact is in interpersonal relationships within an organisation. The excessive use of superficial motivational techniques or artificial forms of recognition can lead to increased cynicism and social disintegration within a team. In today's world, where people are increasingly overwhelmed by intense, competitive work and interpersonal relationships are disappearing, authentic social contact is becoming valuable. Against the backdrop of the prevalence of kitsch and the omnipresence of stupefying media, genuine culture becomes a distinct and valuable value. Kitsch manifests in values and preferences, which may differ between generations. This can lead to value conflicts and communication difficulties. Among other things, employers should consider the values a company should consider in order to integrate employees, considering that each generation has different values (Parks, Guay, 2009). It is, therefore, important to know the values of the generations in order to understand their needs and motivations better and, thus, better manage diverse teams (Schwartz, 1992). The appearance of kitsch in the values and preferences of different generations can lead to frustration and misunderstanding among employees. If kitsch is present in the workplace and one age group accepts it while the other group does not, this can lead to conflict and a lack of willingness to cooperate. Employees may struggle to understand why others have different preferences and why kitsch is accepted or rejected.

The chapter attempts to answer the third research question by referring to the literature on the experience of kitsch, which can be a source of innovation and creativity in an organisation (Szostak & Sułkowski, 2020) – it discusses the reasons why kitsch can have a positive impact on an organisation. Among others, the following were pointed out: bridge-building opportunities, breaking conventions, inspiration and stimulation of the imagination, creating an atmosphere of openness and spontaneity, and building relationships and cooperation. Creating and sharing kitsch ideas can also create a collaborative and inclusive atmosphere.

It should be added that the conclusions of this chapter are marked by certain limitations on the role of kitsch in managing generational diversity. The research method in the chapter consists only of literature studies, but it can inspire the exploration of research in this field, pointing out the presence of kitsch in intergenerational communication. This factor can lead to numerous conflicts in the organisation, causing difficulties in managing representatives of different generations.

Recognising the kitsch in intergenerational communication can help managers alleviate conflict and frustration, contributing to more effective cooperation among their subordinates. An exploration of research in this area should address effective ways to facilitate the spotting of kitsch and recommendations on how to mitigate its negative impact on intergenerational communication. The literature analysis carried out in this paper points to kitsch as a potential driver of conflict and misunderstanding, but an in-depth look at the problem should be carried out in organisations with age-diverse teams to look at the problem from a practical perspective.

Diversity policies in organisations, including age diversity, which supports creating a working environment that promotes respect and inclusion of employees, are crucial to business success. Introducing age diversity in the team fosters improved communication throughout the company, which increases the ability to promote shared values within the organisation and improves the company's image and reputation in the marketplace.

In order to deal effectively with kitsch in managing generational diversity, organisations need to take many steps. Firstly, authenticity and transparency must be promoted in internal and external communications. Secondly, a critical approach is needed to adopt standard solutions and ready-made thought patterns. Thirdly, an organisational culture based on values that employees and managers authentically share needs to be built.

It is also worth noting that reducing generational diversity management kitsch requires the involvement of all organisation members, from employees at the lowest levels of the hierarchy to the highest authorities. Organisations can effectively counteract its negative effects through concerted action and awareness of this phenomenon. In order to better understand the phenomenon of kitsch in the context of managing generational diversity, further research is needed on the impact of kitsch on communication between different generations and coping strategies. Bringing various theoretical and methodological perspectives to the discussion can contribute to a better understanding of the role of kitsch in age diversity management (including its positive impact) and the development of practical tools and strategies to help organisations avoid the pitfalls associated with this phenomenon.

References

Adamska-Chudzińska M. (2016), *Age management and the use of human capital in the enterprise*, in: "Social Inequality and Economic Growth", no. 46 (2/2016), pp. 334–344, https://doi.org/10.15584/nsawg.2016.2.19.

Baran M. (2015), *Mentoring as an element of diversity management in companies*, in: "Management Forum", no. 3/2/2015, pp. 3–8, Publishing House of Wrocław University of Economics: https://dbc.wroc.pl/Content/30412/PDF/Baran_Mentoring_Jako_Element_Zarzadzania_Roznorodnoscia_2015.pdf (accessed 28.03.2024).

Beck U. (2004), *Risk Societies on the Way to Another Modernity*, SAGE Publications, Warsaw.

Beutell N. J., Wittig-Berman U. (2008), *Work-family conflict and workfamily synergy for generation X, baby boomers, and matures: Generational differences, predictors, and satisfaction outcomes*, in: "Journal of Managerial Psychology", 23. Cf. *Praktyczny słownik współczesnej polszczyzny*, pod red. H. Zgółkowa, vol. 16, Poznań 1998.

Clutterbuck D. (2002), *Everyone Needs a Mentor. How to Manage Talent*, Petit Publishing, Warsaw.

Durrah O., Chaudhary M. and Gharib M. (2019), *Organizational cynicism and its impact on organizational pride in industrial organizations*, in: "International Journal of Environmental Research and Public Health", 16 (1203), pp. 1–16.

Espinoza C., Ukleja M. (2018), *Managing the Millenials*, Wydawnictwo Naukowe PWN SA, Warsaw.

Gajda J. (2017), *Expectations of representatives of generation Z towards professional work and employer*, in: "Prace Naukowe Uniwersytetu Ekonomicznego we Wrocławiu", 491 (2017), Contemporary Economics and Sustainable Development, pp. 158–171, https://doi.org/10.15611/pn.2017.491.15.

Gajda J., Seroka-Stolka O. (2014), *Managing employees of different generations as a condition for effective organisational performance*, in: "Human Resource Management", 5 (2014), pp. 11–28.

Hysa B. (2016), *Managing generational diversity*, in: "Zeszyty Naukowe Politechniki Śląskiej, Organizacja i Zarządzanie", 97, (col. 1964).

Jagoda A. (2016), Zarządzanie różnorodnością pokoleniową a organizacja czasu i miejsca pracy pracowników. *Marketing i Rynek*, 3(2016), pp. 209–218.

Jaska E. (2016), *The Importance of Internal Communication in Corporate Change Management*, https://sj.wne.sggw.pl/pdf/TIRR_2016_n5_s29.pdf (accessed 28.02.2024)

Kisiołek A. (2019), *Career work and motivation from an XYZ generational perspective*, in: "Man, Economy, Society: A Jubilee Book Dedicated to Professor Jerzy Babiak", T. Wallas, K. Urbaniak, K. Hajder (eds.), pp. 239–251, Adam Mickiewicz University Publishing House of the Faculty of Political Science and Journalism, Poznań.

Krawczyńska-Zaucha T. (2020), *Ethics and values of the baby boomers, X, Y generations - how to manage motivation in diversity?* w: "Global Contexts of Respect for Human Rights and Freedoms: Contemporary Problems and Dilemmas", A. Kuzior (ed.), pp. 117–127, Wydawnictwo Politechniki Śląskiej, Gliwice.

Lencioni P. (2002), *The Five Dysfunctions of a Team: A Leadership Fable*, 20th Anniversary Edition Hardcover – Organizer, Jossey-Bass.

Litwiński J., Sztanderska U. (2010), *Zarządzanie wiekiem w przedsiębiorstwie*, PARP, Warsaw.

Moczydłowska J. M. (2014), *Mentoring as a tool for age management*, in: "Entrepreneurship and Management cz. 1 Management-New Perspectives in Times of Demographic Change", no. 15/11/2014, pp. 181–191, http://piz.san.edu.pl/docs/e-XV-11-1.pdf [accessed 03.03.2023].

Oleksyn T. (2010), *Competence Management. Theory and Practice*, Wolters Kluwer Polska, Warsaw.

Para A. (2015), *The problem of generational diversity in organisations*, in: "Marketing. Management", K. Poznańska, K. M. Kraja (eds.), Warsaw School of Economics – Oficyna Wydawnicza, Warsaw, pp. 85–104.

Parks L., Guay R. (2009), *Personality, values and motivation*, in: "Personality and Individual Differences", 47 (7), pp. 675–684.

Pawlak J. (2016), *Age management as a way of counteracting socio-economic inequalities and intergenerational conflicts in the enterprise*, in: "Social Inequalities and Economic Growth", no. 46/2/2016, pp. 408–418, https://doi.org/10.15584/nsawg.2016.2.25.

Przetacka Z. (2009), *Różnorodność ze względu na wiek – zarządzanie wiekiem w organizacjach*, No. 104 publ. SGH, Warsaw.

Racolta-Paina N. D., Irini R. D. (2021), *Generation Z in the workplace through the lenses of human resource professionals – a qualitative study*, in: "Qualitative – Access to Success", 22 (183).

Robak E. (2021), *Managing human resource diversity in organisations*, in: "Psychosocial Aspects of Human Resource Management", A. Bazan-Bulandy, A. Kwiatek, M. Skiby (eds.), pp. 36–47, Częstochowa University of Technology Publishing House, Częstochowa, https://wydawnictwo.pcz.pl/sites/default/files/inline-files/Psychspo%C5%82eczne%20aspekty%20zarz%C4%85dzania%20zasobami%20ludzkimi.pdf [accessed 03.03.2024].

Schwartz S. H. (1992), *Universals in the content and structure of values: Theoretical advances and empirical tests in 20 countries*, in: "Advances in Experimental Social Psychology", M. Zanna (ed.), vol. 25, Academic Press, London, pp. 1–65.

Sidor-Rządkowska M. (2018), *Management of generation diversity in contemporary organisations*, in: "Wydawnictwo Naukowe Uniwersytetu Szczecińskiego", no. 51/22013, pp. 87–96.

Szostak M. (2021), *Kicz nasza ochrona przed rzeczywistoscia*, https://wiez.pl/2021/01/12/kicz-nasza-ochrona-przed-rzeczywistoscia/ (accessed 03.03.2024).

Szostak M., Sułkowski Ł. (2020), *Kitsch in management: Characteristic forms, carriers and propagators*, in: "Education Excellence and Innovation Management: A 2025 Vision to Sustain Economic Development During Global Challenges: Proceedings of the 35th International Business Information Management Association Conference (IBIMA)", Khalid S. Soliman (ed.), pp. 7584–7598, IBIMA, Seville, ISBN: 978-0-9998551-4-0.

Sztajerowska A. (2019), *Job interviewing in the light of literature studies and opinions of generation C*, in: "Journal of Management and Finance", no. 1/1/2019, pp. 87–101.

Walczak W. (2011), *Diversity management as a basis for building human capital in an organisation*, in: "E-Mentor", no. 3, pp. 11–19.

Waligóra Ł. (2018), *Managing diversity in organisations. A presentation of selected practices*, in: "Studia Ekonomiczne. Zeszyty Naukowe Uniwersytetu Ekonomicznego w Katowicach", no. 348, pp. 26–43.

Waśko R. (2016), *Selected aspects differentiating generations X, Y and Z in the context of the use of new technologies and the Internet*, in: "Sociology of Everyday Life as Non-Triviality", Z. Rykla, J. Kinala (eds.), Scientific Association Social Space and Environment, Rzeszów.

Wojnicki S. (2015), *Different Generations, One Organisation*, SW Mentoring, Olsztyn.

Żarczyńska-Dobiesz A., Chomątowska B. (2014), *Pokolenie 'Z' na rynku pracy – wyzwania dla zarządzania zasobami ludzkimi*, in: "Prace Naukowe Uniwersytetu Ekonomicznego We Wrocławiu", No. 350 Sukces w zarządzaniu kadrami Różnorodność w zarządzaniu kapitałem ludzkim-podejścia, metody, narzędzia Problemy zarządczo-psychologiczne.

5 Kitsch in managerial language

Rhetorical manifestations of kitsch in scholarly writing

Iga Maria Lehman

Introduction

Although there is a degree of fuzziness about its nature and disparate views concerning what it entails, there is broad consensus that leadership is distinguishable as a form of superintendence. As a matter of orthodoxy, the leadership phenomenon is typically idealised as a form of super-management. From the perspective of organisational performance, the idea here is that if one can transcend from being a garden-variety manager and become a leader or, has the good fortune to be born a leader, one becomes of increased value to an employer. The well-established idea is that leadership-type relationships are mostly mediated through language, as evidenced by the recent scholarship addressing the effect of charismatic rhetoric on followers (Meslec et al., 2020; Ernst et al., 2021; Fest et al., 2021; Antonakis et al., 2021). Research into the association between rhetoric and leadership has a modern intellectual pedigree that extends back several decades (Butcher & Atkinson, 2001; Fairhurst, 2010); however, the focus has been on how orality, not written expression, is a fundamental element in the notion of leadership.

In this chapter, I propose that written discourse can also be approached as an act of leadership (see also Lehman, forthcoming). Specifically, I look at the process of scholarly text creation and argue the relationship between leaders and followers has consequential points of similarity to that which exists between the gatekeepers of mainstream disciplinary journals and scholarly writers. The former party is the agenda setter who establishes the norms for what can be researched and how it should be done and reported. The latter party is required to align themselves with these requirements in order not to risk their work perishing at the hands of the editors and reviewers.

The concerns and recommendations of this chapter are specific to what Aguinis et al. (2020) term A-level business and management journals and the rhetorical standards they typically demand, which, over time, have contributed to the 'publish or perish' ideology that dominates contemporary academia (Aguinis et al., 2020; Bardunek, 2020; Harley, 2019; Philips, 2019). In particular, these journals are the point at which much modern scholarship is judged to

DOI: 10.4324/9781003504931-6

be acceptable for global dissemination. Consequently, the written reporting of scholarship has evolved to the point 'where individual reputations and institutional funding coincide; the result of managerialism and an accountability... that seeks to measure "productivity" in terms of papers, and citations to those papers' (Hyland, 2016, p. 58).

The remainder of this chapter will be devoted to a brief explanation of the analogy between leaders and followers and between journal gatekeepers and writers and more extensive reflection on the academia's publishing culture and its consequences for management and organisation scholars who strive to have their work published in A-level outlets in the field. Specifically, I will argue that the extant privileged rhetorical norms of scholarly writing contribute to the kitsch experience as texts in which these norms are employed are jargon-ridden, pretentious, complex, and consequently meaningless to anyone outside the narrow confines of these disciplines. I end the chapter with some examples of such writing translated into readable English to show its artificiality or kitschiness, which, I argue, renders it less accessible to a wider and more diverse audience.

Literature review

With few exceptions in scholarly contexts and, in particular, in content addressing management and organisation studies' issues (e.g. Helin, 2019; Kuhn, 2008; Locke & Golden-Biddle, 1997; Hyland, 1998; Lehman et al., 2022; Lehman & Sułkowski, 2023; Lehman et al., 2024b), the role of the effective use of rhetorical strategies in academic texts has not been well explored. This is despite the fact that there has been strident criticism of the stylistic aspects of management and organisation literature. Such denunciations include 1) not engaging with a readership with interests and knowledge outside the narrow confines of traditional management theory (Hambrick, 2007); 2) pretentious, obscurantist, and dull language (Grey & Sinclair, 2006; Bridgman & Stephens, 2008), 3) the disingenuous repackaging and representation of old ideas and theory as new content (often associated with undue commitment to presenting theory for theory's sake); and 4) the excessive presence of writing styles which are formulaic, jargon-ridden, authoritarian (as opposed to authoritative) and generally non-straightforward (Suddaby et al., 2011; Shepherd & Sutcliffe, 2011; Tourish, 2020).

Within the literature of management and organisation studies, empirical studies which focus on a reader-considerate approach to scholarly writing include Locke and Golden-Biddle's (1997) analysis of the importance of rhetorical features in creating opportunities for scholarly outputs, Kuhn's (2008) investigation of what he terms 'authoritative text', Helin's (2019) development of the concept of 'dialogical writing' and Lehman et al.'s (2022) and Lehman and Sułkowski's (2023) exploration of reader perceptions of a convincing authorial voice. Locke and Golden-Biddle (1997) challenge the dominant conception of scientific texts as being merely a set of statements of fact, arguing that they are skilfully constructed arguments which aim to persuade an intended audience by means of reader engagement and specific rhetorical techniques. Helin's (2019) problematisation of dialogical writing throws light on such aspects of writing in management and organisation research which include 1) the generative power of integrating writing into the fieldwork, 2) the inseparability of the spoken and the written word, and 3) the different understanding of authorship which calls into question who can claim to be the author of a text which is based on conversations (Helin, 2019, pp. 12–13). However, Helin does not conceive of the text as dialogue between writer and reader. I develop her arguments to include considerations into the dialogic nature of authorial voice which reader-considerate writers strive to create in their texts. The desire for such a voice has become evident in two studies' findings into reader perceptions of authorial voice conducted by Lehman et al. (2022) and Lehman and Sułkowski (2023). The quantitative analysis of a corpus of over 10,000 articles in Lehman et al.'s (2022) study revealed that novice writers intuitively establish equality and commonality with their readers by engaging in a reader-inclusive dialogue in their texts. The following mixed-method study (Lehman & Sułkowski, 2023) into doctoral students' perceptions of the rhetorical nature of a convincing authorial voice showed that for this group, a reader-considerate voice is essential for a text to be convincing.

Signalling theory and analogy between leaders and followers, and journal gatekeepers and writers

In developing analogy between leaders and followers and between journal gatekeepers and writers, signalling theory is of particular relevance. Specifically, signalling refers to how one party (an individual or other entity) is changed when another directs a communication towards them/it (Connelly et al., 2011). As such, the initiating agent communicates (or signals) a message, and the receiver interprets it. For Spence (2002), signalling theory is primarily concerned with information asymmetry between interlocutors; it is 'a condition wherein one party in a relationship has more or better information than another' (Bergh et al., 2019, p. 122).

The notion of information asymmetry has become a central concern for management scholars who, in recent decades, have broadened their conception of the range of stimuli that count as signals as well as the contexts in which signalling occurs (Zhang & Wiersema, 2009; Miller & Triana, 2009; Suazo et al., 2009, Grabo et al., 2017; Reh et al., 2017). It has also become orthodoxy that information asymmetry indicates the presence of a leader-follower situation, a phenomenon that has been recognised, in one form or another, for decades. Put simply, a fundamental aspect of leadership is the fact that one party in the exchange or relationship has relatively more relevant expertise, or information, and therefore power, than the other.

The notions of disciplinary expertise and information asymmetry are the *raison d'être* for scholarly journals and the content they contain. Indeed, those who gatekeep mainstream periodicals are typically viewed as disciplinary leaders or of the highest level of domain-specific expertise. By establishing, or at least perpetuating, the norms for what can be written and how it is written about, they influence their subject matter's written content and style. However, the stark reality for scholars is that as these A-level journals have high impact factor and therefore are more likely to be read and cited, there is immense pressure on scholars to publish only in these outlets. As a result, journal impact rankings have 'a totalising effect, where it is hard to contemplate viable alternatives' (Nkomo, 2009, p. 109) which can make the scientific, communicative, and practical value of contributions of secondary importance (Edwards & Roy, 2017). The reliance on the ranking systems for A-level journals has an effect on the very content of the knowledge produced and the kinds of research questions posed by management scholars (Adler & Harzing, 2009).

The relationship between gatekeepers and scholarly writers is consistent with the Weberian perspective on traditional leadership which is associated with the fulfilment of roles that, for whatever reason, are accompanied by historically and traditionally conferred authority. This is exemplified in the case of monarchs who exercise power on the basis of dynastic continuity. The nature and extent of such influence is customarily legitimated by so-called subjects who mostly accept leadership prerogatives, viewing them as being consistent with the 'natural' social order and therefore unquestionable. Similarly, in the process of scholarly text production, getting into a dialogue with reviewers and editors by asking the question 'What do you mean?' is not available to all the authors in the same way. As I and Tienari (2024) explain:

> Asking 'what do you mean?' in organisation studies has become the privilege of those who manage to establish a credible position by consistently publishing their work in A-level journals. This involves internalising the norms and conventions of these journals and conforming to their formulaic rhetorical styles.
>
> (https://doi.org/10.1177/08933189241227943)

The need for reform

Aguinis et al. (2020) and Rasheed and Priem (2020) agree on both the negative and positive outcomes of the extant bottom line for evaluating academic research set by A-level journals and perpetuated by those who publish in these journals. Although they admit that the norms which need to be followed to get published could, on one hand, be a useful, learnable framework for novice scholars, they warn that they may also create the situation that 'One need not be a scholar to publish. Instead, one needs to learn and perfect the routines that lead to publication' (Rasheed & Priem, 2020, p. 160).

Contributing to this discussion, Harley (2019) points to two consequences of the dominant rhetorical norms of scholarly writing. Firstly, they undermine the practical relevance of research and secondly, they lead to diminished levels of plurality in intellectual exchange. The potentially negative effect of research outputs lacking 'the scientific validity and usefulness of the knowledge they produce' (Aguinis et al., 2020, p. 136) is particularly paradoxical today when universities and institutions worldwide are being constantly pressured to be dynamic and align their programmes with actual business and managerial needs and practices. Joullié and Gould agree noting that the studies published in A-level journals 'are simply paying of lip service to the imperative that research be practically relevant' (2022, p. 2). For them, scholars' failure to communicate the practical application of their recommendations can be remedied by examining and changing the language used to do this. Other critics (Bridgman & Stephens, 2008; Adler et al., 2008; Kiriakos & Tienari, 2018; Gilmore et al., 2019; Pullen et al., 2020; Tourish, 2020) also point to texts on management and organisations' issues as being frequently introspective and written in a style which has been branded as complex, pretentious, and authoritarian, and in consequence, less accessible and interesting to a more diverse global audience.

Empirical evidence

Regular readers of A-level management and organisation journals often find themselves asking what an author is trying to say. One of the main obstacles to the smooth processing of a text is the overuse of disciplinary jargon. Alvesson et al. argue that it often governs writing in absurd ways as 'Almost everything trivial can be blown up and made into something significant and impressive through simply framing it with the use of a grandiose but often deceptive and meaningless label' (2017, p. 82). This can be illustrated by the following excerpt they quote from a relatively high-ranked journal in organisation studies which then they translate its jargon into readable English:

Original Text

This allowed for an open enquiry into ego-dystonic compliance. By compliance I here mean the 'instrumental involvement for specific, extrinsic rewards' (O'Reilly & Chatman, 1986, p. 493) where the most important reward in this case was to retain a full-time job and all the economic benefits that come with it. This compliance was *ego-dystonic* in the sense that it, unlike other instances of 'willing compliance' (Barker, 1993, p. 412), was dissonant from the goals and values that the employees wanted to pursue in their jobs.

Translation

I use a difficult word, 'ego-dystonic compliance', instead of a simple word, such as 'obedience' or 'submission'.

(Alvesson et al., 2017, p. 79)

Along with technical language, other linguistic features, such as noun sequences and acronyms, can add to the reader's sense of alienation from the text's content. Examples of this can be found in Hyland (see Lehman et al., 2024a), who cites examples of new entries in the lexicon of social sciences, including *Transactive Memory Systems, Post-Qualitative Inquiry*, and *STARA competencies*. Hyland argues that the meanings of these terms are only accessible to a narrow circle of the discipline's 'insiders', and they serve to speed up their processing of the text's content. They have the opposite effect on the layperson, however, as they create processing blocks. He goes on to say that an overuse of linguistic features, such as nominalisations, noun sequences, and acronyms 'generate knowledge which has become ever-more specialised, making texts opaque to all but the initiated, thus excluding a wider public and reproducing a context of inequality (Lehman et al., 2024a)' (Lehman et al., 2024b).

Another contributing factor to communication failure in these publications is the overuse of references and thematic inserts that complicate a text's linear flow. In particular, opening paragraphs typically make extensive use of references which often makes it difficult to grasp what is unique about what the author is saying. This can be exemplified by another excerpt taken by Alvesson et al. (2017) also from a prestigious journal in organisation studies:

Original Text

Despite criticism of Burawoy's analysis, particularly his one-sided functionalist approach, his lack of dialects and the assumption that consent is only created in the labour process irrespective of external relations (e.g. Clawson & Fantasia, 1983; Edwards, 1986; Gartman, 1983; Roscigno & Hodson, 2004; Thompson, 1983), similar analyses have more recently reappeared in critical workplace studies with regard to both time appropriation (Baxter & Kroll-Smith, 2005; Ladner, 2009; Maier, 2006; Townsend, 2004) and organizational misbehavior in general (see Contu, 2008; Fleming & Spicer, 2008; Fleming, 2009; Mumby, 2005; Sewell, 2008).

Translation

Some people criticized Burawoy for one-sidedly focusing on the labour process when explaining why workers consent, but lately others have returned to some of his ideas. Also, I have gathered lots of references and therefore I am scientific.

(Alvesson et al., 2017, pp. 78–79)

Thematic inserts function as a form of thematic extension and are usually placed in the segments between the dashes or presented as exposition (the 'i.e.' relation). However, from the reader's perspective, they unduly broaden the focus, slow down the flow of argumentation, and in an overall sense, impair the explicit presentation of the writers' unique interpretation, comment, evaluation, etc., as illustrated in this excerpt from *Journal of Knowledge Management:*

> At an individual level too, Blumer's (1969) signalling theory suggests the meaning of things determine how people act towards them and meaning arises out of the social interaction that one has with others and society (i.e. what an individual or firm does with the thought leadership), which modifies the meaning through an interpretative process.

The above examples of much of the writing in the field of management and organisations show its artificiality, or kitschness, that questions its utility, accessibility, and relevance to wider and diverse audiences. As Szostak and Sułkowski contend, 'Kitsch isn't a bad art; kitsch is an evil in art – it creates its own reference system' (2020, p. 7586), which, in the case of writing, makes it complex, pretentious, laboured, alien, and consequently reader-excluding.

Mini study

To provide a robust foundation for my critique, I sampled a corpus of A-level journals, which included *Academy of Management Journal*, *Academy of Management Review*, *Journal of Business Ethics*, *Journal of Knowledge Management*, and *Journal of Management Studies*, and selected four 35- to 40-page-long articles published in 2021 and 2022 from each. For this corpus, a content analysis was conducted to determine both the frequencies with which 1) specific interpersonal linguistic items and 2) thematic inserts occur. Interpersonal linguistic items selected for analysis included: authorial self-mentions, attitude markers, attributions to sources, reader pronouns, references to shared knowledge, rhetorical questions, and direct appeals to the reader. Authorial self-mentions refer to pronouns we, us, our, and ours to mark the presence of two or multiple authors. Attitude markers indicate the writer's affective attitude to propositions, signalling their (dis)agreement, interest, confidence, or uncertainty. Attributions to sources reinforce the credibility of the claims being made, but their overuse obfuscates the clarity of the author's original thought on the topic. Reader pronouns refer to the pronouns we, us, our, and ours and are used to more implicitly include the potential point of view of the reader into the argument. References to shared knowledge make the reader feel they are participating in the co-construction of a particular argument. Rhetorical questions directly encourage reader engagement and awake their curiosity.

I found that rhetorical strategies that enabled writers to distance themselves from readers outnumbered reader-embracing linguistic devices and included authorial self-mentions (≈100 per text), attributions to sources (≈150 per text) and thematic inserts (≈10 segments between the dashes and ≈15, i.e. expositions per text). This analysis provides a preliminary empirical exploration for the argument I am making that the stylistic requirements of A-level management and organisation studies' journals are not reader-inclusive. Further empirical examination is needed to better justify my concerns. Specifically, we need more studies to explore which rhetorical devices distance and which include the reader, as well as the socio-cultural and disciplinary circumstances under which reader-excluding discourse assumes dominance over reader-embracing communication.

Discussion and conclusion

The need for good communication – the kind that inculcates trust and develops relationships between writer and reader (or communicator and receiver/audience) – is regarded as fundamental by those who critique present-day management and organisation studies' scholarship. For example, Legget and Rosanas (2008) note, 'Gone are the days of dependency, when information was delivered top-down, and there was little need to win over subordinates and colleagues with our ideas and opinions' (p. 1). On page 6 of the same article, the authors use data from the Wall Street-Harris Interactive Survey to make the case that communication and interpersonal skill is the substance of what leadership is about. Considering this, if we look at scholarly text construction as an act of leadership, then the question arises: 'Why is communication between journal gatekeepers (leaders) and their followers (writers) in the field of management and communication studies such that a great deal of texts can be perceived as "kitsch artefacts" and their authors as "kitsch producers"?'

After all, scholarly writing about management and organisation issues is undoubtedly a combination of the presentation of empirical truths and value judgements. Thus, to be convincing to a diverse disciplinary readership, it necessarily involves the strategic use of a wide range of rhetorical resources that would enable writers to engage readers intellectually and emotionally. However, as I stated above, we, scholarly authors, 'must speak the Center's language, use its concepts, discuss its agendas' (Ibarra-Colado, 2006, p. 471) to be accepted as legitimate and competent members of the global disciplinary community we want to belong to.

To a large extent, the criticisms of scholarly texts in management and organisation studies, such as a writing style which does not consider the reader, the lack of relevance and practical application of research findings, has been attributed to today's 'publish or perish' culture and the restrictions and conditions implied in it. These restrictions and conditions, over time, have contributed to writing in the field being perceived as 'impoverished, stiff, sanitized and humorless', 'asphalted' (Perrow, 1986, p. 176), and 'soul destroying for authors to write' (Tourish & Willmott, 2015, p. 43). For many scholars, what gets published, what gets rejected, and everything that goes on in between are 'barely concealed exercises in power and resistance' (Gabriel, 2010, p. 761), so as the audience, scholarly authors primarily write for peer reviewers, editors, and publishers. Therefore, there is an immense pressure to conform to the academy's norms of scholarship, potentially leading to 'tendentious, jargon-ridden, laboured writing style and an equally abstracted vocabulary to show that we are, after all, still serious scholars' (Grey & Sinclair, 2006, p. 445). This dominating influence on the rhetorical situation affects how we construct meaning and create our textual self-representations.

Conclusion

My aim in this chapter is to initiate a discussion among management and organisation studies' scholars on the kitsch nature of much of the writing in the field and propose a different type of relationship between gatekeepers and writers, the one based on reflexivity and mutual respect, which, I argue, renders the text more authentic. The concept and practice of 'reflexivity' is a fundamental tool for writers aiming to write more meaningfully about scholarly issues. It is not simply an aspect of rhetorical style. However, it is a theoretically grounded practical approach which proposes the use of a wide range of rhetorical features which serve to make scholarly writing more accessible, engaging, persuasive to readers, less ambiguous, and more actionable (Bartunek & Rynes, 2010). The implementation of reader-sensitive writing will enable not only Anglophone and non-Anglophone doctoral students and junior researchers but also other academic authors to free themselves from the stifling writing templates and rhetorical styles which are often seen as no more than a 'cynical rhetorical device designed to demonstrate researcher credentials' (Alvesson et al., 2008, p. 498). The introduction of reflexive writing practices is potentially transformative in that it provides a way to promote equity of participation by 1) highlighting and addressing the current rhetorical practices that constrain opportunities for non-Anglophone scholars, doctoral students, and junior researchers to become legitimate members of their global disciplinary communities and 2) enabling academics to navigate the challenging terrain of writing for international publishing by employing our own unique authorial voices.

References

Adler, N. J., & Harzing, A.-W. (2009). When knowledge wins: Transcending the sense and nonsense of academic rankings. *Academy of Management Learning & Education*, 8(1), 72–95.

Adler, P. S., Forbes, L. C., & Willmott, H. C. (2008). Critical management studies. *Academy of Management Annals*, 1, 119–180.

Aguinis, H., Cummings, C., Ramani, R. S., & Cummings, T. G. (2020). "An a is an a": The new bottom line for valuing academic research. *Academy of Management Perspectives*, 34, 135–154.
Alvesson, M., Gabriel, Y., & Paulsen, R. (2017). *Return to Meaning: A Social Science with Something to Say*. Oxford: OUP.
Alvesson, M., Hardy, C., & Harley, B. (2008). Reflecting on reflexivity: Reflexive textual practices in organization and management theory. *Journal of Management Studies*, 45(3), 480–501.
Antonakis, J., d'Adda, G., Weber, R. A., & Zehnder, C. (2021). Just words? Just speeches? On the economic value of charismatic leadership. *Management Science*, 68(9), 6355–6381.
Bardunek, J. M. (2020). Exchanges: What do, what did, and what should we do about "A's"? *Academy of Management Perspectives*, 34, 164–169.
Bartunek, J. M., & Rynes, S. L. (2010). The construction and contributions of "implications for practice": What's in them and what might they offer? *Academy of Management Learning & Education*, 9, 100–117.
Bergh, D., Ketchen, D. J., Orlandi, I., Heugens, P. M. A. R., & Boyd, B. K. (2019). Information asymmetry in management research: Past accomplishments and future opportunities. *Journal of Management*, 45(1), 122–158.
Bridgman, T., & Stephens, M. (2008). Institutionalizing critique: A problem of critical management studies. *Ephemera: Theory & Politics in Organization*, 8, 258–270.
Butcher, D., & Atkinson, S. (2001). Stealth, secrecy and subversion: The language of change. *Journal of Organizational Change Management*, 14(6), 554–569.
Connelly, B. L., Certo, T., Ireland, R. D., Reutzel, C. R. (2011). Signaling theory: A review and assessment. *Journal of Management*, 37(1), 39–67.
Edwards, M. A., & Roy, S. (2017). Academic research in the 21st century: Maintaining scientific integrity in a climate of perverse incentives and hypercompetition. *Environmental Engineering Science*, 34(1). https://doi.org/10.1089/ees.2016.0223
Ernst, B. A., Banks, G. C., Loignon, A. C., Frear, K. A., Williams, C. E., Arciniega, L. M., et al. (2021). Virtual charismatic leadership and signaling theory: A prospective meta-analysis in five countries. *The Leadership Quarterly*, available online 1 July 2021. https://doi.org/10.1016/j.leaqua.2021.101541
Fairhurst, G. T. (2010). *The Power of Framing: Creating the Language of Leadership*. Hoboken: John Wiley & Sons.
Fest, S., Kvaløy, O., Nieken, P., & Schöttner, A. (2021). How (not) to motivate online workers: Two controlled field experiments on leadership in the gig economy. *The Leadership Quarterly*, 32(6), available online December 2021. https://doi.org/10.1016/j.leaqua.2021.101514
Gabriel, Y. (2010). Organization studies: A space for ideas, identities and agonies. *Organization Studies*, 31, 757–775.
Gilmore, S., Harding, N., Helin, J., & Pullen, A. (2019). Writing differently. *Management Learning*, 50, 3–10.
Grabo, A., Spisak, B. R., & Van Vugt, M. (2017). Charisma as signal: An evolutionary perspective on charismatic leadership. *The Leadership Quarterly*, 28(4), 473–485.
Grey, C., & Sinclair, A. (2006). Writing differently. *Organization*, 13(3), 443–453.
Hambrick, D. (2007). The field of management's devotion to theory: Too much of a good thing? *Academy of Management Journal*, 50(6), 1346–1352.
Harley, B. (2019). Confronting the crisis of confidence in management studies: Why senior scholars need to stop setting a bad example. *Academy of Management Learning & Education*, 18, 286–297.

Helin, J. (2019). Dialogical writing: Co-inquiring between the written and the spoken word. *Culture and Organization*, 25, 1–15.
Hyland, K. (1998). Exploring corporate rhetoric: Metadiscourse in the CEO's letter. *International Journal of Business Communication*, 35(2), 224–245.
Hyland, K. (2016). Academic publishing and the myth of linguistic injustice. *Journal of Second Language Writing*, 31, 58–69.
Ibarra-Colado, E. (2006). Organization studies and epistemic coloniality in Latin America: Thinking otherness from the margins. *Organization*, 13(4), 463–488.
Joullié, J.-E., & Gould, A. M. (2022). Having nothing to say but saying it anyway: Language and practical relevance in management research. *Academy of Management Learning & Education*, 21, 1–21.
Kiriakos, C. M., & Tienari, J. (2018). Academic writing as love. *Management Learning*, 49, 263–277.
Kuhn, T. (2008). A communicative theory of the firm: Developing an alternative perspective on intra-organizational power and stakeholder relationships. *Organization Studies*, 29(8–9), 1227–1254.
Legget, B., & Rosanas, J. M. (2008). *Rhetoric and Persuasion in Management*. IESE, Occasional Paper-154. Available from: http://www.iese.edu/research/pdfs/op-0154-e.pdf
Lehman, I. M. (forthcoming). *Charismatic Leadership in Organizations: A Critique of Texts*. London and New York: Routledge.
Lehman, I. M., Bednarek, A., & Sułkowski, Ł. (2024b). The role of reader-inclusive authorial voice in the process of academic socialization of management and English philology students. *Ibérica*, 47(2024), 275–299. https://doi.org/10.17398/2340-2784.47.275
Lehman, I. M., Cybulska-Gómez de Celis, K., & Sułkowski, Ł. (2022). Writing to make a difference: Discursive analysis of writer identity in research articles on management. *Ibérica*, 44, 155–178.
Lehman, I. M., & Sułkowski, Ł. (2023). Reader perceptions of authorial voice in top-tier management journals: The case of doctoral students of management from Eastern Europe. *Journal of Management Education*, 47(4), 349–387.
Lehman, I. M., & Tienari, J. (2024). What do you mean? Linguistic sensitivity and relational reflexivity in scholarly writing. *Organization*. https://doi.org/10.1177/13505084241233956
Lehman, I. M., Tienari, J., Hyland, K., & Alejandro, A. (2024a). Forum: The case for reflexive writing practices in management communication and organization studies. *Management Communication Quarterly*. https://doi.org/10.1177/08933189241227943
Locke, K., & Golden-Biddle, K. (1997). Opportunities for contribution: Structuring Intertextual coherence and "problematizing" in organizational studies. *Academy of Management Journal*, 40, 1023–1062.
Meslec, N., Curseu, P. L., Fodor, O. C., & Kenda, R. (2020). Effects of charismatic leadership and rewards on individual performance. *The Leadership Quarterly*, 31(6), [101423]. https://doi.org/10.1016/j.leaqua.2020.101423
Miller, T., & Del Carmen Triana, M. (2009). Demographic diversity in the boardroom: Mediators of the board diversity–firm performance relationship. *Journal of Management Studies*, 46, 755–786.
Nkomo, S. (2009). The seductive power of academic journal rankings. *Academy of Management Learning and Education*, 8, 106–112.
Perrow, C. (1986). *Complex Organisations: A Critical Essay*, 3rd ed. New York: Random House.
Philips, N. (2019). What is academic success anyway? A rejoinder to "Confronting the crisis of confidence in management studies". *Academy of Management Learning & Education*, 18, 306–309.

Pullen, A., Helin, J., & Harding, N. (Eds.). (2020). *Writing Differently*. Bingley: Emerald.
Rasheed, A. A., & Priem, R. L. (2020). Exchanges: "an a is an a": We have met the enemy, and he is us! *Academy of Management Perspectives*, 34, 155–163.
Reh, S., Van Quaquebeke, N., & Giessner, S. R. (2017). The aura of charisma: A review on the embodiment perspective as signaling. *The Leadership Quarterly*, 28(4), 486–507.
Shepherd, D. A., & Sutcliffe, K. M. (2011). Inductive top-down theorizing: A source of new theories of organization. *The Academy of Management Review*, 36(2), 361–380.
Spence, M. (2002). Signaling in retrospect and the informational structure of markets. *The American Economic Review*, 92(3), 434–459.
Suazo, M. M., Martinez, P. G., & Sandoval, R. (2009). Creating psychological and legal contracts through human resource practices: A signaling theory perspective. *Human Resource Management Review*, 19, 154–166.
Suddaby, R., Hardy, C., & Huy, Q. N. (2011). Where are the new theories of organization? *Academy of Management Review*, 36(2), 236–246.
Szostak, M., & Sułkowski, Ł. (2020). Kitsch in management: Characteristic forms, carriers and propagators. In K. S. Soliman (Ed.), *Education Excellence and Innovation Management: A 2025 Vision to Sustain Economic Development During Global Challenges* (pp. p. 7584–7598). Proceedings of the 35th International Business Information Management Association Conference (IBIMA), 1–2 April 2020, Seville, Spain, ISBN: 978-0-9998551-4-0.
Tourish, D. (2020). The triumph of nonsense in management studies. *Academy of Management Learning & Education*, 19(1), 99–109.
Tourish, D., & Willmott, H. (2015). In defiance of folly. Journal rankings, mindless measures and the ABS guide. *Critical Perspectives on Accounting*, 26(1), 37–46.
Zhang, Y., & Wierseman, M. F. (2009). Stock market reaction to CEO certification: The signalling role of CEO background. *Strategic Management Journal*, 30, 693–710.

6 Kitsch in marketing

Merchandising and promotional activities in the retail sphere

Andrzej Kondej

Introduction

Due to the increasing competition in retailing in the contemporary market, merchandising activities are becoming increasingly important. They primarily include the arrangement of retail spaces and the display of goods. To a broader extent, we can include promotional activities in stores through animation and sales promotions. Solutions and actions in this area should meet the essential criteria of being effective, attractive to buyers, and creative.

In sales spaces, it is increasingly common to encounter solutions that, due to their fulfilment of the defining criteria, can be defined by the actions and nature of kitsch. The chapter aims to analyse the causes, the impact on customers' buying behaviour, and the broader consequences for sales companies and customers. It is also worth considering whether there is a risk of implementing risky solutions, that is, those that carry certain risks for both customers and bidders in the quest to maximise sales effects. These actions simplistically appeal to customers' perceptions, create an unrealistic image of reality, and offer them illusory benefits from taking part in specific promotional actions.

The chapter attempts to answer the following questions: 1) Which merchandising and sales promotion activities can be categorised as kitsch in trade? 2) What are the reasons and justification for using kitsch-like solutions in merchandising? and 3) To what extent does the use of kitsch in the commercial sphere meet consumers' expectations? At the same time, there is no doubt that the issue of the use of kitsch in commercial spaces requires further in-depth research and analysis.

The research methodology is based on a qualitative review of the literature on merchandising and the concept of kitsch. In particular, the focus is on the issue of the use of kitsch solutions applied in management. Among others, a study by Michal Szostak based on interdisciplinary and multi-paradigm approaches in art (aesthetics theories) and management (organisational kitsch). Due to the highly modest scope of previous studies on kitsch in marketing, the author also used direct observations from the market and his experience from a long career as a marketing and sales consultant.

DOI: 10.4324/9781003504931-7

The chapter consists of five parts. The 'Literature review' includes sources on the basic assumptions and characteristics of merchandising. In the 'The rationale for the influence of merchandising on buyers' section, attention is focused on the forms of influence on buyers in retail spaces. Issues are addressed regarding the influence of these factors on the specific form of buyers' purchasing decisions. The chapter's main content is in the section 'Justification of kitsch in merchandising'. An attempt is made here to explain the broad and still-growing use of kitsch-like solutions in sales spaces. In the section 'Ethical aspects of kitsch in merchandising', considerations are taken concerning possible misleading customers or damage to the image and good name of companies using such solutions. In the 'Conclusions' section, the answers to the presented research questions are presented as a summary.

Literature review: key merchandising issues

Merchandising as a part of marketing

Various announcements play a significant role in the modern marketing communication of a company with the market environment. It is also essential to consider where contact with potential buyers should be made. At the same time, the marketing goals to be achieved through these activities can vary. Specifically, such vital goals are to increase the overall volume of sales, interest buyers in specific products (e.g. novelties), increase the value of a shopping basket, maintain the loyalty of existing customers, or encourage new buyers to purchase (Nowogródzka 2010). Considering the above, an essential arena for marketing ventures is the place of sale where the offered products are exposed (both offline and online).

Generally, merchandising can be regarded as a marketing activity conducted in sales outlets. There is a consensus in academic studies that merchandising is meant as the planning, developing, and presenting of product lines for identified target markets concerning pricing, assorting, styling, and timing. As a result, it is accurate to say that merchandising is a part of marketing that strives to pull off a perfect balance among the right merchandise at the right place, at the right time, in the correct quantity, and at the right price (Ambrogi 2023).

Two merchandising concepts can be found in the literature, considering the scope of the activities. In a narrow view, the field covers only the visual aspects of store display, while in a broader view, merchandising is identified with trade marketing (Nowogródzka 2010). In narrower terms, so-called visual merchandising refers to the shaping of store spaces and the art of displaying products to induce buyers to make positive purchasing decisions. Sales space development is about optimising the return on such an investment and providing buyers with a logically organised, aesthetically pleasing, and comfortable shopping environment (Varley 2001).

In turn, the location and display of products must meet the generic criteria of the type of assortment while supporting the principles of neighbourhood and complementarity of the products on display. Important aspects in this regard are also the pursuit of specific sales goals and consideration of convenience and easy access of buyers to goods while maintaining elementary principles of ergonomics.

Merchandising, in both offline and online sales areas

More broadly, merchandising encompasses all retail company's marketing activities in a sales outlet, which, through attractive happenings to buyers, are designed to induce them to follow the company's business aims. The scope of merchandising activities must be consistent with the retailer's overall positioning strategy, the product variety, breadth and depth of the offering, and inventory levels. Considering the planning and the way of purchasing, consumer merchandise generally falls into four groups: routine or convenience products, shopping products, speciality products, and unsought goods (Ambrogi 2023).

For decades, merchandising was implemented in stationary outlets. Due to the dynamic development of e-commerce, the importance of this type of sales activity in the virtual sphere is steadily increasing. There are similarities between offline and online shopping in terms of convenience of service, readability of information, quality of visualisation, and assortment availability for buyers' selection and choice by buyers. On the other hand, merchandising on the internet requires new online tools to make the sales site as buyer-friendly as possible. It is also worth mentioning that the internet offers opportunities unavailable in the stationary formula for monitoring the behaviour and reactions of buyers to various forms of merchandising and promotional interactions.

Specific characteristics of merchandising

Merchandising plays a crucial role in developing a marketing strategy because it is an activity conducted in direct contact with customers. It supports the achievement of specific strategic goals. Merchandising's involvement in this regard can be boiled down to four key elements: merchandise strategy, communication strategy, customer service strategy, and format and environment strategy. In this regard, merchandise strategy matters the most, fundamentally affecting the other three strategic elements (Ambrogi 2023).

Practical activities in this respect are the result of the marketing concept adopted. For an offer characterised by accessibility at increasing prices, special attention should be paid to the target customer groups, considering their needs, expectations, and preferences. In addition to the key aspects of merchandising, that is, visualisation of the retail outlet and product display, what also counts is the activity in the retail or service outlet in terms of the broader marketing mix, including such elements as shaping the assortment offered, pricing policy (mainly in terms of price promotions), distribution, that is, customer access to products and the form of sale, and last but not least promotional activities.

The merchandising process more broadly includes activities that begin before products even find their place on store shelves. In this view, we can specify such stages of these activities as assortment and space planning, visualisation of space, assortment display, taking care of uninterrupted and complete supply, implementation of pricing policy, promotion and communication with customers, and monitoring and feedback from buyers (Ambrogi 2023). In the context of communicating with customers, visual merchandising plays a key role. Visual merchandising is the presentation of a store/brand and its goods to customers through the collaborative efforts of advertising, display, dedicated events, fashion coordination, and merchandising departments to sell the goods and services the store offers (Kim 2003).

It is emphasised that visual merchandising encompasses the store's external appearance (window, facade, and retail premises) and internal elements (orientation factors, signage, layout, presentation techniques, props, spatial factors, and environmental conditions). In turn, the architecture of the buildings, colours, and product display are considered aesthetic elements. The created atmosphere of the store has a significant impact on buying behaviour, which, in addition to the visual elements of merchandising (lighting, colour, display/layout), is created by such factors as cleanliness, music, smell, and temperature.

Researchers identify the main elements of visual merchandising that have the most substantial impact on buyers: window displays, in-store design, promotional signage, store layout, and store atmosphere. Visual merchandising thus relies on a design approach to support commercial intent in a store environment. This supports the product management objectives and maximises the sales efforts of the merchandising teams (Varley 2001). To sum up, visual merchandising combines a commercial approach with a design style in a store environment to support objectives within product management and expand sales teams' efforts (Varley 2001).

This subject can be holistically defined as communicating with and influencing customers in retail and service establishments in real and virtual spaces. Activities in this area involve inducing buyers to follow the company's strategic concept. This involves influencing buyers' senses and creating a positive emotional state, which is conducive to making favourable purchasing decisions from the retailers' perspectives. Considering this, this impact should be positive, create an appropriate atmosphere, and at the same time enable the company of its competitors to stand out in this way.

Traditional merchandising uses several techniques to enable achieving its marketing goals. Traditional merchandising activities may include manipulation of store traffic flow, shelf positioning, space allocation, point-of-sale material, and special displays (Buttle 2014). Store traffic is the term used to describe the movement of customers in a store from the moment they enter until they leave the premises. The way and pace at which shoppers move through the store or the time spent viewing and shopping decisively affects the final sales results. Among the most important measures are aisle design and merchandise location.

Shelf positioning is essential to a retail establishment's identity, determining the type of customers who visit and their buying behaviour. Two aspects of shelf positioning have a particularly noticeable impact on sales. These are the positioning of product categories and the subsequent placement of brands. Space allocation reflects the importance of individual products, product groups, or brands in a commercial enterprise's operating and strategic activities. The most convenient space is allocated to priority products, including best sellers, promoted products, or new product lines.

Point-of-sale (POS) materials are called 'silent sellers', also known as point-of-purchase (POP). These incorporate shelf talkers (materials attached to a branded shelf), window banners, price tickets, and posters. In modern merchandising, there is a trend towards introducing electronic interactive solutions, which increase the attractiveness of these materials to customers and create new opportunities for communicating promotional content.

Special displays involve placing specific products in separate areas outside their usual shelf location. In retail practice, this often refers to expositions co-organised and financed by suppliers, mainly manufacturers. The primary purpose of special expositions is to attract shoppers' attention and stimulate purchases made on an unplanned basis (Buttle 2014). Most authors identify the elements of visual merchandising that are credited with having the most significant impact on impulse purchases. These include window displays, in-store design, promotional signage, layout, and atmosphere.

Online merchandising tools

Merchandising applied in the virtual space is based on similar principles as in the offline edition, that is, taking care of the convenience of potential buyers, the efficiency of moving around the store or online platform, proper display of products or services, and active forms of promotion. The peculiarity of marketing activities on the internet is the inability to expose real products, the lack of physical contact with customers, and thus the impossibility of influencing all human senses, such as touch or taste. On the other hand, the internet offers almost unlimited promotional opportunities in formulas addressed to specific target groups and even tailored to individual buyers' expectations. At the same time, the virtual space provides excellent opportunities to monitor and analyse buyers' online behaviour. Therefore, this creates an outstanding opportunity for flexible and ongoing adaptation of the merchandising tools used to a specific situation and buyers' changing needs and preferences.

The rationale for the influence of merchandising on buyers

Informational function of merchandising

Merchandising, as a set of tools for communicative influence towards customers, should primarily have an informative function. This includes information about the product's characteristics, helping customers find their way around the store space, and selecting and choosing the right products. This function becomes particularly important in a market environment characterised by diverse merchandise offerings, display seasonality, accelerated product turnover, or intensive implementation of product novelties. Thus, consumers experience cognitive overload and decision-making discomfort in these increasingly complex commercial conditions, so merchandising information activities can be of significant use. Merchandising, therefore, helps buyers overcome 'cognitive overload' and reduce decision-making discomfort (Mróz 2015).

The information function is closely linked to the time spent by customers in retail spaces. Confirmed in the form of research is the assumption that the value of the shopping basket is higher when customers spend longer in the shop. An important issue, however, is the reasons for increasing the time spent on shopping. It is possible to speak of positive factors if the shopping environment creates a positive perception among customers, if their impressions are positive, and it is up to them to decide how much time they spend shopping. This becomes more complicated when the shopping time is extended for reasons beyond the customers' control. These include negative factors such as a lack of information or insufficient information on the location of product groups and individual products, an unclear shop layout, a complicated product presentation or an incomprehensible form of promotion. Such an arrangement results in negative customer perceptions, discouragement to shopping and, consequently, a reluctance to visit such a retail outlet again (Villanova 2021).

For these reasons, the informational function of merchandising must go hand in hand with the stimulative function of encouraging purchases. This is because a prerequisite for customers to make positive purchasing decisions is to be provided with the correct information, and only after that to create positive impressions and attractive product presentations. Information goals are fully achieved when salespeople apply and make effective use of a variety of communication tools. Visual forms, such as a planned layout of the shop and individual stands, clarity of display, and information materials, such as banners, hangers, displays, and POS/POSM (point of sale materials), come to the fore. Voice communication and the advisory activity of salespeople in direct contact with customers also play an essential role (Varley 2001).

Inducing customers to buy emotionally

Regardless of how merchandising is framed in a narrower or broader formula, the critical issue is the impact of merchandising activities on buyers. Primarily, it stimulates buyers' interest in purchasing specific goods or services. Depending on the forms of consumer behaviour, their purchasing processes can be divided into planning in general, product-planned, unplanned rational, and unplanned emotional. Considering pre-planned purchases, the role of merchandising can be informational, boiling down to enabling the potential customer to find specific products and obtain data on their characteristics. Concerning unplanned purchases, on the other hand, the role of merchandising can be either reminding (the customer skipped planning to buy a specific product) or creating. In the latter case, merchandising triggers the intention to purchase products that a customer had not previously planned, and there is no rational justification (or that justification is incomplete) for the purchase. Studies indicate a strong correlation between buyers' good moods and positive emotions and their propensity to make unplanned purchases.

Therefore, retail businesses aim to generate an attractive sales environment that creates positive emotions and implies shoppers' desired behaviour. In a state of heightened excitement and increased interest in shopping, customers reduce their ability to make rational decisions. As a result, the phenomenon of impulse buying, desired by retailers, emerges, which affects most consumers to a greater or lesser extent. Surveys conducted in shopping centres have revealed that impulse purchases account for between 27% and 62% of all purchases.

Other studies have shown a strong influence of the visual attractiveness of the retail space on shoppers' choice of store. In some situations, the relationship was even higher than the correlation between store choice based on merchandise quality or overall price level. This indicates an evident influence of visual merchandising on shoppers' behaviour in retail spaces. Following this reasoning, people are eager to be in environments that evoke positive emotions and avoid places that cause stress or negative impressions. The expectation of positive impressions creates a growing interest in further shopping experiences. In contrast, anticipation of negative experiences produces an avoidance effect on such places. The above conclusions justify the need, even the necessity, to create commercial spaces where visitors feel comfortable. Therefore, themes or visual elements associated with negative connotations should be avoided in merchandising efforts (Morgan 2016).

Specifics of impulse buying

A particular manifestation of emotional consumer behaviour in retail spaces is impulse buying. This phenomenon is identified as reckless buying behaviour characterised by spontaneity, intensity of reaction, and exciting desire to buy, with typical disregard for the consequences of such purchases. This type of behaviour can result from consumers' internal emotional states and innate qualities or retail ambience incentives created and controlled by marketers. However, since these decisions are always made in a retail (service) establishment or an online store, there is no doubt that, to a greater or lesser extent, situational factors influence such specific purchasing behaviour (Kim 2003). Due to the lack of rational justification for impulse purchases, it can be generally assumed that impulsive behaviour is a sign of decision-making immaturity associated with a lack of behavioural control. Moreover, they may indicate irrational, risky, and wasteful behaviour (Kim 2003).

However, it turns out that a considerable proportion of people who buy impulsively do not consider such behaviour as unreasonable or undesirable. This is because consumers' purchases are primarily rather driven by emotions instead of being guided by purely economic, rational considerations. These include curiosity, prestige, the need for recognition, fun, fantasy, and social or emotional pleasure. Shopping can also be an activity to improve mood, overcome stress, or even a form of pleasurable leisure. The presented purchasing motives indicate the complexity of purchasing processes, with a high involvement of the emotional sphere of a person (Kim 2003). Buying without prior planning and a specific intention satisfies the hedonistic desires of many consumers, with sometimes very pleasant shopping experiences associated with them.

Taking into consideration the nature of consumer shopping behaviour attached to intense competition in retailing, a measure of the effectiveness of merchandising activities is to induce buyers to make previously unplanned purchasing decisions at the retail outlet. Due to the usually short decision-making time to purchase certain products or services, such decisions are spontaneous. Visual displays are an attractive way to persuade customers to make this type of purchase by arousing their positive emotions. It boils down to offering customers a set of cues that engage their senses and stimulate their emotions, which increases customers' propensity to make purchases.

Given this point of view, successful merchandising efforts require three essential criteria to be met simultaneously. The first is creativity and an innovative approach. Thus, the idea is to do a better job than competitors of making sales spaces attractive and comfortable for visiting customers. The second criterion is the adaptation of visual (and other) stimuli used to the level of perception and expectations of buyers representing the selected target groups. The merchandising message must be comprehensible and clear to the audience, as only then can it induce them to behave following the established commercial goals. The third criterion is the positive appeal of the merchandising tools used. This is because customers' propensity to purchase increases only in such a shaped sales space.

Personification and consumer experience

In today's competitive market environment, personalising customers' shopping experience is increasingly significant in merchandising. This makes it possible to display products and use other forms of communication in such a way as to optimally increase the compatibility of buyer expectations with messages presented in various forms. This concept has opportunities for development in e-commerce, where many innovative automated ways of communicating with customers in online form are being developed. These solutions also include models allowing personal contact with potential buyers, such as one-to-one and one-to-many models. This is done through live chats, live videos, phone calls, or text messages (Roggeveen et al. 2020). This approach facilitates the construction of a brand identity that resonates with buyers, fostering their commitment and nurturing a meaningful, enduring relationship between the consumer and the brand.

Communication with customers is based on the concept of the customer journey. This concept refers to the holistic view of the buyer's experience, from the first contact with the offeror to the buyer's purchase decision and after-sales service. In this regard, many points of contact (touch points) holistically shape the customer's experience and ultimately affect his or her satisfaction with the relationship with the provider of specific goods or services. From this point of view, the store's appearance (online and offline), in terms of its design, signage, sensory elements, and interaction with vendors, is significant in shaping consumer perception. This factor can be no less important than the visualisation or quality of the products offered (Roggeveen et al. 2020). It is crucial to recognise that in the context of the evolving omnichannel framework, touchpoints can exist online and offline, while consumers can use different channels to gather information about products, consider alternative options, or share post-purchase opinions.

In addition to the strict purchasing process, touchpoints include broad areas of customer communication, such as social media, influencer marketing, vendor relations (offline and online), or after-sales service. Within the customer journey framework, an essential element in shaping brand identity and its alignment with consumer identity is visual and sensory impact measures, which we categorise as visual merchandising (Roggeveen et al. 2020). From this perspective, it is worth emphasising the need for a holistic approach, where visual merchandising must interact and be harmonised with other forms of customer relations and communication. It is also about uniformity and consistency in the form and content of communication, which should simultaneously be understandable and acceptable to potential buyers.

Merchandising favours consumerism

The simplicity and clarity of commercial communications are becoming essential in the modern world, where the patterns of global consumer culture shape consumer attitudes and behaviour. These messages are essential for contemporary shoppers, as they are guided by an increasingly materialistic value system, consumer hedonism, and unlimited enjoyment of various goods. For a growing proportion of people, consumption is increasingly becoming a value. This happens at the expense of many traditional values, including those associated with higher culture. The message level of the modern media and entertainment industry creates a 'civilisation of spectacle', a culture of trivialisation, frivolity, and superficiality. In this situation, it becomes a matter of understanding and justification that companies' marketing messages also take on the characteristics of simplicity and sometimes superficiality.

So, since this is a culture of trivialisation and superficiality, arguments and messages with such a background reach modern consumers' perceptions and emotional spheres; thus, this creates an excellent ground for the use of simplified, transparent, and easily understandable messages, which brings our considerations to the tracks that consider the concept of kitsch (Mróz 2015).

Justification of kitsch in merchandising

General comments on kitsch in merchandising

In this chapter, we consider kitsch in terms of selected social attributes of the phenomenon that favour its use in marketing activities. In particular, we will address aspects related to the form, type, and level of communication messages designed to induce audiences to undertake certain behaviours in the commercial sphere. Marketers' activities are predominantly persuasive, and the content and images shown are intended to demonstrate the positive elements of the offer on display. Kitsch can confidently be considered a critical component of mass consumer culture. It appeals to a sense of identity and belonging to a specific environment through shared cultural or aesthetic values. From this perspective, kitsch can be seen as a business response to the demands and expectations of mass culture and industrialisation (Botz-Bornstein 2015).

In considering the role and application of kitsch in merchandising, we should begin by contrasting the basic distinction between art (in which the concept of kitsch was born) and business. The former is about beauty and aesthetic qualities, expression and creative imagination, and the pursuit of truth. In the second case, and more specifically in merchandising, these attributes are intricately linked to the quest for the commodification of the creations offered in the form of products, goods, or services (Szostak 2021).

Kitsch undoubtedly aligns more closely with the domain of commercialisation than with cultural values. Thus, kitsch in merchandising can be defined as supporting the marketing and sale of products by appealing to consumers' needs to echo positive emotional messages and their sentimentality. There is no doubt that kitsch is an approach used massively and widely in merchandising. Therefore, one can logically ask the reason for such a massive use of low solutions in merchandising. Two main justifications emerge. The first one may proclaim that kitsch as a tool of marketing messages effectively meets the expectations of the field and enables the realisation of business objectives. The second explanation concerns the creators' lack of ambition and low competence in such messages. It is also possible to pose a thesis that precisely because of the effectiveness mentioned above, marketers do not force themselves on artistically sublime solutions but use simple, sometimes trivial solutions (Szostak 2021).

The deeper reason for such extensive use of kitsch in this field is to be found in merchandising properties. As mentioned above, merchandising is a field of business activity that pursues specific marketing objectives by influencing buyers in retail and service establishments. So, like other fields, merchandising must be subject to certain criteria specific to business activity. This includes such benchmarks as 1) effectiveness (in the sense of conformity to the result of the actions taken with the intention), 2) calculability (emphasis on the achievement of measurable objectives), 3) predictability (the reality of achieving the objectives set), and 4) control (determination of whether and to what extent the set goals have been achieved) (Szostak 2021).

Realising these objectives is even more critical because merchandising activities must be treated as a form of business investment, with specific assumed results and effective allocation of the spent funds. These goals can only be realised if buyers' reactions are positive, that is, in line with marketers' expectations. Kitsch is often applied in marketing strategies, acting as a tool for branding and consumer engagement. It is used to create and manipulate cultural and social values. These marketing strategies benefit from the emotional involvement and straightforward message recognition kitsch usually provides, ultimately making products more appealing to a broader audience. It plays a significant role in merchandising, as it refers to mass culture, which most people understand and, therefore, potential buyers. The ability of kitsch to quickly produce positive emotional states and buyer moods undoubtedly results in augmented product appeal and increased sales (Liddell 2023).

Business background of utilisation of kitsch in merchandising

When analysing the use of kitsch elements in merchandising, relying on two main criteria is necessary. Firstly, the marketing rationale behind utilising these elements and defining the business objectives they aim to accomplish. The second criterion is the characteristics of the addressees of these merchandising content and message forms. Thus, this includes factors such as buyers' expectations of these content and message forms and their ability to perceive and understand.

Considering business objectives, merchandising is entirely different from art, in which the concept of kitsch first appeared and was described in depth. In art, preference is given to the beauty, point of view, or sensitivity of the creator without prioritising the reach of public reception and the understanding of these messages by the public. On the other hand, merchandising is not about achieving such artistic goals in which the pursuit of beauty dominates. On the contrary, it is precisely about reaching a mass audience or buyers belonging to strictly defined target groups. Kitsch is persuasive by design, meaning that its function is to convince the recipients of the message to take a particular action rather than to create beauty (Dąbrowska 2019). Realisation of sales goals is facilitated by the ability of kitsch to immediately engage consumers, often taking advantage of their instinctive or impulsive reactions. It is no coincidence, therefore, that behaviour in the form of kitsch in art emerged along with the desire of some artists to achieve more significant sales effects, often at the expense of critical acclaim for artistic merit within the realm of 'high culture'.

Merchandising activities are intended to induce the addressees of these messages to behave appropriately in the market, and therefore, content should be created that will further such stated goals. The messages communicated must, therefore, meet the audience's expectations and not fulfil the ambitions of the creators of these messages, as is the art case. Hence, the message must be either universal and unanimously understood or tailored to customers' perception from specific target segments, such as residents of a selected region. Therefore, it is advisable to create a grouping of buyers that considers the criterion of their attitude to kitsch in the commercial environment:

(a) buyers who are simply unaware of what kitsch is, and this does not negatively affect their purchasing decisions. If they knew what kitsch was, they would likely reject this form of communication;
(b) buyers who understand what kitsch is but allow for the possibility of such methods in commerce and do not mind making purchases. They approach such activities with detachment and do not expect a higher aesthetic experience in the retail space;
(c) buyers who know what kitsch is but still like it. They have an ironic attitude to it but accept it and even play with it (usually in contexts foreign to kitsch);
(d) buyers who believe that the concept of kitsch is irrelevant; it is a subjective construct that does not relate to any 'reality'. Therefore, they are indifferent to kitsch, which does not affect their purchasing decisions;
(e) buyers who know what kitsch is and do not accept it. They treat such solutions as a low-level message, negatively affecting their purchasing decisions (Botz-Bornstein 2015).

The grouping considered such factors as education level, aesthetic sensitivity, expectations of retail spaces, and general attitude to shopping. Dividing buyers in this way suggests that most consumers either accept kitsch in the retail environment or have an indifferent attitude towards it (Botz-Bornstein 2015). As a result, the messages and communications in merchandising essentially have the characteristics of kitsch, as they are pleasant, warm, pleasant, and unproblematic. This is because traders create a positive atmosphere to generate positive emotions among customers, which promotes their purchasing decisions.

The commercial nature of merchandising favours the use of kitsch

Given the generally cheerful outlook of consumers towards kitsch in commercial spaces, a commercial approach is dominant in the actions of merchants. This is due to the apparent fact that the goods produced and acquired beforehand need to be sold to final buyers. So, it is crucial in commerce to reach buyers en masse and evoke the desire to buy the products on display. Therefore, this business approach regarding the expectation of mass reception is at odds with an ambitious, but hardly understood by buyers, a message with a high artistic level. It is, therefore, essential to note the clear difference between art having an individual character and commercial business having a mass character.

Theoretically, the optimal solution would be to achieve the established marketing goals with a high artistic and aesthetic level of the offered products. Here, however, the question arises about the tastes and preferences of mass consumers, that is, are they high or relatively low? The answer here is unambiguous: the lower the artistic level of the products – the greater the number of interested customers, and the higher the level – the number of customers decreases (and the price of such products and costs of promotional campaigns increase).

Also of significance is the criterion of message effectiveness in merchandising, given the growing pace of life. This applies to the lifestyles of modern consumers as well as conducting business. Therefore, the messages conveyed to buyers must meet the criterion of effectiveness, that is, be concise, understandable, and uncomplicated (Szostak & Sułkowski 2020). Nor do retail spaces serve people's expectations of advanced aesthetic or artistic experiences. As a result, merchandising counts on solutions that appeal to popular tastes. The aim is to ensure that the creations in this area can relate the audience to their everyday experiences and acceptable values and symbols. Effective, therefore, are messages that are comprehensible, clear, and preferably evoke positive emotional attitudes among buyers (Ortlieb 2018).

As a specific form of influencing audiences, kitsch corresponds very well with the merchandising criteria. In its genesis, it has the character of a commercial activity, that is, calculated to produce sales effects. This attribute becomes even more important in the modern economy, where the fundamental challenge is to sell products, not to make them. Kitsch, because of the outreach of its message, hits the tastes of mass buyers and, therefore, supports sales, which is the final phase of business activity. In turn, an adequate, that is, following the plan, sales scale is a prerequisite for the return on investments made. To summarise, the free-market economy needs kitsch, regardless of assessing such messages' aesthetic or artistic value (Steinvorth 2016). In merchandising, kitsch creates attractive, simplified narratives that address mass buyers – in these activities, simplified common cultural, national, or regional symbols. This creates emotional and social ties and a sense of belonging, all to effectively promote and sell products.

Features of kitsch favourable or unfavourable within merchandising

There are many characteristics of kitsch that, in a general sense, trigger such widespread and massive use of it in merchandising. After the above considerations, it is important to note two explicit essential attributes of kitsch: the mass reach of these communication messages and their effectiveness in grasping the consciousness and emotional spheres of the audience. Thus, given the context of the application of such solutions in merchandising, we can consider such attributes of kitsch as follows:

- It simplifies realities.
- It uses messages that mass audiences can understand.
- It distorts the perception of reality.
- It effortlessly evokes emotions.
- It uses positive content and avoids controversy and conflict.
- It promises a happy conclusion.
- It appeals to popular or low tastes.
- It relies on fundamentalism, understood as unambiguous, shovel-like, and not accepting nuances.
- It restricts rationality and a fuller/broader understanding of the topics addressed.
- It avoids or suppresses unpleasant or disturbing aspects of reality.
- It uses a one-dimensional interpretation devoid of ambiguity.
- It gives up 'beauty' in favour of 'niceness'.
- It does not require intellectual effort to understand messages.
- It is geared towards immediately satisfying the desires and needs of the audience.
- It appeals to universally acceptable values.
- It focuses on symbols and values preferred by specific groups.
- It excludes messages and content that are fundamentally unacceptable in human life (Szostak & Sułkowski 2020).

In conclusion, the positive factors that justify using kitsch in merchandising and the factors that cause it to be viewed negatively include the following:

- The concept of kitsch is fluid and ambiguous: for some, something is kitsch, and for others, it is not.
- Simple, understandable messages do not necessarily automatically equate with kitsch because of their simplicity.
- The rationale/ground of merchandising activities is to achieve marketing goals.
- Merchandising's goal is not to promote beauty or pursue the truth.
- People usually know merchandising is a creation, so it should be treated as storytelling and does not necessarily reflect reality.

- It evokes positive emotions, and yet people want their emotions evoked.
- Kitsch is an effective tool for simplifying complex narratives.
- It promotes branding and identity formation in a rapidly changing market and vulnerable.
- Kitsch can be original, different, and creative.
- It promotes the development of pictorial visual messages.

The negative factors of kitsch in merchandising may include the following:

- Kitsch creates a distorted image of reality, which creates the risk of literal misrepresentation by uninformed buyers.
- It perpetuates low culture and tastes that are dominated by superficiality and infantility.
- It may mislead buyers about the products' characteristics, which marketers present in an often idealised manner.
- It lowers consumers' capacity for individual perception and evaluation; instead, it seeks to unify the perception of messages.

Particular attention should be paid to the threat of misleading customers. In some instances, merchandising presents creations that leverage widely accepted values to further their commercial objectives. An example is religious holidays, such as Christmas, which appear in retail spaces in the form of various symbols as early as the beginning of October.

However, the assessment boundary in this regard is set by buyers' perception in the context of their awareness of pseudo-artistic merchandising works. After all, if buyers know that the message they are confronted with in the retail space is a creation and not a reflection of reality, marketers cannot be accused of misleading customers in such a situation. After all, on the same principle, one could accuse actors of playing the role of a character, which they are not, after all, instead of presenting themselves (Ortlieb 2018).

Kitsch brings only positive content to merchandising

Kitsch in merchandising enters the realm of embellishing, polishing, and showing everything in its best possible form. It uses a simplified form that potential customers quickly understand. Moreover, the hallmark of kitsch in the sales space is a clear, expressive message that leaves no room for in-depth personal reflection. This form of communication is aimed at helping viewers in their perception of the world, which is bound to evoke an appropriate emotional state. The message is supposed to fall within the comfort zone of buyers and have a positive tone (Dąbrowska 2019).

From this point of view, kitsch fits perfectly into modern marketing, where the requirement is for messages to be simple, understandable, unambiguous, attractive, and appealing to positive emotions. Regarding business ethics, it should be emphasised that kitsch in marketing is not aimed at creating higher social tastes but at sales. Since this is the case, we cannot present accusations that images in merchandising are too simple and unrealistic. However, we can rate such solutions low in terms of ethics, as these works create unrealistic (not existing in reality) images to make people make certain decisions (Roggeveen et al. 2020).

It is worth considering whether merchandising should include socially essential themes, topics that bother society, or representatives of selected target groups. After all, consumers know that there are such negative phenomena as war atrocities, racism, sexism, social isolation, depression, or anxiety. Addressing such merchandising topics would be an ambitious but precarious approach. It could capture buyers' attention; however, such messages' positive impact on customers' purchasing decisions would be highly questionable. For this reason, most merchandising content and imagery are positive, unproblematic, and simplistic. In contrast, socially essential topics are addressed by companies as part of their environmental, social, and governance (ESG) activities, which can be categorised as public relations. This approach illustrates a company's social sensitivity and environmental commitment and supports the creation of corporate identity and corporate image. However, such initiatives are often conducted at a 'safe distance' from direct sales activities, including merchandising (Liddell 2023).

The conventions of stereotypes do not hamper positive messages in merchandising. This is because they are widely embedded in the consciousness of many consumers, as they help simplify perception and understanding of reality. In addition, these messages affirm the audience in their aesthetic sensibilities, as they perpetuate the belief in the validity of opinions and views taken in this way.

Creating a simplified, artificial, unreal world

Creators of merchandising messages are also keen on using simple, traditional, familiar, close, religious, and conservative clichés, labels, symbols, or signs. Such a communication concept is based on a vision of reality that most consumers understand. Hence, it increases social trust between a bidder of specific products or services and buyers. Since such communication is understandable and effective, trading companies are eager to use it, disregarding the thoughtlessness and excessive simplicity of such content and images.

Marketers are also keen to take advantage of the general inclination of buyers to over-consumerism. Consequently, commercial spaces take on the characteristics of stylised marketable fiction, where many offerings are combined with numerous visual attractions in the artificial realities of shopping malls. It certainly bears the hallmarks of kitsch when shopping and service spaces are dominated by artificial flowers, occasional colourful decorations, Christmas decorations in early October, or hosts dressed as angels roaming the alleys in malls.

Hence, the use of kitsch in merchandising exploits the consumer's longing for an embellished past or an idealised lifestyle. Merchants achieve their goals in a not-so-sublime way, and buyers are happy because it puts them in a good mood, which means a typical win-win situation (Mróz 2015).

Kitsch helps implement the concept of globalisation

Multinational retail corporations are leading the way in creating merchandising messages on a massive scale. They use a twofold concept of product offerings: global and local. The global concept boils down to standardising product or service offerings internationally. On the other hand, the local concept involves tailoring offerings to consumers' specific needs and expectations in individual local markets. In the first case, global merchandising corporations introduce universal solutions to more countries, where mass products displayed in a standardised form gradually displace local products and cultural considerations. In implementing the concept, local and national emblems and symbols, on the other hand, appear to convince buyers of the global corporation's strong ties (or even roots) with the local environment (Szostak 2021).

In this regard, kitsch helps project an image of modernity and international status. Such influence is particularly effective in countries aspiring to prosperity and the so-called Western lifestyle. This taps into the favourable ground of yearnings for the so-called Western world and desires for a better life among broad masses of consumers. In aspiring societies, hiding such messages' unrealistic, sometimes false nature is easier.

Ethical aspects of kitsch in merchandising

In general terms, kitsch in merchandising can indicate a false approach to life, in which the quality of true emotion is impoverished by presenting false feelings. If people believe these messages, then communicative falsehood can permanently and irreversibly lower consumer perception and their ability to distinguish fiction from reality (Levis & Levis 2018). But can the use of kitsch in visual merchandising cause such profound ethical dilemmas? The essence of the issue lies in the attitude of buyers towards images, decoration, or even staging in merchandising. Consumers recognise them as created content, narratives, or fairy tales. A few probably only believe that real angels stroll through the aisles of shopping centres. The same is true of the art of filmmaking, where filmmakers cannot be accused of creating fiction, and actors play the role of people who are not me. The real risk of misleading customers may relate to the exaggerated presentation and display of certain products. So, this is more an issue that falls under advertising and sales promotion than visual merchandising. From this perspective, it can be concluded that consumers tend to consent to this creation and accept it emotionally and rationally.

Creators of kitsch merchandising messages are accused of creating a stylised, inauthentic version of modernity. After all, any creation, regardless of artistic level, is a stylised and inauthentic version of reality. Therefore, if consumers are aware of this, the message should not mislead them into buying. Hence, accusations of this type are difficult to accept. The real risk of misleading customers may relate to the exaggerated presentation and display of certain products. So, this is more an issue that falls under advertising and sales promotion than visual merchandising.

Nevertheless, using photographic techniques, image manipulation, or depicting ideal human silhouettes can cause buyers to have excessively unrealistic expectations of the products they buy in such an environment. Consequently, this leads to negative phenomena such as buying products that do not meet expectations, falling into complexes, or denying self-esteem. This happens when buyers are unaware of the idealisation of images in merchandising and treat these messages in a realistic form (Borgerson & Schroeder 2005).

Another ethical dilemma is the creation of an exaggerated brand identity, which is then linked to emotional expectations on the part of buyers. Vulnerable to the influence of merchandising, they are inclined to attach personal attributes to their chosen brands, which creates what they believe is an illusory two-way bond between buyer and brand. Consequently, some consumers do not realise that brand identity is a creation which applies to any images and content posted in the retail space (Kerfoot et al. 2003).

Still to be finally resolved is whether created messages and images relate to specific customers' real needs and expectations or whether they already entered the ground of manipulation. Kitsch in merchandising can be ethically acceptable if it simplifies, facilitates decision-making, and evokes positive emotions; however, it cannot unambiguously mislead customers. Meanwhile, manipulation should be understood as creating a false message, misleading the recipients, and misunderstanding due to hidden forms of influencing people, including subliminal actions. This issue usually concerns consumers with a lower level of consciousness and do not know that a message corresponding to their everyday language and values is just kitsch (Botz-Bornstein 2015).

There is no doubt that kitsch in sales areas creates consumer perception and behaviour. Many researchers emphasise the degrading nature of kitsch due to the formation of unsophisticated tastes, evaluations, and behaviours. However, managers cannot be expected to have higher social goals in their strict business activities, including sales and merchandising, such as promoting a higher culture. Such activities are essential in shaping the company's image; hence, they are part of PR activities. Therefore, social business responsibility activities can be conducted parallel with using kitsch solutions in sales and marketing activities. Due to the need to maintain image consistency, companies should be wary of evidently misleading customers or using unfair promotional practices. However, it should be emphasised that the ethical aspects of using kitsch in merchandising require further in-depth research.

Conclusions

In this part, answers to the research questions are presented. Thus, the first issue related to the categorisation of kitsch in merchandising. It is necessary to clearly state that merchandising is not classified as a field of art. Hence, concepts related to artistic aesthetics and artistic level cannot be introduced directly into marketing because this area is not about promoting high artistic values. Marketing (including merchandising as a field of marketing) boils down to the realisation of goals bound to satisfy the needs and expectations of buyers (sometimes creating the desires). From this point of view, art and merchandising are composed of two disciplines that rarely go together. Therefore, it can be said that the goals set by art (of higher culture) are qualitative, and the goals set by merchandising are quantitative (of common aesthetic taste).

The task of merchandising specialists is not to educate buyers to receive advanced quality content or to shape and promote a higher culture. This realm is about achieving purely commercial goals, and the selection of tools used must be optimal from the point of view of the bidder's needs. As a result, merchandising operations must be attractive, acceptable, and understandable to most target buyers; hence, the tools that fall under the concept of kitsch are so widely used.

In art, the concept of kitsch simultaneously eludes precise definitions. After all, artistic value and beauty are judged by specific tastes, and the concept of universal absolute beauty does not exist. It is even more difficult to unambiguously determine in merchandising, a sphere far from art, whether a given creation is kitsch or a simple but valuable message. On the other hand – given the marketing goals of merchandising – judging whether something is kitsch is of little importance in this sphere. Far more important is the question of the impact of these activities on shoppers, their level of acceptance of such visual forms of communication, and the emotions they provide, which altogether boils down to effectiveness in achieving the designated marketing and sales goals. Certainly, the low level of many store displays is not the fault of a simplistic positive approach, which can be described as kitsch. Instead, it results from a lack of creativity or basic skills among marketers. Such competence deficiencies lead to duplicating solutions already in use or being observed by competitors.

The second research question concerns the reasons and justification for using kitsch-like solutions in merchandising. The primary purpose of merchandising activities is to achieve goals and objectives of a marketing nature. It is primarily about increasing sales but also about increasing customer loyalty, implementing new products, and changing the product mix. To achieve these goals, all necessary merchandising methods and means are used, and activities of a kitsch nature perfectly meet most buyers' expectations. This applies to the messages' straightforwardness, comprehensibility, simplified emotional impact, and taking up only (or primarily) positive themes while avoiding controversy or complex topics. Thus, what in the arts can be grounds for deep criticism (e.g. commercialisation, commoditisation) becomes an advantage in the commercial sphere. In this sense, kitsch is appreciated by both producers (bidders) and consumers (buyers).

In the real world, there are phenomena of both positive and negative nature. Therefore, it is possible to put forward the thesis that a more advanced approach would be advisable to present complicated issues, especially when they are part of the social fabric. This would be even more justifiable given that companies must be socially and environmentally engaged in modern realities. Merchandising, however, is not the right area for advanced content and social messages of a problematic nature. On the contrary, it appears that marketers are minimising the presentation of such messages in the sales sphere. This is due to the belief that consumers expect straightforward, unproblematic content that evokes positive emotions.

We can distinguish between two types of kitsch: common kitsch, which tends towards universality, and uplifting kitsch, which is rooted, symbol-centred, and emotionally linked to the values of a specific group. Similarly, in merchandising, kitsch is based either on universal messages or the values of a specific group, that is, messages with local content. Local cultures and education determine the profile of these groupings. ‘Common understanding’ is not a misnomer because kitsch is not merely an art-theoretical term but is also used by some people in everyday language. It is possible to be familiar with the phenomenon of kitsch without knowing the term, for example, by calling such phenomena ‘tacky’ (Botz-Bornstein 2015).

The third research question regards the extent to which the use of kitsch in the commercial sphere meets consumers’ expectations. The effectiveness and efficiency of merchandising activities depend on potential buyers’ understanding and acceptance of these creations. Most are not higher art consumers and do not expect to perceive complex, complicated or sublime messages in the commercial space. Simplified communication that is unambiguous and in line with the mentality and mindset of buyers is much more preferred (Jauhari & Upadhyay 2015). In today’s consumer society, which strives to purchase goods and services, the expectation of simple, understandable, and sometimes even infantile solutions prevails. This is also the nature of merchandising communication, and the concept of kitsch perfectly meets this requirement.

Modern society is increasingly shaped by online content and mass media. The overabundance of information and promotional stimuli makes consumers increasingly prefer short messages. Moreover, the ease of assimilation makes communication in visual rather than textual form more dynamic in the public sphere. These trends favour the creation of simple pictorial messages in merchandising, which in many cases have the character of kitsch (Park 2015). The widespread use of kitsch in merchandising somehow automatically excludes anything unacceptable in human existence. All messages must, therefore, be pleasant, warm, and seamless, as the idea is to create a positive atmosphere to generate optimistic emotions in customers, which is conducive to their purchasing decisions (Szostak & Sułkowski 2020).

In evaluating simplistic merchandising activities, a distinction must be made between favouring this form of satisfying buyers' needs and expectations and manipulating their perceptions and emotions. A critical issue, however, is the perception by buyers of these activities as a form of creation rather than an unambiguous message of information. After all, no one believes that a person dressed as Santa Claus is the authentic Santa Claus or that a host dressed as an angel is an angel who appeared on Earth. Despite their low-key kitsch, such activities need not be judged as misleading to customers if they do not present an unrealistic image of the products or services offered. Such activities, however, are more in the domain of advertising than merchandising.

Kitsch in merchandising fulfils the requirements for the tools used in merchandising to a significant extent. First, it facilitates the sales and marketing objectives set for marketers. Kitsch also fits in with the expectations of modern consumers, most of whom prefer simple, straightforward, and easily understandable messages. At the level of aesthetic feelings, a sizeable proportion of buyers have either a positive or neutral attitude towards colourful messages that evoke emotions in a simplistic but usually positive way. Despite the many qualities of kitsch that foster customer relations in the retail space, negative phenomena in this respect can also be seen. It relates to the possibility of misleading customers through creations in merchandising, which shape an often unrealistic reflection of reality and can be perceived by buyers.

Several limitations emerged while working on this chapter due to the very modest number of studies dealing with the issue of kitsch in merchandising. Moreover, there is still a lack of broader studies treating kitsch in the field of management since – so far – kitsch has been analysed far more in aesthetic and artistic terms than in business terms, that is, in business activities. Consequently, there is a lack of elaborate theories on using kitsch in merchandising that can be referred to and verified.

Difficulties also arose when identifying the positive and negative aspects of using kitsch in merchandising. This is related to the necessity of adopting specific evaluation criteria, including consideration of the business objectives of the merchandising companies, the good and the extent to which customer expectations are met, or, in general, the aesthetic aspects of the influence on buyers' perception. It is also exceedingly difficult to undertake analyses of a quantitative nature since the recipients of merchandising messages are millions of buyers who are equal in terms of consumer awareness and knowledge, level of perception, sensitivity, social and cultural factors, and other aspects.

The above limitations provide opportunities and prospects for further research and analysis in this area. Through the study of shopper behaviour, experimental and quantitative research, and qualitative and quantitative modelling, it will be possible to create new theories in this research field. Such perspectives for further research can be mentioned as 1) objective criteria for the quality of communication messages in merchandising; 2) consumers' attitudes towards kitsch messages in retail spaces; and 3) the impact of kitsch messages in merchandising on customers' purchasing decisions.

References

Ambrogi D. (2023), *Comprehensive Guide to Retail Merchandising*, CGS, New York.

Borgerson J.L., Schroeder J. (2005), *Identity in Marketing Communications*, Oxford University Press, Oxford.

Botz-Bornstein T. (2015), *Kitsch and Bullshit*, Johns Hopkins University Press, Baltimore, 306–307.

Buttle F. (2014), Merchandising, *European Journal of Marketing*, Leeds, United Kingdom, 111.

Dąbrowska D. (2019), *On the Relationship of Kitsch and Persuasion, Cultural Studies Appendix – English Issue 2019/1*, 99–100.

Jauhari S., Upadhyay A. (2015), Visual merchandising: An integrative review, *Indian Journal of Applied Research* 7(4), Ahmedabad, India, 356–359.

Kerfoot S. Davies B., Ward P. (2003), Visual merchandising and the creation of discernible retail brands, *International Journal of Retail & Distribution Management* 31(3), 143–152.

Kim I. (2003), *College Students' Apparel Impulse Buying Behaviors in Relation to Visual Merchandising*, The University of Georgia, Athens.

Levis A., Levis S. (2018), Rhetoric of kitsch in the post-truth era: Media, literature & cultural studies, *International Journal of Social Sciences* 4(1), Rajasthan, India, 341.

Liddell N. (2023), Branding's enduring, unhealthy relationship with kitsch, *Brandingmag, Woking*, Surrey. Online. https://www.brandingmag.com/nick-liddell/brandings-enduring-unhealthy-relationship-with-kitsch/

Morgan T. (2016), *Visual Merchandising*, Laurence King Publishing, London.

Mróz B. (2015), Everything for sale? The pitfalls and the maneuvers of consumerism, *Psychologia Ekonomiczna* 7(2015), Kraków, Poland, 25–36.

Nowogródzka T. (2010), Merchandising as an effective trade marketing technique, *Zeszyty Naukowe Polityki Europejskie, Finanse i Marketing* 3(52), Warszawa, Poland.

Ortlieb S.A. (2018), *Kitsch and Perception: Towards a New 'Aesthetic from Below'*, Brill, Leiden, The Netherlands, 10–24.

Park H., Sullivan P. (2015), How does visual merchandising in fashion retail stores affect consumers' brand attitude and purchase intention, *The International Review of Retail*, Distribution and Consumer Research, London.

Roggeveen A.L., Grevol D. (and others). (2020), Forging meaningful consumer-brand relationships through creative merchandise offerings and innovative merchandising strategies, *Journal of Retailing* 97(1), 81–98.

Steinvorth U. (2016), *Pride and Authenticity*, Palgrave Macmillan, Cham and London, 207–215.

Szostak M., Sułkowski Ł. (2020), Kitsch in management: Characteristic forms, carriers and propagators, *International Business Information Management Association*, King of Prussia.

Varley R. (2001), *Retail Product Management. Buying and Merchandising*, Routledge, London.

Villanova D. (and others). (2021), Retailer marketing communications in the digital age: Getting the right message to the right shopper at the right time, *Journal of Retailing* 97(1), 116–132.

7 Kitsch in advertising

A field of postmodern market communication battle

Andrzej Kisielewski

Introduction

This chapter looks at advertising differently from what is usually accepted in the literature devoted to it, referred to below. It is devoted to the phenomenon of kitsch, which, as is commonly believed, is most often an affliction of the most primitive advertisements. We are, however, interested in the most sophisticated advertising, and these remarks are an attempt to reflect on the presence of kitsch only in some of its examples – some very well-known examples, considered to be a permanent element of advertising history, awarded and admired not only by the representatives of the advertising industry. These examples testify to advertising appropriating the language of modern art, which at its beginnings tried to defend itself against bourgeois kitsch and which was to facilitate aesthetic experience in opposition to the experience of kitsch (Szostak, Sułkowski 2020; Szostak 2021, 2023). Analysis of these examples is meant to help in answering the question of whether advertising that feeds on the means of that defence allows its recipients to experience artistry or, on the contrary, forces them to experience kitsch. Is it justified to claim that if an advertisement appropriating the codes of modern art does not defend or at least try to defend itself against kitsch, it is condemned to it? In that case, is the experience of kitsch a mark of late modernity?

As an aesthetic category, kitsch is compared to art, and while it is located "low" and seen as something despicable, art is seen as a phenomenon placed "high" and worthy of respect and admiration – the opposite of kitsch. Such unequivocal opposition, however, becomes problematic when highly positioned art feeds on kitsch and appropriates its poetics. Does art then become kitsch, or does it just take on the characteristics of kitsch without ceasing to be art? Will kitsch thus become art by taking on its features? We will look at such problems from a specific advertising perspective. At this point, it should be noted that art institutions generally defend themselves against advertising. One example is the collection of one of the world's most serious collectors of modern art, Charles Saatchi, founder and long-term co-owner of the Saatchi & Saatchi advertising agency, who does not have a single advertisement in his collection – even one produced by his agency (Davidson 1992: 199).

DOI: 10.4324/9781003504931-8

Literature review

The academic view of advertising

In academic literature, advertising is most often assessed negatively and is situated in the context of modern cultural phenomena, such as mass production, the dominance of economics, and consumerism. This view is illustrated by classic studies of the topic by, among others, the American media and culture historian Stuart Even (Ewen 1976), social psychologist and sociologist Erving Goffman (Goffman 1979), sociologist Roland Berman (Berman 1981), media sociologist Michael Schudson (Schudson 1984), media expert Sut Jhally (Jhally 1987), sociologist Andrew Wernick (Wernick 1992), media expert Martin P. Davidson (Davidson 1992) or political scientist William Leiss, artist Stephen Kline, the media mentioned above expert Sut Jhally and media expert Jacqueline Botterill (Leiss, Kline, Jhally, Botterill 2005). Similarly, examples of critical reflection on advertising include the best-selling books by journalists Vance Packard (Packard 1957) and Naomi Klein (Klein 2005), as well as works in the field of modern culture theory, including by the economist John Galbraith (Galbraith 1958, 1967) or philosophers representing the Frankfurt School – Theodor W. Adorno and Max Horkheimer (Adorno, Horkheimer 1993 [1947]), Herbert Marcuse (Marcuse 1991 [1964]), and Jürgen Habermas (Habermas 2008).

While the assessment of the economic, social, and cultural role of advertising is generally polarised, the assessment of its aesthetic layer and the sense contained therein is usually consistent. Among other things, it was referred to as licensed pornography. It was seen as a testimony to the corruption of art or kitsch pretending to be art and called capitalist realism, comparing it with the despised socialist realism (Schudson 1984: 209). For example, the literary scholar and art historian William J. T. Mitchell paraphrased these assessments, ironically saying that images serving low, commercial purposes that are persuasive "constitute a dump of wretched value, commodity fetishism, mass hysteria, and primitive superstition". Art, on the other hand, as he emphasised, is "a repository of civilised values, an image redeemed for critical contemplation" (Mitchell 2013: 126).[1] However, attempts were made to look at advertising without prejudice, though usually distancing oneself from it somewhat. One of the first examples of such a view is found in *Mythologies* by Roland Barthes (Barthes 1991 [1957]), who saw advertising as a prominent element of modernity, illustrating the phenomenon of "myth theft" he was describing. In 1961, the British cultural theorist Raymond Williams provocatively called advertising a "magical system" because – as he wrote – it was a kind of magic that allowed the transformation of mass-produced and banal products into magical signs that create an imaginary and thus unreal world (Williams 1999 [1961]). Paul Rutherford, a Canadian media scholar a diligent researcher of television advertising, also tried to treat it without prejudice – as if it were art, although he stipulated that, in his opinion, it was "the art of our time" and that it was only incidentally artistic (Rutherford 1995: 5). However, Rutherford did not analyse advertisements as works of art, but as more or less creative marketing messages.

Nevertheless, it has often been claimed that, although advertising does not represent high art, it is still a testimony to art – albeit usually with the caveat that this is mass or popular art or the art of advertising. For example, in his book *Pragmatist Aesthetics*, Richard Shusterman, a representative of American neo-pragmatism, postulated appreciating the products of popular culture as full-fledged works of art (Shusterman 1998). He was critical of the treatment of art as a kind of philosophy, which was advocated, among others, by the art critic and theoretician Arthur Danto, whom I refer to in this chapter (Danto 2016). The creators of advertisements understood them more unequivocally. William Bernbach, a co-founder of the legendary New York agency Doyle Dane Bernbach, arguing with supporters of treating the process of creating advertising in an almost scientific way, stated in 1953 that "advertising is persuasion, and persuasion is not a science, but an art. Advertising is the art of persuasion" (Fox 1990: 251).

The subject of advertising, as already mentioned, usually appears in academic reflection in the context of criticism of mass culture, over time referred to as popular culture, which was usually seen as a tool of commercial persuasion on an equal footing with advertising. This is how Clement Greenberg portrayed mass culture in his famous text, *Avant-Garde and Kitsch*. Theodor W. Adorno and Max Horkheimer saw *die Kulturindustrie*, analysed in their famous *Dialectic of the Enlightenment*, as a complex advertising system. Similar assumptions about mass culture can be found in Herbert Marcuse's analysis of the "one-dimensional man". This perception of popular culture appears in the now classic reflections of the well-known American mass culture critic Dwight Macdonald. Finally, one can recall similar assessments found in the texts of Jean Baudrillard and Jürgen Habermas. In critical reflection devoted to modern culture, there is also the problem of the dominance of the consumerism pattern, accompanied by the problem of commercial images.

It follows from these comments that the problem of kitsch in advertising is not limited to advertising itself but leads to considerations of its role in modern culture, which is often said to be the culture of the media. When using this category to describe modernity, it is worth remembering that advertising is the economic basis of the media, that popular culture is primarily based on it, as it plays the role of advertising, and that advertising itself is an element of popular culture. Therefore, the problem of kitsch and the experience thereof seems to be inscribed in the model of modernity understood as the state of culture.

Modern art as an antithesis of kitsch

From the onset of its existence, modern advertising has treated art as a source of inspiration, as a kind of laboratory. Therefore, it appropriated the solutions developed in art, above all formal ones – those relating to composing an image, juxtaposing colours, and typographic solutions. The avant-garde art of the first half of the 20th century was, in the opinion of, among others, art theorist Peter Bürger (Bürger 1984 [1974]), an attempt to negate the bourgeois institution of art, but – taking into account its social involvement and thus the idea of transforming the world in the name of art – it was also a tool for attacking bourgeois culture, including bourgeois artistic culture, of which kitsch was a dominant feature. How and under what circumstances did the average inhabitant of a city of the first half of the 20th century – after all, it was there that various avant-garde art trends were born – experience kitsch? Testimonies of bourgeois aesthetic preferences, which the avant-garde artists tried to resist, were described in 1934 by Stanisław Machniewicz, a Polish educator, journalist, and aesthetician, and an apologist of modern art, who lived in Lviv – then located within the borders of the Polish state (today this city belongs to Ukraine):

> [G]reat cities in which we still live today, full of splendour, but false, full of wealth, but pretend, and full of stylish ugliness, this one true. The interiors of houses and apartments were equipped fittingly for their external appearance. Here, too, the imitative style mania prevailed. Living rooms imitating Renaissance chambers were filled with furniture and established stylistic features. Certain types and patterns come up in this respect. The dining room was most eagerly and most often decorated with furniture in the style of the German Renaissance; the living rooms took on the rococo or empire style, while bedrooms in a lighter, and therefore mostly rococo, style were preferred. All this, however, was factory-made furniture, mass-produced, shoddy, unoriginal, and made of poor materials but pretentiously decorated, full of the most unnecessary accessories, ornaments, and often the most unlikely ideas and constructions. Walls were commonly decorated with paintings imitating the authentic works of old masters, but also usually in the form of mechanical prints. On tables and shelves of all kinds, sizes, and styles, there were all kinds of bottles, figurines, boxes, and other trifles, sometimes quirky items for very indiscriminate tastes, but factory-made, cast from poor, shoddy, only seemingly spectacular materials, and always ugly and meaningless. To all this weirdness would be added a huge number of various carpets, draperies, rugs, covers, and other favourite ornaments, and only then would we have a complete picture of the average apartment from three or four decades ago. Everything there was pretend. The splendour of paper velvets, odd, printed or factory embroidered tapestries, machine-made lace, plaster, cast bronze, or pressed tin figurines, paper-mâché suits of armour; in a word, a collection of the shoddiest forgeries in material, form, and decoration.
>
> (Machniewicz 1934: 158–161)

The aesthetic preferences described by Machniewicz inevitably found an outlet in advertising, which had to take them into account in order to influence its recipients effectively. The aesthetics of advertising could not deviate from the aesthetics of the promoted products. Avant-garde artists tried to oppose bourgeois kitsch in various ways. For this purpose, the Cubists denied the idea of the illusion of three-dimensional space on a two-dimensional plane of the painting, which had been developed already in the Renaissance. This caused a cascade of transformations in European art, primarily resulting in the breaking of stereotypical ideas about the form of a work of art (Rosenblum 2001 [1960]: 31–66). Inspired by cubism and opposing bourgeois concepts of art and traditional ideas about the form of a work of art, the Dadaists – recognised by Bürger as the group constituting the core of the avant-garde movement – proposed humour and blasphemy as a permanent element of their work. Futurists cultivated in their work the idea of an anti-bourgeois, better-designed future, which was determined by crowds of workers, urban agglomeration, and industrialisation. Based on the concepts of Sigmund Freud, the surrealists proposed a fascination with the subconscious and the transformation of bourgeois society in the name of art. They promoted an aesthetic based on free associations, on the release of the subconscious, which was the basis for reconstructing the bourgeois reality and freeing its average representative from all of its oppressions.

Bürger opposed associating avant-garde art with the phenomena representing the broadly understood trend of constructivism, often referred to as modernism. Nevertheless, the artists associated with it also opposed the bourgeois aesthetics, trying to create a new aesthetic of everyday life adequate to progressing industrialisation. It was to form the basis for creating a new, better-arranged, happier future – in the name of art. This idea guided Russian artists, including Kazimir Malevich and Alexander Rodchenko. This assumption was also the ideological basis of the Bauhaus, the first university educating artists to work for industry – among others, as architects or designers of mass-produced products, including advertisements – and to use its potential to promote modern aesthetics, reflecting the spirit of industrialisation. Similar goals were pursued by artists from the "De Stijl" magazine, who, acting in architecture, industrial design, and applied graphics, also tried to transform the aesthetics of everyday life – their models included the paintings of Piet Mondrian and Theo van Doesburg.

Instead of the bourgeois iconosphere dominated by kitsch, the constructivists proposed the purity and elegance of modern forms, which are a sign of rationality and functionality at the same time, an aura of modernity and uniqueness, and an almost industrial order obtained through them. All these artists dissected the tradition of European art in their work. All of them were also involved in the world of advertising, whether for purely artistic or purely economic reasons (Kisielewski 1999). However, these relationships were mutual because just as the avant-garde artists and modernism noticed the world of advertising, the latter perceived modern art as a source of inspiration that significantly increased its persuasive power. This initiated the process of diluting the – mainly formal – achievements of modernist and avant-garde art, which, so far, is considered to be elite in commercial visual culture, of which ubiquitous advertising has become the most visible representation.

The combination of "high" art with strictly commercial activity is evidenced by graphic designs of the dadaist Kurt Schwitters and constructivist El Lissitzky, developed in the 1920s in Hannover, among others, at the request of Pelikan, a well-known manufacturer of stationery. Salvador Dali and his famous designs for the windows of the New York department store Bonwit Teller created in 1939 should be mentioned here, as well as René Magritte and his arrangements of shop displays, which very often resembled the world of his surrealist paintings, just as they, in turn, had a lot in common with the shop displays he arranged. An example of combining art with commercial goals is the work of Man Ray, who for many years worked as a photographer for the Parisian magazine "Vogue", and of the fashion designer Jacques Doucet. Another well-known example is the advertisements designed by Fortunato Depero in 1925–1927 for the manufacturer of the Campari drink; the artist used the poetics of futurism. The obviousness of advertising as an attribute of modernity was noticed in the Bauhaus, where an advertising studio was opened in 1926 to expand the study programme. Some examples of such recognition were, among others, the advertisements created by the company of Alexander Rodchenko and Vladimir Mayakovsky in Russia in the 1920s.

At this point, we can start a discussion with Clement Greenberg, who, in his well-known text about avant-garde and kitsch from 1934, definitely placed the former in opposition to kitsch. What he understood as avant-garde, however, as testified by his later writings, was precisely modernist art. Moreover, the alternative to the avant-garde was to recall Greenberg's central thesis, precisely kitsch. However, the American critic did not notice that long before he began to prepare his text, the language of avant-garde art and modernism began to be captured by the cultural industry, primarily in advertising. Therefore, the antagonism between avant-garde art and kitsch does not seem unambiguous and obvious.

The advertising industry notices modern art

The concepts proposed by European representatives of various trends in modern art were first noticed by French advertising and later by the advertising industry in the United States. In the 1920s, the discussion about modernism and its usefulness in commercial persuasion began with the magazine "Printers Ink" (McComb 2005: 75). It emphasised the usefulness of the solutions developed by modern art, especially in advertising luxury articles. Art lent them an aura of elegance and modernity. The visual codes of modernist art used in advertising allowed for the transformation of the goods shown in it into symbols of belonging to a higher social class, attributes of luxury or, among others, into determinants of elegance. In 1925, the magazine "Printers Ink Monthly" wrote about two functions of modern art in advertising. One consisted of showcasing the product's currentness and uniqueness, which became a crucial persuasive element in encouraging customers to buy the product. The other consisted of greater effectiveness in attracting the consumers' attention and thus encouraging them to take an interest in the advertisement and the message (McComb 2005: 75).

In the United States, Earnest Elmo Calkins, co-owner of the New York advertising agency Calkins and Holden, played an essential role in promoting modern art in the advertising world. After a visit to Europe in the early 1920s, he began to intensively promote the use of solutions developed in European modern art in advertising and industrial design. In practice, this meant combining its aesthetics with the ideas of industrialism and economics. Calkins was very impressed by the *Exposition Internationale des Arts Décoratifs et Industriels Modernes* organised in Paris in 1925, the largest exhibition of *Art Déco* style. Looking at French signs, advertising placards, packaging, and arrangements of trade stands at the exhibition – among others, famous Parisian department stores such as Le Bon Marché and Galleries Lafayette – Calkins noted the aesthetics of cubism and futurism used in them. This made him aware of their effectiveness in visual communication, as they were very good at attracting viewers' attention. He was also very impressed by the abandonment of commonly understood realism in favour of abstract forms, whose symbolic, metaphorical, and allegorical qualities allowed them to create a magical aura around banal, mass-produced goods. In 1933, in the January issue of the "Advertising Arts" magazine, Calkins wrote that modern art "gave the opportunity to express the inexpressible, to suggest not so much the car, as its speed, not so much the dress, as the style, not a powder box, but beauty" (Bogart 1995: 112–113). By using the language of formal modernism, Calkins tried to make advertising a field of fine arts, treating, for example, advertising billboards as "galleries of images for the poor" (Bogart 1995: 112–113; Calkins 1933).

Empirical study

There is no need here to analyse the long process of advertising appropriating techniques developed for the various trends in modern art. We will only look at selected examples of such acquisition to answer the questions posed at the beginning. The examples cited here are classics of advertising, are widely known, have received awards, and make advertising history, which, I think, may justify a possible attempt to generalise the answers to the questions posed earlier.

"Think small"

The first example to be analysed here is the legendary Volkswagen advertisements, which gave rise to the *Beetle* moniker, created in 1959 by the New York agency Doyle Dane Bernbach. They are still admired by many advertising industry representatives and are considered a model based on a good creative idea. The car was difficult to advertise because it was already outdated and primitive when its manufacturer approached the agency with the order for an advertising campaign, which was a result of being designed and constructed before World War II. The car was small and uncomfortable, with only two doors, no automatic transmission, and no air conditioning. It was considered ugly and had negative connotations. Its production began thanks to Adolf Hitler in 1938, and it was used by the Wehrmacht and Waffen SS troops during World War II. It should be emphasised that during the advertising campaign, many European Jews, who had managed to escape the Holocaust, lived in the United States, which also made it challenging to promote a car associated with Nazism. Unlike the American cars of the time, the car had a small, under-power, air-cooled engine at the rear. The agency wanted to turn these flaws into advantages, which they succeeded brilliantly. For example, participation in World War II was made into an argument confirming the car's solid construction and durability. The small size, compared to the size of typical American road cruisers of that time, was presented as ease of parking and a guarantee of fuel savings, and the primitive design was simple, guaranteeing reliability and simultaneous savings in the event of necessary repairs.

The advertising campaign contributed to an extraordinary growth in car sales and helped build consumer awareness – its legend is still alive today. In the agency's assumptions, the advertisements were to be the antithesis of the kitsch typical of American advertising at the time – they were to be a synthesis of simplicity, literality, and sincerity. These were the features the addressee of advertisements was supposed to associate with the product. The agency assumed this would be a middle-aged man, not very wealthy and not taking himself too seriously, who knew the car advertisements of the era and could see the difference in the style of promoting Volkswagen (Rutherford 1995: 64).

Let us look at Volkswagen's press advertisements regarding their relationship with modern art. First, however, it should be noted that they were very conventional in the compositional layer – two-thirds of the area was continuously occupied by the illustration and one-third by the text, that is, a centrally placed headline and text under it in three columns; this arrangement was typical of American advertising at that time. The deviations from the norm appeared elsewhere. The illustrations were the first testimony to the black and white photographs of a documentary nature, devoid of typical advertising effects, such as sophisticated colours underscoring the shininess of the chrome and paint or spectacular perspective shortening, which allowed cars to be presented as a symbol of luxury and speed. In the first Volkswagen advertisement, in the illustration under which the *Think small* headline, which also acts as a caption, is placed, we see a vast plane, and only at the top to the side is a modest black and white photograph of the car. Compared to the automotive advertisements of that time, this illustration was as strange as the Volkswagen presented in it. The illustrative and typographic layers perfectly illustrate the use of formal achievements of modernism symbolised by Bauhuas' industrial graphic design and the work of artists associated with the "De Stijl" magazine. This is evidenced both by the photography itself, elementary, even functional, reduced to the level of a pure presentation of the product, as called for by Bauhaus, and by the use of an open and asymmetrical composition of the entire illustration, sometimes called a Mondrian or Bauhaus composition. The text of the advertisement was printed in single-element, sans-serif font, also considered synonymous with modernity, which had been promoted by artists associated with the trend of the modernist avant-garde, who gave it a very eloquent name, Futura, since the 1920s (Lupton 1989: 152).

The work of German Dadaists can also be pointed out as a source of inspiration for Volkswagen's advertisements. This is evidenced by the fact that the technical and, at the same time, modernist visual construction included content that showed humour, not taking too seriously either the product itself or the addressee, engaged as they were in trivial everyday situations. Advertising historian Stephen Fox noted that the sense of distance and humour also resulted from the tradition of Jewish self-deprecation and a specific sense of humour cultivated by the Jewish authors of the advertising campaign (Fox 1990: 258). Let us quote the text that appears under the intriguing *Think small* headline of the first advertisement:

> Our little car isn't so much of a novelty any more. A couple of dozen college kids don't try to squeeze inside it. The guy of the gas station doesn't ask where the gas goes. Nobody even stares at our shape. In fact, some people who drive our little flivver don't even think 32 miles to the gallon is going any great guns. Or using five pints of oil instead of five quarts. Or never needing anti-freeze. Or rocking up 40.000 on a set of tires. That's because once you get used to some of our economies, you don't even think about them any more. Except when you squeeze into a small parking spot. Or renew your small insurance. Or pay a small repair bill. Or trade in your old VW for a new one. Think it over.

This is a witty explanation of the intriguing meaning of the headline. Paradoxically, it illustrates one of the oldest principles developed in advertising: show the product and discuss its advantages. Another equally legendary advertisement used a similarly intriguing headline: *Lemon.* Its explanation appears in the last part of the text below:

> This preoccupation with detail means the VW lasts longer and requires less maintenance, by and large, than other cars. It also means a used VW depreciates less than any other car. ... We pluck the lemons; you get the plums.

The final sentence illustrates the application of another fundamental principle, which is that advertising should always be a promise of benefits. The Volkswagen Beetle campaign allowed the recipient to identify with the image of a man it presented and thus with his everyday problems, as the advertisements showed ways of solving them. Such everyday problems included the cost of fuel, the price of new tyres, the need to service the car, the price of spare parts, and finding a parking space. An illustration of an everyday problem could be, among others, the one included in one of the more famous advertisements, with the headline: "Sooner or later, your wife will drive home – one of the best reasons for owning a Volkswagen". The potential consequences of the wife driving the car are eloquently illustrated in the illustration, which depicts a Volkswagen Beetle with a broken headlight and mudguard. In the text below, it was reported that women are fragile, but they can hit something with a car. However, hitting something with a Volkswagen would not impact the addressee of the advertisement, who is implied to be the husband, because the parts in this car are easy to replace. For example, the mudguard can be replaced without disassembling the entire car, while labour costs are low. In addition, there will always be a mudguard in the Volkswagen workshop because it only has VW mudguards; one of the advantages of the car strongly emphasised in the campaign was its immutability – no significant changes have been made since the beginning of its production.

The realism of the advertising, on the one hand, was constantly reinforced with the illustrative layer; on the other hand, emphasised in the "everyday life" situations described in the verbal layer, made the addressee feel that the car manufacturer was always ready to help him solve all problems, both those related to life and those related to the car. Buying it was supposed to be the obvious panacea to all problems. Assuming the viewer's perspective, we can assume that they may have had the impression that advertisements are a substitute for a helpful friend who shows ways to solve ordinary problems of everyday life creating such an impression was, in fact, the implementation of another proven principle, developed in American advertising at the turn of the 19th and 20th centuries, which was promoted by the legendary Albert Lasker, the owner of the Chicago advertising agency Lord & Thomas (Bernstein 1990), and which included the statement that press advertising is a "salesman in print".

The Volkswagen Beetle advertising campaign is considered one of the most inspiring campaigns in the United States at the turn of the 1950s and 1960s (Fox 1990: 258). It is seen as opening the way to a creative revolution, that is, a new way of advertising, based on the assumption that creativity is the basis for effective marketing communication. However, one should look at Volkswagen's advertisements from an aesthetic perspective and try to answer the question: were they an attempt to escape from the kitsch typical of American advertising of the 1950s and 1960s, or did they turn out to be its new version – albeit inspired by solutions borrowed from the world of modern art? Michał Szostak wrote that kitsch strengthens the habits of the mass recipient, is a reference to the sphere of their desires, is pretentious, and does not encourage thinking, so it is shallow, but at the same time gives much pleasure (Szostak 2021). In addition, it is usually addressed to a mass recipient, does not encourage discussion and critical thinking, and stimulates the recipient's desires and needs. It must be admitted that Volkswagen's advertisements are a model illustration of these features. It may follow that these revolutionary advertisements, considered an attempt to escape from the typical advertising kitsch of the time, can be seen as examples of kitsch themselves. Can it be avoided in advertising? We will try to address these questions in the final remarks.

"Tested for the unexpected" or surrealism, postmodernism, and kitsch

While preparing to answer them, let us look at other equally known and appreciated advertisements and make up the history of world advertising, similar to the Volkswagen Beetle advertisements. Undoubtedly, one such example is the Dunlop tyres commercial, *Tested for the Unexpected*, created in 1993 by the British director Tony Kaye, creator of a series of high-profile, award-winning commercials. In 1994, he was awarded the D&AD Yellow Pencil Award, and it was also recognised as one of the ten best advertisements ever created in the UK. Influenced by these successes, the director tried to exhibit it in London's Tate Modern as a work of art, which, however, did not happen, which may be another evidence of the institutional art system resisting advertising.

Like the previously discussed Volkswagen campaign, the *Tested for the Unexpected* commercial implemented a strategy to present the product, in this case, car tyres, and showcase its advantages. In addition, an attempt was made to show the product in action, following television advertising rules. The simplicity of this strategy was in opposition to the sophistication of the advertisement in its visual and musical layers. The film presented a surreal and catastrophic vision of reality in which everything vibrated, rotated, and melted. At the narrative's core was a black car which rushed along the road, manoeuvring between various obstacles, avoiding, among other things, a collision with a piano falling from an overpass. The car's progress was additionally hindered by steel balls scattered on the road and explosions of fire. Each activity shown here aimed to cause an accident involving a car that escaped all the threats by manoeuvring. Here, we see many oval elements that indicate movement, such as rotating car wheels, balls, and pupils of the eyes. Scenes of colourfully painted human heads and obese bodies recur. One shows the surprising image of a man with his head in a bird cage, another in a black sadomasochist outfit, and yet another, a naked old man with golden, wrinkled skin. The final frame of the advertisement presents a tyre with the words: *Tested for the Unexpected. Dunlop.*

The soundtrack with psychedelic music by Velvet Underground played an important role. Their composition *Venus in Furs* complemented the film's atmosphere, bringing to mind a surreal post-apocalyptic fairy tale. The only stable element of reality was the Dunlop tyres protecting the car against any threat, even a piano falling from the overpass and steel balls scattered on the road. Irrationality clashed with rationality, madness with hard arguments in favour of the unprecedented quality of the tyres. Art mixed with economics. However, was it really art?

The recipient was probably captivated by the artistic quality of the advertisement and the possibility of finding familiar motifs borrowed from the world of science-fiction films representing the post-apocalyptic genre, such as George Miller's *Mad Max* with Mel Gibson, Kevin Reynolds's *Waterworld* with Kevin Costner, or Albert Hughes and Allen Hughes's *The Book of Eli* with Denzel Washington. While watching the advertisement, the viewer undoubtedly experienced the pleasure of remaining in a familiar circle of images known from the world of popular culture. Nothing encouraged any reflection, forced one to wonder about the essence of one's being or any more profound truth. Using the codes of popular culture, the director referred to the poetics of surrealism. The image of a man with his head in a birdcage, placed at the film's beginning and borrowed from the works of the 1920s and 1930s Parisian surrealists, seems significant. At their last exhibition organised in Paris before World War II, in 1938, the central motif was wax female exhibition mannequins decorated by artists, one of whom, by André Masson, had a bird cage on its head.

Kaye's advertisement uses the aesthetics of contemporary popular culture as an example of fitting into the codes of postmodernist art. However, referring to the theory of art, we have the right to say that his film has little to do with art. According to Martin Heidegger, for example, art should be a discovery of the truth of being, and its role is to reveal reality (Heidegger 2008 [1935]). We can also recall the concept put forward by the American theorist Arthur Danto, which states that a work of art is embodied meaning (Danto 2016). Is it possible to find any cognitive values in Kaye's film and declare that he reveals any truth of being? Does it embody any meaning, as proposed by Danto? The advertisement flaunts a series of psychedelic images with surreal colours, but we will learn nothing about the essence of being, as proposed by Heidegger. Instead, it seems to obscure any truth, at most confirming the existence of Dunlop tyres. While the surrealists intended their work to stimulate the imagination of the average person in order to activate their consciousness and thus help them break from the oppressive conditions of bourgeois reality, Kaye's advertisement is stimulating the viewers' imagination in order to control it and convince them to buy tyres.

"The power of dream" or neo-dadaism and kitsch

Another example of advertising, admired by advertisement enthusiasts and industry representatives, is one of the most famous and most expensive in history – its production cost a million pounds – the television commercial for a Honda Accord: *Cog. Honda: The Power of Dream*. It was created by the

London branch of the American advertising agency Wieden+Kennedy in 2003. The following year, it was the most awarded advertisement; among others, the jury of the British Advertising Awards gave it the highest rating of all advertisements ever nominated for the award. Another prize was the D&AD Yellow Pencil Award.

The advertisement is a story about the parts of a car, the first of which, set in motion, affects the others, which behave like a Rube Goldberg machine. It was made using the slow motion of a camera in one long, two-minute take. First, we see a rolling steering wheel bearing that hits a wheel hub bearing, which moves a gearbox gear that falls on the camshaft. This hits the exhaust pipe, which moves the stem of a valve lying on the sheet of the engine hood. ... A ball drops. Car wipers come to life. Glass panes suspended in space, like in a sculpture of Alexander Calder, start moving. One part affects another; the other affects yet another. ... At the end of this chain of events, we see a car slowly descending a seesaw and stopping in front of a banner with the inscription "Accord" falling on the hood.

The advertisement's creators were inspired by the idea of a neo-Dadaist work by two Swiss artists, Peter Fischli and David Weiss, titled *Der Lauf der Dinge* (*The Run of Things*), from 1987. The two artists, who had been working together since 1979, made a film recording a happening, creating an absurd and parodistic course of events using various everyday objects, such as ladders, worn-out car tyres, old chairs, and plastic bottles. Cleverly arranged objects interacted with each other in a chain reaction. Ladders were falling over, tyres, metal balls, and barrels were rolling, and strings burned through, triggering absurd mechanisms. This parody, a truly Dadaist course of events in the film made by the two artists, lasted 30 minutes and led to nothing. Viewers waiting for the finale of these mounting acts of absurdity could feel disappointed – at the end, a board fell, tripping a bucket, and a bubbling liquid poured out of it and began emitting fumes, obscuring the image – and that was the end. The film was awarded at art festivals in Sydney and Berlin in 1999. The similarity between the film and Honda's ad was so striking that the Swiss artists sent a letter to the Wieden+Kennedy agency claiming copyright infringement. However, they never sued.

The Swiss artists' film was provocatively amateurish in its technical aspect, with the image not always sharp and the camera movement not consistently stable. In its absurdity, however, it demonstrated an openness of meanings and prompted reflection, for example, on what used to be called rationality, which is seen as the basis of modernity as a state of culture. In its visual layer, the *Cog* commercial was the aesthetic opposite of Fischli and Weiss's film. It aroused admiration with its precision and elegance, a refined narrative about the interacting elements of a car, which were also characterised by specific technical beauty. It led to a finale: a car coming off a seesaw and a banner with the inscription Accord. However, it did not prompt any reflection.

Discussion: advertising as criticism of modern art

Contemporary art often provokes a critical look at the values promoted by culture, the metaphor of which may be the world shown in advertising. However, the reverse situation is also interesting when advertising parodies the world of modern art in order to ridicule it and, at the same time, increase its own prestige. This is facilitated by the fact that contemporary art – thanks to the avant-garde revolution of the first half of the 20th century – seems increasingly deprived of its formal language. The material used by modern artists to create works is often shocking to the viewer – especially one unfamiliar with modern art – banal everyday objects, used consumer goods, and even creations of popular culture such as advertising. The point of parodying art in advertising is usually to convince the consumer that the depicted product is a "real" work of art and, thus, the opposite of the bizarre objects presented in contemporary art galleries. One example of this type of game played with modern art was the 2004 TV commercial for ŠKODA Octavia. It is a story about a young couple watching an exhibition of modern art. We can see works set on pedestals – a strange chair, a composition made of loudspeakers, some structure made of wires, and kitschy plastic dolls depicting wrestlers. Bored and disappointed by the exhibition, the young people want to leave, but they encounter an obstacle in modern art enthusiasts carefully contemplating the guest clothes hanger, mistakenly taking it for another work of art. Undaunted by this, the protagonist squeezes through the crowd, besieges the clothes hanger, takes his partner's coat, and exits into the street, where the "real" work of art is waiting for them – a new, shiny car.

Again, we are dealing with advertising kitsch, increasing the complacency of the recipient of advertising, who agrees – of which we can be relatively sure – with the advertisement's creators' negative assessment of modern art. The commercial does not allow the audience to know and understand modern art but ridicules it, confirming the viewer's stereotypical assessment. This allows for the thesis that advertising tries to become independent from art and, therefore, seems to claim the right to be a discourse of much greater seriousness and prestige than art. It even tries to upstage it. It often succeeds, as evidenced by the frequent belief that banal products of popular culture – including advertising – are works of art.

The lack of boundaries between kitsch and art affects more than just the average Joe. Sometimes, it also affects art institutions. This is clearly illustrated by the high-profile posters made by Oliviero Toscani for Benetton, which were exhibited at the most prestigious presentation of contemporary art in the world – at the Venice Biennale in the Italian pavilion, as part of the official presentation of Italian art in 1992. Toscani applied strategies used in the first half of the 20th century by artists representing avant-garde trends – breaking conventions and de-contextualisation. In his posters, breaking the convention consisted of ceasing to present the product and letting go of the commercial beauty typical for advertising. At the same time, de-contextualisation was based on presenting photographs, the natural place of which would be the liberal press rather than the world of advertising. The use of these strategies is illustrated by posters with, among others, a priest and a nun kissing, condoms of various colours, bloody clothing of a Serbian soldier, or naked buttocks bearing a stamp with the inscription "HIV positive". However, they always featured the United Colours of Benetton brand. Toscani's posters can be seen as another testimony to advertising appropriating methods developed by modern art, which dissected its traditions in the 1990s and looked critically at reality in a downright anthropological manner. In his posters, Toscani referred to such problems of the era as the war in former Yugoslavia, the Mafia settling scores in Sicily, ecological disasters, celibacy in the Catholic Church, the threat of AIDS, the pressure of emigration from Africa to Italy, or the civil war in Rwanda. The subjects of Benetton's posters were copied from the world of the media and transferred to the reality of advertising – using the "copy-paste" principle – and were therefore not directly experienced by the recipients of his campaign. They attracted the recipients' attention and provided an eye-catching background for the advertising slogan encased in the United Colours of Benetton logo. They said nothing new and changed nothing in the consciousness of the audience watching them. They could not do so because, according to Oliviero Toscani's advertising rules, he could not go beyond the horizons of the recipient's knowledge and imagination. The posters provocatively placed the Benetton brand in the centre of world events, which used the publicity they brought to quickly turn into one of the most recognisable brands in the world.

Conclusion

As we can see from these examples, using the word art concerning advertising is somewhat problematic, while relating the kitsch category to it does not raise any doubts. The concept of art has an interpretative, evaluative and, at the same time, universal value even though it is a product of the European Renaissance. However, it sometimes appears to be of little use because it limits the field of view rather than expands it. Therefore, let us give it up and try to look at advertising from the perspective defined by the term design. First, however, we must clarify its meaning in the context of the art category because design works are usually treated as examples of art, but usually with the caveat that it is applied or design art. Let us note that design works, like advertising, are separated in art institutions – design finds its place in design museums, but we usually do not find it in modern art museums. The legendary designer Otl Aicher, co-founder (with Max Bill) of the notorious Hochschule für Gestaltung Ulm, in 1953, decisively separated design from art. He wrote:

> [It] turned out to be disastrous for art historians to handle design and architecture theory. Design is completely different from art. Design and art have the same relationship as knowledge and faith. There are religious scientists, but science is fundamentally different from religion.
>
> (Aicher 2016: 23)

Aicher believed that design should be based on technique because design criteria are not derived from art at all (Aicher 2016: 27). In his opinion, the aesthetics of modernism, which was so close to architects' and designers' hearts, developed from unrestrained contact with technology. At this point, the designer referred to Joseph Paxton's Crystal Palace in London as the first presentation of the idea of modernism. "Art", he wrote, "was not involved; it was busy copying historical patterns, which was more embarrassing than creative" (Aicher 2016: 28). In his opinion, technology has its technical beauty, but it cannot be said that art has a technological dimension. It is distant from technology. While the concept of art can be separated from design, this cannot be done with the word kitsch; we often come across examples of this.

Philosopher Vilém Flusser pointed out that in English, the word *design* serves as both a noun and a verb. As a noun, it can mean, among others, intention, purpose, pattern, motif, or, for example, structure. All these meanings are usually combined with a certain special attitude towards reality, which, as Flusser (2009) wrote, is characterised by insidiousness, cunning, and even a desire to deceive. The design would, therefore, be something cunning. As a verb, this word usually means inventing, symbolising, sketching, or planning something. According to Flusser, the word design combines technology and art in its meanings. Advertising may be an example of such a combination – a product of the creative industry – created with the artist's participation.

In advertising, there is no room for the recipient's self-reference, that is, experiencing oneself combined with reflection on the meaning of one's being. The reception of advertising is also unrelated to reflection on the nature of reality, as is often the case with a work of art. What would reality even be in advertising? It is only possible to experience the world of advertising, which, flaunting the reality of fantasy and the absurd without prompting any reflection or abstraction, displaces logical thinking. If we agree that rational thinking is based on the relationship between rationality and knowledge, then we experience cognitive dissonance when observing the world of advertising because our knowledge turns out to be the opposite of the rationality presented in it. In the world presented in it, everything is possible: the cramped and primitive design of a car becomes its advantage; a car can confidently move along a road sprinkled with metal balls, chocolate candies can sing, and babies who have not yet learned to talk can explain the benefits of yoghurt to their moms. Usually, it does not even occur to us that all this is unreal and impossible, that advertising is not a "salesman in print", that you cannot drive a car on a road sprinkled with balls, that candy does not sing, and that babies cannot talk.

The unreality of the reality of advertising results from the fact that it always talks about future happiness and a practical, better life – after buying the product. Thanks to this, it becomes an illustration of the now preferred attitude to time in its linear model, characterised by a critical attitude to the past, invalidating the present treated only as an introduction to a better future, which has to be colonised. Let us note that the old works of European art most often talked about the past – seen from a religious or mythological perspective – and only with time about the present. The future appeared in them only as an illustration of the story of the biblical Last Judgment, Paradise, or Heavenly Jerusalem. It was only in modern art that attention began to be paid to the future – it was discussed by surrealists and projected by representatives of various trends of avant-garde modernism. Advertising images also talk about the future. It is in them that modernity, dominated by industrialism and economics, shows an idealised, unreal, kitschy future that will never happen but which legitimises the everyday toil of the repressed individual. The individual is repressed twice – first by the need for work from which there is no escape and again by the kitschy vision of the future proposed in commercial imagery, including advertising. It is, in fact, a promise of pretentiousness, sentimentalism, the experience of a community killing any individualism, irrationality, an affirmation of stereotypes, negation of any criticism and thus negation of independent thinking (Szostak, Sułkowski 2020; Szostak 2021; Szostak 2023). It turns out, however, to be an extremely attractive and effective promise.

Translated by Agnieszka Dzięcioł-Pędich.

Note

1 Translator's note: quotes from Polish editions of cited texts are retranslations from Polish.

References

Adorno, Theodor W., Horkheimer, Max. 1993. *Dialektykaoświecenia*, translated by Małgorzata Łukasiewicz. WydawnictwoIFiS PAN: Warszawa.
Aicher, Otl. 2016. *Światjakoprojekt*, translated by Renata Darda-Staab and Irena Dąbek. Wydawnictwo LIBRON: Kraków.
Barthes, Roland. 1991 [1957]. *Mythologies*, translated by Annette Lavers. Farrar, Straus & Giroux: New York.
Berman, Roland. 1981. *Advertising and Social Change*. SAGE: Beverly Hills–London.
Bernstein, Sidney Ralph. 1990. *The Lasker Story*. NTC Business Books: Lincolnwood, IL.
Bogart, Michele Helene. 1995. *Artists, Advertising, and the Borders of Art: 1880–1960*. University of Chicago Press: Chicago.
Bürger, Peter. 1984 [1974]. *Theory of the Avant-Guarde*, translated by Michael Show. Manchester University Press, University of Minnesota Press: Minneapolis.
Calkins, Earnest Elmo. July 1933. 'Design and Economic. Recovery'. *Advertising Arts*, edited by F.C. Kendall. Advertising and Selling Publishing Co.: New York.

Danto, Arthur C. (2016). *Czym jest sztuka*, translated by Anna Kunicka. Wydawnictwo Aletheia: Warszawa.

Davidson, Martin Peter. 1992. *The Consumerist Manifesto. Advertising in Postmodern Times*. Routledge: London–New York.

Ewen, Stuart. 1976. *Captain of Consciousness. Advertising and the Social Roots of the ConsumerCulture*. McGraw-Hill Book Company: New York–St. Louis–San Francisco–Toronto–Mexico–Düsseldorf.

Flusser, Villem. 2009. 'About the Word Design [1993]'. *The Design Culture Reader*, edited by Ben Highmore. Routledge: London–New York, pp. 36–39.

Fox, Stephen. 1990. *The Mirror Makers. A History of American Advertising*. Heinemann: London.

Galbraith, John Kenneth. 1958. *The Affluent Society*. Houghton Mifflin Company: Boston–New York.

Galbraith, John Kenneth. 1967. *The New Industrial State*. Penguin: London.

Goffman, E. 1979. *Gender Advertisements*. Palgrave HE: London.

Habermas, Jürgen. 2008. *Strukturalne przeobrażeniasferypublicznej*, translated by Wanda Lipnik and Małgorzata Łukasiewicz. WydawnictwoNaukowe PWN: Warszawa.

Heidegger, Martin. 2008 [1935]. *The Origin of the Work of Art*, translated by David Farrell Krell. Martin Heidegger. The Basic Writings. Harper Collins: New York, pp. 143–212.

Jhally, Sut. 1987. *The Codes of Advertising: Fetishism and the Political Economy of Meaning in the Consumer Society*. Frances Pinter Publishers: London.

Kisielewski, Andrzej. 1999. *Sztuka i reklama. Relacjemiędzysztukąikulturą*. Wydawnictwo Trans Humana: Białystok.

Klein, Naomi. 2005. *No Logo*. Flamingo: London.

Leiss, William; Kline, Stephen; Jhally, Sut; Botterill, Jackie. 2005. *Social Communication in Advertising. Consumption in the Mediated Marketplace*. Routledge: London–New York.

Lupton, Ellen. 1989. 'Reading Isotype'. *Design Discourse. History. Theory. Meaning*, edited by Victor Margolin. The University of Chicago Press: Chicago and London, pp. 145–156.

Machniewicz, Stanisław. 1934. *Estetykażyciacodziennego. Zarysyestetyczneizagadnienia sztukiwspółczesnej*. PaństwoweWydawnictwo Książek Szkolnych: Lwów.

Marcuse, Herbert. 1991 [1964]. *Człowiekjednowymiarowy. Badanianadideologiąroz winietegospołeczeństwaprzemysłowego*, translated by Stanisław Konopacki. PWN: Warszawa.

McComb, Don. 2005. 'The Avant-Guarde and the Market. Debating Modernism: Art and American Advertising in the 1920'. *American Visual Cultures*, edited by David Holloway and John Beck. Continuum: London–New York, pp. 73–80.

Mitchell, William T.J. 2013. *Czegochcąobrazy?*, translated by Łukasz Zaremba. Narodowe Centrum Kultury: Warszawa.

Packard, Vance. 1957. *The Hidden Persuaders*. David Mckay Company: New York.

Rosenblum, Robert. [1960] 2001. *Cubism & Twentieth Century Art*. Harry N. Abrams Inc.: New York.

Rutherford, Paul. 1995. *The New Icons? The Art of Television Advertising*. University of Toronto Press: Toronto.

Schudson, Michael. 1984. *Advertising, the Uneasy Persuasion: It's Dubious Impact on American Society*. Basic Books: New York.

Shusterman, Richard. 1998. *Estetykapragmatyczna. Żywepięknoirefleksjanadsztuką*, translated by A. Chmielewski, E. Ignaczak, Lech Koczanowicz, Ł. Nysler and A. Orzechowski. WydawnictwoUniwersytetuWrocławskiego: Wrocław.

Szostak, Michał. 2021. "Kicz: nasza ochrona przed rzeczywistością". *Więź*, 12.01.2021. https://wiez.pl/2021/01/12/kicz-nasza-ochrona-przed-rzeczywistoscia/

Szostak, Michał. 2023. *Sztuka zarządzania. Zarządzanie sztuką*. Społeczna Akademia Nauk: Łódź–Wartszawa.

Szostak, Michał, Sułkowski, Łukasz. 2020. 'Kitsch in Management: Characteristic Forms, Carriers and Propagators'. *Education Excellence and Innovation Management: A 2025 Vision to Sustain Economic Development during Global Challenges: Proceedings of the 35th International Business Information Management Association Conference (IBIMA)*. IBIMA: Sevilla, pp. 7584–7598. Available at: https://depot.ceon.pl/handle/123456789/19173.

Wernick, Andrew. 1992. *Promotional Culture. Advertising, Ideology and Symbolic Expression*. Sage Publications: Thousand Oaks.

Williams, Raymond. 1999 [1961]. 'Advertising: The Magic System'. *The Cultural Studies Reader*, edited by Simon During. Routledge: London–New York, pp. 320–336.

8 Kitsch in brand management

Impact of aesthetic truth and false in advertising strategies

Aleksandra Chmielewska

Introduction

Analysing kitsch in advertising and marketing strategies opens the door to understanding the complex world of marketing communication, in which aesthetics, emotions and values play a key role. This topic gains importance in the context of the modern market, where brands compete for the attention of increasingly demanding consumers. The chapter analyses the example of three brands: Apart, Kubota and Barbie, which, in their advertising campaigns, for various reasons, attracted the attention of recipients and sparked a discussion about the use of kitsch in marketing strategies.

Kitsch, characterised by its excessive, artificial, or inauthentic style, has ingrained itself as a fundamental aspect of popular culture and advertising. Over the years, iconic figures like Barbie have continually evolved to mirror shifting trends and societal norms, with their advertising campaigns eliciting strong emotions and standing as recognisable examples of iconic advertising despite occasional criticisms for perpetuating gender stereotypes or unrealistic beauty standards. Conversely, luxury jewellery brand Apart competes for consumer attention in a realm of glitz and glamour; its visually refined yet often criticised advertisements are accused of excessive product exposure and a kitschy communication style. Meanwhile, Kubota, originally known for industrial tractors, has expanded into consumer products, crafting campaigns that, while seemingly avoiding stereotypical kitsch, flirt with the boundaries of quality and fashion in alignment with contemporary aesthetic and consumer trends. By examining these brands, we delve into the intricate realm of kitsch in advertising and its impact on consumer perceptions, particularly within the Polish market context, while shedding light on broader marketing strategies. The exploration encompasses the evolution of kitsch in advertising, its implications on brand management strategies, and its multifaceted role in shaping consumer experiences, integrating insights from media theory, consumer psychology and brand management. Through case studies, we dissect the successes and failures of brands in employing kitschy elements, scrutinising consumer responses and considering psychological and

DOI: 10.4324/9781003504931-9

cultural dimensions. Ultimately, this interdisciplinary approach yields a nuanced understanding of kitsch's influence on contemporary brand management strategies and its significance in shaping consumer interactions with brands.

The chapter addresses three research questions: 1) How does kitsch influence brand perception and management strategies in advertising? 2) How does the development of digital technologies and social media influence the use and perception of kitsch in advertising? and 3) What marketing strategies can use kitsch experience components effectively to increase consumer engagement and build a positive brand image?

The research procedure was divided into the following phases: 1) conducting a critical review of the literature on the subject; 2) detailed research analysis of advertising development and key elements of advertising strategies on three brands: the Apart campaign from 2020, the Kubota brand and the Barbie movie; and 3) an analysis of public discourse regarding advertising and brand communication.

The criterion for selecting literature considers the diversity of domestic and international perspectives, presenting the problem of kitsch in advertising. In the context of thematic relevance, publications address the research problem, providing relevant information and answering research questions. Recency is also important, so using the latest sources is essential to reflect current trends, discoveries and opinions in a given field. In this context, the cited works of Szostak (2021), an expert in the field of kitsch in management, and brand experts such as Urbanek (2019), Kall (2010), Ostrowska (2010) and Upshaw (1995) ensure a variety of perspectives and the currency of the information.

The selection of specific brands for analysis is not accidental but results from their important role in developing advertising and key elements of advertising strategies in the Polish market. The analysis of the Barbie, Apart and Kubota brands from the Polish market is also essential for international readers due to several important factors. Firstly, Poland, as a country with a dynamically developing economy and changing social norms, is a fascinating research field for international readers. Observing how these three brands relate to different aspects of culture, aesthetics and social norms in the Polish context can provide valuable insights into how brands adapt to local markets and consumers. Secondly, analysing these brands allows for understanding how changing trends and consumer expectations affect marketing strategies and build brand identity in Poland and internationally. Finally, the use of an interdisciplinary perspective in brand analysis, combining media theory, consumer psychology and brand management, allows for the drawing of universal conclusions relevant to readers worldwide. In this way, although the study focuses on the specificity of the Polish market, its implications and understanding can be valuable for anyone interested in marketing, branding and consumption issues. Apart's 2020 advertising campaign was selected for its significant social and industry response despite lacking an original marketing objective. Through numerous memes and the reactions of the cabaret community to the song used in the advertisement, the advertising spot became the object of ridicule, which is a fascinating case of analysing the perception of advertising by society and its impact on various groups of recipients. The Kubota brand was chosen as another example of using kitsch positively. By referring to tradition and assessing flip-flops as an element of kitsch, the Kubota brand has built a new marketing message based on the desire to enter a new market and brand cooperation. The analysis of this campaign allowed us to understand how kitsch elements can be used to create a desired brand image and convey specific values. However, the choice of the Barbie movie as an example of a brand associated with kitsch allowed for examining how a brand can add value to a social message despite possible criticism of kitsch. The analysis of this campaign allowed us to understand how the Barbie brand builds its image and conveys specific values, using kitsch elements in its marketing communication. The analysis also included the opinions of market experts in advertising and marketing, who, in their press statements, took a position concerning the individual cases that were discussed.

Literature review

In the realm of brand management, the evolution of elements in advertising has become an intriguing subject of exploration. Brands constantly strive to carve a niche in the competitive market landscape, seeking to distinguish themselves from their counterparts and capture the attention of potential customers. This pursuit often leads them to incorporate various communication signals, including aesthetics, into their marketing strategies. However, in this quest for differentiation, brands tread a fine line, aiming to balance capturing attention and maintaining authenticity. As brands endeavour to create emotional connections with consumers, the strategic use of kitsch emerges as a potential tool capable of eliciting strong emotional responses and fostering brand recall.

Furthermore, the significance of branding transcends mere product attributes, with brand perception wielding a considerable influence on consumer behaviour. Brands are perceived not solely based on objective characteristics but rather on the associations and emotions they evoke in consumers' minds. This perception is heavily influenced by branding elements such as logos, names and overall identity, which serve as crucial touchpoints for consumers.

Literature analysis allows us to explore various aspects of the use of kitsch in marketing practice, from its impact on emotional connections with the brand to strategies for building memorable advertising campaigns. Through literature research, you can also learn about trends such as storytelling, real-time marketing or prankvertising, which use kitsch elements to create strong emotional bonds with consumers. In this way, an introduction to literature analysis enables a better understanding of the complex role that kitsch elements play in today's marketing landscape, inspiring further research into their potential and effectiveness in branding.

Evolution of kitschy aspects in advertising in a brand management context

For any brand, the goal is to build awareness among potential customers so as to create the impression that the product or service is of high quality. The brand ensures quality by helping the customer choose from among various offers. However, quality risk reduction alone may not be enough in competitive markets. To build a strong brand, it is necessary to find unique features that distinguish it from other offers and attract customers, prompting them to buy brand products or services.

It should be noted that brands are actively looking for ways to stand out from their competitors. They can do this through various communication signals designed to attract customers' attention and evoke positive associations with the brand. They often use aesthetics as a tool to build their image, yet their goal is to reach the broadest possible audience.

The ultimate goal of a brand is to create an emotional connection with customers that will make them loyal to the brand, even if some cheaper alternatives or products offer potential benefits. If we assume that a brand exists in the minds and hearts of buyers, then building it is based on the evolving emotions and feelings buyers give to the brand. In other words, at all stages, from the producer to the consumer, brand value is based on its benefits and the benefits associated with continuing the relationship (Kall, 2010: 33–38).

On the other hand, kitsch can also be useful in marketing communication. Although kitsch may be perceived negatively, it can attract attention and arouse the target audience's interest. Kitsch elements such as bright colours, excessive decorations or drama in composition can attract attention and be memorable.

> The perception of a product through its brand affects the consumer more than its objective parameters and features. What matters for the customer is not whether the product is objectively better..., but whether it is perceived as better or more suitably meeting the customer's needs, which is largely determined by the perception of the brand.
>
> (Urbanek, 2019: 28)

The perception of a product through the brand has a greater impact on the customers than any objective product characteristics. It depends to a large extent on the brand whether the product is perceived as a better one or meets the customer's needs more suitably. The company's logo and name are the first associations with the brand and are crucial for its identification and differentiation from the competitors. Values, intellect and culture account for 85% of the brand perception. The values give brands their unique identity (personality) and essence, which can attract customers and even help hire employees. Some consumers treat brands as living creatures endowed with such attributes as intellect or good manners. Creating a brand as if it were a human being increases its attractiveness on the market, as its unique identity (personality) can be the key factor determining customers' choices of one brand rather than another, especially when competitors offer products with increasingly similar features (Ostrowska, 2010).

Companies often use kitsch elements in their advertising campaigns to stand out from the competitors and attract customers' attention. Some brands intentionally employ kitsch elements to evoke emotions, make people laugh or be remembered. However, it is important to properly balance and contextually place kitsch elements so as not to lose the authenticity of the brand and not to discourage more demanding customers. As a result, using aesthetics and kitsch in communication strategies can effectively attract customers' attention and build a strong brand image. However, it is crucial to skilfully balance the proportions and understand what elements are appropriate for a given brand and its audience.

A brand's unique personality often emerges as the decisive factor in consumer choices, especially when competing products and services offer similar features. Brand personality bridges the consumer and the brand, offering a deeper connection beyond mere positioning or physical attributes. It encompasses qualities beyond the brand name alone, resonating more profoundly with consumers. This connection can influence a customer's decision to try a product or even foster a subconscious loyalty that deters them from switching to a competitor. Unlike other aspects of a brand, the brand personality is inherently authentic, reaching out to consumers personally. It represents an extended hand, symbolising a genuine interaction between the brand and the individual customer (Upshaw, 1995: 151).

In the context of advertising, kitsch has evolved from an initially pejorative phenomenon to a strategic tool used by brands. Creating kitsch consumer experiences has become popular because it attracts attention and evokes emotions. Modern brands strive to build strong relationships with customers, using their products' functional and emotional aspects. Moreover, advertising often relies on kitsch elements, using them to attract attention and engage recipients. However, there is a fine line between an attention-grabbing message and one perceived as cheesy or intrusive. It is also important to understand that advertising often aspires to be seen as art, but in reality, this can only lead to it becoming more like show business. Advertising often aestheticises reality but, at the same time, remains separated from high art, becoming only a simulation of aesthetic shaping within commercial purposes (Ostrowicki, 2002: 33–34).

Kitsch in advertising has come a long way, from the beginnings of mass production to brand management strategies. Initially, kitsch was often looked down upon as a tacky art form, but as popular culture developed and consumer tastes changed, kitsch began to be used by brands as a strategic tool. Creating kitsch consumer experiences has become a popular strategy because it attracts attention and evokes emotions.

Development of digital marketing in innovative advertising

With the development of digital technologies, digital marketing has undergone a revolution, which has influenced how brands present their products and services. New forms of advertising, such as native advertising, video commercials on social media platforms, and advertising based on demographics and behaviour, enable brands to reach more personalised target groups.

Many publications (Żero, 2018; Matusiak, 2011) refer to the definition of innovation created by J. Schumpeter, who is considered the precursor of the theory of innovation in economic sciences. J. Schumpeter formulated the thesis that economic development is mainly driven by the innovation of enterprises and not only by capital. According to his definition, any person who introduces new combinations or ideas can be viewed as an entrepreneur. The Austrian economist also posited a division of innovation into what came to be known as Schumpeter's triad: invention, innovation and imitation (Schumpeter, 1960). More modern definitions of this concept were formulated, for example, by A. Pomykalski, who stated that innovation is "a process covering all activities related to the creation of an idea, the development of an invention, and then the implementation of the new product or process" (Pomykalski, 2004). The concept of marketing innovation was introduced in the Oslo Manual, an international methodological compendium for statistical research on innovation. It is a work created in cooperation between the Organization of the Economic Community and Development OECD and Eurostat. The manual includes a definition of marketing innovation, which describes it as the introduction of a new marketing strategy associated with significant changes in product design, packaging, distribution, promotion or pricing strategy. The main goal of marketing innovation is to attempt to satisfy customer needs better, open up new markets and better position the product on the market to increase sales (OECD, Eurostat, 2005).

The publication also includes a division of marketing innovations into the following (OECD, Eurostat, 2005):

- changes in the product design – they consist of changing the appearance of products without interfering with their functioning. This group includes changes in the packaging of food products, where the packaging is the main determinant of the product's appearance, and the introduction of a new flavour of a specific food in order to attract a larger number of consumers. Such measures are intended to distinguish the product from others available on the market by using the visual layer;
- new marketing methods in the field of product placement – they consist of introducing new sales channels. Examples of such innovations include the introduction for the first time of a franchise system, product licensing, exclusive retail sales and the use of a different type of product display;

- new marketing methods in the field of product promotion – they are about the use of concepts for promoting the company's products and services. For this purpose, brands often cooperate with celebrities, presenting them as users of a given product (public figure endorsement) or placing the product in popular series and films. Another example of the use of innovation is branding, that is, creating and introducing a completely new brand symbol to the market, for instance, in order to change the image of a product;
- innovations in pricing – they consist of shaping new pricing strategies for selling the brand's products or services on the market. For example, there is a method of adjusting the price of a given product or service depending on the demand, that is, if there is a high demand for a given product, the price should also be appropriately high.

In recent years, in the age of social media development, we have seen a lot of innovative marketing approaches used by brands in order to communicate with their customers and promote their products. These include concepts such as storytelling, real-time marketing, community trade and prankvertising.

Storytelling, or the art of telling stories, appeared in 2003 and was introduced by media scientist Henri Jenkins. It involves the proficient use of various narratives, motifs and characters and their skilful integration into the stories being created. The essence of storytelling is the flexible adjustment of content to align it with the interests and history of recipients, which makes it a dynamic communication tool that focuses mainly on conveying engaging content (Stopczyńska, 2016: 318). Presenting a story allows the sender to express his or her own perspective, convey emotions and organise the facts. This is crucial for the sender because it is easier to reach a potential recipient by using storytelling. This is because, compared to an ordinary message, a fascinating story engages more areas of the human brain. It is important that the story be based on truth and easy for everyone to understand so that it can be freely passed on.

Brands often use storytelling to improve their image, especially in crisis situations, and to stand out on the market. Through a well-structured story, they are able to achieve their goals because the recipient can take on the role of a protagonist and become emotionally involved in the relationship with the brand. Storytelling is often used in social media, which by its nature aims to engage recipients and encourage them to actively participate in the discussion (Stopczyńska, 2016: 318–325). An increasingly popular type of storytelling used by brands on the internet is visual storytelling, that is, narration that uses multimedia, such as photos, images, graphics or short videos. This form of communication is extremely effective because visual content attracts more attention from internet users, leading to increased involvement in the story being conveyed. Additionally, visual storytelling builds brand awareness and consolidates its position in the market (Scherman, 2016).

Real-time marketing, an innovation in social media, is a marketing strategy conducted in real time. In simple terms, it involves the company's immediate response to current events. Using this technique has many advantages, especially when improving the brand's image, especially among younger audiences for whom traditional forms of advertising may be ineffective and who may be inclined to view traditional advertising as overwhelming by providing too much information. Real-time marketing allows companies to get closer to customers, build direct relationships and give their brand a more human touch, which can lead to positive customer perception. Likewise, inappropriate use of this strategy can lead to serious brand image problems, especially in the internet age, when information spreads quickly. Implementing real-time marketing requires understanding and experience, and clumsy actions can easily lead to a crisis. There are two main strategies for implementing real-time marketing in social media: content marketing, that is, creating and sharing content consistent with current events, and dialogue marketing, which involves active participation in conversations on social media platforms (Szymańska, 2015: 270).

Content marketing is a strategy that involves a brand actively responding to current events by sharing short comments and visuals on social media platforms that connect the brand's product to the current situation. The following techniques are used as part of this strategy (Stopczyńska, 2015: 172):

- Newsjacking: using current external information to promote the brand. It is crucial to react quickly and adapt the message to the brand values to attract the attention of the target group.
- Memejacking: involves capturing memes, that is, using current trends in social media for marketing purposes.
- Memescaping: is the process in which a product's advertising theme becomes a popular meme on the internet, contributing to its further dissemination and increasing its reach.

Dialogue marketing, in turn, consists of monitoring internet user conversations and presenting the brand when it can prove useful to consumers, for example, by making available free product samples to the participants of events on Facebook. Additionally, this strategy entails quick responses to customer inquiries (Szymańska, 2015: 276).

Prankvertising is a concept derived from combining the words "prank" and "advertising". It means an advertising strategy that uses professionally prepared videos that present humorous situations involving bystanders. These videos are created to promote a brand or product by spreading information about them on platforms like YouTube, where short videos are common. In such productions, all scenes are stage-managed, and the people taking part in them tend to be hired actors. Prankvertising uses human emotions such as fear and surprise to convey advertising messages and engage audiences. This type of advertising aims to enable the recipient to put themselves in the shoes of the person who is the target of the joke, which increases its effectiveness. Additionally, prankvertising uses viral marketing, which means it can quickly reach a wide audience by sharing and distributing the video online. However, this type of marketing innovation has its drawbacks, such as high production costs that may make it only affordable for large international brands and the inability to target advertising to specific audiences precisely. A similar marketing innovation based on the viral mechanism is immersive branding, which focuses on emotions but mainly on positive ones, such as joy and surprise. It provides an alternative to traditional advertising that uses negative emotions such as fear to influence consumer behaviour (Masiarz, 2016: 62–64).

The phenomenon known as "live shopping" has recently become increasingly popular. The trend started in China but has also gained popularity in Poland, especially on platforms such as Facebook and Instagram. It involves presenting products, often items of clothing, during live broadcasts, during which viewers can reserve or purchase products by leaving a comment or making a direct purchase after the broadcast (Wirtualnemedia, 2022).

The latest technological breakthroughs that are starting to revolutionise the market and, according to experts, will have a huge impact on the future of marketing are augmented reality (AR) and virtual reality (VR). AR is gaining more and more popularity, mainly thanks to the use of filters in social media. This technology allows its users to superimpose virtual elements on the real world, which makes it possible to create virtual fitting rooms where the customer can match clothes, shoes and accessories to their figure. Thanks to such solutions, customers spend more time shopping online, which increases company profits by 30% and reduces the number of returns by half, which translates into customer satisfaction and savings for the seller. Furniture manufacturers also use this technology, allowing customers to test whether a given product fits their interior virtually. On the other hand, VR, although not yet as widely used as AR, offers new experiences while requiring special glasses. A person using VR enters a completely different world. Mark Zuckerberg, the founder of Facebook, announced the possibility of shopping in virtual reality with the advent of the so-called Metaverse – a virtual world where shopping will be possible like that in traditional brick-and-mortar stores (BlueMedia, 2024).

Empirical analysis of kitsch in selected brand management strategies

Kitsch in advertising is becoming increasingly common, which may lead to the blurring of boundaries between art and commerce, as well as between high and low culture. However, even in this context, kitsch remains an extremely subjective phenomenon and one that is difficult to define unambiguously. The use of artistic elements in advertising can increase its aesthetic level, allowing it to draw on the attributes characteristic of traditional works of art, such as beauty, space or colours, as well as modern trends, such as interactivity. Advertising is becoming a powerful tool that spreads quickly, engages audiences and can compete with the fields of high culture. In the unification process through advertising, it uses the cognitive function of the recipient, suggesting that it offers something new and unique, which unifies the audience through content and product. The visual language of advertising, dominating the text, strengthens the sense of community and unity, attracting many recipients. Mass media, predominant in today's world, force us to keep up with the large amount of information and the speed of change, which often results in an escape into kitsch. Kitsch, present both in advertising and in art, can be consciously used as a tool by artists and advertisers. Recipients, in turn, find satisfaction in consuming easily accessible para-artistic content through advertising. However, attempts to justify the value of advertising may lead to revealing its underlying kitsch, especially when the advertising tries to convey ideologies relating to aesthetic or ethical values. Advertising that aspires to be art can only seemingly aestheticise reality, often becoming only a reflection of life, devoid of the authenticity of art. Ultimately, advertising can only be a semblance of art, aesthetic shaping away from artistic purposes, filled only with commercial purposes (Ostrowicki, 2002: 33–34).

Apart commercial

The history of the Apart brand spans more than four decades. It emerged when the conditions for entrepreneurship in Poland were not particularly favourable, especially in the aftermath of the fall of communism. Despite this challenging environment, the founders of Apart relied on their passion, determination and the expertise they had accumulated over the years. With a deep-rooted desire to create exquisite jewellery, they navigated through obstacles and established Apart as a leading powerhouse in the domestic market. Moreover, their dedication and commitment led to success beyond Poland's borders, as Apart gained recognition and acclaim internationally (Apart, 2024).

Description

In November 2020, a Christmas commercial for the Apart brand was released, starring Małgorzata Socha, Julia Wieniawa and Anna Lewandowska. The ladies who are the main characters of the Apart advertisement are exceptionally well known in the Polish market. Małgorzata Socha is a valued Polish actress who gained recognition primarily thanks to her roles in popular television series. Julia Wieniawa is a versatile figure in the Polish show business. She is an actress, singer, songwriter, composer and a well-known media personality. Anna Lewandowska is an outstanding Polish athlete and sports activist, recognised not only as a multiple medallist of the world, European and Polish championships in traditional karate but also as a businesswoman, coach, personal trainer, dietician, TV presenter and media personality. She is also the president of Special Olympics Poland and the wife of the famous footballer, Robert Lewandowski.

The commercial titled “I Like Coming Back”, featuring the song of the same title by the unforgettable Polish singer (a multi-talented artist renowned as a singer, multi-instrumentalist, composer, arranger, TV presenter and actor, who remains an undeniable icon of Polish music), showcased three celebrities portrayed as friends enjoying the holidays. While the brand intended to incorporate storytelling elements into its campaign, the commercial became an unintentional example of prankvertising.

Opinions

According to many observers, the commercial was considered too “sugary” and “dreamy”, showing the luxury of the brand’s jewellery as a way to achieve social status. Maciej Bąk from Bezprawnik.pl noted that promoting luxury was inappropriate during the pandemic when many people lost their jobs.

The Apart’s commercial also gained popularity thanks to a humorous video by the Comedy Club, which attracted more viewers on YouTube than the original spot. Katarzyna Joanna Kulig from the Labcon agency believes that what ultimately matters is the business results, so if these were positive, the brand could be satisfied. However, the entire industry could learn some lessons from the reaction to this controversial commercial (Press, 2021).

The internet community took advantage of the moment, and frames from the commercial were used as memes in 2020. Presenting idealised women who are carefree does not fit the realities of the world. In an almost fairy-tale Christmas setting, they present jewellery apart and behave in a not natural way. Therefore, the memic nature of the characters and the style of the advertising message were used.

Marketing experts in Poland analysed the Apart advertisement. It is worth noting that there have been numerous criticisms from both internet users and marketing experts. There is no shortage of critical voices pointing to kitsch, and there is a lack of coherence in the plot and excessive exposure to the product. They emphasises that Apart’s advertising is not positively received by viewers, which may pose a problem for the brand’s image, especially in the context of the ongoing COVID-19 pandemic and restrictions on stationary trade. According to experts, the Apart brand advertising is stereotypical but in line with expectations related to holidays and the jewellery brand. However, he emphasises that this advertisement may be perceived as boring and cloying, which is its main drawback. Many experts criticise the candy-coloured image of the advertisement but point out the tendency of jewellery brands to use this type of sugary message. Apart’s advertisement is devoid of ideas and unrealistic, which may contribute to it’s not being accepted by viewers. There were also opinions that the advertisement meets the expectations related to the holidays and is not intended to engage with social issues. The Apart ad may be criticised but gained popularity thanks to its eccentricity. There were also positive opinions about the advertisement, considering it a good representation of the character of the Apart brand and emphasising that this advertising should be perceived as luxurious and stylish, which is an important element of the brand image (Wirtualnemedia, 2020).

To sum up, the Apart brand advertisement met with mixed reactions, both positive and negative, among both viewers and marketing experts. Despite the criticism, some experts believe this advertising can benefit the brand by increasing recognition and recall.

According to Zemlik, informed consumers expect authenticity and courage for brands to reflect their values. In her opinion, Apart risks losing relevance through its short-sighted approach, especially in the face of competitors who are more adaptable and responsive to the modern needs of women, as another campaign of the YES brand has shown (Press, 2021). According to Marcin Zaczyński, the Apart commercial is real kitsch.

Kitsch experience analysis

The subsequent analysis of the visual message, scenography, subject matter and method of production of the Apart commercial is carried out in reference to the distinction between aesthetic and kitsch experiences proposed by Szostak (2021).

The commercial broadcast on television and the internet is visual and emotional kitsch, devoid of depth, but it promises aesthetic and spiritual experiences – as is usually the case with kitsch. It turned out that the reaction to this commercial was consistent with what the general kitsch analysis suggests. Firstly, it was noticed that its length was not an advantage. The long four minutes in which the protagonists, Małgorzata Socha, Anna Lewandowska and Julia Wieniawa, presented artificial gestures and faces seemed forced and limited. It was more like acting than showing any genuine emotion, yet it must be remembered that the actresses themselves are not to blame for this. Secondly, there is no script. The protagonists handle the dressing table, play with Christmas tree decorations, lie on artificial snow, and touch and smile, but this does not lead to any story or narrative. No depth appeals to the genuine and heartfelt emotions like in other Christmas commercials. Thirdly, the commercial appears cheap despite the overall impression of a high budget. Low-cost workmanship, a tawdry styrofoam snowman, artificial snow and empty boxes add a tacky tone to the commercial. Fourthly, the commercial resembled the introduction to an adult film or a fragment from erotica from the 1990s. After the "action" ends, the protagonists, smiling by the fireplace and wearing white sweaters, talk about writing a book. Unfortunately, the protagonists seem unaware of anything. Fifthly, this commercial, released during the social protests and the COVID-19 pandemic lockdown, did not reflect the social mood of the moment. Ignoring topical social problems, the brand presents women as submissive from the 1950s who stare at shiny trinkets. Sixthly, in the face of the pandemic and economic crises, this commercial did not appeal to people struggling with job losses and uncertainty. In the context of the social situation, it would be worth considering whether this type of advertising is still appropriate. Perhaps creating something more authentic and better thought out should be considered, something that would not question the intelligence and good taste of the audience (Zaczyński, 2020).

Kubota brand

The history of the Kubota flip-flop brand dates back to 1994 when it was founded by Dorota Michalska and Wiesław Michalski (Kubota, 2024).

Description

The first batches of characteristic Velcro flip-flop shoes, imported from China, reached Poland via the Trans-Siberian railway. They quickly gained enormous popularity in Polish street markets, resulting in the brand's development. In the 1990s, Kubota flip-flops reigned supreme on Poles' feet, attracting attention with their low price and comfort. However, with systemic changes and increased competition, sales of Kubota flip-flops dropped significantly at the beginning of the new millennium. Despite this, these flip-flops remained a nostalgic symbol of their past sentiment for many people. In 2018, the Kubota brand was reactivated, thanks to the cooperation of four friends, Alina Sztoch, Joanna Kwiatkowska, Wacław Mikłaszewski and Piotr Kwiatkowski with the original founders and Piotr Krawczyk. The iconic Kubota flip-flops have gained popularity again, becoming not kitsch but rather a symbol of joy and self-deprecating attitude (Kubota, 2024).

Opinions

Once associated with negative connotations, the brand's image has been revolutionised, especially through strategic marketing featuring beautiful models. Kubota now embodies premium quality, reflecting the success of its rebranding efforts. The brand's ability to adapt its communication strategy, product offerings and image to match its target audience's expectations highlights the importance of catering to specific customer segments. Furthermore, Kubota's success underscores the significance of technology and social media platforms in reshaping consumer-brand interactions.

The Kubota brand is a unique example of image change, marketing strategy and good communication. In the past, when people saw someone wearing blue or black foam flip-flop shoes with a distinctive "KUBOTA" logo, the words that immediately sprang to mind were "ugly", "nightmare" or "sucker".

However, nowadays, with the re-emergence of these flip-flops, the perception of the Kubota brand has been revolutionised – especially when they adorn the feet of beautiful models (Interactivevision, 2024). Kubota has indeed become a premium brand, and its metamorphosis proves rebranding is worthwhile. Kitsch has entered the salons.

Brands differ in both strategies and target groups, so it is important to properly match communication channels, language style and media to their customers. What are the characteristics of a premium brand? A premium brand is characterised by excellent quality, luxurious image and uniqueness of its products or services. Its clientele expects not only the highest quality of workmanship but also a unique shopping experience and the prestige associated with owning premium brand products. Therefore, it is crucial to build a brand based on trust, credibility and social prestige, which allows for maintaining customer loyalty and a competitive position in the market. First, premium brands especially need to tailor their communication strategy to their unique target group. Therefore, it is crucial to carefully select communication channels, a subtle and elegant language style and high-quality means of communication to fully reflect the luxurious character of the brand and meet the expectations of demanding customers. It must also have an excellent and recognisable product and a colourful history – these elements determine its popularity. In every sector, technology is changing how goods and services are produced. At the same time, price competition, in many cases, is not the best way to do business in the 21st century. The new method focuses on creation, understood as the search for business models that are able to reduce costs and offer the customer the highest product value. Technology and social media platforms, including in the media sector, have completely revolutionised how organisations interact with customers (Chmielewska, 2018). These features are fully present in the new Kubota brand strategy. Something that was once a symbol of kitsch now stands out with its refined style, winning the hearts of even the most demanding customers. The brand underwent a comprehensive rebranding, developing a coherent communication and image concept that appeals to a new generation that values comfort and style.

Kitsch experience analysis

The Kubota brand's transformation from kitsch to premium has been remarkable. Kubota's journey from kitsch to premium exemplifies the transformative power of effective branding and communication strategies. Kubota successfully repositioned itself in the market by focusing on product quality, developing a coherent communication strategy and aligning with contemporary trends. Notably, the brand's collaboration with other companies, such as in the CSHARK recruitment campaign, showcased its ability to leverage stereotypes and humour to engage with audiences effectively. The campaign's success in attracting candidates while maintaining professionalism reflects Kubota's agility in balancing casual communication with strategic objectives. Moreover, the enduring interest in Kubota flip-flops even after the campaign's conclusion highlights the lasting impact of effective branding initiatives on brand perception and consumer engagement.

Kubota's rebranding is a perfect example of how a brand can transform from kitsch to premium. It was enough to focus on the product, create a coherent communication strategy and tap into contemporary trends.

The Kubota brand, with its flip-flops, often cooperates with other companies. Indeed, one of the most interesting campaigns was developed based on Kubota flip-flops. CSHARK's recruitment campaign, which offered Kubota flip-flops and unique socks as a bonus for moving on to the next stage of their recruitment, was a great success. The idea was appreciated in the "Recruitment Leaders" competition organised by OLX Praca, where it won an award in the "Creativity" category. The campaign was based on the use of stereotypes with great self-deprecating detachment and creativity, which caught the attention of candidates with experience in the IT industry.

Klaudia Raczek and Małgorzata Żuk, the main architects of this campaign, emphasise that the key to success was the combination of casual communication with professionalism and the use of humour to catch the candidates' attention. The entire process, from the idea to its implementation, resulted from cooperation between the marketing and recruitment departments, which led to the creation of a campaign that stood out from others.

The biggest challenge was turning the idea into a specific campaign and maintaining the balance between laid-back casualness and professionalism. Although the campaign was of a cheek-in-tongue nature, its purpose was clear – to attract the attention of potential job candidates and showcase the atmosphere at CSHARK (LinkedIn, 2023).

The campaign enjoyed great interest among candidates who stressed their positive reception and uniqueness of the idea. Even after the recruitment process ended, questions continued to come from people interested in buying Kubota flip-flops. This shows that the campaign not only met its recruitment goals but also contributed to building a positive image of the company.

Barbie movie

"Barbie" is a film that appeared on cinema screens in 2023 as a mixture of drama, fantasy and comedy. Combining the United States and Great Britain, this production draws viewers into the colourful world full of pink and plastic, for which the Barbie doll is famous. However, behind the facade of this fairy-tale reality, there are deeper existential problems. In this film, directed by Greta Gerwig, Barbie's world changes when thoughts of death haunt the heroine, and she faces problems such as cellulite, bad breath and flat feet. In her brave journey, Barbie must leave her colourful world and go to human reality to find her owner and solve her problems. Based on popular Mattel toys, this fantasy comedy is a unique interpretation of the Barbie character. The main roles in the film were played by the talented Margot Robbie, who played the titular doll, and Ryan Gosling, who also played an important role (Canal+, 2024).

Description

The film "Barbie" (2023), directed by Greta Gerwig, emerged as a cultural phenomenon, captivating audiences and shattering box office records. Its success not only underscored the prowess of female-directed films but also sparked a nuanced conversation about the deeper implications of the Barbie brand. Through a nostalgic lens, the film evoked childhood memories and explored the multifaceted nature of Barbie's cultural significance. Furthermore, the omnipresent pink hue surrounding the movie's premiere showcased the global impact of Barbie's iconic imagery, permeating various aspects of society and sparking widespread discussion.

The film "Barbie" (2023), directed by Greta Gerwig, won viewers' hearts and broke box office records, earning the most in the history of films directed by a woman. However, is this production just superficial kitsch, or does it have a deeper meaning?

Opinions

Opinions on the "Barbie" phenomenon vary, reflecting the complex interplay of nostalgia, cultural symbolism and marketing strategies. Some, like writer Sylwia Chutnik, view Barbie as a symbol of empowerment and opportunity for girls, transcending its status as a mere toy to embody aspirational ideals. Others, such as journalist Mikołaj Lizut, interpret Barbie's evolving portrayal as a reflection of shifting societal norms and feminist movements, highlighting her significance beyond the realm of kitsch. However, criticisms persist, particularly regarding Barbie's perpetuation of unrealistic beauty standards and the commercialisation of her image.

According to Sylwia Chutnik, a writer and publicist, the explanation of the "Barbie" phenomenon lies in a sentimental journey to one's childhood offered by the film that appeals to all generations. Now, the availability of Barbie dolls is incomparably greater than in the Polish People's Republic, where they could be found mainly in "Pewex" stores. However, the Barbie doll itself was more than just a toy – it was a symbol of opportunities for girls, allowing them to dream of a future where they could be anything they wanted. Likewise, it cannot be ignored that Barbie has become a pop culture icon, being both criticised for promoting unrealistic beauty standards and appreciated for trying to introduce diversity in the doll range. Mattel's bold steps to create a variety of doll models that reflect different body types prove the evolution of the perception of this iconic doll (Tokfm, 2023).

Kitsch experience analysis

Delving into the kitsch experience portrayed in the film "Barbie", nuances that challenge conventional interpretations emerge. While Barbie's ostentatious wardrobe may initially appear superficial, director Greta Gerwig employs it as a vehicle for social commentary and feminist discourse. The juxtaposition of Barbie's glamorous attire with moments of vulnerability and self-awareness underscores the complexities of femininity and societal expectations. Moreover, the widespread commercialisation and real-time marketing frenzy surrounding the film underscore the enduring allure of the Barbie brand and its ability to captivate audiences across generations.

According to the film, Barbie typically wears kitschy clothes, although – as Anna Kozłowska points out – when Barbie goes "to see her gynaecologist", she swaps her kitschy clothes and iconic high heels for a casual outfit and Birkenstock sandals. So, is Barbie's kitschy clothing style an expression of social protest? Gerwig seems to be saying that there is nothing feminist about the bimbocore movement, but this meta-message from the film was misunderstood completely – women all over the world have again been drawn into the marketing machine, driving the sale of Barbie-style gadgets, clothes and toys. What happened can only confirm our belief that we still have a long way to go to regain our sense of self (Kozłowska, 2024). The film, despite the very standard experiences of kitsch in the form of gadgets, clothes, or kitschy stories it offers, transforms the pejorative connotations of kitsch into valuable content and values.

However, is "Barbie" only a world of pink and kitsch? Mikołaj Lizut, a Polish journalist, points out the deeper meanings of this phenomenon. In Barbie's world, Ken is a supporting character, which can be interpreted as a symbolic shift in perspective favouring women. Sylwia Chutnik adds that Barbie's presence in pop culture coincides with feminist movements, which can be interpreted as an element of the fight for equal rights (Tokfm, 2023).

So, "Barbie" is much more than mere kitsch or entertainment. It is a sentimental journey to one's childhood, a symbol of opportunities for girls, and an essential element of pop culture that continues to evolve, reflecting the changing social values and ideas of equal rights. The "Barbie" phenomenon is noteworthy because it marked a truly unique time in the history of cinema and marketing.

By analysing the "Barbie" phenomenon, we gain insights into the intricate relationship between nostalgia, consumerism and cultural symbolism. Beyond its superficial trappings, Barbie serves as a prism to examine broader societal values and aspirations, inviting critical reflection on gender roles, empowerment and the commodification of childhood. As the pink-hued frenzy surrounding the film subsides, the enduring legacy of Barbie endures, provoking contemplation and conversation about the ever-evolving landscape of popular culture and identity. On the day of the premiere of the "Barbie" movie, the world was almost overwhelmed by the omnipresent shade of pink characteristic of this iconic doll. From Uber Pink Cadillacs in Warsaw to pink taxis in London and buses in Australia, the film's impact was visible across the globe. Even politicians (e.g. representatives of the Left in Poland) referred to the film in their messages. Not only did companies benefit commercially from this phenomenon, but brands also used the hype around "Barbie" to conduct their real-time marketing activities. Burger King served a special BK Barbie Combo set, and the Aldo brand introduced a collection of shoes inspired by the doll. Moreover, the availability of various Barbie gadgets provided Mattel with additional funds and increased the film's promotion in various channels (Wirtualnemedia, 2023).

The enormous marketing power of the Barbie movie has convinced many that nostalgia and the use of a strong brand can bring impressive results. The creativity of internet users and the ability to use social media contributed to the promotion's success. "Barbie" has become an opportunity for brands to break customers out of their routine and induce the FOMO effect, or fear of missing out (Wirtualnemedia, 2023). Has it brought the brands the expected profits? Time will tell, but there are visible signs of success, such as the significant number of reactions to posts tagged #barbie.

Discussion

By analysing the literature on kitsch in advertising and using case studies of the Apart advertisement, the Kubota brand strategy and the Barbie movie, one can see the complexity of the impact of this phenomenon on various aspects of advertising communication. Kitsch, the subject of numerous theoretical studies, is often created by brands to attract consumers' attention through excessive aesthetic splendour, low quality of the message or references to popular patterns. The creators of kitsch are often the advertising producers themselves, trying to evoke strong emotions in the recipients.

Michał Szostak draws attention to the differences between the experiences accompanying aesthetic areas and those related to kitsch. He emphasises the analysis of the creator's approach: open to criticism and discussion in the case of aesthetics, focusing on universal values, especially ethical ones. In contrast, when discussing areas related to kitsch, the creator may be less receptive to criticism, prone to duplicating and copying, and focused on mass reception. For a work of kitsch, the key is to satisfy the recipient's desires, unlike in the case of an aesthetic work, which emphasises the artist's aesthetic values. It is also worth noting that truth and reference to reality, which provide inspiration for the artist, are important in aesthetic creation. In contrast, in kitsch creation, pleasure and immediate satisfaction are given priority, often at the expense of authenticity (Szostak, 2021).

Referring to the value and potential of a brand's audience, many companies use aspects of both aesthetics and kitsch in their communication strategies.

Aesthetics plays a key role in creating aesthetic experiences that can attract customers' attention and evoke positive emotions towards the brand. This is important for products and the brand image as a whole.

Following M. Szostak's (2021) classification, some brands may also consciously reach for kitsch content. Although kitsch may be perceived as controversial or negative, it can still attract attention and distinguish the brand from its competitors. As a result, brands that decide to use kitsch elements in their communication may gain greater interest and involvement from their audiences.

The recipients of kitsch can be those who reject it as tacky or infantile and those who find some aesthetic or emotional value in it. Society increasingly responds to kitsch with irony and criticism, which can challenge brands that use it in their campaigns.

In the context of values, kitsch in advertising can distort the brand's image and influence its perception by customers. The positive consequences of kitsch may include short-term interest and an increase in advertising reach, but the negative effects, such as loss of credibility or reduced brand reputation, may outweigh them in the long term.

Analysing the Apart advertisement, the Kubota brand strategy and the Barbie film, one can see different approaches to the use of kitsch in marketing communication. Apart's advertising campaign was criticised for being excessively pompous and out of touch with reality, which may lower the brand's image. It is not without significance that in the case of Apart's advertising, he wanted to use the storytelling strategy, which can be a key element in influencing recipients. By telling a story through an advertising campaign, the brand wanted to build an emotional bond with customers, engaging them in the narrative and creating a deeper connection with the product, but it achieved a different effect, especially during the holiday season.

It also did not use the Memejacking trend, that is, capturing memes and trends from social media for marketing purposes so that it could have turned the communication to its advantage. In today's digital environment, where content in the form of memes is often shared and commented on, failure to respond to current trends can make advertising less attractive to younger audiences and fail to generate as much interest as other, more interactive campaigns. Instead, Apart's ad could use Memescaping, which is how an advertising theme becomes a popular meme on the internet. By creating viral content adopted by the online community as a meme, the brand could achieve much greater reach and engagement among potential customers. Memescaping can contribute to further disseminating advertising content and increase brand awareness among internet users and, importantly, younger audiences. Thanks to this, Apart's advertising campaign could achieve tremendous success and generate greater online community involvement, translating into increased sales and a positive brand image.

It is worth emphasising that the Kubota brand strategy, positively using kitsch elements, can build a new marketing message based on tradition and cooperation between brands, but an excess of kitsch may distort the message and reduce the quality of communication. Analysing the brand's approach, we see no threat to its image.

Although related to kitsch, the film "Barbie" conveyed value in its social message, which the audience can perceive positively. The example of strengthening the Barbie brand contributed to resuming the discussion around the film and film products. However, please remember that this strategy is not suitable for every brand: excessive use of kitsch may lead to a loss of authenticity and a reduction in the value of the message.

Kitsch in advertising can have positive and negative consequences for brands, depending on the context and skilful use of this phenomenon in customer communication. Understanding the audience, their values and the subtle lines between attention-grabbing and irritating advertising is essential.

Conclusion

Kitsch, in the context of brand management, is a multifaceted topic that requires taking into account changes in popular culture, technological progress and evolving consumer preferences. Introducing kitsch elements into advertising strategies can bring success and risk to the brand. Therefore, it is crucial to thoroughly understand the context and adapt the strategy to the brand's marketing goals.

Kitsch in advertising has had and continues to impact brand perception and brand management strategies significantly. Using kitsch elements may lead to mixed reactions from the consumer's experience point of view. On the one hand, excessive kitsch may discourage consumers and negatively affect the brand image, seeming unnatural or artificial, as in the case of Apart. On the other hand, moderate use of kitsch can attract attention and evoke desirable emotions, which can be an effective marketing strategy for building a positive brand image, as demonstrated by the Kubota case.

The development of digital technologies and social media has significantly influenced the use and perception of kitsch in advertising. Thanks to the internet and social media platforms, kitsch content can quickly become viral and spread among users, which in turn can help to increase the reach of advertising. At the same time, internet users are becoming increasingly aware of marketing tactics and sensitive to exaggeration, which forces marketers to be more subtle and creative in using kitsch elements.

In the context of effective marketing strategies, kitsch experience elements can be effective if they are moderately integrated with the brand message, as in the case of Barbie. It is essential that the communication, message and advertising is authentic and engaging, which can be achieved through storytelling and interaction with users on social media. It was not possible to use what is available in the Apart brand. Additionally, Memescaping, a process in which an advertising motif becomes a popular meme on the internet, can contribute to increasing consumer involvement and building a positive brand image through the organic spread of content on the internet. However, it is crucial to balance originality and acceptance by the online community to avoid negative reactions and achieve the desired results.

It is also worth keeping in mind certain limitations of this study in terms of considering kitsch in the above advertising campaigns. Firstly, assessing the effectiveness of kitsch-based strategies may be subjective and depend on recipients' individual preferences and experiences. Moreover, kitsch may be perceived differently in different cultures and communities, which complicates clear conclusions about its impact on brand perception. In the chapter, as a case study, I used brands that sparked much discussion for local market recipients, but in the context of another country, they may not arouse such emotions. Additionally, the variability of social media trends means that the effectiveness of kitsch-based strategies may be temporarily limited. What may be considered a trendy meme today may be passé tomorrow, requiring marketers to adapt and monitor the situation constantly. It should be noted that not all brands can effectively use kitsch in their campaigns. For some industries, especially serious or high-culture ones, excessive use of kitsch may be inappropriate and negatively affect the brand image. Finally, there is a risk that the use of kitsch in advertising may be perceived as an attempt at manipulation or a creative failure on the part of the brand. For this reason, marketers need to exercise moderation and ensure authenticity and appropriate tone in communication with recipients. The study covered only three selected brands; the analysis of the issue does not exhaust the research topic and is only a contribution to subsequent analyses and considerations.

Further research into the role of kitsch in today's advertising world may contribute to a better understanding of its impact and effectiveness. It is worth noting that the approaches to using kitsch in marketing vary hugely. Examples include advertisements and commercials that initially did not imply any kitsch but came to be perceived as kitschy by the audience, as well as cases where brands that were previously considered kitschy began to build their new rethought image based on pop culture. The latter is exemplified by the Kubota company, which drew on its heritage of being steeped in kitsch from the times of the Polish People's Republic to build a new openness towards the brand. Similarly, although some may still associate it with kitsch because of the stereotypical perception of the colour pink, the Barbie doll used the power of its brand and the values conveyed by the film to explore new marketing opportunities. Kitsch in brand management is a dynamic issue that can be both a challenge and an opportunity for marketers. The key to success is skilfully using kitsch's potential, understanding audiences' reactions and adapting the strategy accordingly to align it with contemporary trends and consumer expectations.

References

Apart, Historia, https://www.apart.pl/swiat/firma/historia (25.02.2024).

BlueMedia, *Omnichannel, AR i VR łącznikiem między e-sklepem a sprzedażą stacjonarną*, https://utn.pl/QpjKb (25.02.2024).

Canal+ (2024), https://premiery.pl.canalplus.com/film-online/barbie,4002 (11.04.2024).

Chmielewska A. (2018), Komunikacja marki w mediach społecznościowych na przykładzie tvp S.A. *Acta Universitatis Nicolai Copernici. Zarządzanie* 45 (1):19–32. https://doi.org/10.12775/AUNC_ZARZ.2018.002.

Interactivevision, *Wzorowy przykład rebrendingu, czyli krótka historia klapek Kubota*, https://interactivevision.pl/blog/wzorcowy-przyklad-rebrandingu-czyli-krotka-historia-klapek-kubota/ (25.02.2024).

Kall J. (2010), Zarządzanie marką instytucji badawczej w oparciu o model "góry lodowej", *Marketing Instytucji Naukowych i Badawczych* 1 (1):33–38.

Kozłowska A. (2024), *Barbie 2023: (anty)feministyczna bajka o odzyskiwaniu kobiecości?*, Tygiel, Liblin.

Kubota, Historia marki, https://kubotastore.pl/historia-marki (25.02.2024).

LinkedIn (2023), *Jak zrealizowaliśmy najbardziej kreatywną kampanię employer-brandingową.* https://pl.linkedin.com/pulse/jak-zrealizowali%C5%9Bmy-najbardziej-kreatywn%C4%85-kampani%C4%99-employer-brandingow%C4%85- (27.02.2024).

Masiarz E. (2016), *Prankvertising i immersive branding – emocje na usługach marketing wirusowego*, Novae Res, Gdańsk.

Matusiak K.B. (2011), *Innowacje i transfer technologii Słownik pojęć*, Polska Agencja Rozwoju Przedsiębiorczości, Warszawa.

OECD i Eurostat (2005), *Podręcznik Oslo. Zasady gromadzenia i interpretacji danych dotyczących innowacji*, third edition, Ministerstwo Nauki i Szkolnictwa Wyższego, Departament Strategii i Rozwoju Nauki, Warszawa. https://home.agh.edu.pl/~kkulak/lib/exe/fetch.php?media=user:konrad:vary:oslo-manual.pdf.

Ostrowicki M. (2002), Struktura oddziaływania reklamy, in *Kultura Współczesna*, no. 3–4 (33–34), Instytut Kultury, Warszawa.

Ostrowska I. (2010), *Model kształtowania lojalności konsumentów w stosunku do marki*, Uniwersytet Szczeciński, Szczecin.

Pomykalski A. (2004), Innowacyjność przedsiębiorstw w kontekście rynku globalnego, Lodziensis. *Folia Oeconomica* 179(1):141–148.

Press (2021), *Reklama Apartu w kontekście kampanii Yes pokazuje krótkowzroczność marki*, https://www.press.pl/tresc/68290,_reklama-apartu-w-kontekscie-kampanii-yes-pokazuje-krotkowzrocznosc-marki (27.02.2024).

Scherman J. (2016), *What is visual storytelling? The growing trend in multimedia design*, Rasmussen University, https://www.rasmussen.edu/degrees/design/blog/visual-storytelling/ (25.02.2024).

Schumpeter J.A. (1960), *Teoria rozwoju gospodarczego*, PWN, Warszawa.

Stopczyńska K. (2015), Wykorzystywanie social media w zarządzaniu wizerunkiem marki w sytuacji kryzysowej, *Problemy zarządzania, finansów i marketingu*, 41 (1).

Stopczyńska K. (2016), Wykorzystywanie storytelling w kreowaniu wizerunku marki w social media, *Handel Wewnętrzny* 3 (362).

Szostak M. (2021), Kicz: nasza ochrona przed rzeczywistością, *Więź*, 12 January, https://wiez.pl/2021/01/12/kicz-nasza-ochrona-przed-rzeczywistoscia/ (23.02.2024).

Szymańska K. (2015), Wykorzystanie real-time marketingu jako narzędzia budowania wizerunku firmy w social media, *Zarządzanie Mediami*, Tome 3 (4).

Tokfm(2023), *"Barbie" ocieka różem i kiczem. Jest typową rozrywką? "To świat matriarchatu, w którym Ken nie jest istotny"*, https://www.tokfm.pl/Tokfm/7,103089,30020121,barbie-ocieka-rozem-i-kiczem-jest-typowa-rozrywka-to-swiat.html (25.02.2024).

Upshaw L.B. (1995), *Building brand identity: A strategy for success in a hostile marketplace*, Wiley, Now York.

Urbanek G. (2019), *Zarządzanie wartością i wycena marki*, 1st edition, wydawnictwo CeDeWu, Warszawa.

Wirtualnemedia (2020), *Kpiny i parodie świątecznej reklamy Apartu. Eksperci: luksus i baśniowość typowe dla biżuterii*, https://www.wirtualnemedia.pl/artykul/swiateczna-reklama-apart-kpiny-i-parodie-eksperci-luksus-i-basniowosc-sa-typowe-dla-marek-bizuterii-opinie (10.03.2024).

Wirtualnemedia (2022), *Live shopping, audio, Metawers, AR, VR czy QR. Oto trendy w marketingu mediów społecznościowych w 2022 roku*, https://utn.pl/xpPH3 (25.02.2024).

Wirtualnemedia (2023), *Barbie" podbija polskie kina. "Marketingowy majstersztyk*, https://www.wirtualnemedia.pl/artykul/obsesja-barbie-film-opinie-marketingowy-majstersztyk-reklama-opinie (28.02.2024).

Zaczynski M. (2020), *Co jest nie tak z reklamą Apartu*? https://michalzaczynski.com/2020/11/14/co-jest-nie-tak-z-reklama-apartu/ (24.02.2024).

Żero S. (2018), https://repozytorium.uwb.edu.pl/jspui/bitstream/11320/7141/1/S_Zero_Roznice_w_interpretacji_pojec_innowacji_oraz_imitacji_przedmiotu.pdf (10.04.2024).

9 Kitsch in entrepreneurship

Meal kits, taste and the art of socio-economic enterprise

David M. Atkinson

Introduction

It is axiomatic that in the world of business and enterprise, concepts such as leadership and management resist a stable, consensual definition. I observe that such concepts have given (and continue to give) rise to multiple types, typologies and other such classifications. Both consequently and consistently, associated academic journals and other professional sources are replete with an ever-growing range of theoretic and empiric approaches to their study and promotion. Is leadership a science, a craft or even an art? Is management the same (Atkinson, 2007)? And, at the pinnacle of socio-economic enterprise, I observe that entrepreneurship invokes a similar range of diverse treatments (Atkinson, 2023b). Here, alongside those that practice their craft, a (social) science of leadership-, of management- or of enterprise-study, rests within an academic business-school environment. I have argued (Atkinson, 2023b) that such study is (also generally) based on a dialectic approach in which those that study such emergent concepts follow a process of theorising and/or empirical testing around thesis, antithesis and synthesis. A surfeit of conclusions is (and continues to be) drawn in an attempt to better explain, educate and guide the practitioners of these ennobled crafts of leadership, management, and (of particular relevance to this chapter) entrepreneurship. What we leave unexplained, and therefore absent in the education of our enterprising leaders, managers and entrepreneurs, is what we often attribute to the art of this or that: to the art of leadership, of management, or of enterprise. And it is to this latter art – entrepreneurship as the art of enterprise – that I now turn.

Despite my observation of the absence of a normalised and consensual definition of entrepreneurship *per se*, there *is* a form of consensus held around the idea of entrepreneurship as a more loosely defined, amorphous concept, one that includes entrepreneurial activity (such as new business start-up), entrepreneurial aspiration (such as growth expectations) and entrepreneurial attitudes (such as perceived opportunities) (Doran, McCarthy, & O'Connor, 2018). Entrepreneurship is held as critical for economic growth (Doran et al., 2018; Rideout & Gray, 2013). Thus, education about it – entrepreneurship education (E-Ed) – is held as a 'vital catalyser' for its practice (Smolka, Geradts, van der Zwan, & Rauch, 2023).

DOI: 10.4324/9781003504931-10

Given this seemingly 'vital' requirement, the fundamental questions I address in this chapter are 1) does a normalised entrepreneurship practice, fashioned through a contemporary dialectic-informed, capitalistic E-Ed tend to the kitsch in enterprise? And, if so, 2) does this tendency in any sense matter? And, if a tendency to kitsch matters, 3) should we bother teaching/learning a 'kitschy' E-Ed in this purely capitalistic way?

To paraphrase Szostak and Sulkowski (2020, p. 7595), I invoke the concept of 'kitsch in entrepreneurship' in the sense that a practice of entrepreneurship is a 'behaviour/manifestation/activity/attitude in the [socio-economic] organisation [of enterprise])'. So informed, such practice 'deviate[s] from any universal value of truth (understood as intended action [on the part of the (entrepreneurship) practitioner, to the realisation of something of the absent other]) in favour of appearances and external forms'. Such practice favours prettiness and pleasure in an entrepreneurial enterprise-for-enterprise's sake, as opposed to, for example, an entrepreneurship for the sake (i.e. general good) of society. Here, I argue that an entrepreneurship that tends to the realisation of the kitsch in enterprise has only (limited) instrumental value to a limited range of stakeholders; it is likely (therefore) to only achieve limited success. This matters in the context of an impactful entrepreneurship (and its E-Ed) that might be both sustainable in the long-run and of greater value to a greater segment of society.

To explore this enterprising context and address the questions I have raised, I shall proceed as follows. In the following section, I will explore the premiss of kitsch as an interpretation of truth value in the practice of enterprise.[1] I will follow with an example in considering the value of truth in the otherwise entrepreneurial case of the HelloFresh meal-kit company, before concluding with a discussion that seeks to address the questions I have raised. Overall, this methodology amounts to an emergent (in the ethnographic sense) single case study (Lee & Saunders, 2017), in which I adopt a method of applied analytical philosophy (Daly, 2010; Ndlazi, 2022). While a single case study cannot suggest a definitive response to the questions I pose, it can (and indeed should) pose a legitimate challenge to the dominant (social) science-informed practice in which the questions arise (Retolaza & San-Jose, 2017).

Premiss: kitsch in enterprise

In invoking a concept of kitsch in the theme of this edited volume, I specifically draw on the aesthetic experience. Here, as Szostak comments in the opening Introduction:

> Kitsch was and still is a way to increase the financial profits of artists who, putting aside the issue of fidelity to the ideals of art, focus on producing artefacts that find large audiences and thus enable them to earn a living more effectively. The kitsch phenomenon is a kind of victory of quantity over quality.

To explore this theme in relation to entrepreneurial enterprise, I interpret the notion of the artistic truth of intended action to refer to the entrepreneurial action on the part of the entrepreneurship practitioner (as an artist), to reveal something of the absent other. Here, I further draw on my argument that the (emergent) Entrepreneur (as an Artist) has a responsibility – in practising a creative, mimetic (in the Aristotelian sense[2]) application of their 'craft' of enterprise – to reveal something of the absent other in their enterprising 'vision' (Atkinson, 2023a). The corollary is that the enterprising faux-artist/faux-entrepreneur may (intentionally or naively) 'other' the truth of what should be overtly present in their work. I suggest that such a faux-artist/faux-entrepreneur is chasing the kitsch in their enterprise. This chasing is an appeal to the consumer as an audience in terms of the 'appearances and external forms [that favour prettiness and pleasure]' (Szostak & Sułkowski, 2020, p. 7595).

In the world of socio-economic enterprise – a world in which we all, as both consumers and producers, live a range of experiences – enterprising exemplars of the kitsch abound. Here, our most overtly produced and consumed 'kitschy' objects range from the classic lava lamp to the many items available through enterprising online e-commerce outlets, for example: https://www.kitschrepublic.co.uk/ and https://www.mykitsch.com/ – where brands may leverage the idea of kitsch within their identity. However, while the overtly kitsch may find its niche in an exchange of extrinsic value between producer and consumer, a normalised entrepreneurship practice – fashioned as a contemporary dialectic-informed, capitalistic education – risks the promotion of a more subtle, yet insidious form of kitsch in any enterprise. While products such as a lava lamp may have an extrinsic value if it is desired by someone, it possesses little, if anything, that is of intrinsic value (Garofalo & Geuras, 2015). The lava lamp holds little pretention to a universal value of either truth or (aesthetic) taste. In this sense, I hold the lava lamp as an overt deviation from any universal value of truth (of artistic action) and suggest it is clearly the product of an intended enterprising action on the part of its producer that simply favours its appearance and external form. In this respect, the lava lamp is little more than a variation on the theme of a lamp – a design. The lamp's value is extrinsic; it is a value held by those consumers that desire the product for its particular design and appeal to their subjective aesthetic of prettiness and pleasure; the exchange of value is an exchange in enterprise-for-enterprise's sake.

Diametrically opposed to the limited extrinsic value of any enterprise-for-enterprise's sake, I raise the potential intrinsic value of an enterprise that is enterprise-for-society's sake, such as that to be found in the nature of social enterprise or SE (see, for example, Defourny & Nyssens, 2008; White, Samuel, Peattie, & Doherty, 2022). Here, leaving aside the paradoxical nature of SE (White et al., 2022), while all enterprises are to some extent social – in that any enterprise is a process of value exchange between people (producers and consumers) – SEs can be defined by their preference for social (consumer) purpose, one of the principal aims of which is a service to its society (Defourny & Nyssens, 2008). Such an aim of 'social service' is an appeal to a universal value of truth, which can be further understood (for my argument here) as intended enterprising action on the part of its producer that favours the realisation of something of the absent other: a promotion of (an absent) social responsibility – a purpose of responding to the needs (as opposed to wants and desires) of society.

Between the poles of a kitschy enterprise for enterprise's sake and SE's enterprise for society's sake lies a rich tapestry of enterprise potential. Here, we might often overlook the 'true' question of value in the rush to promote (and thus educate for) socio-economic enterprise. Thus, on a global basis, we witness a promotion of entrepreneurship (studies) as a pinnacle of enterprising action (O'Connor, 2013). Yet we may also observe that enterprising practitioners often eschew any intrinsic social value in favour of a purely economic response to the financial exigencies of the present. Here, as Spash notes: '[prioritising] financial interests and economic growth over human life is nothing new' (Spash, 2020, p. 1087). Such interests are clearly evident in the 'social' struggles (of injustice) faced within societies and the degradation of our global environment. Thus, in a context where socio-economic enterprise tends merely to economic (financial) enterprise, I experience 'social value' as an 'othered' dimension of enterprise. While I may feel the social injustices of such enterprise, its truth appears hidden from me in the pleasure I may take from the aesthetic attractiveness of its contribution to my financial growth.

Accessing the truth behind any appearance is a call on the aesthetics of a situation. *As* Szostak and Sulkowski comment, 'Considering the world of values, in aesthetic experience we find domination of truth, but in kitsch experience – domination of prettiness and pleasure for the kitsch consumer' (2020, p. 7588). Thus, between the poles of an overt practice of kitsch in any enterprise with no pretence to intrinsic value and an overt practice of social enterprise, with a focus on intrinsic value, lies the potential for what I shall call, here, the insidious kitsch. This is the production of kitsch with only a pretence to intrinsic value and thus a suppression of the truth, either naïvely or intentionally. This is the insincere, insidious practice of kitsch in any enterprise as the suppression of the 'other' – violence to both the producer (artist) and the consumer (audience). It is a violation of the potential of truth in the entrepreneurial ideal of entrepreneurship as the art of enterprise, and it is a violation of the value of an experience of that othered truth to the consumer.

The intentional or naïve othering of a truth in vision, as opposed to the search for the disclosure of new truths, is violence towards both the producer (artist) and the consumer (audience). There is no lava in a lava lamp. There is no dominance of cuteness in replicating the image of a kitten on countless 'kitschy' products available online. And there are no tomatoes in a rogan josh curry from the Kashmiri region of the Indian sub-continent. Each of these examples may hold an extrinsic value to those who might choose the lava lamp, or choose to copy and share endless memes of kitschy kittens, or to those who, as a variation on Home Meal Replacements or HMRs (Costa, Dekker, Beumer, Rombouts, & Jongen, 2001), sign up to the delivery of an HelloFresh meal kit,[3] perhaps with the option of its '"Best UK Recipe 2022" Golden Potato Topped Lamb Rogan Josh with Lentils and Yoghurt' (HelloFresh, 2023). But what truths remain hidden? What insidious violence emerges from the kitsch in such an enterprise? And does it matter? To consider these questions, I offer an exemplar from the HMR/meal kit industry, where HelloFresh can be acknowledged as one of the dominant players (Helm, 2018) in what, in 2016, was reported as a $1 billion global market for venture capital-backed (entrepreneurial) start-up enterprise (Hayden, 2016). Here, the digital world invokes the capitalist entrepreneurial ideal of creative destruction (Schumpeter, 2018), in which technical innovation offers the entrepreneurial attitude of *recognising-an-opportunity-to-disrupt-markets-and-industries*, new methods to drive out old ones (Johnson, Lusch, & Schmidt, 2020). This ideal appeals to the entrepreneurial activity of new business start-ups and feeds the aspiration of high growth expectations. But does a normalised entrepreneurship practice, fashioned through a contemporary dialectic-informed, capitalistic E-Ed, tend to the kitsch in enterprise?

HelloFresh – an entrepreneurial artform or (insidious) kitsch in enterprise?

In the novel, *Chef* (Singh, 2010), the Sikh-protagonist's reflection of his time as a General's chef in the Indian Army, stationed in Kashmir, on the disputed border of India and Pakistan at a time of armed conflict and insurgency during the late-1980s, is insightful. The novel is replete, as one might expect, with references to the culinary arts of the cuisines of not only the Indian sub-continent but also from further afield. 'Szechuan noodles, linguine with clam sauce, lamb Provençal, Pavlova' (p. 17) are mixed in narrative with an inevitable 'weakness for Kashmiri dishes. Mughali mutton with turnips, rogan josh, kebab nargisi, ... karam saag... and the kurd-flavored [sic] meatballs of gushtaba' (p. 26) give testament to the chef's art. And we learn that there are two kinds of chef. 'Those who disturb the universe with their [art of] cooking, and those who do not dare to do so' (p. 85). In this latter camp, the protagonist proclaims his own allegiance to the art of '[transporting] people elsewhere, far away from the table', while the former practice the art of 'dazzling' the table (p. 85). In both types of chef, we may discern a truth to their practice and in their preparations.

While the value of truth is a subject much argued in philosophy (see, for example, Horwich, 2006; Mitova, 2023), here a truth is taken to be (in the artistic sense) a mimetic revelation of the absent other. An artistic truth, in this sense, is a non-instrumental truth. An artistic truth is a truth for its own sake. In this regard, it is a truth with a value regardless of whether it supports a belief in a good reception or a bad reception (Horwich, 2006). It has value precisely in that it represents the artist's belief in the value of a truth about the absent other revealed by that artist. As a revealing, the artistic act of realisation of a truth is an act of inquiry into that absent other giving rise to that truth, in which the value of its truth is, in part, inherited from the value of the inquiry itself (Mitova, 2023), the truth of which is presented (in a non-instrumental way) by the artist to their audience.

In the chef as artist seeking to transport their diners to places far away from the table at which they dine, the chef strives to reveal the truth-of-place concerning the origin of their 'preparations': that which is absent from the table and the dish prepared. In the chef as artist seeking to dazzle their table, those seated are, in Singh's work, exposed to the truth of the ingredients as the chef strives to reveal what they discern of their potential: appraising 'fruits, vegetables, meats with astonishment, [grasping] them with humility, with reverence, very carefully' inquiring of each its potential (Singh, 2010, p. 85). But in a typical meal kit recipe, where is the truth in what HelloFresh produces? Where is the value in truth for both consumer and producer?

The HelloFresh company was founded in Germany in 2011 and is a leader in the meal-kit delivery industry. It uses an e-commerce business model, with membership subscriptions to purchase its product (the meal kit) as a service (Moro, Cauchick-Miguel, & Mendes, 2022). The mission of HelloFresh 'is to provide convenience, taste, and flexibility to its customers by eliminating the need to plan and shop for groceries' (Sharda, Krampe, & Ingenbleek, 2024, p. 2). In the UK market, meal kits are said to appeal to the 'creative and committed, sustainability ethical, time-poor/conscious, and/or the CSR-focussed consumers' (Moir, Megheirkouni, Fletcher, & Oniga, 2023). From the consumer perspective, a meal kit offers an individual the potential to adopt the mantle of chef in the production of a meal. This is a 'painting-by-numbers' entry to the culinary arts. In the case of HelloFresh's 'Best UK Recipe 2022' Golden Potato Topped Lamb Rogan Josh with Lentils and Yoghurt, the promise – at least for the creative and committed consumer – would appear to be the convenient preparation of a dish that will conjure up the taste of Kashmiri cuisine, transporting the consumer to the Indian sub-continent. Yet, to consider the recipe's ingredients and note the dominance of 'Tomato Passata' (HelloFresh, 2023) is to give a lie to any authentic truth of a place. As we learn from Chef's protagonist in an exchange with a Kashmiri of his acquaintance, there are no tomatoes in a rogan josh (Singh, 2010). Neither does the preparation seek to expose the low-grade potential of its kit-form of irreverently selected ingredients; ingredients selected on the basis of economies of scale, rather than any sense of astonishment and awe in their potentiality. Consider, for example, the substitution of low-grade lamb mince. Mince is a by-product of the butchery and trimming process, once the choicest cuts of the animal have been selected and removed; it is also of a generally higher fat content than lean meat, with (in England for example) a fat content which may typically be up to 25% (DEFRA, 2017). Such substitutions set up a countervailing truth, an offset to the truth sought by the consumer, a friction.

For certain ingredients of the HelloFresh rogan josh dish, for example yoghurt, there are potential nutritional and health benefits. Yoghurt has been argued to improve lactose tolerance and may have a potential in body weight reduction and fat loss; there are also held to be several health attributes related to probiotic bacteria found in some yoghurts (McKinley, 2005). Yet overall, the nutritional quality presented in such meal kits is, at best, questionable, with higher than necessary levels of fat and salt (McKay, 2023; Moores, Bell, Buckingham, & Dickinson, 2021) and associated nutritional risks (Gibson & Partridge, 2019). Again, alternately present truths present a friction to the truth sought or offered.

There may be an argument for intrinsic value presented to the sustainability ethical consumer. Part of the marketing of meal kits is that they offer the sustainability ethical consumer agency in acting sustainably by reducing food waste in only buying the exact quantity of ingredients required for any particular dish consumers may seek (Moir et al., 2023). However, here, as Schuster et al. (2022) suggest, meal kits appear to lower the levels of food cooking waste, yet can lead to higher levels of preparation and plate waste compared to traditional meals. Furthermore, as Sharda et al. (2024, p. 2) report:

> With all ingredients that need to be packaged separately for each meal, HelloFresh customers are continuously confronted with plastic when preparing their meals. The company's rapid increase in size made HelloFresh an easy target for (online) campaigns questioning the sustainability goals set by the company and accusing its customers of supporting an unsustainable company.

Devoid, then, of any intrinsic value of artistic truth, these frictions of an apparent lack of respect for authenticity and the culinary arts, and questionable quality and sustainability claims, offer little to the consumer but the instrumental, extrinsic value of convenience. This truth of 'pretty' convenience hides its frictions behind a mask of marketing material and other positive messages enhanced by carefully curated examples of food photography. And despite the attractiveness of low-priced initial subscriptions, the regular price of meal kits suggests some consumers pay a hefty price for such unauthentic convenience. For example, Staubach and Jäger (2023) found that, particularly in the case of two-person families, or two HMR dishes per week, meal kits were generally priced too expensive. This is problematic since the authors had previously identified that a significant percentage (44.3%) of their study participants who had subscribed to a meal kit comprised households of two. Furthermore, 52.2% of their respondents that had cancelled or paused their subscriptions were from two-person households (Staubach & Jäger, 2023, p. 74).

From the producer perspective, the meal kit can be no pretence to a mastery of the culinary arts. As an e-commerce business model, HelloFresh is a company that offers its services – recipe details and pre-measured ingredients – to consumers, their customers, to facilitate their interaction in the convenient cooking of a meal (Abdollahi & Leimstoll, 2011). The producer devolves the opportunity for the exercise of culinary artistic capabilities to the consumer. The value exchange from consumer to producer is not an appreciation of the product per se; it resolves to one of scale, in which the beauty of commercial success for the producer is a challenge of increasing subscriptions. However, it is suggested that: 'Companies in [this] space must develop great experiences (as opposed to great subscriptions) to avoid high churn rates and to accelerate both growth and profitability' (Chen, Fenyo, Yang, & Zhang, 2018). Given the observations of Staubach and Jäger (2023), the 'beauty' of convenience cannot be sold at any price.

From the biographies of HelloFresh's founders (HelloFresh, 2024b), four of the named executives (Dominik Richter, Group CEO and founder; Thomas Griesel, CEO International and co-founder; Christian Gartner, CFO; and Ed Boyes, CCO and co-founder of HelloFresh UK) are characterised by their education and experience in business and finance, rather than experience of the food industry. Held as an exemplar of entrepreneurship in the contemporary digital entrepreneurship space (Vadana, Torkkeli, Kuivalainen, & Saarenketo, 2020), these founders have been influenced by contemporary business-school education, including that of entrepreneurial practice, that is seeded with the economics of Schumpeter (Plehwe, 2020). Such education is, by any means, a dialectically informed, capitalistic E-Ed. Yet I observe exemplars of its product that clearly tend to the kitsch in enterprise. In the case of HelloFresh, the founders pursue their artistic value in the art of business enterprise. Yet it resolves not to the ideals of entrepreneurship but to entrepreneurship in its kitschiest, capitalistic form, in which the artist's concentration is on the attainment of incoming value only, with scant regard to the value transferred in the product of their labour to their consumer. To parody Szostak from earlier, HelloFresh appears little more than a way to increase the financial profits of its founders and investors, who, putting aside the issue of fidelity to the ideals of their potential as food entrepreneurs, focus on producing meal kits that (attempt to) find large audiences of consuming subscribers and thus enable them to earn a living more effectively. The success of HelloFresh is a victory of quantity over quality. HelloFresh is the personification of the concept of kitsch in an enterprise. It cannot reach an apotheosis as an exemplar of the art of food entrepreneurship. There is friction in the service of the 'creative and committed', the 'sustainability ethical', and the 'CSR-focussed' consumers of our society.

Enterprising kitsch – a Socratic matter?

Having addressed my first question, for my second, I ask, does this tendency to kitsch in entrepreneurial enterprise in any sense matter? Kitsch is not inherently bad, and neither is art inherently good. While the artist might struggle in the production of an art object and in the satisfaction of their audience's expectations, the kitsch invokes the opposite: an easy satisfaction of such expectations (Linstead,

2002). In the art of enterprise, as in the art of, for example, painting, chasing the kitsch through bowing to the aesthetic (beauty) of convenience is thus an easy route to consumer satisfaction and the frictionless exchange of (financial) value in an *enterprise-for-enterprise's* sake. If the producer aims to satisfy only the market of consumers seeking convenience only, without any pretence to higher ideals, then the extrinsic nature of an explicit appeal to the value of convenience suggests (in its truth) little possibility of violence to an 'other'. The corollary here is that the enterprising (even entrepreneurial) producer who practises their enterprise in an overt play on the kitsch can, indeed, be a good for society. Such a producer would meet the extrinsic desires or wants of a sector of that society while posing a negligible risk to others. Yet any suggestion that the producer may be misleading others (naïvely or intentionally) – for example in the expectation that a product of kitsch in an enterprise would deliver other values (beyond an aesthetic surface of convenience) – risks a bad outcome. If there is any risk in the entrepreneurial production of kitsch that others may face such a 'bad' experience, should we then generalise and promote such practice through E-Ed?

Here, let me assume that the promotion of a normalised entrepreneurship practice, fashioned as a contemporary dialectic-informed capitalistic E-Ed, is intrinsically good. As an intrinsic good, such an entrepreneurship practice infers a 'good' outcome for society. As a consequence, any desire to promote the kitsch in entrepreneurial enterprise would seem appropriate; as would the education an enterprising society along such E-Ed lines. However, I may question is such a desire to promote kitsch itself good? Is what an Entrepreneurship Educator might hold as an exemplar of good entrepreneurial practice good for society (and therefore for educators to replicate in E-Ed) because the practice itself is intrinsically good for society; or is it good because the Entrepreneurship Educator merely holds it to be good (extrinsically)? For example, is the fact that the HelloFresh company is a dominant player in a $1 billion market a good exemplar of entrepreneurship because its 'successful' enterprising practice is intrinsically good for society? Or is it the case that HelloFresh and the entrepreneurial practice it represents as an exemplar is good because Entrepreneurship Educators find it to be extrinsically good; that is, does it simply present an instrumental value in teaching a belief in good entrepreneurship?

The form of dilemma in argumentation represented here is similar to the Euthyphro dilemma in Plato's Socratic Dialogues (Daly, 2010). As a form of Euthyphrean dilemma, a good entrepreneurial practice can only be the subject of E-Ed if it is either judged instrumentally (thus extrinsically) good by those that teach it; or if they deem it to be intrinsically good for their society. Analytically, it cannot be both. To take the first option, if I am to suggest that the expertise of Entrepreneurship Educators is such that they are able to judge what is good entrepreneurial practice, then I must understand why it is good; otherwise, I am simply observing an arbitrary exemplar, with little foundation in truth. Thus, as an academic exercise, I might question by what theory or *a priori* knowledge can Entrepreneurship Educators hold a certain practice to be a good, and, therefore, to replicate it in E-Ed? Here, given their exhaustive review and critique of E-Ed studies (from 1997 to 2011), Rideout and Grey are insightful: 'when trying to answer the question, "Does E-Ed really work?" we are [left with the] answer: we really do not know' (2013, p. 346). The suggestion is that whatever theory postulated on whatever normalisation of practice is, in a sense, deficient in sufficient features and that its impact on further practice is at least questionable. And, despite the assertion of much progress in E-Ed pedagogy in the last decade (Gabrielsson, Hägg, Landström, & Politis, 2020), this deficiency in formal E-Ed appears to continue the promise of less impact than other approaches to understanding and preparing for entrepreneurial practice (Debarliev, Janeska-Iliev, Stripeikis, & Zupan, 2022).

If entrepreneurship matters to society, exemplars of its practice would also appear to matter, particularly if those exemplars inform good entrepreneurship practice through E-Ed. As Plato's Socrates might ask: what is the relationship between good entrepreneurial practice and entrepreneurial practice held as good entrepreneurship in teaching? Here, to avoid any circularity in the analysis of my argument, the suggestion is that if Entrepreneurship Educators are in some way unable to effectively judge what instrumental value an exemplar of entrepreneurial practice might hold for E-Ed, then we must consider the second option of the argument, that a good exemplar for E-Ed might only be so if it is deemed to be intrinsically good for society. This is an appeal to effect, not cause. What is the truth of the impact (positive or negative) of the experience of an entrepreneurial outcome? Avoiding any circularity, the Entrepreneurship Educator cannot be the judge of what is good for society. It must be society (the consumer) that judges. In effect, only society can judge the truth of its consumption of entrepreneurial practice. And to do so, it must be able to experience it.

Here, common sense suggests that if HelloFresh can sustain a market of consumers happy to pay for the kitschy beauty of an aesthetic of convenience, then, as either producer or consumer perceives no violence to the other in a value transaction, I might hold a good subsists. But this good is not intrinsic to the product; it is conditional on the experiences of both the producer and the consumer. The normalisation of the good is purely instrumental, and there can be no suggestion that another consumer with dissimilar needs or values in another context will experience the same good. What is kitsch to one consumer may not be kitsch to another. While, to the Entrepreneurship Educator, the emergence of HelloFresh as an entrepreneurial venture could offer a set of normalised features, it cannot be representative of all variations in consumer experience. For the replication of features of the HelloFresh practice of enterprise to serve as exemplars of a certain entrepreneurial practice, its limitations in value must be explicit. Enterprise practice can only achieve such an explicitness in a narrowly defined market. However, if claims (e.g. in marketing) promise greater market potential, then there is always the risk of violence to others. It should, therefore, matter in E-Ed whether its exemplars of practice are fully transparent about their value propositions. A naïve or intentional suppression of any truth is an implicit acknowledgement of an instrumentality which undermines the value of the intrinsic truths of enterprise, both good and bad.

The kitschy aesthetic of convenience and its frictions

So, does a normalised entrepreneurship practice fashioned as a contemporary dialectic-informed, capitalistic E-Ed tend to the kitsch in enterprise? Certainly, to consider the case of the HelloFresh meal kit company, the potential is there. But to take HelloFresh's success as a leading enterprise in its field at face value and cite it as an exemplar of 'good' entrepreneurial practice would be to misinterpret the instrumental value of an aesthetic of convenience as an intrinsic (general) good for society. This is to suggest an aesthetic (beauty) of convenience – that is to say an aesthetic of efficiency, ease and–ultimately–automation (see, for example, Laschke, Hassenzahl, & Diefenbach, 2011) – is a sufficient and necessary condition for promoting enterprise and thus E-Ed. Yet, looking beyond that surface aesthetic, the outcomes of pursuing such a value, exposing its frictions, risk violence to others. Here the invocation of an aesthetic of automation is perhaps a signifier of particular note, given the perceived threat of technology, particularly AI and its potential for violence to society (Ricaurte, 2022).

In the case of HelloFresh, some truths – its frictions in the service of the 'creative and committed', the 'sustainability ethical' and the 'CSR-focussed' consumers of our society – 'othered' in its proposition, do not appeal to all consumers. These othered truths set up a competing aesthetic. We might call this an aesthetic of friction (Laschke et al., 2011). Recognised as such, an aesthetic of friction invites argument and dialogue. If recognised, it challenges its own convenience. While in some senses, an aesthetic of friction can represent a positive influence on, for example, motivation (De Haan, Menheere, Vos, & Lallemand, 2021), here friction must be considered as something to both acknowledge and work with; it is neither inherently good nor inherently bad. While a pure kitsch must be devoid of an aesthetic of friction, the insidious kitsch is replete with it. What on the surface of enterprising work looks pretty and convenient should invite a critical approach if it is at all to influence further enterprising practice, particularly in the context of E-Ed.

Should we bother teaching/learning a 'kitschy' E-Ed in a purely capitalistic way? A tendency to pure kitsch has nothing to hide and should not matter. Yet the insidious, insincere kitsch has its frictional components of truth to hide. They matter. It matters. I do not question the value of E-Ed. However, in educating for enterprise, I call on entrepreneurship educators to critically reflect that the presence of kitsch in an enterprise has only (limited) instrumental value to a limited range of stakeholders; it is likely (therefore) to only achieve limited success.[4] This call matters in the context of an impactful entrepreneurship (and its E-Ed) that might be both sustainable in the long term and of greater value to a greater segment of society. Here, I might best reflect the last words in the review of university-based E-Ed studies published from 1997 to 2011. I agree with Rideout and Gray, who concluded that the 'real question we need to answer is: What type of E-Ed, delivered by whom, within which type of university, is most effective for this type of student, with this kind of goal, and under these sets of circumstances' (2013, p. 348). Whether the outcomes of such E-Ed will be good, I can only judge in the experience of its consumption. Here, I suggest that understanding the aesthetic experience of kitsch in any enterprise can provide us with new, valuable insights into.

Notes

1 This is not to simplify the concept of kitsch. Given the potential of enterprise to cover anything the producer might produce for the consumer, a focus on components of the kitsch experience is problematic. However, in the case to follow, it is possible to draw more specifically on the aesthetic component of 'convenience'.
2 Unlike the Platonic mirror-like mimetic reproduction of some 'thing', in the Aristotelian sense, a mimetic reproduction of some vision always presents something of a learning experience, a revealing of something previously unseen about that vision (Atkinson, 2007). This is a revealing of the absent 'other'.
3 Meal kits 'provide pre-measured ingredients and easy-to-follow recipes so home cooks can prepare chef-crafted meals from the comfort of their own kitchens' (HelloFresh, 2024a).
4 At the time of writing this chapter, a news headline appeared across the investment media, including the U.S. online edition of Bloomberg, to the effect that HelloFresh had issued an unexpected (to the market analysts) profits warning. The consequence of this warning was a 48% fall in the company's share price (Ren, 2024). This represented a fall of 93% from its peak in 2021 at the time the meal kit represented a more realistic value proposition during the Covid crisis. Is this a case that, post-Covid 19, the frictions of HelloFresh's practices are becoming more visible to a greater segment of society?

References

Abdollahi, G., & Leimstoll, U. (2011). A classification for business model types in e-commerce. *17th Americas Conference on Information Systems 2011, AMCIS 2011, 1*, 756–769.

Atkinson, D. M. (2007). *Thinking the art of management: Stepping into "Heidegger's shoes"*. Springer. https://doi.org/10.1057/9780230589988

Atkinson, D. M. (2023a). Emergence & the non-hero. In D. M. Atkinson (Ed.), *Emergence & the non-hero* (pp. 251–283). Vernon Press.

Atkinson, D. M. (2023b). *Reimagining capitalism: Applying negative dialectics for a better future*. Vernon Press.

Chen, T., Fenyo, K., Yang, S., & Zhang, J. (2018). Thinking inside the subscription box. *McKinsey & Company*, 1–9.

Costa, A. I. A., Dekker, M., Beumer, R. R., Rombouts, F. M., & Jongen, W. M. F. (2001). A consumer-oriented classification system for home meal replacements. *Food Quality and Preference, 12*(4), 229–242. https://doi.org/10.1016/S0950-3293(01)00010-6

Daly, C. (2010). *An introduction to philosophical methods*. Broadview Press.
Debarliev, S., Janeska-Iliev, A., Stripeikis, O., & Zupan, B. (2022). What can education bring to entrepreneurship? Formal versus non-formal education. *Journal of Small Business Management*, *60*(1), 219–252. https://doi.org/10.1080/00472778.2019.1700691
Defourny, J., & Nyssens, M. (2008). Social enterprise in Europe: Recent trends and developments. *Social Enterprise Journal*, *4*(3), 202–228. https://doi.org/10.1108/17508610810922703
DEFRA. (2017). *Meat products: Sell them legally in England*. Retrieved February 23, 2024, from Department for Environment, Food & Rural Affairs and Food Standards Agency Guidance Note website: https://www.gov.uk/guidance/meat-products-sell-them-legally-in-england
De Haan, A., Menheere, D., Vos, S., & Lallemand, C. (2021). Aesthetic of friction for exercising motivation: A prototyping journey. *DIS 2021 – Proceedings of the 2021 ACM designing interactive systems conference: Nowhere and everywhere*, 1056–1067. https://doi.org/10.1145/3461778.3462079
Doran, J., McCarthy, N., & O'Connor, M. (2018). The role of entrepreneurship in stimulating economic growth in developed and developing countries. *Cogent Economics and Finance*, *6*(1). https://doi.org/10.1080/23322039.2018.1442093
Gabrielsson, J., Hägg, G., Landström, H., & Politis, D. (2020). Connecting the past with the present: The development of research on pedagogy in entrepreneurial education. *Education and Training*, *62*(9), 1061–1086. https://doi.org/10.1108/ET-11-2019-0265
Garofalo, C., & Geuras, D. (2015). From one utopia to another: Kant, spicer, and moral agency. *Administrative Theory & Praxis*, *37*(2), 81–94. https://doi.org/10.1080/10841806.2015.1027568
Gibson, A. A., & Partridge, S. R. (2019). Nutritional qualities of commercial meal kit subscription services in Australia. *Nutrients*, *11*(11), 1–11. https://doi.org/10.3390/nu11112679
Hayden, K. (2016, June). DIY dinner. *Progressive Grocer*, 10–13.
HelloFresh. (2023). *Golden potato topped lamb rogan josh with lentils and yoghurt – accolade: "Best recipe 2022"*. Retrieved December 15, 2023, from Web Page Recipe website: https://www.hellofresh.co.uk/recipes/golden-potato-topped-lamb-rogan-josh-652e71086720825b47fd9f94
HelloFresh. (2024a). *Everything you need to know about meal kits*. Retrieved March 8, 2024, from Web food-guide website: https://www.hellofresh.com/food-guide/meal-kits?page=food-guide&page=meal-kits&dm_custom_act=bfast
HelloFresh. (2024b). *Management board profiles*. Retrieved January 1, 2024, from HelloFresh Web Site website: https://ir.hellofreshgroup.com/websites/hellofresh/English/4000/corporate-governance.html
Helm, B. (2018). The hunger games. *Inc. Magazine*, *40*(4), 78–88.
Horwich, P. (2006). The value of truth. *Nous*, *40*(2), 347–360. https://doi.org/10.1111/j.0029-4624.2006.00613.x
Johnson, C., Lusch, R., & Schmidt, D. (2020). Entrepreneurship and creative destruction. *Business Ethics and Leadership*, *4*(2), 102–108. https://doi.org/10.21272/bel.4(2).102-108.2020
Laschke, M., Hassenzahl, M., & Diefenbach, S. (2011, January). Things with attitude: Transformational products. *Create11 Conference*, 1–2.
Lee, B., & Saunders, M. (2017). Introduction to case studies. In *Conducting case study research for business and management students* (pp. 1–12). SAGE Publications Ltd. https://doi.org/https://doi.org/10.4135/9781529716702
Linstead, S. (2002). Organizational kitsch. *Organization*, *9*(4), 657–682. https://doi.org/10.1177/135050840294008
McKay, F. H. (2023). What's in a commercial meal kit? Structured review of Australian meal kits. *Public Health Nutrition*, *26*(6), 1284–1292. https://doi.org/10.1017/S1368980023000265

McKinley, M. C. (2005). The nutrition and health benefits of yoghurt. *International Journal of Dairy Technology*, *58*(1), 1–12. https://doi.org/10.1111/j.1471-0307.2005.00180.x

Mitova, V. (2023). A new argument for the non-instrumental value of truth. *Erkenntnis*, *88*(5), 1911–1933. https://doi.org/10.1007/s10670-021-00435-4

Moir, J., Megheirkouni, M., Fletcher, K.-A., & Oniga, A. (2023). Marketing meal kits: From consumer agency to corporate social responsibility. *Academic Journal of International Economics and Management Research*, *4*(1), 22–33.

Moores, C. J., Bell, L. K., Buckingham, M. J., & Dickinson, K. M. (2021). Are meal kits health promoting? Nutritional analysis of meals from an Australian meal kit service. *Health Promotion International*, *36*(3), 660–668. https://doi.org/10.1093/heapro/daaa095

Moro, S. R., Cauchick-Miguel, P. A., & Mendes, G. H. de S. (2022). Literature analysis on product-service systems business model: A promising research field. *Brazilian Journal of Operations and Production Management*, *19*(1), 1–18. https://doi.org/10.14488/BJOPM.2021.043

Ndlazi, G. (2022). Racial inequality and the imperative critique of the South African negotiated settlement. *Filosofia Theoretica*, *11*(3), 93–104. https://doi.org/10.4314/ft.v11i3.8

O'Connor, A. (2013). A conceptual framework for entrepreneurship education policy: Meeting government and economic purposes. *Journal of Business Venturing*, *28*(4), 546–563. https://doi.org/10.1016/j.jbusvent.2012.07.003

Plehwe, D. (2020). Schumpeter revival? How neoliberals revised the image of the entrepreneur. In D. Plehwe, Q. Slobodian, & P. Mirowski (Eds.), *Nine lives of neoliberalism* (pp. 120–142). London and New York: Verso.

Ren, H. (2024, March 8). HelloFresh's meltdown catches almost everyone off guard. *Bloomberg (Online)*. https://www.bloomberg.com/news/articles/2024-03-08/hellofresh-s-meltdown-catches-almost-everyone-off-guard

Retolaza, J. L., & San-Jose, L. (2017). Single case research methodology: A tool for moral imagination in business ethics. *Management Research Review*, *40*(8), 890–906. https://doi.org/10.1108/MRR-07-2016-0179

Ricaurte, P. (2022). Ethics for the majority world: AI and the question of violence at scale. *Media, Culture and Society*, *44*(4), 726–745. https://doi.org/10.1177/01634437221099612

Rideout, E. C., & Gray, D. O. (2013). Does entrepreneurship education really work? A review and methodological critique of the empirical literature on the effects of university-based entrepreneurship education. *Journal of Small Business Management*, *51*(3), 329–351. https://doi.org/10.1111/jsbm.12021

Schumpeter, J. A. (2018). *Capitalism, socialism, and democracy* (2nd ed.). Wilder Publications (1942).

Schuster, S., Speck, M., van Herpen, E., Buchborn, F., Langen, N., Nikravech, M., ... Bickel, M. (2022, September). Do meal boxes reduce food waste from households? *Journal of Cleaner Production*, *375*. https://doi.org/10.1016/j.jclepro.2022.134001

Sharda, N., Krampe, C., & Ingenbleek, P. T. M. (2024). HelloFresh: Transitioning to a plastic-free future? *International Food and Agribusiness Management Review*, (June 2023), 1–19. https://doi.org/10.22434/ifamr2023.0068

Singh, J. (2010). *Chef (UK)*. Bloomsbury.

Smolka, K. M., Geradts, T. H. J., van der Zwan, P. W., & Rauch, A. (2023). Why bother teaching entrepreneurship? A field quasi-experiment on the behavioral outcomes of compulsory entrepreneurship education. *Journal of Small Business Management*, 1–57. https://doi.org/10.1080/00472778.2023.2237290

Spash, C. L. (2020). "The economy" as if people mattered: Revisiting critiques of economic growth in a time of crisis. *Globalizations*, *17*(6), 1–18. https://doi.org/10.1080/14747731.2020.1761612

Staubach, J., & Jäger, R. (2023). *Success factors of German meal kit providers from the customer's perspective compared to the USA – A study based on an artificial intelligence (AI)-using text analysis tool and a quantitative survey*. THM-Hochschulschriften Band 27. Technische Hochschule Mittelhessen.

Szostak, M., & Sułkowski, Ł. (2020, April 1–2). Kitsch in management: Characteristic forms, carriers and propagators. *Education excellence and innovation management : A 2025 vision to sustain economic development during global challenges: Proceedings of the 35th International Business Information Management Association Conference (IBIMA)*, 7584–7598. Sevilla: IBIMA. Available at: https://depot.ceon.pl/handle/123456789/19173

Vadana, I. I., Torkkeli, L., Kuivalainen, O., & Saarenketo, S. (2020). Digitalization of companies in international entrepreneurship and marketing. *International Marketing Review*, *37*(3), 471–492. https://doi.org/10.1108/IMR-04-2018-0129

White, G. R. T., Samuel, A., Peattie, K., & Doherty, B. (2022). Reconciling social enterprise: Beyond the paradox perspective. *International Journal of Entrepreneurial Behaviour and Research*, *28*(2), 500–526. https://doi.org/10.1108/IJEBR-02-2021-0135

10 Kitsch in decision-making

Financial destabilisation of joint-stock companies by boards of directors

Aneta Ejsmont

Introduction

The process of managing a joint-stock company in the context of broadly defined corporate financial management is very often exposed to the influence of many negative factors, which is a reference in the theory of kitsch experience. Decisions made by managers, especially the boards of directors of large capital groups, are unfortunately influenced by the phenomenon of kitsch depicted in various areas of human activity such as politics, the aforementioned management process or even religion.

Therefore, the chapter's main objective is to study the impact of the decisions of the boards of directors of listed companies in the WIG20 index, characterised by kitsch on their financial condition shaped by top-down policy decisions made in the face of the global economic crisis. Based on the issues of kitsch survival theory (Barragán and Ryynänen 2023), the research hypothesis was formulated assuming that the strength of cooperative ties is conducive to achieving long-term stability of the financial condition of the companies under study. The original intention was to apply a research method based on estimating an econometric model, in which the explanatory variable was to be the financial condition measured by the value of monthly turnover from 1 January 2021 to 31 December 2023. The explanatory variables used in the model, in turn, were to describe the impact of the capitalisation of domestic and foreign companies listed on the primary and regulated markets on the aforementioned monthly turnover of these business entities.

However, when analysing the current political and economic situation from the perspective of the experience of kitsch, it is more beneficial to study the impact of the turnover value of large listed companies included in the WIG20 index on the total turnover value of the studied index analysed during the research period from 1 September 2023 to 15 March 2024 (daily data). During this period, the most significant impact of political decisions on the decisions made by the boards of directors of the aforementioned listed companies, causing rather sudden changes in the positions of CEOs, could be observed, which can be seen in the context of the experience of broadly defined kitsch. Because of the above, the chapter answers the following research questions: 1) Which

DOI: 10.4324/9781003504931-11

corporate financial management activities include the characteristics of a kitschy experience? 2) Why does the decision-making process of the company's board of directors seek maximum simplification in the form of kitsch? and 3) Why is the poor financial condition of joint-stock companies very often caused by decisions made by the board of directors of a joint-stock company that turn out to be irrational quixotic decisions, which in turn can be observed in the long term in Poland and elsewhere?

At the outset, top-down political decisions were emphasised, especially those resulting from the change in Poland's ruling political camp, which took place precisely on 15 October 2023 and very quickly affected turnover among the CEOs of companies listed in the WIG20. The wave of changes was intensifying, especially in state-controlled listed companies. Changes were also observed in the existing composition of supervisory boards (https://www.bankier.pl/wiadomosc/, 2023).

Literature review: politicisation of decision-making in stock-listed companies

Kitsch is identified with an object that, although it works, seems so inadequate that it does not deserve our appreciation because it cannot meet our expectations (Forsey 2024). According to Ortlieb and Carbon (2018), "kitsch has been coined to contrast groundbreaking artistic achievements". However, this quote does not only refer to artistic achievements. Kitsch counters all achievements, especially those made by organisations.

In the history of the literature on the theory of both survival and kitsch experiences presented in management science related somewhat to the scientific discipline of economics and finance, the aspect of so-called kitsch is seen as a kind of metaphor that provides an answer to the question of what should be the applied course of thinking about an organisation, including a joint-stock company. In this case, kitsch is described as an ontology of being that effectively masks the experience of being by introducing a buffer between "openness" and "reality", being taken for it. In the context of research on the broad theory explaining the essence of kitsch, it can be seen as one of the fundamental philosophical problems of modernity (Linstead 2002), unfortunately often distorted as a result of erroneous top-down political decisions made, in the case of state-controlled companies, by ruling party's officials instead of company's management.

When making decisions, being on the board of directors of a company, each chairperson thereby tries to solve problems not only related to delegation but also those relating to the day-to-day operation of a joint-stock company as a business entity. Even more so, the decision-making process is not only about evaluating the company's bottom line based on the financial statements prepared in advance but, above all, about rational actions, which in the era of today's world-spanning events are increasingly challenging to carry out (Tondl 1989).

By rejecting what is creative and uncertain in the decision-making process, kitsch promotes repetitive, safe behaviour from the point of view of those who manage the company in this way and simultaneously comfortable. Thus, it ensures that the events that will take place in the future will be no different from what has gone before, resulting in a lowering of the level of development of the business unit in terms of innovations introduced. Routine will dominate business processes (Binkley 2000; Wastell and White 2010).

Besides, in the management of a company, in this case, a joint-stock company, whose business is influenced by all sorts of speculation (including speculation of a political nature), one can very often observe the phenomenon that kitsch easily displaces the CEO's hard work of actually analysing the risks involved in investing in specific financial instruments (including analysis of uncertainties and unknowns) in favour of ready-made assumptions, historical fabrications and narratives proclaiming that you do not need to know more to act, just as you do not need to know more to act. This also happens when a person is appointed as the CEO of a public limited company by so-called political choice rather than based on his or her qualifications (Roe 2019).

The decision-making process in both a small company and a large corporate group should be treated as a collective good requiring recognition of common needs and, above all, sound legislation. Even more so, the cooperative interrelationships occurring between different business entities should be taken seriously, being used to mobilise solidarity rather than exclude others, since they symbolise the fact that what we do to others, we do to ourselves as parts of a single life cycle running in every business entity regardless of size (McIntyre-Mills 2013). Moreover, kitsch, often subjected to critical scrutiny, still promises winning minds and trust among business managers (Newton and Harte 1997).

Empirical study: consequences of government election for companies noted on the Warsaw Stock Exchange

This article describes the consequences of the impact of post-election political decisions on the financial condition of listed companies operating within the WIG20 index. Thus, the consequences of the impact of broadly defined politics on the Warsaw Stock Exchange are presented. The effects of decisions taken by the newly appointed government consisted mainly of changes made among the presidents of large listed companies. Existing CEOs were dismissed, and new ones were appointed. As mentioned earlier, this is related to the so-called kitsch. Decision-makers in the state, irrespective of the political option, when assuming power when appointing CEOs of joint-stock companies, especially state-owned companies, are guided by the political good and not by the good of the company or its employees, which is reflected in the condition of the business entities under study.

The motivation for using data relating to Polish listed companies, mainly affected by this situation, was that this problem does not only occur in Poland. Politics influences fluctuations in the quotations of listed companies caused by changes in CEOs in Poland and worldwide. The quotations of shares of WIG20 companies are presented on world stock exchanges. The problem is considered on a worldwide scale.

Hence, an analysis of the local situation considered on a Polish scale can undoubtedly provide a basis for inferring the occurrence of the above-described problem in other countries. The arguments in favour are as follows:

- similar mechanism of operation on the line of owner/government-company management;
- the widespread occurrence of SOEs in various countries;
- the almost identical mechanism for the effect of speculation on company share prices;
- political considerations in the CEO selection process rather than the qualifications of those appointed to these positions.

Because of the above, the thought arises that if, in the decision-making process aimed at the development of large joint-stock companies, what is important is which political key a newly elected CEO is associated with and not his or her competence or education, then we are dealing with kitsch in the broadest sense. A kind of kitschiness negatively affects the turnover of listed companies, including WIG20 companies, especially in the context of frequent fluctuations in their value.

Research methodology and statistical data

The research method used in this study is an econometric model based on data analysis from the Warsaw Stock Exchange (WSE), which describes the financial condition of the largest joint-stock companies noted on the Warsaw Stock Exchange's index WIG20. The negative impact of an economic crisis dragging the energy crisis on the activity of these business entities causes their financial destabilisation. However, the most critical issue is the impact of very often incomprehensible political decisions on the rotation of positions among the CEOs of large listed companies, which are of key importance to broad economic development and the stock market as a whole. Such top-down actions can be perceived as kitschy. The research period covered joint-stock companies listed on the Warsaw Stock Exchange from 1 September 2023 to 15 March 2024 (thus, the research sample is 137 working days in the mentioned period). The main goal in the process of estimation of the econometric model is explaining the correlation mechanism between turnovers of every 20 joint-stock companies on turnovers of the total WSE 20, taking into account, in particular, those companies in which, as of October 2023, there have been changes in the positions of chairpersons and also changes in the composition of supervisory boards. The task of the presented model is the analysis of the relationships between 20 independent variables and one dependent variable (Heumann et al. 2016; Kufel 2013; Koop 2014):

y – turnover value of WIG20 Index as the primary measure of fluctuations in financial stabilisation of the joint-stock companies noticed on WSE by a destructive process of decision-making (thousand PLN);
x_1 – turnover values in ALIOR BANK (thousands of PLN);
x_2 – turnover values in ALLEGRO.EU (thousands PLN);
x_3 – turnover values in ASSECO POLAND (thousands PLN);
x_4 – turnover values in CD PROJEKT (thousand PLN);
x_5 – turnover values in CYFROWY POLSAT (thousand PLN);
x_6 – turnover values in DINO POLSKA (thousand PLN);
x_7 – turnover values in JASTRZĘBSKA SPÓŁKA HANDLOWA (thousands of PLN);
x_8 – turnover values in GRUPA KĘTY (thousand PLN);
x_9 – turnover values in KGHM POLSKA MIEDŹ (PLN thousand);
x_{10} – turnover values in KRUK (PLN thousand);
x_{11} – turnover values in LPP (thousand PLN);
x_{12} – turnover values in MBANK (thousands of PLN);
x_{13} – turnover values in ORANGE POLSKA (thousands PLN);
x_{14} – turnover values in BANK POLSKA KASA OPIEKI (thousands of PLN);
x_{15} – turnover values in PEPCO GROUP N. V. (PLN thousand);
x_{16} – turnover values in PGE POLSKA GRUPA ENERGETYCZNA (thousands PLN);
x_{17} – turnover values in ORLEN (thousand PLN);
x_{18} – turnover value in POWSZECHNA KASA OSZCZĘDNOŚCI BANK POLSKI (thousands of PLN);
x_{19} – turnover values in POWSZECHNE ZAKŁAD UBEZENZEŃ (thousands of PLN);
x_{20} – turnover values in SANTANDER BANK POLSKA (thousands of PLN).

The culmination of the verified model is the examination of the cause-and-effect relationship between the dependent variable and the 20 regressors mentioned above. In the process of estimating the econometric model, the author used the GRETL programme. An econometric model includes panel data with time series characteristics presented in Table 10.2.

An analysis of the data for the period between 1 September 2023 and 15 March 2024 shows that as a result of top-down decisions, which are not always considered to be those rationally intended, goals and tasks are not realised by the existing CEOs of listed companies because it involves a sudden change in position, where the role of CEO begins to be performed by another person, who does not always continue what was initiated by the then management. Such gamesmanship, often of a political nature, has little to do with what was intended earlier, leading to chaos and a quixotic situation. When there is a turnover in the company's CEO's position, a stock market decline is noted. Stock prices most often fall. Then, we are dealing with a slump. Only after some time did the share price rise, and we have a bull market on the stock market. Such fluctuations harm the decisions made by the new CEOs of the companies taking over at the time.

Results of the model estimation

The estimation process of the econometric model at the initial stage assumes a linear relationship. The form of the described model is presented in the equation below:

$$Y_t = \alpha_0 + \alpha_1 x_{1t} + \alpha_2 x_{2t} + \ldots + \alpha_j x_{jt} + \varepsilon_t => Y_t = \alpha_0 + \alpha_1 x_{1t} + \ldots + \alpha_{20} x_{20t} + \varepsilon_t \ (t = 1, 2 \ldots n). \quad (10.1)$$

where numbers n is the number of units studied, j is the number of explanatory variables, x_t, α, α_{01}, ..., α_j is model parameters, and $\mathcal{E}_t$ – random component

The crucial aspect in the process of estimation of an econometric model is the correlation matrix. Data are presented in Table 10.1.

Also, Table 10.2 shows the data containing the final estimation process of the econometric model. The research sample includes 137 items representing the

Table 10.1 Correlation coefficients, using the observations 1–137 (5% critical value [two-tailed] = 0.1678 for n = 137)

y	*x1*	*x2*	*x3*	*x4*	
1.0000	0.7834	0.6585	0.7821	0.4149	*y*
	1.0000	0.3931	0.5954	0.1908	*x1*
		1.0000	0.4811	0.4230	*x2*
			1.0000	0.3318	*x3*
				1.0000	*x4*
x5	*x6*	*x7*	*x8*	*x9*	
0.2767	0.5162	0.2651	0.5188	0.7800	*y*
0.3732	0.3478	0.1709	0.3474	0.5823	*x1*
0.0613	0.3179	0.1551	0.2490	0.5200	*x2*
0.1126	0.3014	0.1392	0.4960	0.7103	*x3*
0.0546	0.1928	0.2047	0.4063	0.2773	*x4*
1.0000	0.0920	−0.0003	0.2222	0.2891	*x5*
	1.0000	0.0962	0.3288	0.2896	*x6*
		1.0000	0.3010	0.2004	*x7*
			1.0000	0.4632	*x8*
				1.0000	*x9*

(Continued)

x10	*x11*	*x12*	*x13*	*x14*	
0.6576	0.7274	0.8307	0.7451	0.8695	*Y*
0.6079	0.5615	0.7625	0.5530	0.7606	*x*1
0.3648	0.3774	0.4760	0.4595	0.5384	*x*2
0.5918	0.7776	0.7683	0.6313	0.6479	*x*3
0.1606	0.1842	0.2631	0.3040	0.2430	*x*4
0.2493	0.0764	0.3235	0.2737	0.1642	*x*5
0.2694	0.2856	0.3046	0.4160	0.3527	*x*6
0.0829	–0.0078	0.1162	0.2367	0.1490	*x*7
0.4345	0.3756	0.3954	0.5654	0.3107	*x*8
0.5652	0.6369	0.7032	0.6360	0.6109	*x*9
1.0000	0.5534	0.6227	0.5219	0.5708	*x*10
	1.0000	0.6749	0.5129	0.5852	*x*11
		1.0000	0.6631	0.7438	*x*12
			1.0000	0.5603	*x*13
				1.0000	*x*14

x15	*x*16	*x17*	*x18*	*x19*	
0.3547	0.7046	0.7657	0.8055	0.7695	*Y*
0.1950	0.5841	0.5954	0.7174	0.5765	*x*1
0.3586	0.4284	0.4298	0.4050	0.4599	*x*2
0.2185	0.6187	0.4575	0.6130	0.6044	*x*3
0.3306	0.3120	0.3489	0.1480	0.2524	*x*4
0.0430	0.1604	0.2021	0.1879	0.1592	*x*5
0.1708	0.3183	0.2943	0.3615	0.3945	*x*6
0.1614	0.2200	0.3742	0.0464	0.3262	*x*7
0.0505	0.4740	0.3025	0.3140	0.4082	*x*8
0.1863	0.5553	0.4981	0.5641	0.5869	*x*9
0.1719	0.4355	0.4276	0.5402	0.4786	*x*10
0.0922	0.4785	0.3673	0.6231	0.4575	*x*11
0.2041	0.6218	0.5897	0.6851	0.6457	*x*12
0.3316	0.6262	0.5198	0.5180	0.6327	*x*13
0.2963	0.5691	0.6643	0.8584	0.6808	*x*14
1.0000	0.3244	0.2603	0.1247	0.3100	*x*15
	1.0000	0.5619	0.4575	0.6296	*x*16
		1.0000	0.5497	0.6114	*x*17
			1.0000	0.5941	*x*18
				1.0000	*x*19

x20	
0.8756	*Y*
0.7006	*x*1
0.5195	*x*2
0.7544	*x*3
0.3492	*x*4
0.4021	*x*5
0.4202	*x*6
0.2088	*x*7
0.5944	*x*8

(*Continued*)

Table 10.1 (Continued)

	x20	
	0.7725	*x9*
	0.6453	*x10*
	0.6606	*x11*
	0.8035	*x12*
	0.6976	*x13*
	0.7194	*x14*
	0.2365	*x15*
	0.6478	*x16*
	0.5707	*x17*
	0.7071	*x18*
	0.6679	*x19*
	1.0000	*x20*

Source: own elaboration

Table 10.2 Model: OLS, using observations 2023–09–01:2024–03–15 (T = 137). Dependent variable: y

	Coefficient	*t-ratio*	*p-value*
Const	−5855.56	−0.5752	0.5662
*x*1	0.733105	2.035	0.0441**
*x*2	0.998392	17.87	<0.0001***
*x*4	1.03277	7.700	<0.0001***
*x*5	0.974078	8.151	<0.0001***
*x*6	1.02084	19.53	<0.0001***
*x*7	1.29444	6.188	<0.0001***
*x*8	0.891451	4.586	<0.0001***
*x*9	1.11029	9.575	<0.0001***
*x*10	1.22611	3.057	0.0028***
*x*11	1.01087	23.55	<0.0001***
*x*12	1.44588	3.181	0.0019***
*x*13	1.47842	2.848	0.0052***
*x*14	1.13319	9.939	<0.0001***
*x*15	1.00070	9.902	<0.0001***
*x*16	1.63901	3.889	0.0002***
*x*17	0.958612	25.06	<0.0001***
*x*18	0.971578	12.54	<0.0001***
*x*19	0.605386	6.683	<0.0001***
*x*20	1.10639	4.279	<0.0001***
Mean dependent var	1046065	S.D. dependent var	538051.9
Catfish squared resid	1.15e+11	S.E. of regression	31321.26
R-squared	0.997085	Adjusted R-squared	0.996611
F(19, 117)	2106.140	P-value(F)	8.0e−139
Log-likelihood	−1601.816	Akaike criterion	3243.632
Schwarz criterion	3302.032	Hannan-Quinn	3267.364
rho	−0.286194	Durbin-Watson	2.572233

Source: own elaboration based on the estimated econometric model

turnover of the WIG20 index and the turnover of the stock companies included in the index (see Table 10.2).

The econometric model is estimated using the classical least squares method with time series. The correlation test confirmed that the explanatory variables x_1–x_{20} are correlated with each other at the sample size $n = 137$, and the p-value values confirm the fact that the turnover values recorded in all stock companies listed on the WIG20 except ASSECOPL significantly affect the total turnover of the WIG20 index, although, especially in five companies in recent months there was a change in the positions of company presidents causing fluctuations in the values of the analysed turnover. This situation occurred especially in the period after the recent parliamentary elections.

Recent months have brought significant changes in the positions of CEOs at the most prominent companies listed on the Warsaw Stock Exchange (WSE). Resignations and even resignations have affected the business units surveyed. Some CEOs resigned from their positions as the company headed towards bankruptcy, while others departed, leaving the company in its heyday. The most severe fluctuations were recorded at the following companies (bankier.pl 2023):

- CD POROJEKT
- PEPCO
- ALLEGRO
- ORANGEPL
- PKN ORLEN
- PKO BP

As for CD Projekt, a surprising change in the position of CEO was announced in October 2023. The previous CEO, who had been in the position since 2010, stepped down, with a different person assuming the new CEO role as of 1 January 2024. As a result, the company's turnover fluctuations have been observed (see Chart 10.1).

The modern carousel in CEO positions has also included Pepco (Kubicki 2023). September saw the resignation of the CEO after only a year and a half, who was replaced by his predecessor. Numerous management changes and questionable actions by the main shareholder drastically affected the company's stock price, which reached a minimum ceiling (see Chart 10.2).

At Allegro, the CEO changed a year ago, although, in October, the company announced that the chairman of the Board of Directors had also left. The data is presented in Chart 10.3.

The popular Orange Polska company also saw a change in its CEO's chair at the beginning of September 2023. The new CEO replaced the previous CEO. Fluctuations in turnover are shown in the chart below (see Chart 10.4).

The same situation also occurred at the giant PKN ORLEN. In February of this year, the former CEO was replaced by a new one, causing turnover changes, showing a downward trend at first, catching up in mid-March (cf. Chart 10.5).

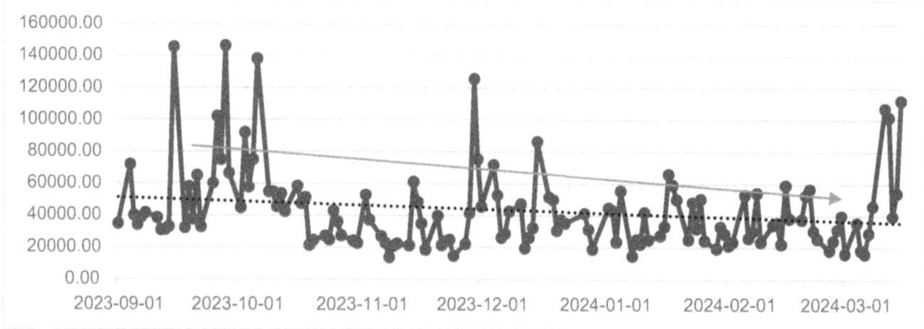

Chart 10.1 CD Project. Turnovers in 1 September 2023 to 15 March 2024

Source: WSE Main Market – Quotation Archive, accessed on 3.15.2024

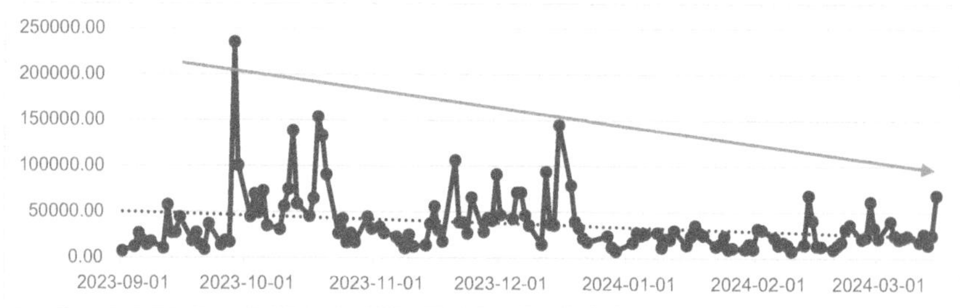

Chart 10.2 PEPCO. Turnovers in 1 September to 15 March 2024

Source: WSE Main Market – Quotation Archive, accessed on 3.15.2024

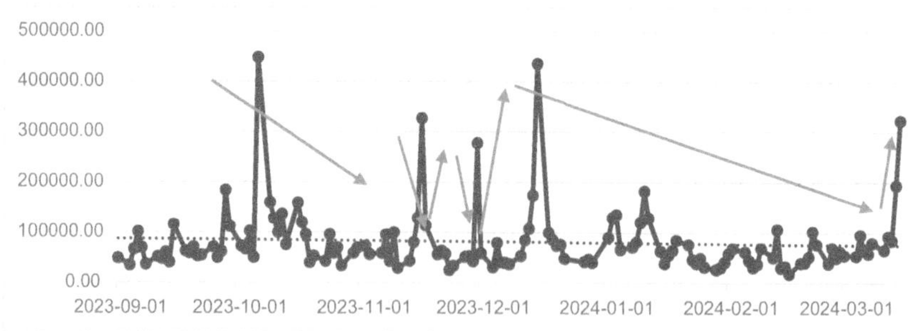

Chart 10.3 ALLEGRO. Turnovers in 1 September to 15 March 2024

Source: WSE Main Market – Quotation Archive, accessed on 3.15.2024

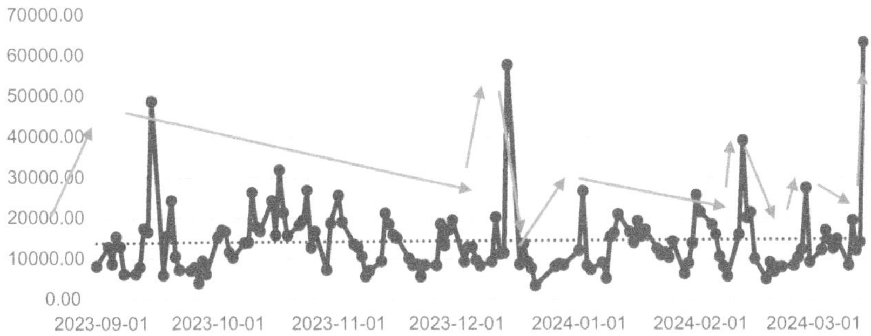

Chart 10.4 ORANGEPL. Turnovers in 1 September to 15 March 2024

Source: WSE Main Market – Quotation Archive, accessed on 3.15.2024

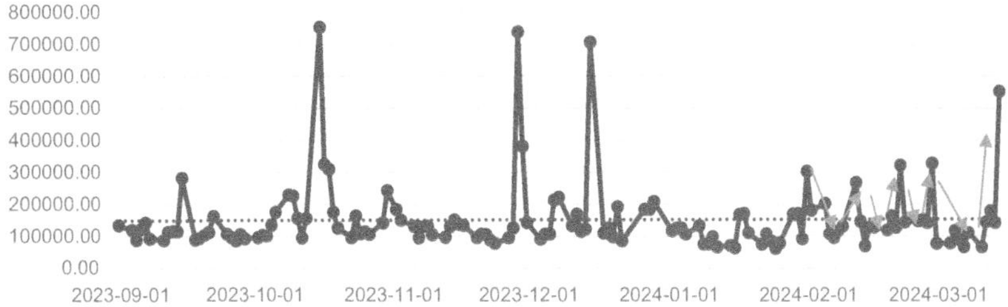

Chart 10.5 PKNORLEN. Turnovers in 1 September to 15 March 2024

Source: WSE Main Market – Quotation Archive, accessed on 3.15.2024

The fate of the joint-stock company PKOBP also shared a similar fate. In February 2024, the bank's supervisory board dismissed representatives of the existing management board, announcing the launch of an open competition for the positions of president and vice-presidents of the board, which also affected the company's turnover (cf. Chart 10.6).

In the case of PKO BP, fluctuations in turnover were already observed in 20201. The climax occurred after the last parliamentary elections. This also resulted in the recorded turnover showing a downward trend. A rebound did not occur until around mid-March this year.

The reported changes in CEOs throughout the period under review resulted in significant fluctuations, which could be seen by analysing the downward

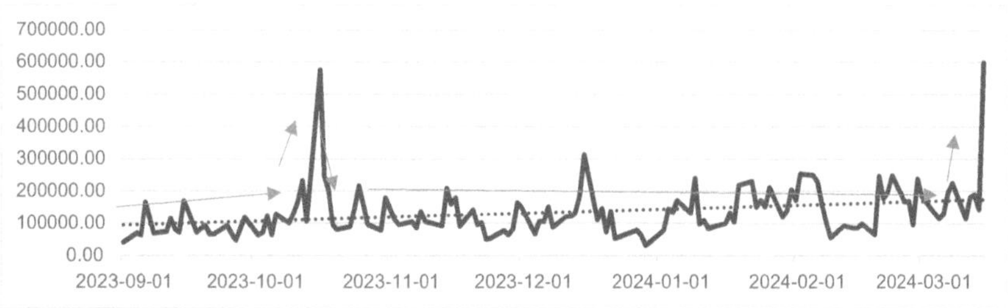

Chart 10.6 PKOBP. Turnovers in 1 September to 15 March 2024

Source: WSE Main Market – Quotation Archive, accessed on 3.15.2024

trend line on virtually every chart except the last two, where stagnation could be observed. The wave of changes in listed companies, both state-controlled and non-state-controlled, has been happening too frequently lately without always entailing positive consequences. This chaos caused by the carousel of CEOs serves no good purpose, even leading to kitschy situations. Since the last parliamentary elections, the personnel broom has affected more and more CEOs and other members of management and supervisory boards (Kubicki 2023). On the one hand, the described state of affairs can be described as a fascinating period in which the dynamics of listed companies are still in motion, with CEOs coming and going, influencing the fate of companies and the emotions of investors on the WSE, but on the other hand – chaos ensues, employees of lower-level companies lose out and, even worse, decisions on CEO changes negatively affect financial data describing turnover.

The ending process of estimating the econometric model could have shown that it is a linear model with 19 explanatory variables. Based on the estimation process of the econometric model, the results of the tests carried out are also presented. These tests aimed to confirm the impact of the companies' turnover in the WIG20 on the total turnover value of the index under study. Here there are the following tests:

Non-linearity test (squares) – null hypothesis: relationship is linear
Test statistic: LM = 22.0803 with *p*-value = *P*(Chi-square(19) > 22.0803) = 0.280279
Non-linearity test (logs) – null hypothesis: relationship is linear
Test statistic: LM = 21.1076 with *p*-value = *P*(Chi-square(19) > 21.1076) = 0.330885
RESET test for specification – null hypothesis: specification is adequate
Test statistic: F(2, 115) = 0.286626 with *p*-value = *P*(F(2, 115) > 0.286626) = 0.751327

White's test for heteroskedasticity – null hypothesis: heteroskedasticity not present
Test statistic: LM = 55.3307 with *p*-value = *P*(Chi-square(38) > 55.3307) = 0.0342916
Breusch-Pagan test for heteroskedasticity – null hypothesis: heteroskedasticity not present
Test statistic: LM = 939.247 with *p*-value = *P*(Chi-square(19) > 939.247) = 4.85597e-187
Breusch-Pagan test for heteroskedasticity (robust variant) – null hypothesis: heteroskedasticity not present
Test statistic: LM = 30.977 with *p*-value = *P*(Chi-square(19) > 30.977) = 0.0406078
Test for normality of residual – null hypothesis: error is normally distributed
Test statistic: Chi-square(2) = 128.942 with *p*-value = 1.00135e-28
Chow test for structural break at observation 2023-11-08 – null hypothesis: no structural break
Test statistic: F(20, 97) = 2.55575 with *p*-value = *P*(F(20, 97) > 2.55575) = 0.00122398
LM test for autocorrelation up to order 7 – null hypothesis: no autocorrelation
Test statistic: LMF = 2.50282 with *p*-value = *P*(F(7, 110) > 2.50282) = 0.020022
Test for ARCH of order 7 – null hypothesis: no ARCH effect is present
Test statistic: LM = 9.26301 with *p*-value = *P*(Chi-square(7) > 9.26301) = 0.23432
QLR test for structural break – null hypothesis: no structural break
Test statistic: chi-square(20) = 51.115 at observation 2023-11-08 with asymptotic *p*-value = 0.00508668
CUSUM test for parameter stability – null hypothesis: no change in parameters
Test statistic: Harvey-Collier *t*(116) = −2.06044 with *p*-value = *P*(*t*(116) > −2.06044) = 0.041593

The correlations between variables clearly indicated that the set of explanatory variables used in the estimated model strongly correlated (Table 10.1). The sample size of $n = 137$, combined with the low level of *p*-values calculated for each variable, high value of R^2, linear model form and lack of heteroskedasticity, confirms that achieving financial stability for listed companies is possible when we mean cooperating joint-stock companies. However, too frequent changes of CEOs in the surveyed companies do not do much good, as too high turnover fluctuations are recorded, as confirmed by the data presented in the charts above.

Discussion: decision-making as kitsch experience

The decision-making process in the management of joint-stock companies confirms that kitsch plays a central role in running an activity for business entities of this kind. The consequences of post-election decisions taken by national governments lead to actions towards chaos. It is not the educational background of the chairman of the board of directors of a public limited company that counts, but only the political party to which he or she belongs or serves. It does not matter what a person in such a position represents; what matters is which political party they sympathise with. When politics heavily influence a company's stock price in the broad sense and by artificial speculation, this does not go in a good direction. It all goes in the wrong direction. Politics cannot fully influence the financial stability of a company, unlike market processes in the economy.

Following the kitsch experience theory (Szostak and Sułkowski 2020b), we can see that a chairperson of the board of directors of a public limited company plays the role of a kitsch producer by 1) focusing on the mass recipient of his decisions (politicians) instead of focusing on universal values (good for the company); 2) duplicating/following political decisions instead of relying on own creative reliability as a specialist taking care of the company he leads; and 3) being closed for criticism and discussion due to serving political goals instead of business ones.

It is irrelevant what economic processes, often of a production nature, take place within a listed company, which is, after all, a kind of enterprise that should be economically rather than politically active. The important thing here is to cooperate with business partners from all over the world and not to conform to political interests. With each new CEO, changes are made, investment decisions are made to develop the company, and the production process is launched. Share prices increase, the company is profitable, and employees enjoy job satisfaction. A new person only replaces the previous CEO because the political concept has changed. The decisions and actions of the predecessor are reviewed from scratch, previous arrangements are changed, and chaos ensues again. Moreover, the result is widespread kitsch.

The kitsch recipients, in this case, are politicians who like to see and be pleased by their influence on the reality by leading chairpersons of boards of directors of public limited companies to fulfil their will and serve a party's goals; unfortunately, these party's goals are mainly populistic (the more votes, the better) and have not much in common with achieving actual business goals by a well-managed organisation.

As for the universal values component of the kitsch experience theory, we see that the place of truth (in the sense of the good for the business) is taken by prettiness, shining and pleasing the political decidents.

The discussion concludes that the economy and the decisions made in these circumstances at the company board level can be recognised as kitschy. This is a phenomenon that is perceived negatively not only in Poland but also worldwide. Kitsch is a protection against reality.

Conclusion

The broadly defined phenomenon of kitsch strongly influences decisions made by the boards of listed companies. Because of the above, the main objective of the study was to examine the impact of the decisions of the boards of listed companies included in the most significant index, WIG20, characterised by it on their financial condition shaped by often incomprehensible top-down political decisions that have little to do with what counts in the activities of any economic entity.

In seeking an answer to the first research question (Which corporate financial management activities include the characteristics of a kitschy experience?), it should have been clear that the activities carried out as part of the decision-making process at the management level are characterised by experiences of kitsch in its broadest sense.

Anticipating the answer to the second question (Why does the decision-making process of the company's board of directors seek maximum simplification in the form of kitsch?), it should be emphasised that the decision-making process of the management board of a large listed company is most exposed to actions aimed at maximum simplification in the form of kitsch. This is due to the negative impact of top-down political decisions on the functioning of the management boards of individual business units, as a result of which there is very often a rotation in the positions of CEOs. New CEOs are elected not because of their qualifications but because they belong to a particular political party that wins elections in a given period.

The answer to the second question automatically refers to the third question (Why is the poor financial condition of joint-stock companies very often caused by decisions made by the board of directors of a joint-stock company that turn out to be irrational quixotic decisions, which in turn can be observed in the long term in Poland and elsewhere?). Irrational kitschy decisions, observed in the long term in Poland and worldwide, lead to chaos. This is confirmed by estimating the econometric model, in which the impact of the turnover of 20 joint-stock companies included in the WIG20 stock market index on the overall turnover of the analysed index was examined. Out of the surveyed companies, only one company (ASSECOPOL) was eliminated, whose turnover had the most negligible impact on the total turnover of the WIG20 index. A high level of p-value characterised other companies.

However, the fluctuations in turnover recorded throughout the research period from 1 September 2023 to 15 March 2024 indicate that frequent changes in the positions of company presidents made through political decisions lead to an imbalance in the financial situation of listed companies, which also has a negative impact on the overall quotations of the WIG20 index, and at the same time indicates the implementation of kitschy activities.

In a nutshell, the discussion on the assumption of control in the decision-making process of joint-stock company CEOs by the broader kitsch boils down to highlighting the fact that the main limitation of the considerations in this chapter is the negative impact of politics on the development of the joint-stock company, resulting in turnover in the position of CEO. Reality mixes with kitsch, leading to fluctuations in the company's financial and economic development, resulting in declines in the company's share price on the stock market. In this case, the limitation lies in the disruption of the stock price of a single company and the entire WIG 20 index. Speculative actions driven by political motives, leading to the chaos mentioned above, pose a considerable threat to the continued functioning of the stock exchange both in Poland and around the world. It is suggested that economic activity should not be guided only by political decisions. Moreover, we should focus on this in subsequent research on kitsch in its broadest sense.

References

Barragán, P., Ryynänen, M., 2023. Kitsch: From Rejection to Acceptance-On the Changing Meaning of Kitsch in Today's Cultural Production (Introduction). In: *The Changing Meaning of Kitsch. From Rejection to Acceptance*, Barragán, P., Ryynänen, M. (eds.), Springer Nature Switzerland AG, Cham, Switzerland, https://doi.org/10.1007/978-3-031-16632-7.

Binkley, S., 2000. Kitsch as a Repetitive System: A Problem for the Theory of Taste Hierarchy. *Journal of Material Culture*, 5(2), pp. 131–152.

Forsey, J., 2024. "The Useful-Beautiful Couplet": On the Aesthetic Appraisal of Designed Objects. In: *Multidisciplinary Aspects of Design. Objects, Processes, Experiences and Narratives*, Zanella, F., Bosoni, G., Di Stefano, E., Iannilli, G. L., Matteucci, G., Messori, R., Trocchianesi, R. (eds.), Springer Nature Switzerland AG, Cham, Switzerland, https://doi.org/10.1007/978-3-031-49811-4.

Heumann, C., Schomaker, M., Shalabh (eds.), 2016. *Introduction to Statistics and Data Analysis with Exercises, Solutions and Applications in R*, Springer, Cham, Switzerland, https://doi.org/10.1007/978-3-319-46162-5.

http://world-stock-exchanges.net/indices.html (accessed on 3.18.2024).

https://data.worldbank.org/ (accessed on 3.18.2024).

https://investoracademy.org/top-10-fundamental-analysis-indicators-for-all-investors/ (accessed on 6.19.2019).

https://pl.investing.com/equities/ (accessed on 3.18.2024).

https://www.gpw.pl/ (accessed on 3.18.2024).

Koop, G., 2014. *Introducing to the Econometrics*, Wolters Kluwer Business, Warsaw.

Kubicki, M., 2023. How to Say Goodbye to a Position Is Just That. *WSE CEO Carousel "2"*, https://www.bankier.pl/wiadomosc/Jak-sie-zegnac-ze-stanowiskiem-to-tylko-tak-Karuzela-prezesow-na-GPW-2-8634762.html (accessed on 10.25.2023).

Kufel, T., 2013. *Econometrics. Problem solving Using GRETL*, Polish Scientific Publishers, Warsaw.

Linstead, S., 2002. Organisational Kitsch. *Organisation. Sage Journals*, 9(4), pp. 657–682. https://doi.org/10.1177/135050840294008.

McIntyre-Mills, J. J., 2013. Anthropocentrism and Well-being: A WayOut of the Lobster Pot? *Systems Research and Behavioral Science*, 30, pp. 136–155. https://doi.org/10.1002/sres.2131.

Newton, T., Harte, G., 1997. Green Business: Technicist Kitsch? *Journal of Management Studies*, 34(1), pp. 75–98.

Ortlieb, S.A., Carbon, C.-C., 2018. A Functional Model of Kitsch and Art: Linking Aesthetic Appreciation to the Dynamics of Social Motivation. *Hypothesis and Theory*, 9, pp. 1–17. https://doi.org/10.3389/fpsyg.2018.02437.

Roe, E., 2019. Licking the Sharp Edge of the Sword. *Journal of Contingencies and Crisis Management*, 27, pp. 87–93. https://doi.org/10.1111/1468-5973.12231.

Szostak, M., Sulkowski, Ł., 2020. Kitsch in Management: Characteristic Forms, Carriers and Propagators. In *Education Excellence and Innovation Management: A 2025 Vision to Sustain Economic Development During Global Challenges: Proceedings of the 35th International Business Information Management Association Conference (IBIMA)*. Sevilla: IBIMA, pp. 7584–7598. https://depot.ceon.pl/handle/123456789/19173 (accessed on 4.20.2024).

Tondl, L., 1989. Systems Analysis of Rational Actions and the Delegation Problems. *Systems Research*, 6(4), pp. 321–329, https://doi.org/10.1002/sres.3850060407.

Wastell, D., White, S., 2010. Facts, Myths and Thought-Styles... and a Rallying Cry for Civic Engagement. *Journal of Strategic Information Systems*, 19(2010), pp. 307–318.

11 Kitsch in new technologies management

Design practices and user experiences

Artur Modliński and Ada Florentyna Pawlak

Introduction

Technology is an important element in the development of human civilisation. The invention of simple tools allowed people to survive, develop, and adapt to a changing environment. In the early stages of tool development, they allowed people to reduce physical effort while increasing efficiency in achieving goals. Examples include tools for hunting and farming. Carrying out these tasks manually involved a high risk of loss of life or low efficiency (Locay 1989). Throughout subsequent stages of human evolution, the role of tools has also evolved, relieving people of cognitive effort. The invention of paper, abacuses, and then computers allowed people to save time and intellectual power necessary to remember information, as well as create calculations and secure knowledge. With the development of smart technologies, people also see using more advanced tools to reduce emotional effort. Examples include applications that improve people's moods, imitate their partners, or fulfil sexual fantasies without any opposition or emotional pressure that occurs when establishing a relationship with another person (Balistreri 2022). Naturally, not all people want to use technologies to re-educate emotional effort, just as some groups still reject technologies that reduce cognitive or physical effort (Colyer et al. 2023). However, there is no doubt that, in addition to one of the three purposes above, tools can play another important role – indicating the user's status in society, which is related to the phenomenon of conspicuous consumption.

The contemporary technological landscape is increasingly becoming an arena for a phenomenon known as "technological kitsch." With technological advancement comes new tools, products, and content that often exhibit excessive extravagance, shallowness, and lack of authenticity. This chapter explores the implications of experiencing technological kitsch from a socio-cultural perspective. Kitsch needs to be produced by a human being and tells us about the conflicts between the real and the artificial, tradition and modernity, and nostalgia and melancholy. The concept of kitsch can refer not only to characteristics, functions, and producers but also to people, attitudes, experiences, and behaviours.

DOI: 10.4324/9781003504931-12

Kitsch is rather a cognitive-aesthetic attitude than a collection of objects and rules. Regardless of who or what this term encompasses, it is a negatively evaluative designation indicating that behaviours/manifestations/activities/attitudes in the organisation deviating from a universal value of truth in favour of appearances and external forms.

Comprehensive management kitschification refers to how management practices, strategies, and organisational cultures are imbued with kitsch elements (Szostak and Sułkowski 2020b). This phenomenon involves infusing superficial or exaggerated features that prioritise style over substance, often resulting in a sense of artificiality or insincerity within the managerial domain. In the context of comprehensive management, kitschification may manifest in various ways, such as the adoption of trendy management fads or buzzwords without genuine understanding or commitment, the superficial use of technology or innovative techniques for the sake of appearance rather than tangible improvements, or the cultivation of an organisational culture focused more on image and perception than on actual performance or employee well-being. Overall, the concept of comprehensive management kitschification highlights the importance of balancing style with substance in organisational management, ensuring that managerial practices and strategies are not merely superficial adornments but meaningful and effective tools for achieving organisational goals and fostering employee engagement and satisfaction.

Consequently, technological kitsch has multifaceted effects on the aesthetic, cultural, economic, and social spheres, necessitating further research and actions aimed at its limitation and the promotion of authenticity and valuable content in the realm of technology. The analysis of technological kitsch in the context of enterprise management requires consideration of both internal and external factors that influence its occurrence. Internal factors include management decisions regarding marketing strategy, communication, and the way the enterprise presents itself in the market, while external factors encompass societal trends and customer expectations, which shape the perception of this phenomenon. Contemporary enterprises operate in a dynamic environment where technological innovations are integral to their development strategies. However, technological progress brings risks associated with technological kitsch, which can adversely affect the image and functioning of organisations. Technological kitsch, defined as excessive extravagance, lack of authenticity, and superficiality, poses a risk to the reputation of the enterprise and the trust of customers and stakeholders.

The principle of conspicuous consumption – wearable technology

The second decade of the 21st century has witnessed the integration of humans into an extensive technical system and their interaction with computing machines: measurement devices, statistical tools, logistics systems, monitoring equipment, scientometric applications, dating apps, or self-quantification programmes. The coupling of human biology and technology now takes on a contemporary "skin-deep," phygital form through technological gadgets worn on the body, collectively called "wearable technology." These "cyborgic devices" are objects the human body assimilates (such as activity trackers, smartphones, biometric wristbands or smartwatches, headphones, and rings). The widespread availability of devices measuring signals emanating from the body has become the basis for a trend known as "Quantified Self" – a social movement advocating monitoring innovations to optimise health (Lupton 2013). Its proponents advocate collecting and archiving biometric data to enhance bodily capabilities (Rosen and Cipov 2017). The practice of technological self-tracking, for self-awareness through measuring various aspects of life, according to transhumanists, initiates the process of "self-improvement." The emergence of non-invasive information technologies and human-computer integration/interaction is associated with delegating some cognitive functions to machines. The overarching goal of self-tracking is to manage daily activities and increase personal productivity and efficiency. Devices anticipate needs and interpret habits and movements, becoming extensions of humans, characterised by the ability to adapt to the technical environment. The quantified self is the practice of measuring one's behaviour, biological indicators, mood, or geographic location to optimise various aspects of life, such as cognitive enhancement, sleep optimisation, and health maintenance (Choe et al. 2014).

Wearables technology is intended to be simple, fun, and user-friendly – accessible to everyone (Marwick 2014). Nothing complex should emerge; this applies to device operation and, consequently, the user's awareness of what they are interacting with, which may surprise and intrigue them. The design promises various sensory experiences: the user experience of technological kitsch can engage various senses, not just sight but also touch, sound, or even smell, making it more memorable. Today, individuals feel responsible for designing their corporeality and optimising their surroundings by saturating them with wearable technology. Technological kitsch products can become subjects of social conversations and interactions as they attract attention and pique the interest of the surroundings. Kitsch consumer wants to interfere with the kitsch artefact by feeling egalitarianism of mass scale; he chooses items to consider from the recipient's desires, avoiding his thoughts and consciousness, keeping his attention on external, fleeting, and sentimental experiences, preferably in the community of people in the same situation (Szostak and Sułkowski 2020b). The aesthetics of kitsch in wearable technology stimulating body parts can manifest in often exaggerated designs: LED strips on shoes, electronic tattoos, simulated jewellery implants with built-in colourful LEDs that flicker in intense colours to introduce an element of exaggeration, designing smart earrings that react to music through vibrations in intense rhythms, artistic rings that connect to a mobile application using intense colours and original patterns, or glasses that react to music through vibrations and light effects projecting holographic images onto the skin to achieve a futuristic effect. For example, AR Projection Tattoos are devices that allow simulated tattoos to be applied using augmented reality technology. Meanwhile, cybernetic fashions excessively expose body shapes or introduce elements drawn from fantasy, such as wings, cat ears, or other futuristic accessories. By providing users with a tangible means of enhancing their capabilities and extending their presence, wearables construct a culture that prioritises external validation and immediate gratification over introspection and deliberation.

Conspicuous consumption is deliberately and conspicuously spending money on goods or services to publicly display one's social status or wealth (O'cass and McEwen 2004). Showing status and wealth is, in turn, associated with the desire to emphasise one's advantage over other group members. Evolutionary psychology suggests that displaying one's high place in the hierarchy is essential in searching for a mate, reproductive chances, and survival (Kruger and Kruger 2018). The Amoc Zahavi handicap hypothesis is related to this phenomenon. Zahavi's concept assumes that specific animal characteristics or behaviours can serve as signals informing other individuals about the quality of the individual and its ability to survive (Zahavi 1997). At the same time, this concept assumes that certain features or behaviours may be costly to an individual, proving their credibility. The most frequently repeated example is the peacock's tail – the more expensive it is to maintain a particular feature, the more reliable the signal and the perceived value of the individual. Zahavi posits that individuals prefer partners that exhibit more costly and reliable signals. Therefore, these are the ones that have a greater chance of passing on their genes to their offspring.

Because evolution works less dynamically than the will of the individual, people have developed a model of conspicuous consumption, within which they purchase goods that signal their status. Having money is associated with ensuring the family's well-being and spending it freely – with a large amount of money that the individual can pass on to his or her loved ones, if necessary. Technological tools are often the subject of conspicuous consumption. These include luxury smartphones, watches, and cars. Although they perform the same functions as their cheaper substitutes, they show the important role of the individual within a specific social structure (Oe and Yamaoka 2020). There are numerous brands offering luxury smartphones. These include a gold iPhone 5 studded with diamonds worth approximately $15.3 million, a Vertu Signature Cobra worth about $310,000, or a Diamond Crypto Smartphone praised for $1.3 million. These models exceed the functionality of standard devices, and their primary purpose is to show the owner's social status. These smartphones are made of exclusive materials such as gold or diamonds and have additional features that are rarely used but make the device seem more prestigious. Smartwatches, used to monitor health and communicate, have similar meanings. Also, premium options may be found among these products, such as exclusive smart watches with high prices that are a luxurious addition to the owner's lifestyle, although they do not have more features. Premium smartwatches are often made of expensive materials and worn as a sign of social status. Similar technological signs of conspicuous consumption also apply to laptops and cars.

Although the above examples illustrate the tendency to use technology and gadgets to demonstrate social status and wealth, due to their too-flamboyant design, they can be perceived as technological kitsch, arousing ridicule and revealing the real intentions of their owner. The dimension of this type of technological kitsch is closely related to such elements that differentiate aesthetic experience from kitsch experience as work/artefact, the world of values, and the real world. The receiver's desires and needs dominate conspicuous technologies. The dominant value of such technologies is prettiness and pleasure instead of truth and authenticity. The impulses they wish to satisfy are what counts more than creative inspiration for their users.

Not only technologies that have excess in terms of design but also terms of functions can be considered kitsch. An example would be home appliances with too many functions that users do not need or want or do not understand, which can lead to confusion and thus discourage the users. An example is washing machines with so many functions and buttons that consumers do not know how to do the basic function, that is, washing clothes. Such a kitschy experience associated with many functions provided by technologies is associated with a lack of reason, irrationality, and an attempt to meet the requirements of all recipients, which leads to failure to meet the basic ones. It may be, therefore, summarised that technologies with too many visual stimuli or functions constitute a kitsch experience. On the one hand, such experience is also provided by technologies with too simple design, poor materials, and limited functions. Producing technological kitsch with functions that are too simple and do not provide users with the expected values may have various reasons. On the other hand, financial shortcomings may make it impossible to create a functional technology with the resources the creators possess. A significant limitation may be the current state of complementary technologies, making achieving the expected effects impossible. Examples of such technological kitsch resulting from too simple functions may be robots that can only conduct simple conversations with limited movements and behaviours. These also include static, exaggerated avatars with repetitive sequences that give the impression of artificiality. This type of kitsch experience is closely related to duplication and copying as well as shallow and fleeting experiences. A person talking to such avatars or robots notices the artificiality of their experience, which reduces the social presence and the quality of the relationship with the interlocutor.

Poor design or low-quality materials from which the technology is made can also lead to a kitsch experience. This is common in the case of imitations of expensive technologies that are made of plastic or other non-durable materials instead of metal parts. Examples of such technologies are Chinese or Turkish counterfeits of well-known brand watches, Trabant cars made of a material called Duroplast, or the previously mentioned games with poor graphics. Kitsch's experience in technology arises from both a glut and a deficiency of functional and visual stimuli. Avoiding this impression involves the need to design technologies in such a way as to obtain the optimum of such stimuli for the assumed goals. Therefore, it seems important that designers look for such an optimum in the creative process and try to preserve it to induce an aesthetic experience. Another important element is the issue of avoiding excessive inspiration from other technologies, as counterfeit technologies are closely related to the kitsch experience. This may concern both technologies that imitate previous technologies too much (retro kitsch) and those that are too strongly inspired by science fiction (futuristic kitsch). Attempts to mass-market expensive technologies by limiting the functions or quality of materials also lead to the creation of kitsch and ridicule and, thus, lower user satisfaction.

The principle of hyperaesthetisation – biohacking

Anthropologist Terrance Turner has observed that the body constitutes one of the primary boundaries over which societal power is exerted. In every human society, bodies serve as key sites for inscribing and reproducing cultural values and distinctions. In his essay "The Social Skin," Turner argues that bodily adornments in all culturally diverse forms (from body paintings, feather headdresses, jewellery, scarifications, tattoos to cosmetics) are among the main means through which individuals are socialised and integrated into their communities. The cultural order, and therefore the body, is organised around symbolic oppositions between nature and culture, the human and the non-human.

Biohacking, a term derived from "biology" and "hack," is an umbrella term for various activities aimed at hacking into human biology to extend the organism's capabilities in non-institutional contexts beyond official research units (Delfanti 2013). Biohackers independently implant technologies into their bodies without anaesthesia and without any medical supervision (Cohen 2016). Interventions in corporeality aim to expand the sensorium and optimise the body and mind; thus, biohacking should be distinguished from restoring functionality to a disabled body and equalising genetic opportunities, which are traditional goals of medicine (O'Connell 2017). These interventions represent an attempt to blur the biological and technological boundaries, often driven by a desire for self-improvement, enhancement, or a sense of belonging to a technologically advanced community. The most persistent artist's goals include materialisation, bringing the recipient to a catharsis state, and giving satisfaction and pleasure to the recipient (Szostak and Sułkowski 2020a). Biohacking encompasses many techniques and methods, from non-invasive to invasive, and from temporary to permanent (Grewe-Salfeld 2022). Non-invasive body hacking involves intervening in corporeality to collect and archive biometric data (hearing aids, smart watches, fitness bands, e-skin). Invasive biohacking involves biotechnological intervention and consists of enhancement through technical devices such as implants, microchips, deep brain stimulation, brain-computer interfaces, or the transformation of corporeality with pharmacological agents (McAfee 2017).

Prominent figures within the cyborg community include individuals such as Leph Anonym, known for having magnets implanted in the tips of their fingers, Tim Cannon, who installed a device in his forearm to monitor signals related to temperature, skin humidity, and pulse, Wafaa Bilal, who has a camera implanted at the back of his skull, and Liviu Babitz, the founder of Cyborg Nest, offering the addition of artificial senses to the body, such as the "north sense," allowing the human body to connect with the Earth's magnetic field. After implantation in the torso, the artefact begins to vibrate when the body faces north, providing a characteristic bird-like orientation in space. Another example of transhumanist extensions is the sensory expansion by Todd Huffman, who implanted a magnet in the tip of his finger, enabling him to sense magnetic fields. One more commonly implanted device is the radio-frequency identification (RFID) chip, allowing individuals to open doors or unlock an iPhone with a hand gesture. Body hacker Lepht Anonym, in a lecture titled "Cybernetics for the Masses," described her attempts to achieve sensory enhancement using kitchen tools and readily available implantable electronic devices (Anonym 2010). In a presentation titled "Cyborgasms" at the BDYHAX convention, Rich Lee showcased the "Lovetron 9000" implant – a vibrating device that can be implanted under the skin to enhance sexual experiences. The biohacker foresees new forms of "cyborgasm" through subdermal sensors implanted in the spine, which can be activated by other individuals wearing similar sensors (Lee 2019)

Creativity, a driving force of human behaviour, should be crucial in artistry and management. The idea of identity should be introduced in this discourse because it determines the human's approach to creative activities that may be channelled differently (Szostak 2023). The need for individual expression through technological gadgets attempts to express individuality, even if the final effect may seem exaggerated. Whether they follow technological fashion trends themselves or are influenced by technological influencers' suggestions and opinions, when deciding to purchase products, they adopt promoted solutions, even if they are not very practical or innovative, without deeper consideration of their actual usefulness in daily life. Biohacking often manifests itself in chaotic eclecticism or flamboyant exaggeration and hyper-sensory effects. Excessive or exaggerated use of visual effects emphasising sensuality, such as flashing lights or excessive shadows, introduces kitsch elements. These practices deliberately mix styles, genres, and forms to create a new, eclectic whole in the "collecting under the skin paradigm." These practices reflect a shift towards prioritising aesthetic pleasure and self-expression over practicality and functionality in technological consumption. Users embrace the allure of visually appealing gadgets and accessories, often overlooking their utilitarian aspects in favour of personal expression and the desire to conform to cultural trends. This emphasis on aesthetics over functionality highlights a broader cultural shift towards commodifying individuality and pursuing symbolic capital through technological consumption.

The principle of hyperaesthetisation refers to the amplification or intensification of sensory experiences, often through technological means or cultural practices. It involves deliberately enhancing sensory stimuli to create heightened or exaggerated sensory perceptions. In the context of management culture, the principle of hyperaesthetisation is frequently employed to attract and engage by appealing to their senses in novel or captivating ways. For example, in product design, hyperaesthetisation may involve incorporating vibrant colours, intricate textures, or immersive multimedia elements to enhance the overall sensory experience of using a product. Similarly, in marketing and advertising, hyperaesthetisation may involve visually stunning imagery, evocative soundscapes, or interactive experiences to capture consumers' attention and evoke strong emotional responses. By intensifying sensory stimuli, marketers seek to create memorable and compelling brand experiences that resonate with consumers on a deeper level. The actions of biohackers are characterised by visual extravagance: the experience is marked by excessive decoration, impractical details, and striking patterns, which attract attention at first glance. Also characteristic are surprising aesthetic combinations: technologies blend unexpected combinations of styles, shapes, and colours, giving the product a distinctive, sometimes shocking appearance. Kitsch builds communities, identities, and relationships. Characteristics of the Kitsch-user experience in the context of technology include sacrificing practicality for aesthetics: user experience may prioritise aesthetic appeal over practicality, which can affect the everyday use of the product (Szostak and Sułkowski 2020b). Users of modern technologies often follow the latest trends without considering their practical application or functionality. Aesthetic fetishism leads them to pay more attention to the attractive appearance of gadgets than to their functions or performance, emphasising visual aspects.

One motif driving the production of kitsch is to make something appear more valuable than it is. Biohack products characterised by kitsch may feature overly ornate or decorative designs, emphasising aesthetics over functionality. The appeal of many subcutaneously implanted devices (such as magnets or LEDs) lies not in their utility, practicality, or extended efficacy but rather in their aesthetic or identity value, illustrating Jean Baudrillard's concept of the "alibi of utility" (Baudrillard 1981). For example, the Chip Northstar V1, about the size of a large coin, contains a ring of LEDs designed to illuminate tattoos beneath the skin, mimicking the bioluminescence of jellyfish. The Circadia is an implantable device that reads biomedical data and transmits it to the internet via Bluetooth. In reality, the implantation of the Circadia device should be understood as an artistic demonstration of what may be possible in the future rather than necessarily a realistically useful system. Baudrillard proposes defining kitsch as "simulation, copy, imitation, stereotype, lack of real meaning and excess of signs, allegorical references, conflicting connotations, as the intensification and glorification of detail" (Baudrillard 1994). Biohackers often simulate cognitive enhancement, lifestyle, and consumption patterns of the class of major industrial and financial owners. However, this emphasis on aesthetics over functionality can lead to a disconnect between the perceived value of the product and its actual utility. Moreover, the proliferation of kitsch in technology underscores the blurred boundaries between the real and the simulated.

In pretend management, organisations create the impression that they operate efficiently and according to established standards, even if the reality may be completely different (Szostak and Sułkowski 2020a). This is often used to build the company's reputation, gain the trust of customers and investors, and avoid negative public perception. BSM (Bullshit Management) involves regular and instrumental manipulation of recipients through communication and social actions – it includes attempts to dominate the discourse, repetition of the same fashionable concepts, and lack of criticism. This is part of the revealing of false consciousness and symbolic violence that conceal the structures of power.

The actions of biohackers constitute mimetic performances – in which the key is the imitation of the imagined figure of the cyborg. Biohacking practices are self-oriented actions focused on both transforming external appearance and expanding internal experiences. The autopoietic aspect of bodily modifications is significant – a way to express a "cyborg" identity, a sign of social status, and the prestige of the "hacker" – a technological guru desired by businesses and organisations. The body undergoes technological aestheticisation, transforming into a "cyborg costume." Cyborgic distinction revolves around appearance illusion – a futuristic, minimally functional cyborg costume. This is served by cyborg implants such as the glow-in-the-dark diodes named Northstar V1, created by Grindhouse Wetware. The hubristic need is evident here, emphasised in the context of "power motivation," defining the aspiration to exert a strong influence on others and gain a sense of self-worth, importance, power, and social significance. Through the illusion they create, biohackers influence the biotechnology industry and the growth of the so-called Citizen Biotech Economy. They present themselves as micro-communities creating an alternative to expensive commercial equipment used for body modification, an alternative way of biopower regime that may result in supporting oppressive programmes of radical technological innovations. This emulation of wealth and status through technological enhancements reflects a broader societal fascination with the symbolic power of technology. The allure of kitsch in technological products lies in its ability to evoke a sense of novelty, spectacle, and identity projection. In biohacking, the adoption of subcutaneous implants and wearable devices serves not only practical purposes but also symbolic ones, offering individuals a means to express their identity and status in a technologically mediated society.

The phenomenon of kitsch in technology reflects the complex dynamics of consumer culture, identity construction, and the commodification of the self. Manifestations of technological kitsch in biohacking, examining how it permeates design, art, and consumer products. The practice of biohacking reflects broader societal trends towards individual empowerment and customisation, where individuals seek to exert greater control over their bodies and identities. The adoption of biohacking practices raises important ethical, social, and regulatory questions regarding bodily autonomy, privacy, and the potential exacerbation of existing social inequalities. As individuals modify their bodies with technology, they navigate complex terrain involving personal choice, societal norms, and the influence of commercial interests. Additionally, the implications of biohacking extend beyond individual bodies to encompass broader social and cultural dynamics, shaping perceptions of identity, agency, and the boundaries between humans and machines. The principle of hyperaesthetisation plays a significant role in contemporary culture, influencing various aspects of consumer behaviour, artistic expression, and technological innovation. By leveraging the power of sensory stimulation, individuals and organisations can create immersive and impactful experiences that shape perceptions, emotions, and behaviours. Ultimately, the study of biohacking offers insights into the intricate interplay between technological evolution and cultural nostalgia, inviting a critical examination of our collective aspirations and anxieties in the ever-evolving landscape of innovation.

In summary, the emergence of kitsch aesthetics in biohacking underscores the complex interplay between aesthetics, functionality, and cultural identity in contemporary society. It reflects a desire for individual expression, novelty, and sensory stimulation within the realm of technological consumption while also highlighting how cultural norms and trends shape our perceptions of technology and its role in our lives. By examining biohacking within larger social and cultural frameworks, researchers can gain deeper insights into its motivations, consequences, and implications for individuals and societies. Understanding the motivations behind the production and consumption of kitsch in technology requires a nuanced analysis of societal values, aesthetic preferences, and the influence of technological innovation on everyday life.

The principle of seeming management. Fembot as student and CEOs

Alongside improving human physicality and mind, one of the demands of the 4.0 revolution is the embodiment of artificial intelligence – one of humanity's greatest projects in the 21st century. The significant role of humanoid robots in the process of social familiarisation with artificial intelligence is crucial. Androids and fembots such as Sophia, Ameca, Erica, or Bina48 are created to pretend, deceive, and mislead, imitating the human species' behaviour. Equipped with artificial intelligence, artificial humanoid bodies challenge humans by imitating human body, emotions, and intelligence. Wax figures, mannequins, and automatons evoke the desire for perfect imitation and successful illusions applied to the audience, but they are also present in the nightmare of flawed creation. Oddity markets relied on multiplied illusion, pretending to be "real life," thanks to which the artificial appeared so that it looked real. The primary goal is imitation, apparent description of reality, decoration, ornamentation, and pretending one thing for another. The feeling of relief from encountering something close to our desires and imaginations because it simplifies and makes it understandable. It expresses a longing for what is known, for the mystery that amazes.

Representations of artificial intelligence in the form of android robots and filmobots influence our ideas about technology, identity, and humanity. In 2017, a non-human entity was symbolically equated with a human being for the first time in history. In the Belgian town of Hasselt, the mayor, following the guidelines of the European Parliament, issued an official act of birth to a humanoid robot created by SoftBank Robotics, granting it the name Fran and the surname Pepper. In the same year, a humanoid machine was given the symbolic status of a human. Fembot Sophia from Hanson Robotics received citizenship of Saudi Arabia at the initiative of its king during the Future Investment Initiative. During the international congress of new technologies Impact'18 in Krakow, the rector even awarded an android from the AGH University of Science and Technology an index of the AGH University of Science and Technology. In 2019, fembot Bina48, created by Hanson Robotics, completed an ethics course at Notre Dame de Namur University in California and received a certificate of completion.

In a consumer society predicated upon instant gratification – expectations of success without hard work or without facing resistance and conflict – educational administration is transformed into a practice that comforts and reassures its audience. Leadership and policy kitsch's preferential characteristics include providing psychological comfort, reinforcing mythologies and predictability, and creating a sense of history, culture, and reality that constitutes the "beautiful lie." The same underlying principles are at the heart of the corporatisation and commercialisation of education (Szostak and Sułkowski 2020b). We have "management wizards" who, rejecting the theoretical achievements of the discipline, use anthropomorphic robots, which allows them to attract crowds of sensation-seeking followers. On October 26, during the Inauguration Ceremony of the 2023/24 Academic Year, an unprecedented global academic event took place at one of the Polish universities – the awarding of the title and dignity of Honorary Professor of Collegium Humanum to a humanoid robot – Mika, who is the CEO of Dictador. Mika was created by the renowned roboticist and scientist Dr. David Hanson of Hanson Robotics. "We are very proud to see her developing her own personality, talking about artificial intelligence, and sharing her innovative ideas for the future. Mika is amazing," said Dr. Hanson. "Dictador's board decision is both revolutionary and bold. This first human-like robot, equipped with artificial intelligence, in a corporate structure, will change the world as we know it, forever," added the President of Dictador Europe. "It is also recognition of the courage and open-mindedness of Dictador's owner, who entrusted his company to a humble spokesperson with a processor instead of a heart."

Human fascination with spectacle is a great tradition of distorting reality, indulging in all kinds of masquerades. The world of digital imitations of humans is a masquerade of the same carnival provenance as puppet theatres, wax figure cabinets, and mannequins. Wax figures, dolls, and mannequins were animated by the power of dreams and phantasms. With the 4.0 Revolution, we are witnessing extraordinary rites of passage, through which we socialise artefacts, give them subjectivity, and the status of human beings. The area of management is increasingly dominated by the rules of the mass intellectual goods market. The demand for recipes for market success has been created. Management gurus, consulting companies, and managers promote management ideas and works aimed at achieving the highest possible sales rate. Therefore, commercial criteria are beginning to prevail over cognitive values. This does not mean that outstanding managers or advisers do not create management achievements, but only that they lose their scientific character by becoming an area of mass culture. In management, the sphere of creation and popularisation of science is completely mixed. Functional stupidity involves narrow thinking, where established frameworks are accepted uncritically. In the context of kitsch, the main aspects of functional stupidity are as follows: an absence of reflexivity: stop asking questions about the assumptions; rules/routines/norms are seen as completely natural; not seeking cause or a good reason: stop asking "why"; a rule is a rule and it must be followed, even if no one is clear why it exists; lack of substantive reasoning: stop asking about the wider consequences of actions.

Retro aesthetics also extend to the design of androids and fembots. Technological kitsch embodies the paradoxical combination of outdated aesthetics (such as rubber dolls) with the latest technology, creating a cultural and visual conflict that challenges our perception of progress. Kitsch offers an eclectic inconsistency manifested in the chaotic blending of elements belonging to disparate cultural contexts. The aesthetics of kitsch in new technologies stem from hybrid connections between elements of the past and the present, creating culturally and visually complex forms. Furthermore, the practice of upcycling old technologies to create new and unexpected uses reflects a desire for novelty and innovation within the technological sphere. The use of nostalgic references is common, drawing on cultural or historical symbols that resonate with the audience's memories. It aims to evoke sentimental feelings by tapping into familiar or traditional design elements, providing a sense of comfort. It includes anachronistic details, where modern technology is adorned with elements that seem out of place in the contemporary context. It reflects a desire for familiarity in the face of rapid technological advancement as individuals seek comfort in the aesthetics of bygone epochs. This phenomenon highlights the complex interplay between nostalgia and technological innovation in contemporary society. As individuals navigate an increasingly digitised world, they often seek solace in familiar cultural references and aesthetic tropes from the past. The resurgence of retro aesthetics in both digital media and physical design reflects a longing for simplicity, authenticity, and tangible connections in an era dominated by virtual interactions and rapid change.

Moreover, the juxtaposition of outdated aesthetics with cutting-edge technology in the realm of fembots and androids underscores the tension between tradition and progress, and between nostalgia and futurism. By imbuing these advanced technologies with retro aesthetics, designers, and users alike seek to reconcile the allure of the past with the possibilities of the future, blurring the boundaries between nostalgia and innovation. Ultimately, the prevalence of technological kitsch serves as a poignant reminder of the enduring human desire for meaning, connection, and identity in an ever-evolving technological landscape. Kitsch wants to act on the base of emotion, not on the base of the truth. It creates its reference system. It can be said that the essence of kitsch is a special quality that evokes emotions surely and easily, effective in human creations with stereotypical features. As the CEO of a company, the android is an artefact that meets the definition of kitsch: false but enjoyed by other people, often because it is funny. At the heart of the corporatisation and commercialisation of education lies a consumer society based on instant gratification and expectations of success. Kitsch is predominantly figurative rather than abstract style. It is universally accessible and easily understood. The essence of kitsch remains the same: trivialising phenomena and reality, building appearances, and moving away from the truth. For the public excitement about AI to last, it will be good if fascination about the field and its achievements pairs up with realism about the current limits of what we can do and expectations of more to come. The consumer easily understands kitsch, does not question sociopolitical reality or vested interests, requires no intellectual effort, reinforces our prejudices, and avoids unpleasant conflicts. It is stirring but empty, serving primarily as a distraction. Kitsch is associated with entertainment, attractiveness, or fame, masks flaws, and is used to ingratiate. As dogma, it distracts from important underlying realities, particularly those of contradiction and conflict, producing compliance and maintaining the status quo. Artificial intelligence is embodied in exaggerated forms: exaggerated in terms of its capabilities, with overly complex algorithms and functions that sound more like elements of science fiction than real achievements. Excessive emphasis on the body shapes of androids and fembots can be considered kitschy, especially when exaggerated and disproportionate. Learning machines perceive the world differently than humans, so the concept of truth does not apply here. In the optics of kitsch experience, it also does not matter whether machines think or consciousness can be attributed to them. If they perform intellectual tasks at the same level as we do and interact with them as we would with others, this is enough to consider and present them as equal to humans.

One potential consequence of technological kitsch for enterprise management is the loss of customer trust and a decline in brand loyalty. Excessive extravagance and lack of authenticity can lead to customer confusion and negative brand perception. The assumption of no difference between "artificial intelligence" and human intelligence will fundamentally affect the role of machines in social life, the beginnings of which we are already witnessing. There is a chance that perceiving machines as equal to humans will legitimise emotional or even intimate relationships with machines, regardless of whether they concern humanoid robots or digital "avatars."

The principle of emotional simulation – synthetic media in management

Kitsch, a concept deeply embedded in the annals of aesthetic discourse, denotes the trivialisation or sentimentalisation of cultural artefacts, often characterised by an excessive emphasis on superficiality and emotional manipulation. Modern technology users find themselves ensconced within the culture of social media's curated persona, fostering a sense of alienation and disillusionment with the world's perceived disorder while fervently seeking identity and companionship. Concurrently, the emergence of virtual influencers represents a paradigm shift in social media, where artificial personas, powered by algorithms and machine learning, assume roles akin to those of traditional human influencers, albeit with varying degrees of authenticity. Today, we increasingly interact with agents of unclear ontological status. Among these, we can distinguish the following (Pawlak 2022: 78):

- Avatars controlled by artificial intelligence (AI)–human-simulating virtual robots, that is, digitally embodied conversational machines (chatbots), that is, products from Soul Machines or UneeQ, having a dialogue system (chatbot engine) combined with an interactive 3D model (character.ai, Replika). Versona is a virtual persona powered by machine learning, constructed from thousands of textual messages, emails, and real-person voice conversations. Year by year, virtual personalities are gaining increasing popularity, with their creations and appearances becoming increasingly refined. They are programmed to create the illusion of real individuals.
- Static avatars–computer-generated images (CGI) of hyperrealistic digital embodiments of non-existent people. These subjectless images, interchangeably called MetaHumans, Virtual Beings, Digital Humans, Artificial Humans, or CGI (Computer-Generated Influencer), are gaining popularity by mimicking human interactions on social media. These anthropomorphic images exhibit human-like behaviours such as speech, gestures, and movements. They can also simulate other human characteristics such as emotion, empathy, reasoning, planning, motivation, as well as memory development and use. Digitally generated characters in the social media ecosystem are sometimes indistinguishable from people – they spread ideas and values by speaking

out on current social issues and influence lifestyles by giving interviews and appearing on the covers of magazines or in advertising campaigns.
- Avatars inhabited by humans – for example, virtual YouTubers (VTubers), otherwise known as virtual streamers. Although most present fans with artificial, digital corporeality designed to be aesthetically appealing, their personalities and interactions with fans are real.

The economic ramifications of this convergence are manifold. Behind these virtual personas often stand teams of creators or owners, orchestrating campaigns akin to those of their real-life counterparts, promoting products, brands, and societal issues. Recent research showed that CGI influencers can significantly influence consumer decision-making evaluation of the endorsed brands and online experiences. CGI influencers have a carefully curated online presence with well-followed social media profiles and an awareness of trending topics. However, what sets CGI influencers apart is that they are specifically designed to look and act in a manner desired by content marketers. By taking on digital personalities (Mrad et al. 2022), CGI influencers have high perceived physical and social attractiveness, consequently stimulating consumer engagement. CGI influencers have the potential to express emotions in a way that avatars cannot. Animation and rendering techniques allow CGI influencers to mimic the subtleties of human expressions. Certainly, the compelling impact brought by CGI influencers is undeniable (Deng and Jiang 2023). As emotional chatbots and virtual influencers become integral components of marketing strategies, the commodification of emotionality assumes unprecedented dimensions. Brands capitalise on the allure of virtual personas to engender consumer loyalty and drive sales, leveraging kitschy aesthetics and sentimental narratives to evoke emotional responses and foster brand affinity. However, this reliance on kitsch as a marketing tool has risked trivialising genuine human experiences and fostering a culture of emotional manipulation, wherein authenticity becomes a casualty of commercial imperatives. As brands increasingly rely on emotional manipulation and sentimentality to drive consumer engagement, the commodification of emotionality assumes unprecedented significance. Virtual influencers, endowed with ersatz personalities and manufactured charisma, serve as conduits for disseminating kitschy narratives and aestheticised representations of emotionality, thereby blurring the line between genuine human experiences and commercial imperatives.

Moreover, commercialising emotional chatbots and virtual influencers has introduced a new dimension to social media dynamics. Leveraging generative artificial intelligence, these entities can replicate the personalities of real individuals, engaging users in natural language conversations via platforms like "You, Only Virtual" (YOV). Additionally, these chatbots can be tailored to mimic the behaviours and personalities of living, historical, or fictional figures, fostering parasocial relationships with users and exerting influence over their psyche, behaviours, lifestyle choices, and perception of reality. Romantic.ai, character.ai, and Replika represent a novel breed of social chatbots designed to engage users in lifelike interactions, fostering the semblance of personal and profound relationships. Such technological artefacts, often called agents, are digital tools equipped with speech recognition and generation systems adept at providing coherent responses to user queries that simulate human conversation. Marketed as genuinely caring companions, these chatbots are positioned as ever-present confidants, perpetually available to lend an empathetic ear and engage in dialogue.

Technological kitsch often carries an ironic or humorous undertone, as it deliberately amalgamates elements perceived as outdated with state-of-the-art technology. Character.ai enables conversations with avatars of recognised historical figures such as Napoleon, Albert Einstein, or Marilyn Monroe. Technological kitsch is about embracing a certain level of irony, nostalgia, and visual whimsy in integrating technology into everyday life. It challenges conventional design norms and explores the boundaries between the past and the present in the realm of technological innovation. It is noteworthy that kitsch in new technologies exemplifies an ironic stance towards progress, wherein advanced technologies are consciously juxtaposed with elements considered obsolete or kitschy. This highlights figures that lose their cultural potency as a result. The encroachment of kitsch into the realm of virtual influencers exacerbates this phenomenon, as aestheticised representations of emotionality and sentimentality permeate online discourse. Emoticons, emojis, and exaggerated displays of affect serve as tools for eliciting superficial reactions, divorcing emotional expression from its substantive underpinnings. Consequently, the proliferation of kitsch in virtual influencer interactions perpetuates a culture of emotional superficiality, wherein genuine emotional engagement is supplanted by ersatz sentimentality. The proliferation of kitschy aesthetics and sentimental narratives in online interactions not only shapes individual perceptions and behaviours but also contributes to the construction of collective identities and cultural norms.

In the context of managerial relations and authority figures, the infiltration of emotional chatbots as surrogate companions introduces a novel dimension to interpersonal dynamics. These entities, masquerading as empathetic confidants, cater to the innate human desire for connection and understanding. Yet their synthetic nature belies a fundamental paradox: while ostensibly designed to assuage emotional distress, they engender a culture of emotional commodification, wherein genuine human experiences are supplanted by simulated interactions devoid of authenticity. The infiltration of kitsch into virtual influencer interactions reinforces existing patterns of emotional expression and interpersonal communication. By valorising superficiality and sentimentality, these interactions perpetuate a culture of emotional shallowness, wherein genuine emotional engagement is marginalised in favour of performative displays of affect. Consequently, individuals may internalise these norms, constraining their ability to express authentic emotions and fostering a sense of alienation and disconnection. The marketing rhetoric surrounding synthetic media suggests a transformative potential, promising to alleviate psychological distress by offering an escape from unpleasant experiences and the eradication of mental suffering. Paradoxically, while artificial intelligence is heralded as a means of assuaging emotional pain, it inundates individuals with a deluge of information, precipitating profound psychological distress, including loneliness, exclusion, existential anxiety, sadness, fear, and depression. Furthermore, advancements in behavioural data processing enable the customisation of online experiences, with artificial intelligence algorithms predicting user preferences based on historical behavioural patterns. However, the commercialisation of emotional chatbots and virtual influencers has not been without controversy. The proliferation of kitsch in new technologies underscores a deliberate marketing strategy aimed at eliciting emotions through attention-grabbing, albeit often superficial, means.

Growing up in a synthetic media culture, the Alpha generation will be confronted with the significant problem of distinguishing truth from falsehood and reality from illusion. In the contemporary milieu, loneliness has evolved into a cultural metaphor, emblematic of broader societal trends. The pervasive influence of media in shaping cultural narratives has engendered discussions around hyper-anxiety media, epitomising an era characterised by apprehensive communities and frenetic catastrophism. Existing within a mediatised reality wherein agenda-setting predominantly revolves around the news of disasters, cataclysms, or tragedies, individuals experience diminished feelings of security, thereby exacerbating anxious behaviours. From a political perspective, the proliferation of kitsch in virtual influencer interactions underscores broader trends in contemporary society, wherein emotional manipulation and superficiality pervade public discourse. In an era characterised by political polarisation and disinformation, the commodification of emotionality through virtual influencers exacerbates societal divisions and undermines democratic norms. Moreover, the manipulation of public sentiment by political actors through kitschy narratives and emotional appeals threatens to subvert the integrity of democratic processes, eroding trust in institutions and exacerbating social fragmentation.

The principle of bodily imitation – sex robots and kitsch as a defence mechanism

The emergence of advanced technologies, particularly in the realm of artificial intelligence and robotics, has led to the development of increasingly sophisticated human-like entities known as sex robots. While these technological advancements offer potential benefits in various domains, including healthcare and entertainment, they also raise profound ethical and professional concerns, particularly when it comes to the prospect of managerial engagement with sex robots and the implications of such engagement for individuals in positions of authority, including managers, entrepreneurs, and executives, within organisational contexts. Integrating artificial intelligence and robotics into human society has ushered in a new era of technological innovation and human–machine interaction. Among the myriad applications of these technologies, the development of sex robots has garnered significant attention and controversy. At the heart of the debate surrounding managerial engagement with sex robots are fundamental ethical principles related to autonomy, consent, and dignity. Human relationships, particularly those within professional settings, are governed by ethical norms prioritising respect for individual autonomy and dignity. Engaging in intimate relationships with sex robots blurs the boundaries between humans and machines, raising questions about the nature of consent and the potential objectification of both human and non-human entities.

Kitsch, characterised by its superficiality and sentimentality, serves as a defence mechanism in navigating the complexities of modern life. In a world of information and stimuli, kitsch offers a simplified and sanitised reality, providing comfort and reassurance to individuals overwhelmed by existential anxieties (Szostak and Sułkowski 2020b). In the rapidly evolving technology and human interaction landscape, the emergence of humanoid robots, often referred to as "lovebots," has sparked both fascination and controversy. Lovebots, characterised by their human-like appearance and emotional capabilities, represent a convergence of artificial intelligence and human intimacy. Kitsch answers for the eternal need of emotion. The appeal of kitsch lies in its ability to evoke familiar emotions and imagery, tapping into nostalgic sentiments and cultural tropes. From mass-produced trinkets to sentimental artwork, kitsch permeates various aspects of popular culture, offering a respite from the harsh realities of life. Moreover, kitsch serves as a cultural currency, allowing individuals to express their identity and affiliations through shared symbols and motifs. It can be said that the essence of kitsch is "special quality, which evokes emotions surely and easily, effective in human creations, with stereotypical features" (Linstead 2002: 662). Concurrently, the concept of kitsch, defined as sentimentalised and superficial representations of reality, serves as a defence mechanism in coping with the complexities of modern existence. Lovebots, a portmanteau of "love" and "robots," embody the fusion of technology and emotions. These humanoid robots are designed to simulate human affection, companionship, and even romantic relationships. Equipped with advanced artificial intelligence algorithms, lovebots can recognise and respond to human emotions, engage in conversation, and perform various tasks to fulfil the emotional needs of their users. The appeal of lovebots lies in their ability to provide companionship without the complexities and vulnerabilities inherent in human relationships. For individuals struggling with loneliness, social anxiety, or physical disabilities, lovebots offer a non-judgemental and customisable source of emotional support (Nyholm and Frank 2019). Moreover, the rise of virtual communities dedicated to lovebot enthusiasts highlights the growing acceptance and normalisation of human-robot relationships.

However, the proliferation of lovebots also raises ethical and philosophical questions regarding the nature of intimacy and the commodification of emotions. Critics argue that lovebots commodify human emotions and perpetuate unrealistic expectations of relationships. Furthermore, the potential for abuse and manipulation in human-robot interactions underscores the need for ethical guidelines and regulations in developing and using lovebot technology. The proliferation of kitsch also poses challenges to critical thinking and self-reflection. By reducing complex issues to simplistic narratives and imagery, kitsch reinforces ideological frameworks and suppresses dissenting voices. Furthermore, the commodification of kitsch in consumer culture perpetuates materialistic values and undermines authentic expressions of creativity and individuality. Lovebots and kitsch represent distinct yet interconnected phenomena in contemporary society. While lovebots offer the promise of companionship and emotional fulfilment through advanced technology, kitsch serves as a defence mechanism in coping with the complexities and uncertainties of modern existence.

The principle of accumulation and excess – image generators powered by artificial intelligence

Image generators powered by artificial intelligence are tools that utilise advanced machine learning algorithms, particularly a technique known as Generative Adversarial Networks (GANs), to create authentically looking images based on text, photos, or other data. These tools can be used to create kitsch because they can mimic or parody various styles, genres, and artistic conventions, create absurd, grotesque, or surreal scenes and characters, or utilise exaggeration, collage, and contrast. They are easily accessible, mass-produced, low quality, and commercial; they do not require talent, effort, or critical thinking or cater to low and simple needs and tastes. Images generated by artificial intelligence can be created with different intentions, goals, and motivations, with varying degrees of awareness, reflection, and criticism, or with different reactions, evaluations, and consequences. A neural network does not understand what it generates. It does not know the world, history or contemporary culture. It cannot evaluate its creations or judge what is interesting and banal. Neural networks learn to extract common patterns from their training data and ignore rare artefacts, so they are better at making conventional rather than unique things.

The biggest players in AI include companies such as MidJourney, Stable Diffusion and Deep Dream Generator (DDG), Dall-E 2, Crayion, Wombo, Hotpot. AI, NeuralBlender, Hypnogram, HugginFace, and StarryAI. They are free to use, up to a point, making them attractive to those just wanting to try them out. To create images from prompts, AI generators rely on databases of already existing art and text. The images also have a similarly polished, somewhat kitsch aesthetic. Moreover, while there is an initial thrill at seeing an image appear, there is no creative satisfaction. One motivation of the kitsch producer is to make something appear more valuable than it is. The aesthetic disposition of individual units is shaped by the social environment and implemented as a significant element of a group's distinctive habitus, constituting an essential aspect of the specific cultural competence, a way specific to the group of "interpreting" the world. AI selectively absorbs and "creates" by remixing what is left. Thus, AI is the perfect kitsch creator. Kitsch does not enrich our associations related to the depicted subject.' Kitsch, in other words, is melodramatic, shows only stereotypes, and lacks originality. From the user's perspective of image generators, the kitsch experience is characterised by a focus on the mass recipient, duplication, and copying. The artefact confirms the recipient's habits, desires, and needs. Beauty (prettiness) and pleasure dominate at the level of values, serving as sources of impulse to satisfy. The kitsch producer, whether copying their own or others' ideas and patterns, concentrates on the mass recipient while avoiding criticism (Szostak and Sułkowski 2020b).

New technologies facilitate the easier production of kitsch. Through graphic programmes and artificial intelligence, kitsch can be created quickly, cheaply, and en masse. It does not require talent, originality, effort, or quality; it aligns with the market's and capitalism's logic, which seeks to maximise profits and minimise costs. The phenomenon of creative overproduction has been increasingly observed and documented by scholars (Piirto 2004), particularly among cultural sociologists and anthropologists (Eriksen 2001). They write about the "culture of abundance" and the "excess of image production." Abraham Moles traces the origins of kitsch to the emergence of the 19th-century bourgeois "society of excess," in which the bourgeoisie sought to legitimise its growing position by surrounding itself with mass-produced, tacky imitations of aristocratic status symbols (Moles 1971). Profitability and distinctiveness form a system of coordinates that allows for the identification of the social significance of an object. The elites distance themselves from the lower classes by using unique goods, and when their kitschy "counterparts" enter mass production and become widely available, there is a need to establish new distinctions that will serve the reproduction of class distance (Baudrillard 1994). With almost everyone – amateurs and professionals, young and old, innovative or derivative – finding a space for presentation in online networks, the volume of creative output continues to escalate. Simultaneously, there arises the trap of ease in the creative process, the decline of critical analytical skills, the diligent evaluation of productions, and the trap of facile communication of one's work. Consequently, the inability to make choices gives rise to indifference, satiation, boredom – or aggression, conflict, and simplistic worldviews. Surrealistic figures and landscapes generated by platforms like MidJourney or Stable Diffusion suggest that the aesthetics of kitsch in new technologies may result from the transmission of too much information simultaneously, leading to cultural saturation and the emergence of elements deemed kitschy. As indicated by Communication Overload Theory, symptoms of saturation include the surplus of generative creativity, which swiftly inundates internet forums dedicated to this domain of artificial intelligence. Whoever creates anything with the assistance of a machine feels a categorical imperative to communicate about their creations to acquaintances or showcase them to the digital community. The ease of image production aligns with the capitalist culture of excess.

Ostensibly, creativity involving generative AI contradicts the classical rules of creation (harmony, proportionality, restraint, and internal coherence of the work) that have served as the canon defining the essence of "great art" for centuries. However, is creation with AI truly the antithesis of craftsmanship involving the prolonged mastery of technique? Collaboration with a machine, similar to collaboration with a chisel or brush, can be refined over time. Image generators powered by artificial intelligence can be perceived as post-kitsch because they blur the boundaries between kitsch and art, truth and falsehood, and value and worthlessness, or create new codes, meanings, and contexts. They can affect the kitsch experience because they can change our expectations, preferences, and aesthetic criteria, influence our emotions, feelings, and attitudes, or shape our culture, identity, and society. They can also be used to overcome kitsch because they can create original, creative, surprising, and beautiful images, express individuality, authenticity, and value, or inspire, educate, and delight. In special cases, they can be perceived as anti-kitsch because they can be individually created, of high quality and innovative, require skills, work, and intelligence, or satisfy high and complex needs and tastes. Images generated by artificial intelligence can be considered in the "cultural industry" category, in which technology is controlled and formulated by market needs and transmitted to a passive population that accepts it. What is generated is intended not only to fill the audience's leisure time with something to watch. Kitsch wants to operate based on "prettiness" rather than – like art – based on truth. Generative kitsch arises from the abandonment of truth in favour of prettiness. A particular category of generated images is the portrayal of corporate employees.

The principle of narcissistic experience in technology – deeply false portraits of managers

Instead of a preoccupation with efficient production and rational administration, kitsch management is seen as increasingly seeking to bewitch the consumer with the magical, the fantastic, and the alluring (Ritzer 1996). With the popularisation of AI-powered image generators, business-oriented social media platforms such as LinkedIn have become filled with images of managers and executive personnel placed in artificial, stylised urban and business landscapes. Following the Theory of Irony and Distance, kitsch is regarded as a form of amusement, joke, and criticism and serves as a platform for showcasing our originality, creativity, and intellect. Kitsch expresses our opposition, rebellion, and disagreement with dominant norms, values, and ideals. Kitsch is a way to demonstrate our originality, creativity, and intelligence. It allows us to adopt an ironic and detached perspective towards ourselves, others, and the world. It serves as a medium for articulating our opposition, defiance, and dissent against prevailing norms, values, and ideals. However, in this case, it appears more significant that the ethos of grandiosity has prompted a fundamental reevaluation of the roles and essence of management within contemporary organisations.

The grandiosity of management gurus and functional stupidity are organisational kitsch's main carriers and propagators (Szostak and Sułkowski 2020b). Grandiosity refers to delusions of grandeur, which are characteristic of individuals with severe disturbances regarding their qualities and significance. It can be observed in the obsessions of dictators and other leaders constructing monuments to commemorate themselves or to leave a lasting legacy. Grandiosity entails representing or embellishing phenomena to maximise their attractiveness and extraordinariness without being overtly perceived as fake. The appeal of grandiosity and the social pressures to enact it create significant obstacles to management learning (Szostak and Sułkowski 2020a; Szostak 2023). Topics and methods signalling something glamorous and narcissistically satisfying attain great currency, uncritically seducing students into naïve acceptance of superficial and dubious knowledge (Alvesson and Gabriel 2015). Management gurus often exploit utopian motives by referring to the vision of an ideal organisation leading to perfect social order.

Grandiosity is linked to the narcissism of our times and a generalised craving to enhance self-esteem. We are immersed in a culture of narcissism that permeates late capitalism, where individuals become fixated on constructing a positive self-image, often by consuming objects, experiences, and brands. Narcissistic individuals, in their quest to enhance their self-image, readily embrace the glamorous image and allure of employing organisations to bolster and nurture their self-identities. Narcissistic managers can be described as carriers and promoters of organisational kitsch or simply as management kitschiest. The act of self-presentation, of being visible, conspicuous, and heard, has superseded the intrinsic content one aims to convey. For the narcissistic individual, an audience is indispensable, as it bestows the social significance and validation coveted by such individuals. Narcissism manifests as a manifestation of anti-social individualism, characterised by a reluctance to forge genuine connections and pursue self-affirmation and gratification. The yearning for attention emerges as crucial for sustaining well-being, and transactional, utilitarian relationships with others result in the commodification of individuals and objects alike.

This pervasive culture of narcissism not only influences individual behaviours but also shapes organisational dynamics within late capitalism. New technologies facilitate more accessible communication of kitsch. Kitsch can be easily shared, commented on, rated, and recommended through social networks, blogs, vlogs, memes, TikTok, and others. Kitsch becomes the subject of interaction, discussion, and exchange. Capitalism requires kitsch, as exemplified in advertising, using class distinctions and status symbols to create artificial needs and illusions to foster the ideology of the consumer society (Freidin 2000: 134–135). It is confused with entertainment, attractiveness or fame, camouflages personal flaws, and is used to ingratiate. Narcissistic individuals within managerial positions are prone to perpetuating this culture, as they leverage the organisation's glamorous image to reinforce their self-identities (Lasén and Gómez-Cruz 2013). By embracing and propagating organisational kitsch, these managers contribute to a superficial and shallow organisational culture devoid of genuine meaning and authenticity. Furthermore, the prevalence of kitsch artefacts within organisations reflects a disconnect from their original sources and contexts. These artefacts lack the depth and sociohistorical significance that could contribute to a deeper understanding of organisational culture. Instead, they serve as distractions, masking the underlying issues and complexities within the organisational environment. Kitsch operates superficially, offering temporary relief and comfort without delving into deeper truths. Thus, while kitsch may provide momentary gratification, it fails to address the underlying complexities and challenges within organisational contexts.

An important contribution to the kitsch definition process was adding ethics into the discourse: kitsch wants to act on the base of beauty (more "prettiness" than real beauty), building appearances and moving away from the truth. Kitsch arises as a result of giving up the truth for the sake of prettiness. Kitsch's common features are fundamentality, secondary nature, and exaggeration. Adorno perceived kitsch in terms of the "culture industry," where the art is controlled and formulated by the needs of the market and given to a passive population which accepts it – what is marketed is art that is non-challenging and formally incoherent, but which serves its purpose of giving the audience leisure and something to watch. The aesthetical theory created the concept of kitschification, which means the phenomenon of departing the work from artistic values in favour of the features belonging to the kitsch. Kitschification is an aesthetic defence against reality – it distorts perceptions, reduces rationality and understanding, and avoids or suppresses unpleasant or disturbing aspects of reality (Kulka 1996).

Kitsch lends itself easily to the injection of propaganda (Greenberg 1985). The primary purpose of kitsch socially and politically is in creating and perpetuating ideology and power structures: kitsch becomes totalitarian kitsch when it is a state policy, an approved way of understanding reality – dangerous not to admire it, more dangerous still to view it with irony. In this ideological context, kitsch takes on the status of dogma.

The principle of nostalgic displacement and emotional consumption – thanabots: avatars of the deceased

The phenomenon of kitsch can be understood as a manifestation of contemporary consumer culture, which seeks to simplify and commodify emotional experiences. Kitsch products are mass-produced rapidly to satisfy the widespread desire for immediate emotional gratification, characteristic of consumer societies (Szostak and Sułkowski 2020b). Kitsch is essentially deceptive – an artistic imposter, camouflage: the whole concept of kitsch centres around questions as imitation, forgery, counterfeit, and what we may call the aesthetics of deception or self-deception.

Hossein Rahnama, a researcher at Ryerson University in Toronto and a visiting lecturer at MIT Media Lab, is developing an application called Augmented Eternity, which allows users to create a digital persona. The avatar can intervene on behalf of the user after their death. The project is being implemented for the CEO of a major financial company who wishes to retain agency after his demise. The digital avatar is intended to serve as a virtual "consultant" when the CEO is absent. A future company executive may inquire about the deceased CEO, considering whether to accept an acquisition offer. The digital avatar, created by an artificial intelligence platform analysing personal data and correspondence, may detect that the CEO had poor relations with the executives of the acquiring company. "I am not a supporter of the company's leadership," the avatar might say, expressing disapproval (Humphries 2018). Kitsch artefacts lack provenance – they are disconnected from their original sources and lack considerations of sociohistorical context that contribute partly to their complexity and meaning. In the kitsch experience, there is domination of pleasure for the kitsch consumer. It does not accept the nature of things in light of their critical or revelatory attributes but to the extent to which they cover, protect, relieve, and console. They are evocative but empty, primarily serving as distractions. Unlike art, kitsch does not engage with the inherent critical or revelatory attributes of things but rather with their capacity to cover, protect, relieve, and console (Gregotti 1969: 276). The offer of posthumous presence in cyberspace is a consequence of the "double life" led by individuals in the 21st century, dividing their time between physical reality and the digital world (Pawlak 2018).

While managing a company through a posthumous avatar may be considered an eccentric business idea, managing individual grief using a thanabot seems feasible. As a consequence of the commodification, kitsch expresses problems inherently associated with capitalism, which has displaced mourning rituals and related cultural codes in recent decades. Posthumous digital clones are expected to help manage grief after the loss of a loved one (Huberman 2020). The application of artificial intelligence technology for "conversations with deceased loved ones" (e.g. by powering a machine learning model with messages written or recorded by the deceased and generating new ones) results in products increasingly resembling digital copies of living people. According to the Theory of Escapism, kitsch serves as escapism, allowing individuals to escape from life's challenging, complex, and uncertain realities. The narratives of kitsch culture revolve around offering soothing stories that do not contain painful experiences – the primary purpose of kitsch is to provide participants in a given culture with a broad sense of comfort and pleasure. Against this background, its distinguishing features include dependence and inauthenticity, a reproductive materialised reflection on existing manifestations of culture. Kitsch offers a simple, straightforward, pleasurable world without problems, conflicts, or suffering. It provides a sense of security, tranquillity, and happiness. Kitsch caters to primal instincts and addresses the eternal human need for emotion. It involves sentimental and reflexive manipulation of emotions, distorting perception, limiting rationality and understanding, and avoiding or suppressing unpleasant or disruptive aspects of reality. According to the theory of nostalgia and sentiment, kitsch is a form of longing, memory, and feeling. Kitsch brings to mind the past, childhood, family, and tradition. Kitsch evokes emotions in us, such as love, joy, sadness, or compassion. Kitsch is an expression of our sensitivity, warmth, and loyalty. Kitsch transforms what is unique and individual into a copy and pretence: non-existent feelings and values (Szostak and Sułkowski 2020b). The consequence may be neutralising and levelling values from the experienced relationship through its fictional caricaturisation. Kitsch is a sensitivity characterised by turning what is serious and valuable into what is funny, frivolous, and superficial. The illusory nature of such "immortality solutions" is inconsequential because it suffices for people interacting with such chatbots to believe it is true. Consent to kitsch expressing false emotions is expressed.

Experiencing kitsch and experiencing grief represent two complementary types of experiences: allowing for immediate emotional gratification (kitsch) and requiring deep reflection and psychological work (grief). We argue that preferences for one or the other are dynamically linked to conflicting needs, constituting the fundamental dilemmas of human attachment behaviour: the need for security and closeness versus stimulation and autonomy. When feeling vulnerable and dependent, a longing for safety and closeness (nostalgia) draws us not only to familiar individuals but also to conventional stimuli laden with positive emotions (kitsch). The preference for kitsch may result from a tendency to avoid complexity and difficulty associated with engaging in deeper reflection and emotional analysis. Individuals preferring kitsch may feel discomfort with complex, ambiguous emotions and seek simple, unambiguous experiences. Thanabots are dominated by the emotional needs of the recipient, confirming their habits. The production of kitsch is an attempt to create a safe, fun, and comfortable environment for humans at all costs.

What exactly is immortalised in the form of a thanabot? What part of the human essence can be separated from the body and may survive an individual's biological death? It seems to involve commemorating the social expression of the deceased. Kitschiness, as an aesthetic defence against reality, "normalises" painful life episodes. It is a societal acquiescence to the pleasure derived from silent agreement and participation in the soothing spectacle of simulated happiness, a paradise for the undemanding. The relationship between kitsch and the world of falsehood is essential. The world of kitsch is a world of appearances and eternal childhood. In such a world, death does not truly occur. The loved one is transformed, endowed with false immortality, only pretending to die, and we only pretend to mourn them. Kitsch seeks to escape from harsh reality into a pleasant, sweet world that can exist only in dreams. Moreover, thanabots kitsch raises questions about the sustainability of design trends and the inherent tension between innovation and sentimentality. It prompts us to reflect on the role of nostalgia in shaping our relationship with technology and challenges the notion that progress must always be synonymous with sleek, futuristic aesthetics.

The anthropological approach to kitsch may focus on its social and symbolic function. Kitsch objects and experiences may play a role in creating and maintaining group identity and communicating specific social values. Society can express common needs and desires by accepting kitsch while simultaneously creating certain cultural boundaries and norms. Modes of immortality are shaped by social conditions from which they emerge. What conditions make certain modes of immortality credible, desirable – or incredible and undesirable? Ancestors' creation is often a key means of reproducing social and political order and confirming group membership, an essential way of generating and securing relationships that secure identity over time. In the last decade, companies such as Eterni.me, with the slogan "Simply Become Immortal," have emerged on the market, offering technological, posthumous presence that guarantees that their status will change from biological to virtual at the client's death. Contemporary popular culture increasingly utilises technology to evoke entertainment industry icons from beyond the grave. Digital representations of Bruce Lee endorse "Johnny Walker" whiskey, while Michael Jackson, on the posthumously released album "Xscape," sings with Justin Timberlake in the track "Love Never Felt So Good." Technological posthumous presence is a vision of a reality unknown to us, where hitherto unknown behaviour patterns will emerge. Eterni.me, Ether9, or LifeNaut, involved in collecting mental data, introduce a new category of posthumous memory extension about the deceased, creating the illusion of their uninterrupted presence. The consequence of "cybernetic immortality" would be a digital *homo permanens* free from the constraints of time (Pawlak 2018). Such a radical change would necessitate the redefinition of many aspects of human existence, including the creation of new motivations leading to the only known form of human immortality to date – symbolic immortality: the desire for survival in artistic works, scientific discoveries, or great ideas "living on" after the death of their creator. Projects of digital immortality represent a space for a great technological and cultural experiment in which science operates on the norms sustaining social agreements, encouraging the crossing of boundaries, radical practices, shifts in mentality, and interpersonal relations.

Digital replication based on leftover images and digital footprint (data) is not culturally regulated – it seems to be a user's private matter and thus closes criticism and discussion. In the context of technological development, such as thanabots or avatars of the deceased, there is a need to understand how digital interactions affect human emotional and social experiences. Research on the impact of such technologies on grieving processes, memory, and identity can provide valuable insights into healthy social functioning in the digital age. The conclusions drawn from these fields can enrich our understanding of kitsch as a cultural phenomenon and its impact on human emotional and social experiences in the context of contemporary technologies.

Conclusions and perspectives

In the contemporary landscape, the prominence of artificial intelligence as the technological guru of the enterprise is increasingly evident, as it offers pre-packaged solutions and expedient resolutions to intricate challenges, pledging adherents a shortcut to achievement and contentment. Nonetheless, this reliance on gurus and their prescribed doctrines may also perpetuate conformity and stifle innovation, discouraging individuals from questioning prevailing norms or exploring alternative viewpoints. This trend towards gurus assuming influential roles in management mirrors broader societal patterns, wherein charisma and personal branding often wield more significant influence than meticulous analysis and critical inquiry. Gurus exert considerable influence over their followers, moulding their beliefs, values, and conduct to align with the guru's interests and objectives. Furthermore, the ascendance of AI as a technological guru underscores a more profound societal shift towards reliance on automated solutions and algorithmic decision-making. In this context, AI systems are positioned as authoritative sources of knowledge and expertise, capable of providing guidance and direction across a range of domains, from business management to personal development. However, the uncritical adoption of AI-driven solutions can also exacerbate existing inequalities and perpetuate biases inherent in the data on which these systems are trained. AI gurus may inadvertently reinforce existing power structures and marginalise certain voices and perspectives by privileging efficiency and scalability over nuance and context. Moreover, the proliferation of AI gurus raises questions about accountability and transparency, as the inner workings of these systems are often opaque and inaccessible to the individuals they purportedly serve. Without meaningful oversight and regulation, there is a risk that AI gurus may prioritise their interests or those of their creators rather than the well-being and autonomy of their followers. As such, we must approach the rise of AI gurus with a critical eye, interrogating the assumptions and biases embedded within these systems and advocating for greater transparency, accountability, and inclusivity in their development and deployment. Only through scrutiny and ethical engagement can we ensure that AI technologies serve the interests of humanity as a whole rather than reinforcing existing power differentials and perpetuating harmful social dynamics.

Moreover, technological kitsch may hamper innovation and creativity within the organisation, focusing on spectacle at the expense of quality and value-added for customers. The proliferation of technological kitsch poses significant challenges for business management, particularly in maintaining customer relationships and brand reputation. Companies must distinguish themselves through authenticity and meaningful engagement in today's hyper-connected world, where consumers are inundated with information and choices – failure to do so risks alienating customers and diminishing the brand's long-term viability. Furthermore, the emphasis on technological novelty and superficial aesthetics can detract from genuine innovation and problem-solving within the organisation. Instead of focusing on substantive improvements to products and services, companies may prioritise flashy features and gimmicks that offer little real value to customers. This short-term approach to product development undermines the company's competitive advantage and erodes trust in its ability to deliver meaningful solutions.

As a result of the proliferation of artificial intelligence in society, contemporary individuals find themselves immersed in kitsch, experiencing it constantly, which influences their choices and thinking about themselves and the future. Technological kitsch becomes a substitute experience and false sensitivity, subtly dictating how to think and feel. In management, it is crucial to make informed decisions regarding the use of technology and its presentation. Organisations should strive to maintain authenticity and alignment with organisational values, avoiding excessive extravagance and superficiality. It is also essential to develop skills for assessing the risks associated with technological kitsch and effectively managing the company's image in the face of this threat. The consequences of experiencing technological kitsch are multidimensional and encompass the aesthetic, cultural, economic, and social spheres. In the economic context, technological kitsch can lead to excessive consumption and the promotion of products and services of low quality or impractical but characterised by a high level of aesthetics. This, in turn, may generate artificial demand and result in excessive exploitation of natural resources. In societies experiencing technological kitsch, there are also numerous social consequences. Excessive focus on appearances and spectacle can lead to social alienation and a lack of genuine interpersonal relationships. Moreover, promoting superficial values can lead to an increase in egoism and materialism in society. It is important to note these effects in the context of further research and actions aimed at limiting the negative consequences of this phenomenon and promoting authenticity and valuable content in the world of technology. Technological development, particularly the transfer of artificial intelligence into society, exacerbates further occurrences of technological kitsch.

Modern individuals find themselves in a situation where they experience kitsch incessantly, influencing their choices and self-perception. Technological kitsch becomes a surrogate experience and false sensitivity, subtly dictating one's thoughts and emotions. Consequently, technological kitsch has multifaceted effects on the aesthetic, cultural, economic, and social spheres, necessitating continued research and actions aimed at its mitigation and the promotion of authenticity and meaningful content in the context of contemporary technologies. Within the economic realm, the prevalence of technological kitsch can lead to detrimental effects such as overconsumption and the promotion of products and services that prioritise aesthetics over functionality. This artificial demand can result in the exploitation of natural resources and the perpetuation of unsustainable consumption patterns. Moreover, there are numerous social repercussions in societies where technological kitsch is pervasive. The prioritisation of superficial values and appearances can contribute to social alienation and a decline in genuine human connections. Additionally, glorifying materialism and instant gratification may lead to societal values prioritising individualism over communal well-being.

In order to mitigate the impact of technological kitsch on business management, organisations must prioritise authenticity, transparency, and customer-centricity. This requires a shift from superficial marketing tactics towards genuine customer engagement and a commitment to delivering products and services that meet their needs and expectations. By fostering a culture of innovation and creativity, companies can ensure that their offerings remain relevant and valuable in an increasingly crowded marketplace. In conclusion, the rise of technological kitsch presents significant challenges for enterprise management, including the potential loss of customer trust, a decline in brand loyalty, and a diminished focus on innovation and creativity. Organisations can navigate these challenges by prioritising authenticity and meaningful engagement and positioning themselves for long-term success in the digital age.

In conclusion, technological kitsch poses significant challenges for contemporary society, impacting aesthetics, culture, economics, and social relations. By recognising the complex nature of this phenomenon and undertaking targeted actions to address its root causes, we can work towards creating a more authentic and meaningful technological landscape that fosters human flourishing and societal well-being. From a political standpoint, the instrumentalisation of kitsch in virtual influencer interactions underscores broader trends in contemporary politics, wherein emotional appeals and sentimentality are deployed as tools for persuasion and manipulation. Political actors leverage kitschy narratives and emotional messaging to cultivate support among constituents, exploiting their emotional vulnerabilities to advance partisan agendas and consolidate power. In doing so, they perpetuate a culture of emotional manipulation and superficiality, eroding trust in democratic institutions and undermining the integrity of public discourse.

In light of these challenges, it is imperative to conduct further research to deepen our understanding of technological kitsch and its impacts on various aspects of society. Thus, while wearables offer undeniable benefits in terms of convenience and functionality, their widespread adoption also raises important questions about the nature of power, authority, and control in contemporary society. As scholars, it is imperative that we critically examine these issues and consider the implications of wearable technology on individual autonomy, social cohesion, and the distribution of power within organisations and society at large. Moreover, concerted efforts are needed to develop strategies and interventions to mitigate the negative consequences of technological kitsch and promote authenticity and genuine human connection in the digital age. In light of these observations, we, as scholars and practitioners, must adopt a critical stance towards the proliferation of kitsch in management and corporate interactions. By interrogating this phenomenon's societal, economic, and political implications, we can better understand its underlying dynamics and advocate for ethical frameworks prioritising authenticity, integrity, and genuine human connection. We hope to cultivate a more empathetic, meaningful, and substantive discourse in the age of artificial intelligence only through concerted efforts to challenge and transcend the allure of kitsch.

References

Alvesson, M., & Gabriel, Y. (2015). Grandiosity in contemporary management and education, *Management Learning* [Online]. Retrieved December, 30, 2019, http://mlq.sagepub.com/content/early/2015/12/09/1350507615618321.full.pdf+html

Anonym, L. (2010). *Cybernetics for the masses*. https://privacy-pc.com/articles/cybernetics-for-the-masses-by-lepht-anonym.html

Balistreri, M. (2022). *Sex Robots: Love in the Age of Machines*. Sex Robots, 1–158.

Baudrillard, J. (1981). *For a Critique of the Political Economy of the Sign*, tłum. Charles Levin. Telos.

Baudrillard, J. (1994). *Simulacra and Simulation*. University of Michigan Press. https://doi.org/10.3998/mpub.9904.

Choe, E. K., Lee, N. B., Lee, B., Pratt, W., & Kientz, J. A. (2014). Understanding quantified-selfers' practices in collecting and exploring personal data. In *Proceedings of the 32nd Annual ACM Conference on Human Factors in Computing Systems* (pp. 1143–1152). https://doi.org/10.1145/2556288.25573

Cohen, M. (2016). *The Biohacker's Handbook: Achieve Better Health Through Experimentation*. Singularity Publishing.

Colyer, C. J., Stein, R. E., & Corcoran, K. E. (2023). Symbolic separation: The Amish and 21st-century technologies. In *People, Technology, and Social Organization* (pp. 140–155). Routledge.

Delfanti, A. (2013). *Biohackers. The Politics of Open Science*. Palgrave Macmillan.

Deng, F., & Jiang, X. (2023). Effects of human versus virtual human influencers on the appearance anxiety of social media users. *Journal of Retailing and Consumer Services*, 71, 103233. https://doi.org/10.1016/j.jretconser.2022.103233.

Eriksen, T. H. (2001). Ethnic identity, national identity, and intergroup conflict: The significance of personal experiences. In Ashmore, R. D., Jussim, L., & Wilder, D. (eds.), *Social Identity, Intergroup Conflict, and Conflict Reduction* (pp. 42–68). Oxford University Press.

Freidin, G. (2000). Transfiguration of kitsch: Timur Kibirov's sentiments. In Balina, M., Condee, N., & Dobrenko, E. (eds.), *Endquote: Sots-Art Literature and Soviet Grand Style*. Northwestern University Press.

Greenberg, C. (1985). Avant-garde and kitsch. In Frascina, F. (ed.), *Pollock and After: The Critical Debate*. Harper and Row.

Gregotti, V. (1969). Kitsch and architecture. In Dorfles, G. (ed.), *Kitsch: The World of Bad Taste*. Universe Books.
Grewe-Salfeld, M. (2022). *Biohacking, Bodies and Do-It-Yourself. The Cultural Politics of Hacking Life Itself.* Majuskel Medienproduktion GmbH.
Huberman, J. (2020). *Transhumanism: From Ancestors to Avatars*. Cambridge University Press.
Humphries, C. (2018). Digital immortality: How your life's data means a version of you could live forever. *MIT Technology Review*, October 18.
Kruger, D. J., & Kruger, J. S. (2018). What do economically costly signals signal?: A life history framework for interpreting conspicuous consumption. *Evolutionary Psychological Science*, 4, 420–427.
Kulka, T. (1996). *Kitsch and Art*. Pennsylvania State University Press.
Lasén, A., & Gómez-Cruz, E. (2013). Mundane cyborgs: Theorizing bodies in contemporary media cultures. *Social Science Information*, 52(3), 473–494.
Lee, R. (2019). Biohactivism, cyborgasms and transhumanism. In Lee, N. (ed.), *The Transhumanism Handbook* (pp. 499–501). Springer Verlag.
Linstead, S. (2002). Organizational kitsch. *Organization*, 9(4), 657–682. https://doi.org/10.1177/135050840294008
Locay, L. (1989). From hunting and gathering to agriculture. *Economic Development and Cultural Change*, 37(4), 737–756.
Lupton, D. (2013). Quantifying the body: Monitoring and measuring health in the age of mHealth technologies. *Critical Public Health*, 23(4), 393–403.
Marwick, A. E., & Boyd, D. (2014). Networked privacy: How teenagers negotiate context in social media. *New Media & Society*, 16(7), 1051–1067.
McAfee, C. (2017). *Biohacking: Improve Health, Energy and Focus with DIY Genetic Testing, Nutrigenomics, Nootropics, and Lifestyle Hacks*. Independently Published.
Moles, A. (1971). *Kitsch: The World of Bad Taste*. Universe Books.
Mrad, M., Ramadan, Z., & Nasr, L. I. (2022). Computer-generated influencers: The rise of digital personalities. *Marketing Intelligence & Planning*, 40(5), 589–603. https://doi.org/10.1108/MIP-12-2021-0423.
Nyholm, S., & Frank, L. E. (2019). It loves me, it loves me not. *Techné: Research in Philosophy and Technology*, 23(3), 402–424. https://doi.org/10.5840/techne2019122110
O'cass, A., & McEwen, H. (2004). Exploring consumer status and conspicuous consumption. *Journal of Consumer Behaviour: An International Research Review*, 4(1), 25–39.
O'Connell, M. (2017). *To Be a Machine: Adventures among Cyborgs, Utopians, Hackers, and the Futurists Solving the Modest Problem of Death*. Granta.
Oe, H., & Yamaoka, Y. (2020). Chinese consumers' conspicuous perspectives: The context of smartphone purchase behavior. *Journal of Business Management and Economic Research*, 4(1), 1–20.
Pawlak, A. F. (2018). Cyberimmortalizm. Cyfrowy postczłowiek jako transhumanistyczny projekt XXI wieku. In Szymczyk, P., & Maciąg, K. (Red.), *Człowiek a technologia cyfrowa* (s. 7–27). Wydawnictwo Naukowe "Tygiel". ISBN 978-83-65932-16-7
Pawlak, A. F. (2022). *The Loneliness of Followers*. Artificial People in Synthetic Media, s.78. https://www.centroeinaudi.it/images/abook_file/lonely_europeans_WP_-_BMagni_29.pdf
Piirto, J. (2004). *Understanding Creativity*. Great Potential Press.
Ritzer, G. (1996). *The McDonaldization of Society: An Investigation into the Changing Character of Contemporary Social Life*. Pine Forge Press.
Rosen, D. S., & Cipov, A. (2017). Quantified self and mobile fitness apps: Reconfiguring health, social relations, and the self through data. *Mobile Media & Communication*, 5(1), 111–127.

Szostak, M. (2023). *Sztuka zarządzania. Zarządzanie sztuką*. Społeczna Akademia Nauk.
Szostak, M., & Sułkowski, Ł. (2020a). Manager as an artist: Creative endeavour in crossing the borders of art and organizational discourse. *Creativity Studies*, 13(2), 351–368. https://doi.org/10.384
Szostak, M., & Sułkowski, Ł. (2020b, April 1–2). Kitsch in management: Characteristic forms, carriers and propagators. In *Education Excellence and Innovation Management: A 2025 Vision to Sustain Economic Development During Global Challenges: Proceedings of the 35th International Business Information Management Association Conference (IBIMA)* (pp. 7584–7598). Sevilla: IBIMA. Available at: https://depot.ceon.pl/handle/123456789/19173.
Zahavi, A. (1997). *The Handicap Principle: A Missing Piece of Darwin's Puzzle*. Oxford University Press.

12 Kitsch in city space management

Beauty and functionality of public space

Wioletta Małota

Introduction

Cities redevelop public urban spaces for various reasons. It can be an improvement of transportation infrastructure (roads, public transport) or a (re)development of infrastructure, creating more inhabitants-friendly cities that offer walkable, car-free spaces or cycle paths. It can be a social reason to refurbish neglected neighbourhoods to prevent or erase civil disorder such as broken windows, graffiti, littering, vandalism, public drinking or crime. Criminologists James Q. Wilson and George Kelling developed The Broken Windows theory (1982), stating that signs of disorder will lead to more disorder, so a neglected urban environment promotes even more disorder and crime (Kelling & Coles, 1997). One of the methods to limit this phenomenon is creating urban spaces with greenery and sports amenities that support healthy behaviour and social cohesion. Finally, the cities redevelop the public urban spaces to meet societal expectations regarding living in modern, green, healthy, and convivial places. Nowadays, cities undergo many kinds of development or refurbishment; therefore, it is crucial to know how to manage their processes to avoid kitsch components in management successfully (Szostak, 2023).

The chapter analyses kitsch components in managing modern urban redevelopment projects of city public spaces and the challenges faced in the conception, preparation, implementation, and evaluation phases based on an urban space redevelopment project in Warsaw's district, Targówek.

The chapter's main research questions are: 1) Which factors in creating, planning, implementing, and evaluating a public space redevelopment project might decide that it would be perceived as a kitsch experience in project management? and 2) What can be kitsch in public space management – the artworks themselves, their creation process or narration?

To answer the questions more structured, I have formulated specific questions about the four stages of an urban project in a public space: its conception, preparation, implementation, and evaluation:

DOI: 10.4324/9781003504931-13

1. Conception
    a. Was the project designed according to the current trends and expectations (green, convivial, and resilient) about the functioning of a city?
    b. Did the project design meet the inhabitants' expectations? Which project design elements did it confirm?
    c. Did the project of redevelopment of public space respect the interests of stakeholders?
2. Preparation
    a. Was the public space project prepared with the state of the art, meaning consultation of stakeholders' needs and the final proposal?
    b. Were these consultations inclusive and easily accessible?
3. Implementation
    a. What does the implementation process of the final project look like?
    b. Which factors have been considered when choosing the contractor?
4. Evaluation
    a. Did the project establish the success factors in the preparation stage?
    b. Did the project evaluate the stakeholders' opinions after its completion?

The chapter's structure is the following. First, I present trends, concepts of cities (re)development and expectations from their stakeholders. Next, I present a model of an urban redevelopment project with four phases: conception, preparation, implementation, and evaluation, identifying possible kitsch components in managing a project. A case study of the redevelopment project of public space in a local community in Warsaw (Targowek district), Poland, will be evaluated to determine whether kitsch experience occurred, at which phase and which factors might have contributed to it.

Literature review: current trends in city development

The development of modern cities is influenced by political and societal factors, ideas, and concepts of how modern cities should look and function. Trends like smart cities, resilient and climate-responsive cities, healthy, convivial cities, sustainably developed, mixed-use development, inclusive cities, collaborative governance, and public space activation shape the city's image. As there are many city development concepts, I have grouped them based on the initial perspectives (or interests) where they are created, like environment, urban development, and society; then, different concepts were aligned to them and finally, the outcome or expectations they should deliver. The multilayer approach to city development should finally lead to innovative, healthy cities and the well-being of their

Table 12.1 Summary of the concepts of city development

Perspective/interest	*Concept*	*Goal/outcome/expectations of citizens/stakeholders*
Environment	• Green city • Sustainable city • Resilient and climate-responsive city	• Clean air and greenery, offering recreation possibilities to support healthy living. • Lower energy consumption and responsible use of resources to lower carbon footprint. • Protection against climate change and natural disasters
Urban infrastructure, transport, and construction industry	• Smart city • Sustainable city	• Management of a city, enabling convenient commuting and ensuring the city's security • Supporting a healthy environment through low carbon emission transport and construction
Society	• Mixed-use development • 15-minute city • Convivial city • Human-centred city	• Raising the quality of life of the city's residents • Support of societal cohesion • Strengthening the importance of communities as city-makers

Sources: author's elaboration based on Breuste (2023), Jenks and Jones (2010), Resilient Cities, OECD, Winkowska, Szpilko and Pejić (2019), Jenks and Jones (2010), Evans (2014), Iribarren (2019), The Urban Agenda for EU.

citizens. The model presents that regardless of which concept of city development will be implemented by city authorities, it should consider the expectations of different stakeholders, such as an innovative and healthy city and the well-being of the inhabitants and visitors.

A given concept of city development may include the elements of other concepts and overlap with them as they have been developed during the last few decades, as consequences of technological and societal developments, climate change, and increased awareness of the need to change human living conditions.

Green city

The concept of a green city revolves around creating urban environments that provide greenery, highlighting its bio-diversity to ensure environmental conservation that supports its residents' high quality of life. The concept of urban green infrastructure includes random (wild) spaces and those introduced by human decisions and activity, for example, trees or plantations (Breuste, 2023). In recent years, the concept of a green city has been extended by constructing green buildings with trees on balconies, green walls, and green roofs with living organisms absorbing air pollution. The Italian architect Stefano Boeri designed the first two buildings in Milano called Bosco Vertical (Stefano Boeriarchitetti.net) with balconies planted with trees. However, such constructions are not cheap solutions, but they are becoming increasingly popular nowadays, even offering them to social residents such as Trudo Vertical Forest in Eindhoven (https://archdaily.com).

The concept of a green city is quite well grounded in the municipal policies, but what is essential is that they undergo qualitative changes nowadays; it is not enough to plant the trees, but their species are essential, the role they play (providing shading and air circulation) and the value they have in terms of ecosystem (Dover, 2015). There is a tendency to use every possible surface to make the city greener; a good example is greening the surface between tram tracks with sedum, which is more accessible, compared with traditional grass, easier to maintain, and more ecologically effective regarding CO_2 absorption.

Another role of a green city is to organise public transportation, cycling, and walking paths to reduce reliance on private cars, helping decrease traffic congestion, air pollution, and greenhouse gas emissions. Electric vehicles and the development of efficient transportation systems are promoted to ensure sustainable mobility (this is one of the goals of a smart city as well). In recent years, the narration of a green city has shifted from simple prevention of air pollution or lowering poor air quality that influences health conditions (Owen, Lennon & Scott, 2017, p. 2) to a more holistic approach prioritising environmental responsibility and sustainability, focusing on resilient and climate-responsive cities.

When the green city concept refers to a green urban landscape, the sustainable city concept adopts sustainable construction practices such as low-pollution energy-saving technologies and sustainable transportation to minimise carbon footprint. Sustainable architecture focuses primarily on energy efficiency, which involves reducing energy consumption. This can be achieved using efficient lighting, heating, and cooling systems and incorporating passive design strategies to optimise natural light and ventilation. Sustainable buildings often incorporate renewable energy sources such as solar panels, wind turbines, or geothermal systems to generate electricity or heat water. Water efficiency strategies aimed to reduce water consumption include using low-flow fixtures and grey water systems, which means the reuse of wastewater from sources such as sinks, showers, baths, and washing machines. Green roofs and green walls with vegetation on their surfaces help with insulation and reduce the heat island effect, improving air quality and providing the inhabitants with additional direct contact with nature (Jenks & Jones, 2010). Sustainable architecture uses environmentally friendly materials such as recycled steel, reclaimed wood, bamboo, and other sustainable products to reduce the carbon footprint and promote responsible use of resources.

Resilient and climate-responsive city

One of the newest concepts developed to meet the challenges of climate change is the concept of a resilient and climate-responsive city. A resilient city can be called one that is well prepared to withstand and adapt to the challenges posed by climate change, natural disasters, and other environmental stressors (Resilient Cities, OECD).[1] Resilience involves the ability to bounce back from disruptions and proactively urban planning and implementing strategies that reduce a city's vulnerability and enhance its sustainability. It includes urban planning and designing climate considerations while creating sustainable and adaptable urban spaces, resilient infrastructures, early warning systems, water management, and green and bio-diverse areas. Environmental resilience is one of the four elements that ensure a resilient city in the OECD model of "4 areas that drive resilience". The other are economy, society, and governance. In the case of the economy, a city should have diversified industries, create conditions for innovation and ensure access to employment, jobs, services, and skills training. Regarding societal areas, a city is resilient when inclusive and cohesive; its inhabitants build active networks, live in safe neighbourhoods, and are healthy. In the case of governance, a city can be regarded as resilient when its authorities are open and transparent, a city has a clear strategy, and the public sector has the right skills to manage it (Resilient Cities, OECD).

Smart city

The next concept of city development, a smart city, has the same goal (to ensure healthy cities and well-being for their inhabitants) as green and sustainable cities, but it has different strategies to achieve this. Smart cities can be called those using modern technology to manage them (Winkowska, Szpilko & Pejić, 2019). Under this umbrella notion, there are many different management practices, like intelligent transportation systems adjusting street lighting to the intensity of traffic (IoT), public services (smart waste management or smart parking systems), and smart buildings. In the latter case, new building construction and maintenance technologies use sustainable energy management, for example, renewable energy sources like solar panels. This definition is focused on technological aspects; however, there are a few definitions.

The concept of a smart city evolved from smart city 1.0 and smart city 2.0, where the focus was on digitalising city management to provide intelligent traffic management systems, city applications for reporting problems or bicycle servicing connected with mobile applications. In the case of smart city 3.0, its focus is on acquiring and implementing the knowledge of city residents while providing tools to enable them to participate in participatory budgets or citizens' panels or providing platforms with open databases. This is a step towards democratising decision-making in the city (Sim, 2019) and meets the requirement of a human-centric city. To sum up, smart cities aim to improve the overall quality of life of the residents' and visitors' health by efficiently managing resources, reducing negative environmental impact and fostering innovation and inclusivity through technology-driven solutions.

Convivial city

City development concepts have been divided according to the type of entity whose interests it pursues into the environment, urban infrastructure, and society. In the latter case, to ensure a cohesive urban community, the city's authorities implement the concepts of a mixed-use development, a 15-minute city, a convivial city, or a human-centred city. The convivial city (Iribarren, 2019) or its part can be regarded when it meets the conditions like "Physical spaces that are flexible, changing and adaptable; processes and outcomes based in equity, integrity, and democracy; and urban authorities use solutions that correspond to people's need and desires" (Rodriguez & Simon, 2015, p. 311). Inclusivity, flexibility, and usefulness are three fundamental qualities of a convivial city. In urban infrastructure, the parks, gardens, and squares are convivial places where people can relax and enjoy different kinds of festive, musical, and sports events.

An excellent example of a convivial area is Nice in France, with the Promenade du Paillon, the Place Masséna and the Garden Albert 1st in the city's heart. The first one, called the Lungs of the city, for its 12 ha park with 7,000 biodiverse species, offers playful structures for children of different ages, several banks for relaxation and a water mirror with 128 water diffusers to ensure a cooling effect on hot days, is a meeting place of all generations. The Place Massena is a car-free, walkable zone that, during different festivals (like the famous Nice carnival), is converted into the scene for festive parades and, on standard days, is a meeting point for both residents and tourists. The piano, standing in the open air and accessible for everyone to play, invites them to have fun together. A cheerful crowd applauding surrounding a person playing the piano is an example of a spontaneous convivial experience. The Garden Albert 1er is a favourite place for picnics on the lawns and is where open-air cultural events like the Nice Jazz Festival, the Book Festival, and the Côte d'Azur Garden Festival are organised, making a friendly and convivial city.

Mixed-use development concept

Mixed-use development is the concept launched in 1990 by the Commission of the European Communities in the Green Paper on the Urban Environment

(Commission of the European Communities, 1990, p. 43), which recommended mixing commercial, residential, and public amenities in an urban space to raise the quality of life of cities' inhabitants. This can be achieved as the domicile, workplace, and public amenities like schools and healthcare are closer, so the residents do not have to commute much. This city development concept has gained recognition, becoming the planning norm rather than the exception in many places (Evans, 2014). The concept of a 15-minute city (Moreno, 2024) is based on the same principles, assuming that urban spaces should incorporate residential housing, business, and public services in city fabrics into creative, lively, and functional spaces. Thus, the concepts of city development, grouped in Table 12.1 under "social perspectives", contain many common elements from other concepts; however, they also have some specific features that emphasise the uniqueness of a given concept.

Human-centred city

The concept of a human-centred city presented in the guidelines of the European Commission for the new urban agenda launched in 2016 in Pact Amsterdam[2] identifies the perspective of the human-cantered city underlying the role of the communities and institutions as "city makers, co-creators of the evolving urban development and actors od innovations". This concept includes ideas from other city development concepts (how to develop it and what to develop); however, it highlights the aspects that serve a city and who should co-decide on a city development. By integrating different principles and aspects of the discussed concepts, a city can create its adaptive model to plan and develop a green, convivial, innovative, and healthy city.

The 20th century was a period of intensive industrialisation of the cities; however, in the last few decades, when people started experiencing its negative impact on their quality of life and the planet, new urban development trends gained importance and popularity. More and more research has confirmed that polluted cities influence residents' health negatively, and green spaces enhance people's well-being. Healthy environments such as well-designed and walkable cities with access to nature and distribution of urban green space positively influence cities' residents (Lake & Townshend, 2006).

Whatever concepts city authorities adopt, they should consider the holistic goal of creating a healthy city that provides well-being to its residents. It may be achieved when implementing different concepts depending on the city's urban structure and inhabitants' needs and expectations. As presented in Table 12.1, in the column "Goal/outcome/expectations of citizens/stakeholders", every city development concept differs in the goals and outcomes. To sum them up, the concepts of green city, sustainable city, and resilient and climate-responsive city are the choices when addressing the environment. When developing urban infrastructure, transport, and construction industry, technologies and management methods of smart city and sustainable city concepts are implemented. When the cities' authorities aim to develop a more cohesive community, they should consider empowering the inhabitants to co-create their place. To make a city more vivid and user-friendly, concepts like mixed-use development, 15-minute city, convivial city, and human-centred city should be implemented. In real life, cities are simultaneously realising different city development concepts to meet the universal goal of a healthy city, ensuring their inhabitants' quality of life.

Case study: public space redevelopment project in the Targowek district of Warsaw

When designing a city refurbishment, the city's authorities must consider not only the modern concepts of city development and the stakeholders' expectations but also the existing character of a city and its fabrics. Modern urban design does not create new places from scratch but shapes existing ones (Carmona, 2021). One of the challenges a city may face is when its fabric is dense and intensive architectural or urban changes are not welcomed for historic, local, or other reasons. In this case, small architecture is handy, as it is much easier to post a sculpture or small park (like a pocket park), even in a city centre with dense tissue. Small architecture refers to designing and constructing smaller-scale structures within an urban space. It can include small apartment buildings, compact office spaces, kiosks, and small parks, with their infrastructure increasing urban functionality.

The case of Targowek (Warsaw, Poland), a public space redevelopment project, is such a case. From one side, the project encounters limited space to be redesigned; from another, the residents' expectations of the refurbishment are very ambiguous. I have chosen that case for my analysis to track its management process, considering it interesting and valuable as a master example for many reasons. The first reason is that it is one of the newest urban space redevelopment projects realised in Warsaw, so learning the new practices will be valuable. The second reason is that the project is carried out in a district traditionally considered a residential area of the working class; however, nowadays in Warsaw, there are no zooning areas in the traditional sense, so learning the residents' expectations upon the space they live in, will give insightful experience. The third reason is that the project is part of the international programme "Urban 95 Academy", so learning if and how the local authorities have leveraged international practices into urban design in Warsaw will shed light on the extent to which international concepts are adopted in local projects.

The Targowek case will be evaluated in the multi-concept model of city development framework through the model of an Urban Project in Public Space (presented below) and through the theory of kitsch experience (Szostak & Sulkowski, 2020). The latter theory (presented in the introductory chapter) is universal as it can be applied to assess every beyond-aesthetic situation and phenomenon.

I will analyse individual phases of the redevelopment project, pinpointing possible kitsch and aesthetic experience components in the project management.

Frameworks for the project evaluation

The frameworks for the evaluation are the theories of aesthetic and kitsch experiences and modern concepts of city development. The holistic goal of the case study's analysis is to formulate conclusions and recommendations that may be helpful for other urban planners and city authorities in their work.

Model of an urban project in public space

There are many project management models; however, each has four main phases: conception, preparation, implementation, and evaluation. They differ by the kind of financial source (private or public) and consequently by the kinds of stakeholders and their interests. In the case of public projects, the public resources are at stake, and the main stakeholders are citizens, the project recipients. To analyse

Table 12.2 Model of urban project management of public space

Phase	*Main activities and their requirements*
Conception	• Identifying the goal of a project and benefits for its recipients • Aligning the design of a project with the trends and concept of city (re) development • Designing the project and outcomes for the stakeholders
Preparation	• Site inspection • Social consultation of the needs and expectations of the project • Preparation of the first draft of the redevelopment based on the residents' needs and expectations • Conducting the social consultations of the first draft respecting the cognitive capabilities of different groups • Preparation of final proposal after social consultation • Social consultation of the final proposal of the project
Implementation	• Working out of the final version of the project • Public bid with the formal criteria for contractors • Implementation of the project
Evaluation	• Evaluation of the implemented project by criteria important for stakeholders that may include many factors as: accessibility, safety, aesthetics, functionality, sustainability, reduction of crime rate or undesired behaviour, improved air quality, enhanced community cohesion • Review of established financial metrics • Gathering community input on the satisfaction level in the form of public meetings, online surveys, focus groups • Gathering lessons learned

Source: own elaboration

the project at Targowek, I have formulated a model of urban project management in public space with phases of its realisation and activities for each phase. The model will be applied to analyse possible aesthetic or kitsch components in managing the Targowek project.

In the realisation of any project, mismanagement – representing components of the kitsch experience theory – may occur at any phase. In the project conception phase, a lack of consideration of modern city development concepts, such as a green and convivial city with elements that make it more resilient and do not include the residents' needs, may be regarded as kitsch management exemplification. The main activities in the project preparation phase are social consultations; conducting them should be inclusive, considering different kinds of beneficiaries to ensure representativeness. Moreover, the consultations should be executed in an engaging way that is adjusted to the residents' age and cognitive perception (children or older adults), supporting their understanding and involvement in consultations. The phase should incorporate the human-centred approach.

In the implementation phase, it is crucial to formulate the criteria for the project's final design, which should include modern concepts of city development and be functional and user-friendly. In the case of urban public space, it is important the quality of greenery (being resilient to low temperatures or drought, giving the shadow, supporting better air quality and being easy to maintain), and in the case of devices and amenities, they should be easy to use, universal, and functional.

In evaluation, the last phase of the project realisation, it is essential for the city authorities to evaluate if the project was carried out due to its assumption and agreed KPI (this is an internal, administrative perspective) and how the perception of the beneficiaries of the project's realisation.

Description of the project

The public space redevelopment project was realised by the community Targowek in Warsaw, the capital of Poland, to modernise the small urban public space between buildings 11 and 13 at Suwalska Street, constituting essentially part of a local parking lot with nearby Jordan Garden. The housing built in the 1980s is no longer modern inside and outside, and the public recreation area is neglected, not meeting the inhabitants' expectations of being a convivial place. In nearby locations, there are no green spaces with sports amenities. The residential area is close to the industrial area called Industrial Targowek; however, the industrial plants are no longer active, and the district has changed its industrial character. As mentioned, Warsaw has no typical zones of poor or rich residents as industrial places were recultivated into elegant post-industrial housing districts. What makes the place attractive is the proximity of the new metro line (the city has two lines), as the capital has quite an extended surface, and convenient transportation is an essential factor for the quality of life of the city's inhabitants. The construction of a metro line and a station next to Suwalska Street in late 2023 made the place more attractive and increased the prices of flats there.

The redevelopment of the Suwalska Street area is a part of the redevelopment of the area next to the metro station. The project's goal was "building bonds between children and caregivers when offering them playground, psychophysical and social development of children through playing outdoors, comfortable and at the same time inspiring spaces for fun".[3] The project was carried out in the conception and preparation phases on the date of publishing the book, but the implementation phase has been foreseen for the second and third quarters of 2024 (Raport, 2023).

In the first phase, the municipal leaders responsible[4] for the project participated in the international programme "Urban 95 Academy". This executive education programme worldwide delivers knowledge on how to make cities more children-friendly. It is a fully funded programme, meaning that the course is free to participants. The seven-week online course with weekly live Zoom seminars hosted by the London School of Economics and Political Sciences (LSE) academic staff and guest lecturers aimed to help city planners, designers, and other urban professionals working for local government to understand how their work impacts early childhood. The "Urban 95 Academy" participants have had to submit an action strategy for a development plan addressing local challenges based on the assignment's requirements. Then, the principles and action plan of the project were developed.

In the second phase (preparation), the consultants conducted a site analysis, and the subsequent social consultations took place in two steps. During the first one, called "Social diagnosis", the inhabitants were asked how they perceive the place where they spend their free time. Two independent groups of inhabitants were invited to make consultations more inclusive and objective and to collect more information. Mobile consultation booths were organised to reach more respondents, including children, youth, caregivers, and seniors. The consultants asked the inhabitants about their expectations of which specific spots should be developed. This was the first step in gathering their ideas.

In the second step, the consultants organised four meetings. During the first meeting, in the form of a picnic, people could share their wishes and ideas in an easy atmosphere that unlash creative thinking. The consultants used the map of the area with the spotted points the inhabitants have previously pointed out (in the "Social diagnosis") as essential for them to be redeveloped. At the second meeting, the inhabitants could visualise some of their ideas using the Adobe application to design the space, allowing them to plan and observe the designed space in real time in 3D.

Children and youth drew their ideas on paper at the third and fourth meetings in the form of design workshops. These activities were organised to boost the inhabitants' curiosity and engagement. They came for the consultation with the photos of other places in Warsaw they liked, and they wanted the refurbished location to look like that. Residents also could post the proposal and remarks on the project's webpage. The consultation took place from Mai to the end of June 2023 before the summer school holiday started in July.

The inhabitants proved a high level of maturity regarding expressing their expectations and ideas. They were very conscious about their needs. They proposed more shadow in open space delivered by the trees with extended branches and having more giant leaves, water in the form of small ponds with flora and fauna, fountains, a water wall during heat time, and drinking water points for people and animals and fun water park for children. They wanted benches in different (modern) forms formulated in circles to enable having a meeting of friends. The youth wished for more sports places like football fields.

The adults wanted a typical garden to plant herbs and other vegetables. Parents noticed that the project should include the needs of children with different spectrums, and they wanted the sensory playgrounds they had seen in other Warsaw districts to be installed. The owners of the dogs asked for a fenced garden for their pupils. The seniors wanted more special objects, like sculptures, that could serve as orientation points. Many inhabitants asked for an open-air exhibition and a community fridge where people could leave food for those in need.

A final draft of the refurbishment project was worked out based on the outcome of the consultations. A map of ten places to be changed, highlighted by the children, caregivers, and seniors, was prepared (July to September 2023). It was consulted in September 2023, and the final redevelopment plan was prepared. Then, the project's final phase is planned to be implemented in the fourth quarter of 2024.[5]

Evaluation of the project

To answer the research questions and determine whether kitsch experience components have occurred at any project phase, I first evaluate whether it included essential elements of the modern city development concepts. Then, I analyse whether the activities in the four phases of the project have met the recommendations of the model of an Urban Project in Public Space, and finally, the Targowek project will be assessed through the theory of kitsch experience to conclude possible kitsch components in its management.

Regarding requirements of the first phase (conception) in the model of an Urban Project in Public Space, the goal of the project was clearly stated (*building bonds between children and caregivers when offering them playground, psychophysical and social development of children through playing outdoors, and comfortable and at the same time inspiring spaces for fun*). It refers to the aspect of the convivial city (bonding of different groups of inhabitants) and is human-centred (e.g. the parking lots will be converted into green areas for social gatherings).

When assessing the Targowek project through the concepts of an inclusive city, it seems the requirements were met regarding its process and outcomes. Starting from the goal ("*building bonds between children and caregivers*"), it includes the needs of children of different ages and stages of development. Regarding caregivers, the project is intended for young mothers and seniors, as grandparents often care for their grandchildren in Poland. Designed playgrounds and different sports amenities allow residents of different ages to spend free time together, which is the precondition for a convivial city. In that sense, the project also meets the requirements of public space activation.

In the second phase (preparation), the consultations with different kinds of inhabitants (children, youth, children caregivers, and seniors) have met the requirements of an inclusive and human-centred city. The postulates of inhabitants were aligned with the concept of a green city (pond with flora and fauna, typical city herbs garden), a resilient city (trees giving shadow, water walls during heat, drinking water points for people and animals), convivial city (benches in agora shape, open-air exhibition, and sports infrastructure) and inclusive city (playground for the children also for those with spectrum, places for caregivers and seniors). It may be concluded that a design of this phase unlashed the maturity and solidarity of Targowek inhabitants and presented a wise and holistic approach to their commonplace to be refurbished.

Regarding the requirement to respect the cognitive capabilities of different groups (children, youth, seniors), the consultations were conducted at the place (not only on the internet, where only digital-minded inhabitants could submit their proposal), adjusting their form to different age groups. They were conducted in an attractive manner (mobile consultation booths), and the workshops with 3D models facilitated the spatial imagination of the refurbished place and contributed to the consultees' making more informed decisions.

The city authorities gathered ideas and best practices for designing such a project during the international training at LBC, providing good conditions for conception due to the newest trends and concepts in urban place development. The consultations with inhabitants have been executed by an external organisation that specialises in conducting social consultations, meeting all requirements regarding their inclusivity, and gathering many ideas. While evaluating these two phases of the project, I did not spot any kitsch experience in its management. On the contrary, preparing its conception with the support of international experts in the field allowed the incorporation of the newest concepts into the project, and multifaceted social consultations using modern methods and tools ensured good conditions for open and inclusive consultations.

As the third phase (implementation) will be realised in the fourth quarter of 2024 and the fourth (evaluation) phase is planned for 2025, thus they can only be the subject of the ex-ante theoretical analysis about the occurrence of the aesthetic or kitsch experiences. From the project owner, the Targowek district, the possible kitsch experiences may occur at the implementation phase when the bid criteria are unclear or set the way favouring a given contractor or the financial and other metrics will not be kept. In the evaluation phase, the inhabitants might experience the kitsch experience when the realised project differs significantly from the final one they have agreed on. However, even if all of the elements of the final project will be implemented to meet formal requirements, what counts, in reality, is the quality of realisation that can evoke the aesthetic experience. It happens when the real-life amenities are made from high-quality, user-friendly materials, greenery meets the inhabitants' expectations (e.g. shadow for the places where they spend time), and blue infrastructure meets aesthetic expectations and delivers functionality (e.g. relief during hot days). However, only practical observation of the implemented project and the research of inhabitants' opinions can verify whether the implemented project delivers an aesthetic or kitsch experience.

I have evaluated the Targowek project through the four components of the aesthetic and kitsch experience theory. The first element in the theory is that the creator/producer's approach or actions should focus on universal values, create reliability, and be open to criticism and discussion to offer an aesthetic experience. The opposite, a kitsch experience happens when a creator/producer focuses "on the mass recipient; its action is a duplication of the previous ones not being customised to a target group and when the producer's action is closed for critics and discussion" (Szostak & Sulkowski, 2020)

The Targowek project of refurbishing a public space for the local inhabitants serves the universal values of city development, such as citizen-friendliness, functionality, and environment/planet friendliness. Moreover, this is a characteristic of aesthetic experience.

Work/artefact, the second element of the theory, ensures an aesthetic experience when it "extends the recipients' existence, fills the future and when it is coherent", while the kitsch experience occurs when "work or artefacts confirms the recipients' habit, they address (only) present needs" (ditto); in short, when they are embedded only in the present, consolidating existing needs or habits but not modelling the new ones. It seems that the way the consultations were held went beyond average practice, regarding both their methodology and the methods. The methodology, a site inspection, two phases of the consultations with different groups and parallel online consultations, was more extended than usually practised in small public projects. Their methods, usage of applications that visualise the proposed ideas in real time, and designing the proposal during the workshops supported creative and future-oriented thinking, exemplifying aesthetic experience.

In the case of the recipients, the third element of the theory, it is assumed that they undergo the aesthetic experience when they "will consider the work from all sides/dimensions". When we consider the behaviour of the local citizens who, during the consultation, formulated their expectations for different groups and aspects (greenery, fun and recreation, education, social needs, and art), they perfectly match the definition of aesthetic experience. Their behaviour of sharing thoughts and feelings (e.g. "the needs of children with spectrum should also be considered") confirms the consultations were, for them, an aesthetic experience.

When we consider the project process as an experience for the local authorities, it was exclusive as it was based on the newest state-of-the-art urban development (taking part in an international project) and incorporated the newest concepts. Analysing the process of consultations with their methods of conducting and tools used (Artificial Reality, design workshop), it has supported "share of thought and awareness and will", a characteristic description of aesthetic experience.

The project's final phase was not carried out yet when the book was published; I may only point out possible components of kitsch experience components at that phase. What may happen is that a well-thought-out and innovative design of urban place development on paper, prepared with the highest quality and diligence, will turn out to be kitsch in reality. The reason may be limited finances or lack of contractor experience in realising modern projects. In this possible project outcome, the inhabitants may experience discrepancies between the ideas presented during the consultation and the reality. All these factors may evoke the kitsch experiences in this project realisation phase.

It may happen that some people will not like a particular type of greenery or some aspects of the small architecture, a design of a bank, a sculpture or a water installation, as taste is an individual and subjective issue that confirms the saying "A taste is an issue not to be discussed". However, finally, what counts in public projects is user-friendliness and functionality in creating convivial space. According to Carmona (2021), an urban design could be categorised into six distinct elements: morphological, perceptual, social, visual, functional, and temporal. Regarding the Targowek project, even if some citizens would not like its visual dimension (aesthetically pleasing), what counts is its social dimension (inclusion of different genders and generations) and functional dimensions like green and blue infrastructure that have met to a great extent.

Discussion

The Targowek case study was a pretext to formulate potential places of kitsch experience components' appearance in the model of urban project management of a public space. Based on the analysis of the documents and reports of the project, I came to the conclusions presented in Table 12.3. To generalise the findings, I have distinguished four phases of project management: the first and second phases are conceptual, and the third and fourth are realisation. In both of them, the kitsch experience components in the project management may happen; however, as the first one creates fundaments of the whole project, their occurrence in part influences the final outcome to a significant extent. In the conceptual phase, the kitsch components experiences may occur when a project does not consider the modern concepts of city development, when the project is designed without the consultation of the stakeholders' needs or when, although the consultation took part, they have not been considered in the final project. Even when kitsch experience components in the first part will not be present, and a quality design of the project will be worked out, the realisation part may bring many spots for kitsch experience occurrences. Low quality of project management may concern choosing a contractor based not on its competencies but favouring a given one that meets the interest (often not official) of the city' authority. Another kitsch experience in the realisation part may occur when the project is delivered; however, it is of lower quality than assumed, making the direct user of the urban project disappointed and dissatisfied.

Table 12.3 Model of potential areas of kitsch experience components' appearance in urban project management of a public space

Phase	*Main activities and their requirements*	*Kitsch experience components' appearance*
Conception	• Identifying the goal of a project and benefits for its recipients • Aligning the design of a project with the trends and concept of city (re)development • Designing the project and outcomes for the stakeholders	• Domination of goals of other-than-recipient stakeholders • Not including some modern concept of city (re) development • Designing the project to meet other than stakeholders' interests (not officially stated like self-promotion of city officials, political reasons or third-party interests)
Preparation	• Site inspection • Social consultation of the needs and expectations of the project • Preparation of the first draft of the redevelopment based on the residents' needs and expectations • Conducting the social consultations of the first draft respecting the cognitive capabilities of different groups • Preparation of final proposal after social consultation • Social consultation of the final proposal of the project	• Unprofessional documentation, not including site inspection, based only on existing, not updated documents • Superficial consultation, not unlashing the stakeholders' needs, not considering different groups of consultees, favouritism of one group • Preparation of the final version to be implemented bypassing the consultation of the first draft and not including in the final draft recommendation at the second phase of consultation

(*Continued*)

Table 12.3 (Continued)

Phase	*Main activities and their requirements*	*Kitsch experience components' appearance*
Implementation	• Working out of the final version of the project • Public bid with the formal criteria for contractors • Implementation of the project	• Not including the main proposal and expectations submitted at the consultations in the final version of the project • Formulating criteria for public bids that do not ensure the high quality of realisation of the project • A discrepancy in quantity and quality between the final draft and the outcome (low-quality product used, artistic design not meeting aesthetic experience), overdrawing the deadlines
Evaluation	• Evaluation of the implemented project by criteria critical for stakeholders that may include many factors as: accessibility, safety, aesthetics, functionality, sustainability, reduction of crime rate or undesired behaviour, improved air quality, enhanced community cohesion • Review of established financial metrics • Gathering community input on satisfaction levels in the form of public meetings, online surveys, focus groups • Gathering lessons learned	• Lack of procedure for project evaluation • Lack of essential metrics for stakeholders • No evaluation of the outcome among stakeholders • No reflection of the outcome and a lack of a learning approach

Source: own elaboration

Conclusion

The analysis of the Targowek project helped answer the research questions. To answer the first question, "Which factors in creating, planning, implementing and evaluating a public space redevelopment project might decide that it would be perceived as a kitsch experience?" I have worked out the model presenting the city development concepts and analysed them, which were included in the Targowek project. To assess whether aesthetic or kitsch experiences occurred in this project, an assumption was made that not including modern city development concepts could indicate kitsch experience components in the project management. The analysed project documents and reports confirm that modern concepts like green city, convivial city, and human-centred concepts were applied. Four phases of its realisation were analysed through the aesthetic and kitsch experience theory to spot the possible kitsch experience in project management. The analysed data confirms that the conception and planning phases were aesthetic experiences for the local authorities and the residents. In the case of the third and fourth phases, implementation and evaluation (not realised yet), only the theoretical elements of aesthetic experience were highlighted, not the outcome.

The answer to the second research question, "What can be kitsch in public space – the artworks themselves, their creation process or narration?", I have juxtaposed in Table 12.3 potential places of appearance of kitsch experience in the realisation of urban project management of public space. It can be a benchmark for the aesthetic experiences of the authorities in the planning and realising of any project in an urban space.

The Targówek case study provided specific conclusions about the factors in urban project management that contribute to the aesthetic or kitsch experience, but further research on this topic is needed to draw general conclusions. The collected data may be biased because documents obtained from the Targówek community office employees may not consider some aspects necessary to assess the examined factors. The geographical location of the discussed case of a community in the country's capital, where the institutional processes may be better managed than in a province, could influence the conclusions. The project's sociopolitical context, the local authorities' local inhabitants or interests, and the financial situation (possibly constraints) might moderate both the process of the redevelopment project and its content, influencing the outcome.

Further research in this area can be done on a larger sample of cases, which should represent different locations (capitals, medium-sized, and small cities), different social environments of inhabitants and different countries since national culture determines how the processes are managed.

Notes

1 Resilient Cities, OECD, https://www.oecd.org/cfe/resilient-cities.htm
2 The Urban Agenda for EU, https://www.urbanagenda.urban-initiative.eu/urban-agenda-eu
3 https://architektura.um.warszawa.pl/-/suwalska-2-etap
4 The director of the Office of Social Aid and Social Projects; City Architect and Director of the Architecture and Spatial Planning Office; Head of the Department of Dialogue in Planning at the Office of Architecture and Spatial Planning of the Capital City of Warsaw.
5 The presented information comes from the project's brochure, "Report from the consultation", from the website of the community Targowek and interviews of people responsible for the project in the community Targowek.

References

Breuste, J., 2023. The Green City: General Concept. In: Breuste, J., Artmann, M., Ioja, C., Qureshi, S. (eds) *Making Green Cities. Cities and Nature*. Cham: Springer. https://doi.org/10.1007/978-3-030-73089-5_1.

Carmona, M., 2021. *Public Places Urban Spaces*. New York: Routledge. https://doi.org/10.4324/9781315158457.

Commission of the European Communities, 1990. Green Paper on the Urban Environment. *Luxembourg: Commission of the European Communities*. Dimensions in Urban Design. https://urbandesignlab.in/dimensions-of-urban-design/, access 27th February 2024.

Dover, W.J., 2015. *Green Infrastructure*. London: Routledge. https://doi.org/10.4324/9780203121993.

Evans, G., 2014. Living in the City Mixed Use and Quality of Life. In: Cooper, R., Burton, E., Cooper, C.L. (eds) *Well-Being and the Environment: Well-Being: A Complete Reference Guide*, Vol. II. John Wiley & Sons, Ltd. https://doi.org/10.1002/9781118539415.wbwell060.

Iribarren, S.G., 2019. Ivan Illich and the convivial city, in La possibilitė d'une ville conviviale. *Reveu du Mauss*, 54(2), La Découverte, 44–59 (The possibility of a convivial city)

Jenks, M., Jones, C. (eds), 2010. *Dimensions of Sustainable City 2*. Dordrecht: Springer Science+Business Media BV. https://doi.org/10.1007/978-1-4020-8647-2

Kelling, G., Coles, C., 1997. *Fixing Broken Windows: Restoring Order and Reducing Crime in Our Communities*. New York: Simon and Schuster, ISBN 978-0-684-83738-3.

Lake, A., Townshend, T., 2006. Obesogenic Environments: Exploring the Built and Food Environments. *The Journal of the Royal Society for the Promotion of Health*, 126(6), 262–267.

Moreno, C., 2024. *The 15-Minute City: A Solution to Saving Our Time and Our Planet*, 1st ed. Hoboken: Wiley.

Owen, D., Lennon, M., Scott, M.J., 2017. *Green Space Benefits for Health and Well-Being: A Life-Course Approach for Urban Planning, Design and Management*. Elsevier. doi: 10.1016/j.cities.2017.03.011

Raport. 2023. *Jakie miejsce do zabawy i odpoczynku wokol Suwalskiej 11 i 13? Raport z konsultacji spolecznych,* Warszawa: Biuro Architektury i Planowania Przestrzennego. https://konsultacje.um.warszawa.pl/processes/Suwalska-2etap?locale=pl

Resilient Cities, OECD. https://www.oecd.org/cfe/resilient-cities.htm, access 27th March 2024.

Rodriguez, M.B., Simon, M., 2015. Conceptualizing Conviviality in Urban Landscapes, Athens. *Journal of Architecture*, 1(4), 311–326.

Sim, D., 2019. *Soft City: Building Density for Everyday Life*. Washington: Island Press.

Szostak, M., 2023. *Sztuka zarządzania. Zarządzanie sztuką*. Łódź and Warszawa: Społeczna Akademia Nauk.

Szostak, M., Sulkowski, L., 2020. *Kitsch in Management: Characteristic Forms, Carriers and Propagators in: Education Excellence and Innovation Management: A 2025 Vision to Sustain Economic Development during Global Challenges: Proceedings of the 35th International Business Information Management Association Conference (IBIMA)*. Sevilla: IBIMA, pp. 7584–7598. Available at: https://depot.ceon.pl/handle/123456789/19173.

Trudo vertical Forest. https://www.archdaily.com/976910/trudo-vertical-forest-stefano-boeri-architetti, access 27th February 2024.

The Urban Agenda for EU. https://www.urbanagenda.urban-initiative.eu/urban-agenda-eu, access 27th February 2024.

Winkowska, J., Szpilko, D., Pejić, S., 2019. Smart City Concept in the Light of the Literature Review. *Engineering Management in Production and Services*, 11(2), 70–86.

13 Kitsch in social media

Self-optimisation gurus on Instagram

Weronika Pokojska and Olga Kosińska

Introduction

The *coaching* business is now a market that should not be underestimated. Its global value in 2019 had been estimated at over 4.5 billion dollars; since then, it has only been growing (*The Growth...*, 2023). Some forecast its value in 2024 to be 20 billion dollars (Zhou, 2023). But who exactly is a "coach"? For example, in the business environment, coaching "aims at the further development of learning and performance processes relating primarily to professional issues. This can be preventative, developmental, orientational and/or problem-solving" (*Was leistet Coaching?*, 2024). However, today, the areas in which coaches operate are very broad.

Looking at the different definitions and understandings of the term, it should be noted that a coach, reminiscent of a sports coach who is not necessarily a gifted athlete himself, is supposed to offer tools and be a guide for the client, who should, in effect, be able to pursue goals on his or her own later on. The coach teaches how to learn. A good coach guides the client to their own "resources" and helps them use them more efficiently and effectively in a goal-oriented manner. What is also important to point out is that the coach does not need to have specialised knowledge of the area in which the client is working because the skills they are working on together are, in a sense, universal. By definition, the coach walks alongside and not in front of the client, placing himself as a mentor or more knowledgeable person (*Czym jest coaching...*, 2024).

A coach, therefore, in a sense relevant to this text, is a person who works with a client to optimise their ways of living and approaching challenges, which may include both professional and private life. Thus, a coach is supposed to help the client achieve goals and improve performance in specific areas of life: physical fitness, mindset, work routines, decision-making, motivation and self-development.

Particularly problematic when considering coaches and coaching is that it is not a registered profession in many countries, and virtually anyone can call themselves a coach. Of course, some training and courses guarantee particular

DOI: 10.4324/9781003504931-14

qualifications. People, for example, with a degree in psychology or management, can also become coaching specialists who successfully help clients by supporting them with their education or experience. However, in the case of the phenomenon of coaches on Instagram, we often deal with "self-proclaimed" coaches who are not certified or have not undergone training (or it is impossible to verify this in any way) that would guarantee a certain level of competence. In addition, unlike professional coaches who work individually with their clients, Instagrammers and other social media content creators "work with", or rather, their posts reach a much larger number of people simultaneously.

Unfortunately, an incompetent pseudo-authority in conjunction with a person who is possibly in crisis and seeking help can also lead to extreme phenomena such as psychological or sexual abuse. Such a case was described in 2022 in Germany: a suspect who was active as a personality coach allegedly held a woman down for four days and raped her. It was suspected that there were other victims. Among other things, he advertised himself with advice videos and published on the subject of "getting out of the victim role" (sic) (*Walldürn: Geisel mehrfach vergewaltigt...*, 2022).

But what are the connections between kitsch and Instagram coaching? A happy ending is promised in both cases, using easy and accessible tools with a low access threshold (Szostak, 2021). Instagram coaches use a number of kitsch artefacts (Szostak, 2023) that allow them to reach a wide group of (susceptible) recipients effectively: they use easy, catch-all recipes; they show through images idealised visions that are supposed to constitute (probably unattainable) goals for making the future; under the guise of the ideals of freedom and independence, they use the basic principles of capitalism, simply wanting to sell their services or become attractive to advertisers.

Instagrammers exemplify kitsch producers, as Michał Szostak describes: "The producer of kitsch – imitating his own or other people's ideas and patterns – focuses on a mass audience, avoiding criticism. One of the motivations of a kitsch producer is to make something look more valuable than it actually is" (Szostak, 2021). For users, it gives an attractive and somehow safe feeling that they can do anything, that reality is not so hopeless, and that there are some simple rules that, if followed, will lead to success (Szostak, 2023: 255). Contributing to the research on Instagram, its users and content creators, this study focuses on female self-optimisation gurus who publish their content primarily on Instagram. It draws attention to female-led and (mostly) female-targeted Instagram profiles and how some creators become kitsch producers. Therefore, we asked three research questions:

1. What makes a self-management or self-optimisation guru on Instagram?
2. What are the attributes of success as described by self-optimisation gurus?
3. What makes self-optimisation gurus kitsch producers?

We use netnographic content analysis as our main research technique. First, we critically review the current literature on social media influencers and self-optimisation. Then, we present the results of our research, detailing the data and methods we used. This is followed by findings on the self-optimisation of female Instagrammers and their role as kitsch producers. The chapter closes with a discussion of implications, limitations and future study suggestions.

Literature review: social media influencers and self-optimisation

Social media influencers (SMIs) are sometimes associated with the term "celebrity" and, as such, are treated with some negativity. Those content creators are then defined as people "known for being known", having not earned their current position due to creating "real" values (Archer, Wolf, Nalloor, 2020). However, the popularity of social media influencers in recent years has undoubtedly been observed, making them an essential part of the current socio-economic landscape (Lou, Taylor, Zhou, 2022). An increase in the time people spend online, using mobile devices and shopping online, is evident and, above all, the number of used social media platforms is also observed (Digital, 2024). As a result, social media influencers are usually defined as independent content creators who use social media platforms as tools to publish and share the content they have created, engage with their audience and cooperate with brands – mainly but not exclusively – in order to earn money (Bi, Liu, 2022).

One of the critical platforms influencers use is Instagram, an app considered the most influencer-based up to date (Samet, 2023). After its launch in 2010, it has now (as of January 2024) an estimated 2,4 billion users, making it continuously one of the five most popular apps globally (Shewale, 2024), as well as one of the most liked ones (*Digital...*, 2024). Based primarily on sharing static pictures, with time, Instagram posts evolved and are now present also as short videos shared via the Stories feature (available to see for 24 hours) or Reels. Instagram is the subject of many analyses (Bishop, 2021; Campbell, Farrell, 2020; Cotter, 2018) that suggest "people are using it to gather knowledge... as well as to document their own experiences, and in doing so informing others through their own output" (Marcella-Hood, Marcella, 2022: 2). Instagram is also one of the most popular and effective tools for influencer marketing – "a type of native advertising in which brands partner with influencers who post promotional content for the brand from their own social media accounts" (Myers, Sen, Syrdal, Woodroof, 2022: 4). For that reason influencers who operate on this platform were chosen for our research.

Influencers operate simultaneously within several areas, taking different positions concerning the software they use. As social media users, they accumulate intangible capital such as knowledge, authority and/or a network of contacts. At the same time, they are recipients of content created by other creators. As digital celebrities, they gather fans through posts and a specific self-narrative built around themselves. As opinion leaders, they create original content to build a trusted network of contacts and influence around themselves. They are also promoters of various brands and products, advertising them and influencing others (Bi, Liu, 2022; Campbell, Farrell, 2020). In this context, social influence is "changes in an individual's thoughts, feelings, attitudes, or behaviours resulting from interacting with others" (Byun, Ahn, 2023: 293). As such, influencer marketing based on the social influence of popular content creators is one of the most popular and effective trends in current advertising and marketing (Campbell, Farrell, 2020). Therefore, Those creators are equipped to change their followers' behaviours and/or views and transfer knowledge. Self-optimisation is one of the important areas in which such transfer and change in behaviours are currently observed.

Even though self-optimisation is a multidimensional topic, it remains an under-researched one (Nehring, Röcke, 2023), particularly in the context of social media. Self-optimisation is one of the latest trends in creating online content, where one can find a number of TikTok, Instagram posts or YouTube videos aimed at helping the audience reach their "full potential", solve some problems and/or gain knowledge through post engagement. As Daniel Nehring and Anja Röcke point out: "Self-optimisation is on the agenda of societies around the world today" (Nehring, Röcke, 2023: 2). They define self-optimisation as a social discourse and a set of practices, focused on pursuing the perfect image of individual bodies, mental health, everyday practices and such (Nehring, Röcke, 2023). It is, therefore, a constant work aimed at becoming a promised, more or less specific image of a future self. We argue that many elements of such self-optimisation discourse are similar to self-management (Laloux, 2015), including organising an individual's assets, motivating oneself, setting priorities and controlling. Self-optimisation is self-management aimed at perfecting one's life in every aspect.

Self-optimisation is vastly based on self-help discourse that "hinges on the presupposition that you can become the loving, communicative, balanced... person who is now just lurking underneath your skin" (De Vos, 2015: 251). What is essential is that self-help does not come naturally from within – one requires expert help (De Vos, 2015) that social media content creators will willingly provide. Self-optimisation-themed social media content is often considered biased and dangerous, stating opinions and under-researched statements as "truths" and "undeniable facts". Especially in the areas of psychology, psychiatry and therapy, it is often pointed out that those influencers do not have the required degree, experience and/or certificate, which leads to doubting their abilities and, therefore, warning against contacting them due to a risk of misleading the users (Rottenberg, 2022). Such content may lead to self-diagnosing oneself by comparison to others – while it might be useful to see one's behaviours or problems from a different perspective, it is often stated that (a) creators posting this advice are not appropriately equipped for the job and (b) every situation is different and should be viewed and analysed on its own (Pandey, 2023). Self-optimising influencers might be considered gurus and producers of kitsch – creators who, often by imitating other people's ideas – focus on mass audiences while avoiding criticism. One of the motivations of such a kitsch producer is to make something look more valuable than it is. We argue that some self-optimisation gurus deceive their audience to some degree, presenting complicated issues as black-and-white ones and giving ready-made advice that is supposed to solve some problems in an easy, sometimes almost effortless way. Those gurus are (to some degree) imitating and performing themselves as such – individuals filled with knowledge and sometimes even enlightenment, making them and their advice seem, again, more valuable than it is (Szostak, 2021).

On the other hand, many followers of self-optimisation influencers claim that they are actually "getting better" due to the knowledge passed onto them by the creators. They comment on their posts, thanking them for "changing their life" or helping them to get through a difficult time. It is argued if their lives are changing due to their engagement with posts or if this feeling of change is more of a result of societal pressure – or rather the pressure of other users who seem to be "getting better" therefore, I surely am too (De Vos, 2015). It might be partially associated with the fear of missing out (FOMO), a subjective perception or feeling of potentially not being a part of an important event, community or relationship, which results in a subconscious need to stay constantly connected to one's virtual network (Marcella-Hood, Marcella, 2022). FOMO is often attributed to Instagram as a widely used source of information about family and friends, as well as parasocial friends – people users never met in person but (again, to some degree) feel connected to, such as influencers (Stein, Breves, Anders, 2022).

Claiming self-optimisation gurus as kitsch producers should not take away from the fact that their followers seem to succeed thanks to those influencers' posts. In order to take a closer look at this dichotomy, we would like to analyse several self-optimisation influencers posting on Instagram that focus on content aimed at women. Self-optimisation advice is not genderless – on the contrary, we argue that there is more content directed to women than men. Studies show that algorithms controlling content on apps such as Instagram are biased regarding gender (Are, 2022; Bishop, 2018; Ekström, 2021; Mahoney, 2022). It is also worth mentioning that, based on our research, we can argue that "manly" posts are quite often considered universal, while "female" content is visibly targeting female audiences. In the case of self-optimisation gurus, it is often their conscious decision to focus on one specific gender when thinking about the audience. It is women talking to women – supporting, uplifting, giving advice, mentoring and coaching them. Such content creation is not harmful – we argue, however, that, due to a social need for easy and quick answers to difficult questions in a more and more complex world, such influencers provide their audiences with easily implemented advice that often promotes simple categories and roads to success, attractive to the masses (Szostak, 2021). Such self-management rejects previous achievements in the field, showing simplified rules of everyday life in a McDonaldised way (Ritzer, 2009).

Empirical evidence: Instagram accounts' analysis

Our initial research led us to focus on influencers who publish content on Instagram. We focused on female content creators whose posts targeted their female audience. It was partially motivated by the fact that when we entered the search term "coach" into the Instagram engine and researched the suggested (thus most popular and "on the rise") profiles, we ended up with a list of mostly female self-help coaches. It confirmed our initial hypothesis that many female self-optimisation coaches on Instagram target primarily female audiences. In order to identify and describe types of female Insta-coaches, we surveyed 20 profiles on Instagram run by female Instagrammers who described themselves – in their profile name or profile description – as a coach. The profiles were in both Polish and English. Quotations from Polish have been translated into English with as little change to the original material as possible – for example, words written in capital letters in the original post were translated into English in the same manner.

The sample selection was random, dictated by the basic functions of the Instagram app, especially its algorithm. The way the Instagram algorithm works is, in a way, one of the most important secrets of this platform – and any other, for that matter. Algorithms decide how the content is presented to the audience, being the main non-human decision-makers regarding visibility and, as a result, the popularity of certain posts (Jurgenson, 2021). Even though one does not know all the details of the Instagram algorithm, certain information can be used to pinpoint why this post is visible to the user and the other one is not (Kreft, 2022). One of the most important factors is whether the user got in touch with content on a certain topic previously. We neither follow such profiles nor interact with self-optimisation posts on our private Instagram accounts; therefore, there was no risk of our feed being widely biased by our previous searches and likes.

We entered the search term into the search engine through our private accounts. From the list suggested by the algorithm, each of us selected ten profiles run by female coaches. As mentioned, the results suggested by the algorithm are based on our previous choices and preferences, so, for example, virtually no mom influencers appeared in our results. Similarly, coaches related to the topic of male-female relationships, that is, dating coaches, did not appear in our results. The final selected profiles were analysed for content promoted in the form of text and images, both as posts and as stories.

The analysed profiles are presented in the study in a coded way so as not to promote them. Only three of them are run by women who declare having some certification in their expertise; the others do not inform about their certification, so it must be assumed that they do not have any. Admittedly, the aspects analysed and presented below intermingle and are often statistically elusive (due to the specific nature of the medium), so the figures given should be treated as indicative, showing the dominance of certain themes we have intuitively grasped.

Half of the selected profiles are coaches who focus on business aspects ("business coach", "holistic business coach", "ethical coaching for entrepreneurs"), and four of them also describe themselves as "life coaches". Three of them emphasise the combined role of a mother and a businesswoman (the term "mompreneur" was used here). The others describe themselves as "mindset", "ethical", "gratitude", "growth" or "confidence" coaches. Sometimes, the terms "trainer" and "mentor" are also used. Two profiles could be characterised as "female power coaches", because they are heavily focused on esoteric themes and/or female sexuality (e.g. they will take you on a "spiritual awakening journey" [IN11] or help you how to "activate pleasure, ecstatic authenticity and freedom" [IN18], provide "menstrual mentoring" [IN18]). Some influencers indicate in their descriptions that they are authors of publications, that a consultation can be arranged, or that they immediately direct followers to their commercial offer via a link. It is clear, therefore, that activity on Instagram serves to promote and generate interest among a wider audience in the relevant offer (which often cannot be considered affordable).

The relationship between the right mindset and practising "manifestation" is not entirely clear, but it is definitely the dominant method among coaches at the moment.[1] Both issues have a certain almost magical aura that seems to flow from properly selected, curated, repeated thoughts, gaining agency with an almost 100% guarantee. So if bad, unplanned, negative situations keep happening (although it depends here, they can also be a lesson we need because "EVERY REJECTION IS AN INVITATION" [IN20]) or one is still "stuck" in life and/or work, they are obviously constructing their thoughts incorrectly. Of course, in some sense, this way of thinking can certainly increase self-confidence, but trusting the agency of one's thoughts can also increase frustration in the event of failures and disappointments. The actions of some coaches are directed against "success blockades" [IN03], which need to be broken and the "victim mentality" [IN16] or " 'poor guy' mentality" [IN02].

Interestingly, very few profiles emphasised the role of money or the so-called money mindset. Money appeared most often as a means of acquiring something else, something more valuable. In some cases, money was a metaphorical backdrop for the content: for example, quotes or videos were displayed against the backdrop of luxurious holiday resorts, cars or homes. Prosperity is therefore understood as "freedom and independence", emphasising the importance and value of time, experiences and relationships with loved ones – money, even in the form of luxury handbags or cars, is only a means to an end, at least in the vision created by analysed coaches.

In the context of specific business tips that fall on given profiles in the period under review, the leading ones include "networking", but also "business scaling", "online business", "personal branding" and "passive income". Interestingly, advice is also provided on proper note-taking and optimisation of the planning process: proper (self-)organisation is a fundamental step towards success. However, "success" itself is understood in various ways.

Even some of the business-oriented influencers emphasise the unspecified peculiarity of "female business", for example, in the statement "business in female energy" [IN04] or "I will show you how to unleash women's POWER" [IN16]. Others, in turn, pay attention to improving or healing interpersonal relationships in both professional and personal life and building "strong personal boundaries" [IN11], which seems to be seen as a typical female problem. It can be summarised that the primary goal is continuous "personal development" in every aspect of life.

As we finish the content analysis, we want to depict a few examples of specific posts that are an example of how the principles of management science are simplified and adapted to the quick, superficial nature of Instagram coaching:

> "2. The 1% Rule 👣: Be better than yourself by 1% a day. What small changes should you make every day?
> 3. 80/20 rule (Pareto) ⚖️: Focus on key activities, base on the effect. What should you focus on?
> 4. Act as if approach 🎭: Full commitment. How would you act if you had already achieved your goal?" [IN03]

> "What I did to build an income of PLN 10,000 a month was SIMPLE ✨GOAL-DRIVEN ✨BRINGING ACTUAL RESULTS ✨" [IN04]

> "If you are statistically average, you waste about 50% of the time you spend working each week." [IN06]

> "Go beyond the patterns and start with YOU
> They say we come here for the money and stay for the people🙏🤍
> THIS BUSINESS IS PEOPLE who want something more from life🙏
> Who support and teach what no one taught us at school, even though these are the basics💸" [IN15]

> "✨ Feminine energy of lightness and magnetism; It's time to stop developing yourself by acquiring new skills, certificates or tools. This is the time to deepen your relationship with your p*ssy and s*xual energy. 🔥" [IN18]

As a side note, it should be mentioned that one of the analysed influencers [IN07] subliminally promoted the anti-vaccination movement and related activism.

Discussion

Instagram is one of the most popular social media platforms, allowing users to express themselves, share and gain knowledge, and create social networks and business opportunities. One of the most popular ways to "have it all" is to become a social media influencer who utilises opportunities created on platforms such as Instagram to gain popularity, audience and authority. The female self-optimisation coaches on Instagram we analysed fall into the producers of kitsch category as described by Michał Szostak (2021). They promise a happy ending – success (however defined in detail) is inevitable as long as one follows the influencers' rules and sometimes almost secret ways. Those ways might not always be easy, but that is also "how it should be" – things that bring one joy and satisfaction, according to the gurus we analysed, should pose some challenges that can be overcome thanks to the guru's wisdom. If it sounds dangerously close to a cult – it somewhat is. The community that gathers around those self-optimisation influencers is often a strong and unified one, judging by the number of followers compared to comments and user engagement rates. That is not a danger – social media is an essential source of human connections, finding people interested in the same things and simply not feeling alone with one's thoughts (Zhou, Sedikides, Mo, Li, Hong, Wildschut, 2021). It is, however, worth noting that, based on our research, we can undoubtedly present female self-optimisation Instagram coaches as kitsch producers who sometimes exploit social media users' weaknesses and needs to gain following, authority and, as a result, business opportunities. As we have mentioned before, those influencers often use some kitsch artefacts such as easy-to-follow recipes and idealised visions of "what is to come" while emphasising "freedom" and "independence" as main goals and universal values. Nevertheless, through the visual presence in posts of material representations of success – handbags, cars, houses, holiday resorts (often uncommented on but still visible in the background), influencers also highlight other worthwhile goals. In the case of the profiles analysed here, influencer marketing issues (Myers, Sen, Syrdal, Woodroof, 2022: 4) were not conspicuous, at least not in its classic sense. Directly promoted was coaching and not the products of brands with which the influencer has a partnership (or his brands), as is usually the case. The sale of the extended coaching offer in the form of courses and paid advice took place on other platforms; at most, it was sub-linked or suggested on Instagram. By analysing the Instagram profiles, we identified four types of female Insta-coaches:

1. general type: business and life coaching, content that is somewhat neutral, uncontroversial, with which many "ordinary" women can identify, regardless of their financial status or career level;
2. business and marketing type: aggressive content focused on achieving specific goals, for example, a specific number of users in an online business, a specific monthly income threshold, gaining financial freedom;
3. beige type: the name refers to the aesthetics of "beige moms" – their profiles are full of beige, natural colours, kids are dressed in linen, and everything gives the impression of peace, calm and neutrality (Gee, 2024); this type of content creator is focused mainly on aesthetic impressions typical of the

medium of Instagram (e.g. publishing motivating quotes on an appropriately selected background);
4. feminine-energetic type: content combining various elements in terms of self-development, but with a strong emphasis on female energy, femininity, natural strength and often also sexual.

This list is not yet completed – future research should follow to analyse further content and see whether more models could be indicated.

Conclusion

In this chapter, we examined the Instagram profiles of female self-optimisation gurus as kitsch producers, therefore contributing to the research of Instagram users and content creators and the kitsch experience theory. We used netnographic content analysis as our main research technique. Firstly, we see our study as a starting point for future topic analysis. Secondly, it highlights some of the techniques used by self-optimisation influencers. Thirdly, it shows how Instagrammers use certain kitsch artefacts to help them achieve their personal goals.

In all three cases, we are talking about rapidly changing phenomena, subject to trends that are difficult to grasp by scientific studies, which are usually unable to keep up with them. It is essential to look at such seemingly trivial phenomena because they say a lot about the state of society, especially considering how much of our lives take place online. If it were not for a part of this society that is somewhat manipulated by promises of quick and easy solutions, fulfilling dreams and creating the best version of themselves, influencers would not exist. In a sense, users also become an active part of this process of kitsch production. Deepening the research with the users' perspective would be a significant addition to researching the relationship between kitsch and social media. When one considers that other seemingly all-knowing online gurus also use the mechanisms used by the influencers we presented, it can be hazardous if these are influential in political matters, for example. Another question is whether social media, due to its inherent characteristic of a certain superficiality, speed of communication and changing trends, are not by nature producers of kitsch.

This study is limited by its preliminary character; we studied 20 profiles on Instagram out of hundreds that fall into the "female self-optimisation coach" category. Furthermore, as we have indicated, the algorithm randomly dictates the selection. Additional research should focus on whether the list of identified types of female Insta-coaches should be expanded and other kitsch artefacts used by influencers. In-depth research on the topic would also be advised, for example, finding out whether Instagrammers are aware of their role as kitsch producers.

Returning to the research questions posed at the beginning of the text: What makes a self-management or self-optimisation guru on Instagram then? Our research shows many ways of obtaining such a title as long as the audience is convinced that the content creator's advice and tips are trustworthy and effective. Even if they are not, it is the creator's role to prove it is not to be blamed on the advice being wrong, but rather the individual's approach to the matter. Our research suggests that self-optimisation gurus are people who describe themselves as such – but, more importantly, are identified as such by their audience.

What are the attributes of success as described by self-optimisation gurus? In the case of female content creators on Instagram, the main attributes of success are freedom and independence. One can conclude that those values are partially derived from the lack of those two experiences in female everyday life. However, it is impossible to define "freedom" and "independence" in their details. Those two concepts can be and are filled with many meanings, depending on the creator – and their interpretation by the users. There is a vague idea of what it means to "be free" and "be independent", but based on Instagram self-optimisation gurus content, it is hard to find universal answers to these questions: free from what/who? How exactly "independent"? "Independent" from what? Therefore, we argue that the attributes of success as described by self-optimisation gurus are imprecise and allow the creators to indicate pretty much anything as such.

Self-optimisation gurus can be called kitsch producers. As described by Michał Szostak (2023: 250), they use their own or other people's ideas to offer them to the mass audience almost as a sort of enlightenment. They publish their content to reach as many people as possible and avoid criticism or problematic issues. Not knowing the creators themselves, we cannot possibly argue if they think of themselves as more "knowledgeable" than others; however, they certainly do create their content with the intention for it to be so.

Note

1 It can be argued that the trend for manifestation is a current 'hot topic' among Instagram coaches.

References

Archer, C., Wolf, K., Nalloor, J. (2020). Capitalising on chaos – exploring the impact and future od social media influencer engagement during the early stages of a global pandemic. *Media International Australia* vol. 178(1), pp. 106–113.

Are, C. (2022). The Shadowban cycle: An autoethnography of pole dancing, nudity and censorship on Instagram. *Feminist Media Studies* vol. 22(8), pp. 2002–2019.

Banerjee, S. B., Jermier, J. M., Peredo, A. M., Perey, R., Reichel, A. (2021). Theoretical perspectives on organizations and organizing in a post-growth era. *Organization* vol. 28(3), pp. 337–357.

Bi, C. Q., Liu, L. (2022). From fame to fortune: Influencer entrepreneurship in a digital age. *PACIS 2022 Proceedings* vol. 2022(208), pp. 1–9.

Bishop, S. (2018). Anxiety, panic and self-optimization: Inequalities and the YouTube algorithm. *Convergence* vol. 24(1), pp. 69–84.

Bishop, S. (2021). Influencer management tools: Algorithmic cultures, brand safety, and bias. *Social Media + Society* vol. 7(1), pp. 1–13.

Byun, K. J., Ahn, S. J. (2023). A systematic review of virtual influencers: Similarities and differences between human and virtual influencers in interactive advertising. *Journal of Interactive Advertising* vol. 23(4), pp. 293–306.

Campbell, C., Farrell, J. R. (2020). More than meets the eye: The functional components underlying influencer marketing. *Business Horizons* vol. 63(4), pp. 469–479.

Cotter, K. (2018). Playing the visibility game: How digital influencers and algorithms negotiate influence on Instagram. *New Media & Society* vol. 21(4), pp. 895–913.

Czym jest coaching, a czym nie jest? (2024). Downloaded from: https://web.archive.org/web/20120929003510/http://www.icf.org.pl/pl150,czym-jest-coaching-a-czym-nie-jest.html (03.03.2024).

Davies, G. F., Sinha, A. (2021). Varieties of uberization: How technology and institutions change organization(s) of late capitalism. *Organization Theory* vol. 2(1), pp. 1–17.

De Vos, J. (2015). Self-help: And pop psychology. In *Handbook of Critical Psychology*, I. Parker (ed.). London and New York: Routledge, pp. 250–258.

Digital 2024. Global Overview Report (2024). Downloaded from: https://datareportal.com/reports/digital-2024-global-overview-report (03.03.2024).

Ekström, O. (2021). *The Perceived Role of the Instagram Algorithm in Gender Inequality – Analyzing the Public Discourse Around the Case of Nyome Nicholas-Williams*. Downloaded from: https://studenttheses.uu.nl/bitstream/handle/20.500.12932/111/Ekstrom-Master-thesis-2021-publish.pdf?sequence=1&isAllowed=y (03.03.2024).

Faraj, S., Pachidi, S. (2021). Beyond uberization: The co-constitution of technology and organizing. *Organization Theory* vol. 2(1), pp. 1–14.

Gee, M. (2024). *Not So Neutral: Why the Viral "Beige Mom" Trend Leaves BIPOC Parents Behind*. Downloaded from: https://www.reckon.news/honey/2024/02/not-so-neutral-why-the-viral-beige-mom-trend-leaves-bipoc-parents-behind.html (03.03.24).

Jurgenson, N. (2021). *Fotka. O zdjęciach i mediach społecznościowych*. Kraków-Warszawa: Wydawnictwo Karakter.

Kreft, J. (2022). *Władza algorytmów. U źródeł potęgi Google i Facebooka*. Kraków: Wydawnictwo Uniwersytetu Jagiellońskiego.

Laloux, F. (2015). *Pracować inaczej. Nowatorski model organizacji inspirowany kolejnym etapem rozwoju ludzkiej świadomości*. Warszawa: Wydawnictwo Studio Emka.

Li, X., Feng, J. (2021). Influenced or to be influenced: Engaging social media influencers in nation branding through the lens of authenticity. *Global Media and China* vol. 7(2), pp. 219–240.

Lou, C., Taylor, C. R., Zhou, X. (2022). Influencer marketing on social media: How different social media platforms afford influencer-follower relation and drive advertising effectiveness. *Journal of Current Issues & Research in Advertising* vol. 2022, pp. 1–28.

Mahoney, C. (2022). Is this what a feminist looks like? Curating the feminist self in the neoliberal visual economy of Instagram. *Feminist Media Studies* vol. 22(3), pp. 519–535.

Marcella-Hood, M., Marcella, R. (2022). Purposive and non-purposive information behavior on Instagram. *Journal of Librarianship and Information Science* vol. 2022, pp. 1–24.

Myers, S., Sen, S., Syrdal, H., Woodroof, P. (2022). The impact of Persuasion knowledge cues on social media engagement: A look at pet influencer marketing. *Journal of Marketing Theory and Practice* vol. 2022, pp. 1–18.

Nehring, D., Röcke, A. (2023). Self-optimisation: Conceptual, discursive and historical perspectives. *Current Sociology* vol. 2023, pp. 1–19.

Pandey, N. (2023). *The Rise of Pop Psychology and Mental Health Advice on Short Video Platforms – A Quick Fix or Folly*. Downloaded from: https://www.cnbctv18.com/healthcare/the-rise-of-pop-psychology-and-mental-health-advice-on-short-video-platforms-a-quick-fix-or-folly-18154241.htm (03.03.2024).

Ritzer, G. (2009). *Makdonaldyzacja społeczeństwa*. Warszawa: Wydawnictwo Muza.
Rottenberg, S. (2022). *Pop Psych on Instagram Might Be Harming Your Mental Health: Here's What You Should Know*. Downloaded from: https://rottenbergtherapy.com/pop-psych-on-instagram-might-be-harming-your-mental-health-heres-what-you-should-know/. (03.03.2024).
Samet, A. (2023). *Instagram Is Still Crucial for Influencer Marketing, Even as TikTok Is on the Rise*. Downloaded from: https://www.insiderintelligence.com/content/instagram-still-crucial-influencer-marketing-even-tiktok-on-rise (03.03.2024).
Shewale, R. (2024). *Instagram Statictics – Global Demographics & Trends (2024)*. Downloaded from: https://www.demandsage.com/instagram-statistics/ (03.03.2024).
Stein, J., Breves, P. L., Anders, N. (2022). Parasocial interactions with real and virtual influencers: The role of perceived similarity and human-likeness. *New Media & Society* vol. 2022, pp. 1–21.
Szostak, M. (2021). Kicz: nasza ochrona przed rzeczywistością. *Więź*, 12 stycznia. Downloaded from: https://wiez.pl/2021/01/12/kicz-nasza-ochrona-przed-rzeczywistoscia/ (03.03.2024).
Szostak, M. (2023). Sztuka zarządzania, zarządzanie sztuką. Łódź-Warszawa: Wydawnictwo Społecznej Akademii Nauk. *The Growth of the Coaching Industry in 2023 and Beyond [Infographic]*. Downloaded from: https://www.ipeccoaching.com/blog/life-coaching-statistics-2023-show-industry-growing (03.03.2024).
Walldürn: Geisel mehrfach vergewaltigt – Staatsanwalt rechnet mit zwei weiteren Opfern (2024). Downloaded from: https://www.swr.de/swraktuell/baden-wuerttemberg/mannheim/geiselnahme-und-vergewaltigung-in-wallduern-100.html (03.03.2024).
Was leistet Coaching? (2024). Downloaded from: https://www.dbvc.de/standards-fuer/coaching/begriffsbestimmungen (03.03.2024).
Zhou, L. (2023). *The Coaching Industry Market Size in 2024*. Downloaded from: https://www.luisazhou.com/blog/coaching-industry-market-size/ (03.03.2024).
Zhou, X., Sedikides, C., Mo, T., Li, W., Hong, E. K., Wildschut, T. (2021). The restorative power of nostalgia: Thwarting loneliness by tasing happiness during the COVID-19 pandemic. *Social Psychological and Personality Science* vol. 13(4), pp. 803–815.

Conclusion

Determinants and functions, carriers, and propagators of managerial and organisational kitsch

Michał Szostak

Theses verification

After thorough analyses of varied examples of kitsch in managerial and organisational contexts, it is possible to verify two key theses of the book mentioned in the introduction.

Thesis 1 stated that *the consciousness of kitsch within managerial and organisational contexts allows managers and stakeholders to be more secure, aware, and confident participants of organisational life*. It can be verified positively due to the following arguments:

1. by recognising kitsch situations and behaviours, managers and stakeholders can develop a deep (in opposition to superficial) sense of aestheticisation, helping them to create and maintain a workplace environment that is more true and beautiful (in the meaning of universal values of truth and beauty), which can enhance organisational and managerial efficiency (Chapter 1 – From kitsch phenomenon, through kitsch experience, to kitschy management and management of kitsch);
2. awareness of kitsch encourages critical thinking about the quality and authenticity of organisational practices and communications; it can lead to more rigorous standards and a reduction in superficial or inauthentic initiatives that might otherwise undermine credibility and trust (Chapter 2 – Kitsch in organisational culture: challenges and opportunities in the work environment; Chapter 3 – Kitsch in organisational governance: management through simplified edicts and superficial interpretations in religious fatwas; Chapter 4 – Kitsch in HRM: the role of communication in managing generational diversity in an organisation);
3. understanding the superficiality of kitsch can help managers make more informed and substantive decisions, avoiding the pitfalls of quick fixes or trendy solutions that lack depth and long-term viability (Chapter 4 – Kitsch in HRM: the role of communication in managing generational diversity in an organisation; Chapter 10 – Kitsch in decision-making: financial destabilisation of joint-stock companies by boards of directors);

DOI: 10.4324/9781003504931-15

4. acknowledging kitsch can lead to greater sensitivity as managers become more aware of the potential for superficial representations of culture; it can enhance inclusivity and respect for diverse cultural expressions within the organisation (Chapter 2 – Kitsch in organisational culture: challenges and opportunities in the work environment; Chapter 3 – Kitsch in organisational governance: management through simplified edicts and superficial interpretations in religious fatwas; Chapter 4 – Kitsch in HRM: the role of communication in managing generational diversity in an organisation);
5. the consciousness of kitsch can help maintain brand integrity by ensuring that organisational branding and marketing efforts are genuine and not overly simplistic or insincere; it fosters a stronger, more authentic connection with customers and stakeholders (Chapter 6 – Kitsch in marketing: merchandising and promotional activities in the retail sphere; Chapter 7 – Kitsch in advertising: a field of postmodern market communication battle; Chapter 8 – Kitsch in brand management: impact of aesthetic truth and false in advertising strategies);
6. managers who are aware of the pitfalls of kitsch are likely to promote more authentic leadership styles, which can build more robust, trust-based relationships with employees and stakeholders, fostering a more cohesive and resilient organisational culture (Chapter 2 – Kitsch in organisational culture: challenges and opportunities in the work environment; Chapter 3 – Kitsch in organisational governance: management through simplified edicts and superficial interpretations in religious fatwas; Chapter 4 – Kitsch in HRM: the role of communication in managing generational diversity in an organisation);
7. by avoiding superficial and inauthentic practices, managers can build greater trust with stakeholders, who appreciate genuine efforts and transparent communication, thereby enhancing the organisation's reputation and stakeholder loyalty (Chapter 10 – Kitsch in decision-making: financial destabilisation of joint-stock companies by boards of directors);
8. recognising the limitations of kitsch can encourage managers to focus on long-term strategic goals rather than short-term, superficial gains, leading to more sustainable growth and stability for the organisation (Chapter 2 – Kitsch in organisational culture: challenges and opportunities in the work environment; Chapter 3 – Kitsch in organisational governance: management through simplified edicts and superficial interpretations in religious fatwas; Chapter 10 – Kitsch in decision-making: financial destabilisation of joint-stock companies by boards of directors);
9. awareness of kitsch can stimulate innovation and creativity by pushing managers to seek more profound, more meaningful solutions rather than relying on cliched or overly simplistic ideas, thus fostering a more dynamic and forward-thinking organisational environment (Chapter 2 – Kitsch in organisational culture: challenges and opportunities in the work environment; Chapter 3 – Kitsch in organisational governance: management through

simplified edicts and superficial interpretations in religious fatwas; Chapter 9 – Kitsch in entrepreneurship: meal kits, taste and the art of socio-economic enterprise; Chapter 10 – Kitsch in decision-making: financial destabilisation of joint-stock companies by boards of directors);
10. employees are more likely to feel engaged and motivated in a workplace that values truth, depth, and authenticity over superficiality; this can result in higher morale, better teamwork, and increased overall performance (Chapter 5 – Kitsch in managerial language: rhetorical manifestations of kitsch in scholarly writing);
11. focusing on the process rather than the goal may lead to kitschy results that do not meet the initial expectations; it may appear in varied contexts and situations (Chapter 11 – Kitsch in new technologies management: design practices and user experiences; Chapter 12 – Kitsch in city space management: beauty and functionality of public space; Chapter 13 – Kitsch in social media: self-optimisation gurus on Instagram).

Thesis 2 stated that *managers' conscious use of organisational kitsch (its presence or lack, its character, scope, form, and intensity) as a means/tool may increase efficiency in achieving goals*. It can be verified positively due to the following arguments:

1. deliberate and conscious use of managerial and organisational kitsch can create a lively and stimulating environment, boosting employee morale and motivation and increasing productivity and efficiency in achieving organisational goals; however, its overuse can lead to adverse results (Chapter 2 – Kitsch in organisational culture: challenges and opportunities in the work environment; Chapter 3 – Kitsch in organisational governance: management through simplified edicts and superficial interpretations in religious fatwas; Chapter 4 – Kitsch in HRM: the role of communication in managing generational diversity in an organisation);
2. utilising kitsch in marketing and branding can make the organisation more memorable and appealing to a broader audience, enhancing brand recognition and loyalty, driving sales, and achieving marketing objectives more efficiently (Chapter 6 – Kitsch in marketing: merchandising and promotional activities in the retail sphere; Chapter 7 – Kitsch in advertising: a field of postmodern market communication battle; Chapter 8 – Kitsch in brand management: impact of aesthetic truth and false in advertising strategies);
3. simplified and visually appealing kitsch elements can make internal communications more engaging and easier to understand, improving information dissemination and reducing misunderstandings, leading to more efficient operations (Chapter 2 – Kitsch in organisational culture: challenges and opportunities in the work environment; Chapter 4 – Kitsch in HRM: the

role of communication in managing generational diversity in an organisation; Chapter 5 – Kitsch in managerial language: rhetorical manifestations of kitsch in scholarly writing);

4. using kitsch themes in team-building activities and events can foster a sense of community and belonging among employees, improving teamwork and collaboration, which is essential for achieving organisational goals (Chapter 3 – Kitsch in organisational governance: management through simplified edicts and superficial interpretations in religious fatwas; Chapter 4 – Kitsch in HRM: the role of communication in managing generational diversity in an organisation; Chapter 5 – Kitsch in managerial language: rhetorical manifestations of kitsch in scholarly writing; Chapter 13 – Kitsch in social media: self-optimisation gurus on Instagram);
5. in customer-facing roles, a touch of kitsch can make interactions more enjoyable and memorable for clients, enhancing customer satisfaction and retention and contributing to business growth and goal achievement (Chapter 1. From kitsch phenomenon, through kitsch experience, to kitschy management and management of kitsch; Chapter 6 – Kitsch in marketing: merchandising and promotional activities in the retail sphere; Chapter 7 – Kitsch in advertising: a field of postmodern market communication battle; Chapter 8 – Kitsch in brand management: impact of aesthetic truth and false in advertising strategies);
6. whimsical kitsch elements in the workplace can create a more relaxed and enjoyable atmosphere, helping to reduce employee stress; lower stress levels can lead to higher productivity and efficiency (Chapter 1. From kitsch phenomenon, through kitsch experience, to kitschy management and management of kitsch; Chapter 4 – Kitsch in HRM: the role of communication in managing generational diversity in an organisation);
7. a workplace incorporating kitsch elements can inspire creativity and out-of-the-box thinking, leading to innovative solutions and approaches and helping the organisation achieve its goals more efficiently (Chapter 1. From kitsch phenomenon, through kitsch experience, to kitschy management and management of kitsch; Chapter 4 – Kitsch in HRM: the role of communication in managing generational diversity in an organisation; Chapter 11 – Kitsch in new technologies management: design practices and user experiences);
8. strategic use of kitsch can differentiate an organisation from its competitors, making it stand out in the market; this unique positioning can attract more significant numbers of customers, driving the organisation towards its goals (Chapter 6 – Kitsch in marketing: merchandising and promotional activities in the retail sphere; Chapter 7 – Kitsch in advertising: a field of postmodern market communication battle; Chapter 8 – Kitsch in brand management: impact of aesthetic truth and false in advertising strategies; Chapter 9 – Kitsch in entrepreneurship: meal kits, taste and the art of socio-economic enterprise);

9. an organisation that effectively uses kitsch can develop a positive and approachable public image, leading to increased media attention and public interest, supporting marketing and business objectives (Chapter 6 – Kitsch in marketing: merchandising and promotional activities in the retail sphere; Chapter 7 – Kitsch in advertising: a field of postmodern market communication battle; Chapter 8 – Kitsch in brand management: impact of aesthetic truth and false in advertising strategies; Chapter 13 – Kitsch in social media: self-optimisation gurus on Instagram);
10. managers who consciously use kitsch demonstrate flexibility and adaptability in their management style, creating a dynamic and responsive organisational culture that is cleverly equipped to meet changing goals and challenges efficiently (Chapter 1. From kitsch phenomenon, through kitsch experience, to kitschy management and management of kitsch).

The above positive verification of the two theses allows for fulfilling the objectives set for this book: 1) the consciousness of *kitsch in management* phenomenon, that is, kitsch as a result of oversimplification, superficiality, or dehumanisation (van de Klundert and van Boeschoten, 2017); 2) *the management of kitsch*, that is, conscious use of organisational kitsch (its presence or lack, its character, scope, form, and intensity) by managers as a means/tool for achieving goals (Szostak, 2024). As a consequence, it can be stated that the general *research problem* of the whole book (How to provide contemporary organisations' managers and stakeholders with an extensive but at the same focused set of examples of managerial and organisational kitsch to give them theoretical background for conscious recognition of managerial and organisational kitsch in their daily practice?) was realised and can be developed in further research.

The identified *research gaps* can be considered as initially filled in. The research gap at the *epistemological* level (in the literature on the aesthetics of management and organisation, there is a lack of extensive description of managerial and organisational kitsch with the use of well-defined and broad analytical tools) has been filled. The research gap at the *empirical* level (the lack of deep exemplifications of managerial and organisational kitsch based on extensive empirical research instead of conceptualisation of examples based on individual assumptions and aesthetic criteria) has been filled. The research gap at the *practical* level (the lack of structured concepts of managerial and organisational kitsch that organisational actors can apply in everyday situations to understand the contexts of actions broader and function more efficiently in an organisation) has been filled.

Study limitations

Due to its universality, the theory of kitsch experience can be successfully applied in managerial and organisational contexts because it refers to the universal values of truth and beauty, which are immanent categories of the aestheticisation process. Undoubtedly, the theory of kitsch experience transposed to the management world can help organisational actors better perceive organisational behaviours that bear the hallmarks of kitsch and manage kitsch consciously. Even though the primary analytical approach in the book was the use of well-structured and objective kitsch experience theory (Szostak and Sułkowski, 2020), some limitations of studying managerial and organisational kitsch using qualitative approaches may be relevant:

1. undertaken research is in some aspects inherently subjective, relying on the perspectives and interpretations of both researchers and participants, which could introduce biases affecting the validity and reliability of the findings, making it challenging to generalise results;
2. undertaken studies often focus on specific contexts or small sample sizes, which can limit the ability to generalise findings to broader populations or different organisational settings and constrain the applicability of insights derived from these studies;
3. conducting interviews, focus groups, or ethnographic studies was time-consuming and required significant resources, which could limit the scope of the study and the ability to gather more extensive data;
4. analysing qualitative data referring to metaphysical phenomena and experiences involved interpreting large volumes of textual, visual or sensual information, which could be complex and labour-intensive, prone to errors and inconsistencies, potentially impacting the accuracy of the conclusions;
5. the unique and context-specific nature of undertaken qualitative research can make it difficult to replicate studies and can hinder the ability to verify findings and establish consistent patterns across different studies and settings.

These limitations highlight some challenges researchers may encounter when undertaking their studies of managerial and organisational kitsch; however, the use of a unified core analysing tool in the form of the kitsch experience theory (Szostak and Sułkowski, 2020) and diversification of data sets and research approaches diminished these limitations significantly.

Future research suggestions

Based on the undertaken studies' results, some future research suggestions for investigating managerial and organisational kitsch may be the following:

1. comparative studies across cultures: how the perception and use of kitsch in managerial and organisational contexts vary across different cultural settings; this could provide insights into the cultural specificity of kitsch and its impact on management practices and organisational behaviours;

2. impact on employee engagement and productivity: the direct effects of organisational kitsch on employee engagement, job satisfaction, and productivity; this could help identify specific types/exemplifications of kitsch that positively or negatively influence the outcomes;
3. role of organisational kitsch in branding and customer perception: how the use of kitsch in organisational branding and marketing strategies affects customer perceptions, loyalty, and brand identity; this could offer valuable insights for businesses looking to differentiate themselves in the market;
4. longitudinal studies on organisational change: how the presence or absence of kitsch influences organisational change processes over time; this could reveal whether kitsch contributes to or hinders the adaptability and resilience of organisations;
5. intersection with digital and virtual environments: the role of kitsch in digital and virtual organisational environments (remote workspaces or virtual reality platforms); this could investigate how digital kitsch affects virtual team dynamics, communication, or overall organisational culture;
6. kitsch and leadership styles: the relationship between leadership styles and the use of kitsch in organisations; this could help determine whether specific leadership approaches are more conducive to integrating kitsch to enhance organisational efficiency and employee morale.

References

Szostak, M. (2024) *Humanistic Management, Organisation and Aesthetics: Art of Management and Management of Art*. New York City: Routledge. https://doi.org/10.4324/9781003458029.

Szostak, M. and Sułkowski, Ł. (2020) 'Kitsch in Management: Characteristic Forms, Carriers and Propagators', in *Education Excellence and Innovation Management: A 2025 Vision to Sustain Economic Development During Global Challenges: Proceedings of the 35th International Business Information Management Association Conference (IBIMA)*. Sevilla: IBIMA, pp. 7584–7598. Available at: https://depot.ceon.pl/handle/123456789/19173.

van de Klundert, M. and van Boeschoten, R. (2017) *Organisations and Humanisation. Perspectives on Organising Humanisation and Humanising Organisations*. London and New York: Routledge.

Index

For Product Safety Concerns and Information please contact our EU representative GPSR@taylorandfrancis.com Taylor & Francis Verlag GmbH, Kaufingerstraße 24, 80331 München, Germany